This book is part of a series ASPECTS OF PORTUGAL

So far published: MICHAEL TEAGUE: *In the Wake of the Portuguese Navigators* □ *CAMÕES* translated by Keith Bosley; illustrated by Lima de Freitas □ MAURICE COLLIS: *The Grand Peregrination* □ ROSE MACAULAY: *They Went to Portugal Too* □ L.M.E. SHAW: *Trade, Inquisition and the English Nation in Portugal 1650-1690* □ A.J.R. RUSSELL-WOOD: *A World on the Move* □ C.R. BOXER. The following: *The Portuguese Seaborne Empire 1415-1825* □ *The Christian Century in Japan 1549-1650* □ *The Golden Age of Brazil 1695-1750* □ FERNANDO PESSOA: *The Book of Disquietude* translated by Richard Zenith □ FERNÃO MENDES PINTO: *The Peregrination* translated by Michael Lowery □ EÇA DE QUEIRÓS. The following: *Cousin Bazilio* translated by Roy Campbell □ *The Illustrious House of Ramires* translated by Ann Stevens □ *The Maias* translated by Patricia McGowan Pinheiro and Ann Stevens □ *The Yellow Sofa and Three Portraits* translated by John Vetch and others □ *The Sin of Father Amaro* translated by Nan Flanagan □ *The City and the Mountains* translated by Roy Campbell. □ *To the Capital* translated by John Vetch

A

Centenary
PESSOA

Edited by Eugénio Lisboa with L.C. Taylor

Translations: *poetry* by Keith Bosley;
prose by Bernard McGuirk, Maria Manuel Lisboa
and Richard Zenith

With an introductory essay by Octavio Paz
and contributions from Antonio Tabucchi,
José Blanco and others

CARCANET
in association with
The Calouste Gulbenkian Foundation
The Instituto Camões
The Instituto da Biblioteca Nacional e do Livro

Published by Carcanet Press Limited
Conavon Court, 12–16 Blackfriars Street, Manchester M3 5BQ
First edition May 1995; Second edition (revised) December 1995
First paperback edition 1997

This selection and editorial matter
Preface: Eugénio Lisboa
Unknown to Himself: Octavio Paz
Poetry translations: Keith Bosley
Life and Times: L.C. Taylor
Prose translations: Bernard McGuirk and Maria Manuel Lisboa
Book of Disquietude: translation Richard Zenith
A Conversation in the Autumn of 1935: Antonio Tabucchi
Fernando Pessoa, Europe and the Portuguese Discoveries: José Blanco
Bibliography: José Blanco.

Book design: Kim Taylor

This book belongs to the series *Aspects of Portugal*, published in Great
Britain by Carcanet Press in association with the Calouste Gulbenkian
Foundation and with the collaboration of the Anglo-Portuguese Foundation.

Series editors: Eugénio Lisboa, Michael Schmidt, L.C. Taylor

A CIP catalogue record for this title is available from the British Library

ISBN 1 85754 368 8

The publisher acknowledges financial assistance from
the Arts Council of England

Typeset in TimesTen Roman by XL Publishing Services, Nairn
Printed and bound in England by SRP Ltd, Exeter

To the memory of
JONATHAN GRIFFIN
pioneer translator of Pessoa into English

The Trunk and the Fable. From a painting by Emilia Nadal

CONTENTS

ILLUSTRATIONS

Photographs from the Pessoa Archive: between pages 114/115
Sketches on title page & verso of sub-titles by Júlio Pomar,
unless otherwise accredited

ACKNOWLEDGEMENTS

THE EDITORS WOULD LIKE TO THANK:

Donors of financial support essential to this publication:

The Trustees of the Calouste Gulbenkian Foundation; The Instituto Camões, Lisbon; The Instituto da Biblioteca Nacional e do Livro, Lisbon.

Authors and publishers who allowed previously published works to be included in this anthology:

Octavio Paz: 'Introduction' to *Fernando Pessoa: Antologia*, Mexico 1962; its translation by Michael Schmidt first appeared in *Numbers, 4*, Cambridge 1988; Antonio Tabucchi: *Uma Conversa no Outono de 1935* Imprensa Nacional-Casa da Moeda, Lisbon 1935; Richard Zenith: *The Book of Disquietude* Carcanet, Manchester 1991. Some of Keith Bostley's translations of Pessoa's poetry, done for this book, were given advance journal publication in *Cultura*, *The Time Literary Supplement*, *Stand*, and *Translation*.

Artists, and/or owners and publishers, who generously allowed their art-work to be included:

Júlio Pomar (and the Calouste Gulbenkian Foundation) who gave permission for his sketches – originally done for decoration of the 'Alto dos Moinhos' station on the Lisbon Underground – to be used extensively; they appear on the title-page and on the seven half-titles; Emilia Nadal (and Margarida and José Blanco) whose painting 'The Trunk and the Fable' – here in black-and-white – has been used as half-title for the Contents page; Alfredo Margarido whose painting 'A Biblioteca', in black-and-white, accompanies the Bibliography; a new painting, kindly sent by him, (sadly here reproduced only in black-and-white) concludes that section. Other drawings in the text by Martins Correia and David Levine.

Owners of photographs, or other items, reproduced in this book:

Many photographs of Fernando Pessoa, and other personal effects, are part of the collection of the poet's family, and are here used with permission, gratefully acknowledged, from Manuela Nogueira.

Thanks for particular items are also due to: Espólio de Fernando Pessoa at the Biblioteca Nacional in Lisbon; Colecção da Casa Fernando Pessoa – Câmara Municipal de Lisboa; Arquivo de Maria da Graça Queiroz Seruya; Arquivo do José de Almada Negreiros; Arquivo de Manuel Vilhena de Carvalho; Arquivos fotográficos do *Diário de Notícias, A Ilustração Portuguesa* and *O Notícias Ilustrado.*

The photograph of Pessoa's tomb was taken especially for this book by Manuel J. Palma, courtesy of the Monastery of Jerónimos/IPPAR, Lisbon.

Authors and publishers of books central to the compilation of this anthology:

A. Editions of Pessoa's own works: ed. José Aguilar: *Fernando Pessoa: Obra poética* Rio de Janeiro 1960; ed. Jorge de Sena: *Fernando Pessoa: Páginas de Doutrina Estética* Editorial Inquérito, Lisbon 1946; ed. Georg Rudolf Lind e Jacinto do Prado Coelho: *Fernando Pessoa: Páginas Íntimas e de Auto-interpretação* Edições Ática, Lisbon 1966; ed. Georg Rudolf Lind e Jacinto do Prado Coelho: *Fernando Pessoa: Páginas de Estética e de Teoria e Crítica Literárias* Edições Ática, Lisbon 1967.

B. Other key books: Maria José de Lancastre: *Fernando Pessoa: Uma foto-biografia* Imprensa Nacional-Casa da Moeda/Centro de Estudos Pessoanos, Lisbon 1980; and the revised and extended version of the above, *Pessoa: une photobibliographie* Christian Bourgois Editeur, Paris 1990. The above books are 'classic' in their field. Of similar status is: ed. João Rui de Sousa: *Fernando Pessoa: Fotobibliografia 1902-1935* Imprensa Nacional-Casa da Moeda/Biblioteca Nacional, Lisbon 1988. Other books or works that have proved of value in this compilation have included: Margarida Barahona and Pierre Léglise – Costa: 'Chronologie Synoptique' in *L'Univers Pessoa* Metropolitano de Lisboa/Europalia 1991; Peter Rickard: 'Introduction' to his translations of *Selected Poems by Fernando Pessoa*, Edinburgh 1971; ed. José Blanco: *Fernando Pessoa: A Galaxy of Poets* accompanying an exhibition by the London Borough of Camden/Portuguese Ministries of Foreign Affairs and Culture, Lisbon; ed. Fernando Pernes: *Fernando Pessoa e a Europa do Século XX* Fundação de Serralves/Commissariat Portugais de Europalia 1991; ed. Philippe Arbaizar: *Fernando Pessoa: Poète Pluriel* BPI/Centre Georges Pompidou/Éditions de la Différence, Paris 1985.

Others who have helped in various ways:

Professor George Steiner, who kindly sent the comment on Pessoa quoted on the front flap, specifically for this edition.

Kim Taylor, designer of this book, whose detailed care and helpful suggestions have extended far beyond normal 'design' expectations.

Janet Allan, who has co-ordinated the passage of this complex book through type-setter and printer.

Mike Eltenton, who has acted as invaluable intermediary and organizer in numerous transactions and arrangements in Lisbon.

Brian Scragg, who wrestled with some dense pieces of French literary criticism for the 'Comment and Response' section, and Adam Taylor who contributed translations from the Italian.

The Trustee, Director and Staff of the Calouste Gulbenkian Foundation's office in London for indispensable administrative and general support. Frequent, cheerful and willing 'hands-on' help, which has lightened the labours of editing, has been received from: Brian Neville, Jayne Eustace, Joy Eaton, Andrée Mas, and Lynne Cope, who made sense on a word-processor of a particularly awkward text.

As befits a work of this sort, contributions have been received from many persons and sources; the editors may inadvertently have omitted or wrongly made some due acknowledgement. If so, they sincerely apologize.

PREFACE
Eugénio Lisboa

HAROLD BLOOM, PROFESSOR OF HUMANITIES AT Yale and dean of American literary critics, has recently written about twenty-six authors – from Dante and Shakespeare to Joyce and Proust – who comprise, he considers, *The Western Canon* of literature.[1] Among that select twenty-six he has placed Fernando Pessoa. In France, say, or Italy, Spain, Latin America… that would cause no blank amaze: but in the English-speaking world, alas, news of Pessoa has scarcely leaked beyond the walls of Academia. *Time* magazine, in its review of *The Western Canon*, wondered who on earth Pessoa was, and reckoned his inclusion in such select canonical company had to be put down to Bloom's addiction to 'academic obscurities'. This curious parochialism explains why – despite books of Pessoa's translations in the last twenty-five years by Griffin, Rickard, Honig and others, and paraphrases of his poems by writers as various as John Betjeman and Thomas Merton – a comprehensive introductory volume of Pessoa is still needed in English. Pessoa's poetry and prose (in a more copious selection than ever before) we have therefore had newly translated and, to help appreciation, we have added contributory pieces about him and artworks inspired by him.

Both Pessoa's strange personality and his singular literary achievement make him and his works quintessentially modern, indeed contemporary. Many people experience, intermittently, that sense of incredulous detachment, of strangeness, of disquietude… that *alienation*, which Pessoa constantly felt and acutely expressed. He is, indeed, the archetype of the alien, the 'foreigner'. He spent his first six years in Lisbon and was then 'exiled' to Durban; the return to Lisbon, alone, aged seventeen, was a second exile. He had discovered a new language – English – so that Portuguese had to be the object of re-discovery, mainly through the poetry of Cesário Verde and the prose of António Vieira. As with so much else – friendship, love – language had to be seen from the perspective of the outsider. In a way, in a deep and painful way, Fernando Pessoa acted systematically as the amazed discoverer of realities to which he did not belong. The very dis-

---

[1] *The Western Canon* by Harold Bloom. Harcourt Bruce, New York 1994; Macmillan, London 1995. Bloom describes his 'canonical' authors as 'authoritative in our culture' and 'selected both for their sublimity and their representative nature'.

tance between himself and the environment, his non-involvement, allowed him a new and creative perspective; he saw the 'obvious' in a new and different light. Taking nothing for granted, because he was never a natural part of it, he was free to question reality afresh. He even 'reinvented' Portuguese – because he knew English.

Eternal traveller, always passing by and never entering, brilliant virtuoso, unashamed grabber of conquests achieved but not fully exploited by other writers, dazzling literary manipulator of human ecstasies and nauseas that others felt more deeply or simply more genuinely than he did – Fernando Pessoa soon became aware of his acute foreignness, of his being the incurable outsider at the very centre of life, of an excruciating inability really to feel 'the pains of happy people or the pains of people who live and complain'.

Wounded by lucidity, by frigidity, by a sense of distance from living, this same distance, this omnipresent perspective, made his inquisitive mind see things in a clearer or, at the least, in a different way. People like Pessoa learn early in life that the country most of us inhabit, made comfortable by familiar presumptions, is forbidden to them. But this awkward exclusion, an embarrassment in everyday living, this disability that amounts at times to a disease, can prove a fertile dis-ease. Unable to integrate with the habitual, forbidden from happy absorption, unable to see evidence as evident and the obvious as obvious, gazing in always from outside, wondering about 'facts' and 'things' that others accept at once without question – such an affliction can lead to a productive amazement. It is this which permeates Pessoa's work: nor do we need to find texts to prove it implicitly, for Pessoa himself draws our attention to his odd disease explicitly: for him, 'poetry is astonishment, admiration, as of a thing fallen from the skies taking full consciousness of his fall, astonished by things'.

Graham Greene once remarked, in a foreword to a novel by a dissident Czech writer, that 'exile is like some herb which gives its distinct bitter flavour to many different forms of writing: the comic, the ironic, the tragic. You can taste it in the irony of Conrad – it is completely absent from home-based tragedies of Hardy – it is there in *The Cherry Orchard*. For to experience exile a man doesn't necessarily have to leave his country. The sense of banishment can be felt on one's own hearth-stone. Exile is deprivation...'. Fernando Pessoa felt that 'sense of banishment' all the time, and in every kind of human experience. But if exile is deprivation, it may also be a bizarre form of wealth, to the extent that it makes a mind powerfully inquisitive and subversively creative. Such was the case with Pessoa, as the poetry and prose in this collection will show.

INTRODUCTION

OCTAVIO PAZ

Translated by Michael Schmidt

OCTAVIO PAZ : *Unknown to Himself*

POETS DON'T HAVE BIOGRAPHIES. THEIR WORK IS their biography. Pessoa, who always doubted the reality of this world, would readily approve if I were to go straight to his poems, forgetting the incidents and accidents of his earthly life. Nothing in his life is surprising – nothing, except his poems. I do not think his 'case history' – one must resign oneself to using that unpleasant term – explains them; I think that, in the light of his poems, his 'case history' ceases to be one. *Pessoa* means person in Portuguese and derives from *persona*, mask of Roman actors. Mask, character out of fiction, no one: Pessoa. His history could be reduced to the passage between the unreality of his daily life and the reality of his fictions. These fictions are the poets Alberto Caeiro, Álvaro de Campos, Ricardo Reis and, above all, Fernando Pessoa himself. Thus it is not pointless to recall the salient features of his life, so long as we know that it is the footprints of a shadow we are following. The real Pessoa is someone else.

Born in Lisbon in 1888. Father dies, mother re-marries. In 1896 she and her children move to Durban, South Africa, where her second husband is sent as Portuguese Consul. English education. Bilingual poet, the Anglo-Saxon influence will be constant on his thought and in his work. In 1905, on the verge of matriculating at the University of Capetown, he must return to Portugal. In 1907 he drops out of the Faculty of Letters at Lisbon and sets up a printing works. Failure, a word that will be repeated often in his life. Then he works as 'foreign correspondent', that is, as a freelance translator of commercial correspondence in English and French, a modest employment which will keep him fed most of his life. True, from time to time, with discretion, the doors to a university career open to him; with the pride of timid men, he refuses the offer. I wrote *discretion* and *pride*; I should probably have said *reluctance* and *realism*: in 1932 he aspires to the post of archivist in a library and they reject him. But there is no rebellion in his life: just a touch of modesty that looks like disdain.

After his return from Africa, he never again leaves Lisbon. First he lives in an old house with a spinster aunt and a mad grandmother; then with another aunt; for a time with his mother, again widowed; the rest of the time, in temporary accommodation. He meets his friends in the street or at the café. Lone drinker in taverns and inns in the old quarter. Other details? In 1916 he plans to set up as an astrologer. Occultism has its perils and on one occasion Pessoa finds himself involved in a row, set up by the police against the magician and 'satanist' E.A. Aleister Crowley, passing through Lisbon in search of neophytes for his mystical-erotic order. In 1920 he falls in love, or thinks he does, with an office girl; the relationship is short-lived: 'my destiny,' he says in the letter that breaks it off, 'belongs to a different law, whose existence you do not even suspect...' No other loves are known of. In the 'Maritime Ode' and the 'Salutation to Whitman' there is a strain of anguished homosexuality; these are great compositions which make one think of those that García Lorca was to write fifteen years later in *Poet in New York*. But Álvaro de Campos, expert at provocation, is not the whole Pessoa. There are other poets in him. Chaste, all his passions are imaginary; or rather, his great vice is imagination. That is why he never gets up out of his chair. And there is another Pessoa who belongs neither to everyday life nor to literature: the disciple, the initiate. Nothing can or should be said about this Pessoa. Revelation, deception, self-deception? All three together, perhaps. Like the master in one of his hermetic sonnets, Pessoa 'knows and is silent'.

Anglomaniac, myopic, courteous, evasive, dressed darkly, reticent and agreeable, cosmopolitan who preaches nationalism, *solemn investigator of futile things*, humorist who never smiles but chills our blood, inventor of other poets and destroyer of himself, author of paradoxes clear as water and, as water, dizzying; *to pretend is to know yourself*, mysterious man who does not cultivate mystery, mysterious as the mid-day moon, taciturn phantom of the Portuguese mid-day, who is Pessoa? Pierre Hourcade, who knew him at the end of his life, writes: 'Never, when I bade him good-bye, did I dare to turn back and look at him; I was afraid I would see him vanish, dissolved in air.' Did he forget something? He died in 1935, in Lisbon, of a hepatic colic. He left two *plaquettes* of poems in English, a slim volume of Portuguese poems and a trunk full of manuscripts. His complete works have yet to be published.

His public life (one has to call it by some name) passes in shadow. Literature from the suburbs, ill-lighted zone in which move – conspirators or lunatics? – the irresolute shadows of Álvaro de Campos, Ricardo Reis and Fernando Pessoa. For a brief moment, the harsh reflectors of scandal and polemic illuminated them. Afterwards, darkness once more. Near-anonymity and near-celebrity. Everyone knows the name of Fernando Pessoa but few know who he is or what he does. Portuguese, Spanish and Latin American reputation: 'Your name rings a bell, are you a newspaper reporter or a film director?' I imagine Pessoa would not have minded the confusion. On the contrary, he cultivated it. Periods of literary agitation followed by stretches of lethargy. If his appearances are isolated and spasmodic, like hand-claps to scare off the fat cats of official literature, his lonely work is constant. Like all the great lazy geniuses, he spends his life making catalogues of the works he will never write; and as also happens with lethargic people, when they are impassioned and imaginative, in order not to burst, not to go crazy, almost on the sly, in the margins of their great projects, each day he writes a poem, an article, a reflection. Dispersion and tension. Everything marked with the same sign: those texts were written of necessity. And this, fatedness, is what distinguishes an authentic writer from a merely talented one.

His first poems he writes in English, between 1905 and 1908. At the time he was reading Milton, Shelley, Keats, Poe. Later he discovers Baudelaire and haunts various 'Portuguese sub-poets'. Imperceptibly he returns to his mother tongue, though he will never stop writing in English. Until 1912 the influence of Symbolist poetry and of *saudosismo* is dominant. That year he published his earliest things in the magazine *A Águia*, the organ of the 'Portuguese renaissance'. His contribution consisted in a series of articles on Portuguese poetry. It is very characteristic of Pessoa to launch his writing career as a literary critic. No less significant is the title of one of his texts: 'In the Forest of Estrangement'. The theme of estrangement and the search for self, in the enchanted forest or in the abstract city, is rather more than just a theme: it is the substance of his work. In those years he sought himself; he will soon be inventing himself.

In 1913 he meets two young people who will be his fastest friends in the brief Futurist adventure: the painter Almada Negreiros and the poet Mário de Sá-Carneiro. Other friendships: Armando Côrtes-Rodrigues, Luis de Montalvor, José Pacheco. Imprisoned still in the enchantment of 'decadent' poetry, those young men try in vain to revive the Symbolist current. Pessoa invents 'Paulism'. And suddenly, by means of Sá-Carneiro, who lives in Paris and with whom he keeps up a feverish correspondence, the revelation of the great modern insurrection: Marinetti. The fecundity of Futurism is undeniable, though its brilliance has faded since as a result of its founder's renunciations. The repercussion of the movement was instantaneous perhaps because, more than a revolution, it was a mutiny. It was the first spark, the spark that ignites the powder-keg. The fire ran from one corner of Europe to the other, from Moscow to Lisbon. Three great poets: Apollinaire, Mayakovsky and Pessoa. The next year, 1914, would be the year of discovery or, rather, of birth for the Portuguese poet: Alberto Caeiro and his disciples, the futurist Álvaro de Campos and the neoclassicist Ricardo Reis, appear.

The irruption of the heteronyms, an inner event, prepares the public action: the explosion of *Orpheu*. In April 1915 the first issue of the magazine appears; in July, the second and last. Little? Rather, too much. The group was not homogeneous. The very name *Orpheu* shows the Symbolist mark. Even in Sá-Carneiro, despite his violence, Portuguese critics perceive the survival of 'decadentism'. In Pessoa the break is clean: Álvaro de Campos is a complete Futurist but Fernando Pessoa continues as a 'Paulist' poet. The public received the magazine with indignation. The texts by Sá-Carneiro and Campos provoked the usual outrage from journalists. Insults were followed by jeers, jeers by silence. The cycle was complete. Did anything remain? In the first issue the 'Triumphal Ode' appeared; in the second, the 'Maritime Ode'. The first is a poem which, despite its tics and affectations, already has the direct tone of 'Tobacconist's Shop', the vision of how little a man weighs when set against the brute weight of social life. The second poem is something more than the fireworks of Futurist poetry: a great spirit raves aloud and its cry is never bestial nor superhuman. The poet is not a 'little god' but a fallen being. The two poems remind us more of Whitman than of Marinetti, a Whitman abstracted and denying. This is not all. Contradiction is the system, the form of Pessoa's vital coherence: in the same period when the two odes are composed, he writes *The Keeper of Flocks*, the posthumous book of Alberto Caeiro, the Latinizing poems of Reis and 'Epithalamium' and 'Antinous', 'two English poems of mine, very indecent, and therefore unpublishable in England'.

The adventure of *Orpheu* is brusquely interrupted. Some, faced with the journalists' attacks and perhaps frightened by the intemperateness of Álvaro de Campos, take French leave. Sá-Carneiro, always unstable, returns to Paris. A year later he kills himself. A new attempt in 1917: the only issue of *Portugal Futurista*, edited by Almada Negreiros, in which 'Ultimatum' by Álvaro do Campos appears. Today it is difficult to read that stream of diatribes with interest, though some retain a salutary virulence: 'D'Annunzio, Don Juan on Patmos; Shaw, cold tumour of Ibsenism; Kipling, scrap-iron imperialist.' The *Orpheu* episode ends in the dispersion of the group and the death of one of its guiding lights. One must wait for fifteen years and a new generation. None of this is unusual. The astonishing thing is the appearance of the group, well ahead of its time and its society. What was being written in Spain and Latin America in those years?

The following period is one of relative obscurity. Pessoa publishes two booklets of English poetry, *35 Sonnets* and *Antinous*, which *The Times* and the *Glasgow Herald* review very courteously but without enthusiasm. In 1922 appears Pessoa's first contribution to *Contemporanea*, a new literary magazine: 'The Anarchist Banker'. From those years also date his political whims: eulogies of nationalism and of the authoritarian regime. The reality disabuses him and obliges him to recant: on two occasions he stands up to public power, the church and social morality. The first time to defend

António Botto, author of *Canções*, poems of homosexual love. The second time against the 'Student Action League', which attacked free thinking with the pretext of doing away with the so-called 'literature of Sodom'. Caesar is always a moralist. Álvaro de Campos distributes a handout: 'Warning on a moral count'; Pessoa publishes a manifesto; and the aggrieved party, Raúl Leal, writes a pamphlet: 'A moral lesson to the students of Lisbon and the impudence of the Catholic Church'. The centre of gravity has shifted from free art to artistic freedom. The cast of our society is such that the creator is condemned to heterodoxy and opposition. The lucid artist does not evade that moral risk.

In 1924, a new magazine, *Athena*. It runs for only five issues. The supporting talents were never very good. In fact, *Athena* is a bridge between *Orpheu* and the young writers of *Presença* (1927). Each generation when it emerges selects its tradition. The new group discovers Pessoa: at last he has found people to talk with. Too late, as usual. A little later, a year before his death, the grotesque incident of the poetry competition of the Secretariat for National Propaganda occurs. The theme, of course, was a hymn to the glories of the nation and the empire. Pessoa sends in *Mensagem*, poems which are an 'occultist' and symbolic interpretation of Portuguese history. The book must have puzzled the officials in charge of the contest. They gave it a 'second category' prize. It was his final literary experience.

It all begins on 8 March 1914. But it's better to transcribe an extract from a letter Pessoa wrote to one of the young poets of *Presença*, Adolfo Casais Monteiro:

Around 1912 I got the idea of writing some poems of a pagan nature. I drafted some things in irregular verse (not in the style of Álvaro de Campos) and then gave up the attempt. All the same, in the confused half-light, I glimpsed a vague picture of the person who was doing it (without my knowing it, Ricardo Reis had been born). A year and a half or two years later, it occurred to me to play a trick on Sá-Carneiro – to invent a bucolic poet, a little complex, and present him, I don't recall in what form, as if he were a real entity. I spent a few days at this without getting anywhere. One day, when I had at last given up – it was 8 March 1914 – I drew near a high chest of drawers and, taking a handful of paper, began to write standing up, as I always do when I can. I wrote 30-odd poems, one after another, in a sort of ecstasy whose nature I could not define. It was the triumphal day of my life and I will never have another like it. I began with a title, 'The Keeper of Flocks'. And what followed was the appearance of someone in me whom I immediately called Alberto Caeiro. Excuse me for the absurdity of the expression: my master appeared in me. That was the immediate sensation I had. And it was such that, as soon as the 30 poems were written, on another paper I wrote, also without stopping, 'Oblique Rain', by Fernando Pessoa. Immediately and complete...

It was the return of Fernando Pessoa-Alberto Caeiro to Fernando Pessoa himself. Or better said: Fernando Pessoa's reaction against his inexistence as Alberto Caeiro... When Caeiro had appeared, I tried unconsciously and instinctively to find him some disciple. I wrenched the latent Ricardo Reis away from his false paganism, I found him a name and adjusted him to himself, because at that peak of excitement I could already see him. And suddenly, from an opposite source to Reis, another individual surged up impetuously. At a stroke, without interruption or revision, the 'Triumphal Ode' of Álvaro de Campos sprang forth. The ode with that title and the man with the name he has.

I do not know what could be added to this confession. Psychology offers us various explanations. Pessoa himself, who was interested in his case, proposes two or three. One crudely pathological: 'I am probably an hysteric – neurasthenic... and this explains, well or ill, the organic origin of the heteronyms.' I wouldn't say 'well or ill' but inadequately. The fault of these hypotheses is not that they are false: they are incomplete. A neurotic is a man possessed: if he controls his disorder, is he then sick? The neurotic suffers his obsessions; the creator is their master and transforms them. Pessoa recounts that from childhood he lived among imaginary characters. ('I don't know, of course, if it is they or I who don't exist: in these cases we ought not to be dogmatic.') The heteronyms are surrounded by a fluid mass of half-beings: the Baron of Teive; Jean Seul, satirical French journalist; Bernardo Soares, a phantom of the phantasmal Vicente Guedes; Pacheco, a poor copy of Campos... not all of them are writers: there is a Mr Cross, tireless participant in the charade and crossword competitions in the English magazines (an infallible means, Pessoa believed, of ending up broke), Alexander Search and others. All this – like his solitude, his discreet alcoholism and so many other things – casts light on his character but does not explain his poems for us, and that is all that really matters to us.

The same thing happens with the 'occultist' hypothesis, to which Pessoa, far too analytical, does not openly resort but which he does not fail to evoke. It is known that the spirits which guide the pens of mediums, even the spirits of Euripides or Victor Hugo, reveal a disconcerting literary dullness. Others hazard a guess that it is a case of 'mystification'. The error here is doubly coarse: Pessoa is not a liar nor is his work a fraud. There is something extremely vile in the modern mind; people, who tolerate every kind of unworthy lie in real life, and all kinds of unworthy realities, will not tolerate the existence of the fable. And that is what Pessoa's *oeuvre* is: a fable, a fiction. To forget that Caeiro, Reis and Campos are poetic creations is to forget too much. Like all creation, those poets were born of play. Art is play – and other things. But without play there is no art.

The authenticity of the heteronyms depends on their poetic coherence, their verisimilitude. They were necessary creations, otherwise Pessoa would not have devoted his life to living and making them; what matters now is not that they were necessary to their author but that they should also be so to us. Pessoa, their first reader, did not doubt their reality. Reis and Campos said what perhaps he himself would never had said. In contradicting him, they expressed him; in expressing him, they forced him to invent himself. We write to be what we are or else to be what we are not. In either case, we seek ourselves. And if we have the luck to find ourselves – sign of creation – we will discover that we are an unknown. Always the other, always he, inseparable, alien, with your face and mine, you always with me and always alone.

The heteronyms are not literary masks: 'What Fernando Pessoa writes belongs to categories of work which we could call orthonyms and heteronyms. It cannot be said that they are anonymous or pseudonymous because they really aren't. The pseudonymous work is by the author in his own person, except he signs it with another name; the heteronymic work is by the author *outside* his own person...' Gérard de Nerval is the pseudonym of Gérard Labrunie: the same person and the same work; Caeiro is a heteronym of Pessoa: impossible to confuse them. Closer is the case of Antonio Machado, which is also distinct. Abel Martín and Juan de Mairena are not entirely the poet Antonio Machado. They are masks, but transparent masks: a Machado text is not different from a Mairena text. What is more, Machado is not possessed by his fictions, they are not creatures who inhabit him, contradict him or deny him. By contrast, Caeiro, Reis and Campos are the protagonists of a novel which Pessoa never wrote. 'I am a dramatic poet,' he confides in a letter to João Gaspar Simões. Nonetheless, the relationship between Pessoa and his heteronyms is not the same as that between a playwright or novelist and his characters. He is not an inventor of character-poets but a creator of poets'-works. The difference is crucial. As Casais Monteiro says: 'He invented the biographies to accompany the works, and not the works to go with the biographies.' Those works – and Pessoa's own poems written in the light of, for and against them – are his poetic *oeuvre*. He himself turns into an *oeuvre* of his *oeuvre*. And he doesn't even have the privilege of being the critic of that coterie: Reis and Campos treat him with a certain condescension; the Baron of Teive does not always greet him; Vicente Guedes, the archivist, is so like him that when he finds him, in a neighbourhood tavern, he feels a little pity for himself. He is the bewitched enchanter, so wholly possessed by his phantoms that he feels himself to be watched by them, perhaps despised, perhaps pitied. Our creations judge us.

Alberto Caeiro is my master. This declaration is the touchstone of all his work. It could be added that the work of Caeiro is the only affirmation Pessoa ever made. Caeiro is the sun and around him Reis, Campos and Pessoa himself keep their courses. In all of them there are particles of negation and unreality: Reis believes in form, Campos in sensation, Pessoa in symbols. Caeiro doesn't believe in anything: he exists. The sun is life stuffed full of itself; the sun does not look because all his rays' glances are transformed into heat and light; the sun is not self-conscious because in him thinking and being are one and the same. Caeiro is all that Pessoa is not and, moreover, all that no modern poet can be: man reconciled with nature. Before Christianity, yes, but also before work and before history. Before consciousness. Caeiro denies, by the mere fact of existing, not only Pessoa's Symbolist aesthetic but all aesthetics, all values, all ideas. Is nothing left? Everything is left, scoured of the phantoms and cobwebs of culture. The world exists because my senses tell me so; and in telling me so, they also tell me I exist. Yes, I will die and the world will die, but to die is to live. Caeiro's affirmation annuls death; when he suppresses conscience, he suppresses nothingness. He does not affirm that everything is, because that would be to affirm an idea; he says that everything exists. Moreover, he says that it is all that exists. The rest are illusions. Campos sets himself the task of dotting the 'i': 'My master Caeiro was not pagan; he was paganism.' I would say: an idea of paganism.

Caeiro hardly went to school. [1] When he learned that he was being called a 'materialist poet' he wanted to know what that doctrine consisted of. When he heard Campos' explanation, he did not conceal his surprise: 'It's an idea of priests without religion! You say that they say space is infinite? In what space have they seen that?' In the face of his disciple's stupefaction, Caeiro maintained that space is finite: 'What is limitless doesn't exist...' Campos replied: 'And numbers? After 34 comes 35, then 36 and so on...' Caeiro stayed gazing at him with pity: 'But those are *only* numbers!' and he went on 'like a formidable child': 'Is there by any chance a number 34 in reality?' Another anecdote: they asked him: 'Are you content with yourself?' He replied: 'No, I am content.' Caeiro is not a philosopher: he is a sage. Thinkers have ideas; for the sage, living and thinking are not separate acts. That is why it is impossible to expound the ideas of

---

[1] Born in Lisbon in 1889, he died in the same city in 1915. He spent most of his life in a Ribatejo villa. Works: *The Keeper of Flocks* (1911-12); *The Amorous Shepherd: Uncollected Poems* (1913-15).

Socrates or Laotse. They did not leave doctrines, but a fistful of anecdotes, riddles and poems. Chuangtse, more faithful than Plato, does not pretend to communicate a philosophy to us but to tell us some little stories: the philosophy is inseparable from the story, is the story. The doctrine of the philosopher encourages refutation; the life of the sage is irrefutable. No sage has proclaimed that the truth can be learned; what all of them, or almost all, have said, is that all that is worthwhile is to live the experience of truth. The weakness of Caeiro rests not in his ideas (that is, rather, his strength); it consists in the unreality of the experience he says he embodies.

Adam in a villa in provincial Portugal, without woman, children or creator: without conscience, work or religion. A sensation among sensations, an existing among existences. Rock is rock and Caeiro is Caeiro, at this moment. Later on, each will be something different. Or the same. It's the same or it's different: everything's the same by being different. To name is to be. The word with which he names the rock is not the rock but has the same reality as the rock. Caeiro doesn't set himself to name the beings and that is why he never tells us if the rock is an agate or a cobble-stone, if the tree is a pine or a holm-oak. Nor does he pretend to establish relations between things: the word *like* does not figure in his vocabulary; each thing is sunk in its own reality. If Caeiro speaks it is because man is a creature of words, as the bird is a winged creature. Man talks as the river runs and the rain falls. The innocent poet does not need to name things; his words are trees, clouds, spiders, lizards. Not these spiders I see, but these I say. Caeiro is astonished at the idea that reality is ungraspable: why, there it is, in front of us, it's enough to touch it. It's enough to speak.

It would not be hard to show Caeiro that reality is never at hand and that we must conquer it (even at the risk that in the act of conquest it might evaporate before us or turn into something else: idea, utensil). The innocent poetry is a myth, but a myth which institutes poetry. The real poet knows that words and things are not the same, and for that reason, to re-establish a precarious unity between man and the world, he names things with images, rhythms, symbols and comparisons. Words are not the things they name: they are the bridges we extend between the things and ourselves. The poet is the conscience of the words, that is, the nostalgia for the actual reality of things. True, words were also things before they were the names of things. They were things in the myth of the innocent poet, that is, before language. The opaque words of the real poet evoke the speech of the time before language, the glimpsed paradisal accord. Innocent speech: silence in which nothing is said because everything is said, everything is saying itself. The poet's language feeds upon that silence which is innocent speech. Pessoa, real poet and sceptic, needed to reinvent an innocent poet to justify his own poetry. Reis, Campos and Pessoa speak mortal, dated words, words of perdition and dispersion: they are the presentiment of a nostalgia for unity. We hear them against the silent background of that unity. It isn't by chance that Caeiro dies young, before his disciples begin their work. It is his *raison d'être*, the silence that sustains them.

The most natural and simple of the heteronyms is the least real. He is least real because of excess reality. Man, above all modern man, is not entirely real. He is not a compact entity like nature or things; self-consciousness is his insubstantial reality. Caeiro is an absolute affirmation of existence and hence his words strike us as truths from another age, that age in which everything was one and the same. Sensible and untouchable present: we hardly name it and it evaporates! The mask of innocence which Caeiro turns to us is not that of wisdom: to be wise is to resign oneself to the knowledge that we are not innocent. Pessoa, who did know it, was nearer to wisdom.

The opposite extreme is Álvaro de Campos.[2] Caeiro lives in the timeless present of children and animals; the Futurist Campos in the now. For the first, his hilltop retreat is the centre of the world; the other, cosmopolitan, has no centre, exiled in that nowhere which is everywhere. Nonetheless, they do resemble one another; they both practice free verse; both trample on the Portuguese language; neither avoids the prosaic. They believe only in what they touch, they are pessimists, they love concrete reality, they do not love their peers, they despise ideas and live outside history, one in fulness of being, the other in its most extreme privation. Caeiro, the innocent poet, is the one Pessoa could not be; Campos, the dandy vagabond, is the one he could have been but wasn't. They are the impossible vital possibilities of Pessoa.

The first poem by Campos has a deceptive originality. The 'Triumphal Ode' appears to be a brilliant echo of Whitman and of the Futurists. But as soon as this poem is compared with those which were being written in France, Russia and elsewhere in those years, the difference is apparent. Whitman really believed in man and in machines; or rather, he believed that *natural man* was not incompatible with machines. His pantheism extended also to industry. Most of his descendants do not share these illusions. Some see machines as marvellous toys. I think of Valéry Larbaud and of

---

[2] Born in Tavira, 15 October 1890. The date corresponds with his horoscope, Pessoa says. Studies at the *liceu*; later in Glasgow, reads naval engineering. Jewish ancestry. Travels to the Orient. Artificial and other paradises. Adherent to a non-Aristotelian aesthetic, which he sees fulfilled in three poets: Whitman, Caeiro and himself. Wore a monocle. Irascible and impatient.

Barnabooth, who resembles Álvaro de Campos in more ways than one. Larbaud's attitude to the machine is epicurean; the attitude of the Futurists was visionary. They see it as the destroyer of false humanism and, of course, of *natural man*. They do not set out to humanize the machine but to construct a new human species similar to it. Mayakovsky would be one exception and even he... The 'Triumphal Ode' is not epicurean, romantic or triumphal: it is a song of rage and defeat. Its originality resides in this.

A factory is 'a tropical landscape' inhabited by huge, lascivious beasts. Infinite fornication of wheels, pistons and tackle-blocks. As the mechanical rhythm grows louder, the paradise of steel and electricity becomes a torture chamber. The machines are sexual organs of destruction: Campos would like to be chewed up by those furious propellers. This strange vision is less fantastic than it appears and it is not just an obsession of Campos's. The machines reproduce, simplify and multiply vital processes. They seduce and terrify us because they give us at one and the same time the sensation of intelligence and unconsciousness: all that they do, they do well, but they don't know what they are doing. Isn't this an image of modern man? But the machines are one fact of contemporary civilization. The other is social promiscuity. The 'Triumphal Ode' ends in a howl; transformed into a package, box, parcel, wheel, Álvaro de Campos loses the use of the word: he whistles, chimes, hammers, cracks, explodes. Caeiro's word evokes the unity between man, rock and insect; Campos's evokes the incoherent noise of history. Pantheism and universal mechanism, two ways of abolishing conscience.

'Tobacconist's Shop' is the poem of recovered consciousness. Caeiro asks himself: what am I? Campos: who am I? From his room he watches the street: cars, passers-by, dogs, all real and all hollow, all close at hand and all remote. Opposite, sure of himself like a god, enigmatic and grinning like a god, rubbing his hands like God the Father after his horrible creation, the proprietor of the Tobacconist's appears and disappears. He arrives at this cave-temple-shop, Steve the chap with nothing on his mind, *metaphysical being*, who talks and eats, has feelings and political opinions and keeps the feast-days of obligation. From his window, from his consciousness, he watches the two puppets and seeing them, sees himself. Where is reality, in me or in Steve? The proprietor of the Tobacconist's smiles and does not answer. As a Futurist poet, Campos begins by affirming that the only reality is sensation; a few years later he asks himself if he himself is real at all.

When he abolishes self-consciousness, Caeiro suppresses history; now it is history that suppresses Campos. Marginal life: his siblings, if he has them, are the whores, the vagrants, the dandy, the half-wit, the rabble from upstairs and down. His rebellion has nothing to do with ideas of redemption or justice: *No: anything but being right! Anything but caring about mankind! Anything rather than give in to humanitarianism!* Campos also rebels against the idea of rebellion. It is not a moral virtue, a state of consciousness – it is the consciousness of sensation: 'Ricardo Reis is a pagan by conviction: Antonio Mora by intelligence; I by rebellion, that is, by temperament.' His sympathy for the underdog is tinged with disgust, but he feels that disgust above all for himself:

> *I feel sympathy for all those people,*
> *Especially when they do not merit it.*
> *Yes, I too am vagrant and I crave...*
> *To be vagrant and a beggar is not to be those things*
> *But to be outside the social hierarchy...*
> *Not to be Supreme Court Judge, of fixed employment, whore,*
> *Solemnly poor, exploited worker,*
> *Sick with an incurable disease,*
> *Longing for justice, or cavalry captain,*
> *Not, finally, those social persons, novelists,*
> *Who gorge themselves with letters because they have reason to*
> *   shed tears*
> *And who rebel against social life because they have more than*
> *   enough reasons to...*

His vagrancy and penury have no circumstantial source; they are irremediable and unredeemable. To be a vagrant thus is *to be isolated in the soul.* And later on, with that brutality that scandalized Pessoa: *I don't even have the excuse of being able to have social opinions... I'm lucid. None of your heart-felt aesthetics... I'm lucid. Bloody hell! I'm lucid.*

Consciousness of exile has been a constant note in modern poetry, for the last century and a half. Gérard de Nerval pretends he is the Prince of Aquitaine; Álvaro de Campos chooses the mask of vagrant. The transition is revealing. Wandering minstrel or beggar, what does that mask conceal? Nothing, perhaps. The poet is the consciousness of his historic unreality. But if that consciousness draws back from history, society subsides into its own darkness, becomes Steve or the Proprietor of the Tobacconist's. There will those who say that Campos's attitude is not 'positive'. Casais Monteiro answered such critics in these terms: 'The work of Pessoa *really* is a negative work. It does not serve as a model, it teaches neither to govern nor to be governed. It serves exactly the opposite purpose: to undiscipline spirits.'

Campos does not set out, like Caeiro, to be everything but to be everyone and to be in all places. The fall into plurality is paid for by the loss of identity. Ricardo Reis chooses the other possibility latent in his master's work [3]. Reis is a recluse as Campos is a vagabond. His hermitage is a philosophy and a form. The philosophy is a mixture of stoicism and epicureanism. The form, the epigram, the ode and the elegy of the neo-classical poets. but the neo-classicism is a nostalgia, that is, a romanticism that does not recognize itself or masks itself. While Campos writes his long monologues, each time coming closer to introspection than to hymn, his friend Reis polishes little odes on pleasure, ephemerality, Lydia's roses, the illusory freedom of man, the vanity of the gods. Educated at a Jesuit College, a physician by profession, a monarchist, exiled to Brazil since 1919, pagan and sceptic by conviction, Latinist by education, Reis lives outside time. He seems, but is not, a man of the past: he has chosen to live in a timeless *sagesse*. Cioran recently pointed out that our century, which has invented so many things, has not created the one thing we most lack. It is not surprising therefore that some seek it in the Eastern tradition: Taoism, Zen Buddhism; in fact those doctrines fulfil the same function as the moral philosophies of the end of the ancient world. Reis's stoicism is one way of not being in the world – without ceasing to be in it. His political ideas have a similar meaning: they are not a programme but a negation of the contemporary state of affairs. He does not hate Christ or love him; he abhors Christianity though, aesthete to the end, when he thinks of Jesus he admits that 'his sober, dolorous form brought us something that was lacking'. Reis's real god is Fate and we all – men and myths – are subject to its rule.

Reis's form is admirable and monotonous, like everything that achieves artificial perfection. In those little poems one perceives, more than the poet's familiarity with Latin and Greek originals, a wise and distilled mixture of Lusitanian neo-classicism and of the *Greek Anthology* translated into English. The correctness of his language troubled Pessoa: 'Caeiro writes Portuguese badly; Campos does it well enough, though he perpetrates expressions like "I proper" for "I myself"; Reis writes better than I but with a purism I consider exaggerated.' The sleepwalking exaggeration of Campos, by a very natural movement of contradiction, turns into the exaggerated precision of Reis.

Neither form nor philosophy protect Reis: they protect a phantom. The fact is that Reis does not exist either, and he knows it. Lucid, and with a

---

[3] Born in Oporto. He is the most Mediterranean of the heteronyms: Caeiro was blonde with blue eyes, Campos 'between light and dark', tall, thin, and with a cosmopolitan air; Reis, 'dull dark skin', closer to the meridional Spanish and Portuguese. The *Odes* are not his only work. He is known to have written 'An Aesthetic Debate between Ricardo Reis and Álvaro de Campos.' His critical notes on Caeiro and Campos are models of verbal precision and aesthetic misunderstanding.

more penetrating lucidity than Campos' exasperated kind, he contemplates himself:

> *I do not know from whom I recall my past,*
> *I was another, nor do I know myself*
> *When with my soul I feel*
> *That alien I remember as I feel.*
> *From one day to the next we forsake ourselves.*
> *Nothing that's certain binds us to ourselves,*
> *We are who we are and it is*
> *Something inwardly perceived, the thing we were.*

The labyrinth in which Reis is lost is the labyrinth of himself. The poet's inturned look, something quite distinct from introspection, makes him resemble Pessoa. Though both used fixed metres and forms, it is not traditionalism that unites them because they belong to different traditions. They have in common a feeling about time – not as something which passes before us but something which becomes us. Imprisoned in the instant, Caeiro and Campos affirm in a single stroke being or lack of being. Reis and Pessoa get lost in the fastnesses of their thought, catch up with themselves at some bend or turning and, at the point of joining up with themselves, embrace a shadow. The poem is not the expression of being but the commemoration of that moment of fusion. Hollow monument: Pessoa raises a temple to the unknown; Reis, more soberly, writes an epigram that is also an epitaph:

> *Let Fate deny me everything, except to see it,*
> *For I, a Stoic without obduracy,*
> *In the sentence engraved by Destiny*
> *Wish to enjoy the characters.*

Álvaro de Campos used to quote a sentence of Ricardo Reis: 'I hate a lie because it is an inexactness.' These words could also be applied to Pessoa, so long as lie is not confused with imagination or exactness with rigidity. The poetry of Reis is precise and simple as a line-drawing; Pessoa's exact and complex like music. Complex and various, it moves in different directions: the prose, the Portuguese poetry and the English poetry (the French poems have to be set aside as insignificant). The prose writings, which have still to be published in full, can be divided in two main categories: those signed with his own name and those of his pseudonyms, principally the Baron of Tieve, an aristocrat fallen on hard times, and Bernardo Soares, 'impregnated with commerce'. In various passages Pessoa stresses that they are not heteronyms: 'both write in a style which is, for better or for worse, my own'. It is not necessary to linger over the English poems;

their interest is literary and psychological but they do not add much, it seems to me, to English poetry. The poetic *oeuvre* in Portuguese, from 1902 to 1935, includes *Mensagem*, the lyric poetry and the dramatic poems. These last, in my view, are marginal in value. Even if they are left aside, an extensive poetic *oeuvre* remains.

First difference: the heteronyms write only in one direction and in a single current of time; Pessoa branches out like a delta and each of its branches offers us the image, the images, of a moment. Lyric poetry ramifies in *Mensagem*, the *Cancioneiro* (with the unpublished and scattered pieces) and the hermetic poems. As is always the case, the classification does not correspond to the reality. *Cancioneiro* is a Symbolist book full of hermetic elements, though the poet does not have specific recourse to the images of the occult tradition. *Mensagem* is, above all, a book of heraldry – and heraldry is a part of alchemy. Finally, the hermetic poems are, in form and spirit, Symbolist; it is not necessary to be an initiate to get into them and to understand them as poems does not require special knowledge. These poems, like the rest of his work, require a *spiritual* understanding, the highest and most difficult form of understanding. The knowledge that Rimbaud was interested in the cabbala and identified poetry and alchemy is useful and helps us approach Rimbaud's work; really to get into it, however, we need something more and something less. Pessoa defined that something in this way: sympathy; intuition; intelligence; comprehension; and the most difficult, grace. This list may seem excessive. I do not see how, without these five conditions, Baudelaire, Coleridge or Yeats can be really read. In any event, the difficulties of Pessoa's poetry are less great than those of Hölderlin, Nerval, Mallarmé... In all the poets of the modern tradition, poetry is a system of symbols and analogies parallel to that of the hermetic sciences. Parallel, but not identical: the poem is a constellation of signs endowed with their own light.

Pessoa conceived *Mensagem* as a *ritual*; that is, as an esoteric book. If one looks at its external perfection, this is his most complete book. But it is a made-up book, by which I do not want to suggest that it is insincere but that it was born of the poet's speculations, not his intuitions. At first glance it is a hymn to the glories of Portugal and a prophecy of a new empire (the Fifth), which will not be material but spiritual; its dominions will extend beyond historic space and time (a Mexican reader immediately recalls the 'cosmic race' of Vasconcelos). The book is a gallery of historic and legendary personages, displaced from their traditional reality and transformed into allegories of another tradition and another reality. Perhaps without entire awareness of what he did, Pessoa vaporizes the history of Portugal and presents another in its place, one purely spiritual that is a negation of what it replaces. The esoteric nature of *Mensagem* prohibits us from reading it as a simple patriotic poem, as some official critics would like. It has to be added that its symbolism does not redeem it. For symbols to work effectively, they must cease to symbolize, become sensible, living creatures and not museum emblems. As in any work where will plays a greater rôle than inspiration, there are few poems in *Mensagem* which achieve that state of grace that distinguishes poetry from *belles lettres*. But those few live in the same magic space as the best poems in the *Cancioneiro*, alongside some of the hermetic sonnets. It is not possible to define what the space consists of; for me it is that of poetry properly speaking, a real territory, tangible, which *another* light illumines. No matter that the poems are few. Gottfried Benn said: 'No one, not even the greatest poets of our time, has left more than eight or ten perfect poems... For six poems, thirty or fifty years' asceticism, suffering, battle!'

The *Cancioneiro*: a world of beings and many shadows. Woman, the central sun, is missing. Without woman, the sensible world vanishes, there is not even firm ground, water, nor the embodiment of the impalpable. The terrible pleasures are missing. Passion, that love which is desire for one unique being whoever it may be, is also lacking. There is a vague fraternal feeling with nature: trees, clouds, rocks, all fleeting, all suspended in a temporal void. Unreality of things, a reflection of our own unreality. There is denial, exhaustion, mournfulness. In the *Livro de Desassossego [Book of Disquietude]*, of which only fragments are known, Pessoa describes his moral landscape:

I belong to a generation which was born without faith in Christianity and which ceased to have faith in all other beliefs; we were not enthusiasts for social equality, beauty or progress; we did not seek in easts or wests other religious forms ('each civilization has a relationship with the religion which represents it: when we lost ours, we lost them all'); some among us devoted themselves to the conquest of the everyday; others among us, of better stock, abstained from public affairs, wanting nothing and desiring nothing; others gave themselves up to the cult of confusion and noise: they thought they were alive when they heard themselves, they thought they loved when they crashed into the externals of love; and others of us, Race without End, spiritual limit of the Dead Hour, *lived in denial, discontent and mournfulness.*

This is not a picture of Pessoa, but it is the ground against which his figure stands out and with which it is sometimes confused. Spiritual limit of the Dead Hour: the poet is an empty man who, in his helplessness, creates a world in order to discover his true identity. All Pessoa's work is a search for the lost identity.

In one of his most quoted poems he says that the poet is 'a pretender who pretends so thoroughly that he comes to pretend that the pain he really feels is pain'. When he tells the truth, he lies; when he lies, he tells the truth. We witness not an aesthetic but an act of faith. Poetry is the revelation of his unreality:

> *Between the moonlight and the foliage,*
> *Between the stillness and the grove,*
> *Between the fact of night and the fact of the breeze,*
> *A secret passes.*
> *My soul follows it as it passes.*

Is the one who passes Pessoa or someone else? The question is repeated down the years and throughout the poems. He does not even know if what he writes is his own. Or rather, he knows that even if it is, it is not: 'why, deceived, do I judge to be mine what is not mine?' The search for the I – lost, found, again lost – ends in disgust: 'Nausea, will of nothing: to exist in order not to die.'

Only from this perspective can the complete significance of the heteronyms be perceived. They are a literary invention and a psychological necessity, but they are something more. In a sense they are what Pessoa could and would have liked to be: in another, deeper sense, what he did *not* want to be: a personality. In the first movement, they erase the idealism and intellectual convictions of their author; in the second, they show that innocent *sagesse*, the public square and the philosophical hermitage are illusions. The present instant is as uninhabitable as the future; stoicism is a killing remedy. And yet the destruction of the I – since that is what the heteronyms are – provokes a secret fecundity. The real desert is the I, not only because it locks us up in ourselves, and thus condemns us to live with phantoms, but because it withers all that it touches. Pessoa's experience, perhaps without his intending it, takes its place in the tradition of the great poets of the modern age, from Nerval and the German romantics on. The I is an obstacle, is *the* obstacle. That is why any merely aesthetic judgement of his work is inadequate. If it is the case that not everything he wrote was of the same quality, everything, or almost everything, shows the traces of his search. His work is a step towards the unknown. A passion.

The world of Pessoa is neither this world nor the other. The word 'absence' could define it, if by absence we understand a fluid state, in which presence vanishes and absence heralds... what? – a moment in which the present no longer is, and that which may be about to be just begins to dawn. The urban desert is covered with signs: the rocks say something, the wind speaks, the lighted window and the solitary corner tree speak, everything is saying something, not this that I am saying but something else, always something else, the something that is not said. Absence is not only privation but presentiment of a presence which never shows itself entirely. Hermetic poems and the songs coincide: in the absence, in the unreality we are, something is present. Amazed among people and things, the poet walks along a street in the old quarter. He goes into a park and the leaves move. They're on the point of saying... No, they haven't said anything. Unreality of the world, in the last light of the afternoon. Everything is still, expectant. The poet now knows he has no identity. Like those houses, almost gold, almost real, like those trees suspended in the hour, he too weighs anchor, leaves himself. And the other, the double, the true Pessoa does not appear. He will never appear: there is no other. What does appear, insinuates itself, its otherness, which has no name, what is not said and our poor words invoke. Is it poetry? No: poetry is what is left and consoles us, the consciousness of absences. And again, almost imperceptible, a rumour of something: Pessoa or the imminence of the unknown.

Pessoa-Hamlet by João Abel Manta

POETRY

Selected and translated by **KEITH BOSLEY**

POETRY

FERNANDO PESSOA

Ulissabon, latter-day Ithaca
to one whose name means Person, many-sided
poet for whom a humdrum job provided,
stepson of Adamastor's Africa.

At seventeen, home from English and Natal,
he stayed and after thirty years said 'I
do not evolve, I travel', soon to die,
his roots in Portuguese, not Portugal.

The child was father to companions who
became *pessoas*, masks for speaking through –
the seer glad not to know the names of things,

the bard of roses and mortality,
the noisy engineer: beside them, he
who wonders who he is and quietly sings.

                                              K.B.

Drawing by David Levine

FERNANDO PESSOA

CONTENTS

Drawing by
José de Almada Negreiros

from MESSAGE

The Castles

Resting upon its elbows Europe lies:
Stretching from East to West it lies at gaze,
Romantic locks hang down across its eyes,
Greek, full of memories.

The elbow on the left is tucked away;
The right stands at an angle in its place.
That one, where it comes down, marks Italy;
This one marks England where it distantly
Ends in the hand, upholder of the face.

Its eyes, as fateful as the sphinx's, fall
Westward, towards the past that is to be.

The face with gazing eyes is Portugal.

Dom Sebastian, King of Portugal [1]

Mad, yes, mad, for I wanted to be great,
My assurance uncontained
Within me, my design undreamed by Fate;
Hence of me on the sand
What used to be, but not what is, remained.

My madness let the others take from me
And with it all the rest;
For without madness what can mankind be
More than a healthy beast,
A corpse that breeds before its juices waste?

[1] Dom Sebastian: Sebastião (1554-78), whose death in the battle of Alcácer-Quibir (Al-Qasr al-kabir), Morocco, led to the end of Portugal's Golden Age with annexation by Spain in 1580. Rumours of his survival generated the messianic cult of *Sebastianismo*, which persists to this day in some educated circles.

Sea of Portugal

O bitter sea, how much of all your gall
Is bitter tears of Portugal!
That we crossed you, how many mothers wept,
How many sons vain vigil kept!
How many maids betrothed remained unwed
That you, sea, might be ours instead!

Was it worth while? Anything is, if
A soul of man is great enough.
He who would round the Cape must not give up
But in its Storms see his Good Hope.
Danger and depth God to the sea has given
But in it he has mirrored heaven.

Slanting Rain

I

Across this landscape runs my dream of an infinite harbour
And the colour of flowers is transparent with the sails of big ships
That set out from the quay trailing in the waters through shadow
The bulks in the sun of those ancient trees...

The harbour I dream of is dark and pale
And this landscape is full of sun on this side...
But in my mind this day's sun is a dark harbour
And the ships leaving harbour are these trees in the sun...

A freedman twice over, I have despaired of the landscape below...
The bulk of the quay is a clear calm road
Rising and rearing like a wall,
And the ships pass inside the treetrunks
With a vertical horizontality,
And they drop cables in the water among the leaves one by one...

I don't know who I dream I am...
Suddenly all the harbour's sea water is transparent
And I see on the bottom, like a huge print unfolding there,
This whole landscape, an avenue, a road burning in that harbour,

And the shadow of a vessel older than the harbour passing
Between my dream of the harbour and my view of this landscape

And draws me near, and comes inside me,
And passes on the other side of my soul...

II

The church lights up within this day's rain,
And every sail that flashes is more rain beating on the windowpane...
I rejoice to hear the rain because it is the temple being lit,
And the panes of the church seen from outside are the sound of the rain heard
     inside...

The splendour of the high altar is that I can hardly see the hills
Through the rain that is gold so solemn on the altar cloth...

The singing of the choir rings out, Latin and wind shaking my pane
And the water feels itself creaking with the fact of having a choir...

The Mass is a car passing
Through the faithful who kneel on today being a sad day...
A sudden wind shakes in greater splendour
The cathedral festival and the noise of the rain drowns everything
Till only the priest's voice is heard as water running far away
With the sound of car wheels...

And the church's lights go out
As the rain stops...

III

The Great Sphinx of Egypt is dreaming inside this paper...
I write – and it appears to me through my transparent hand
And as the paper sings the pyramids rear up...

I write – I am troubled to see my pen nib
Being the profile of King Cheops...
I stop short...
Everything has gone dark... I fall into an abyss made of time...

I am buried under the pyramids writing poetry in the bright light of this lamp
And all Egypt crushes me from above through the pen strokes I make...

I hear the Sphinx laughing inside
The sound of my pen running over the paper...
A huge hand comes across the fact I cannot see it,
Sweeps everything towards the corner of the ceiling that remains behind me,
And on the paper where I write, between it and the pen that writes

Lies the corpse of King Cheops, looking at me with wide open eyes,
And between our exchange of looks the Nile runs
And a merriment of boats flying flags wanders
Spread out at an angle
Between me and what I am thinking...

Funerals of King Cheops in old gold and Me!...

IV

What tambourines the silence of this room!...
The walls are in Andalusia...
There are sensual dances in the steady glare of the light...
All space stops short...
Stops, slips, unrolls...
And in a corner of the ceiling, much further away than it is,
White hands open secret windows
And there are bunches of violets falling
Because it is a Spring night outside
Above me with my eyes closed...

V

Outside goes a whirl of sunlight the horses of the *carrousel*...
Trees, stones, hills dance stopped within me...
Absolute night at the fair lit up, moonlight on the sunny day outside,
And all the lights of the fair make noises of the garden walls...
Swarms of girls with pots on their heads
Passing outside, full from standing in the sun,
Mingle with large groups of people clinging together at the fair,
People all mixed with the lights of the stalls, with the night and the moon
    light,

And the two groups meet and pass through each other
Till they form only one that is both...
The fair and the lights of the fair and the people at the fair,
And the night that clings to the fair and lifts it into the air,
They go above the tops of the trees full of sunlight,
They go visibly below the rocks that shine in the sun,
They appear on the other side of the pots the girls carry on their heads,
And all this spring landscape is the moon above the fair,
And all the fair with noises and lights is the floor of this sunny day...

Suddenly someone shakes this twofold hour as in a sieve
And, mixed together, the dust of the two realities falls

Upon my hands full of drawings harbours
With big vessels going off and not thinking of returning...
A dust of white and black gold on my fingers...
My hands are the steps of that girl quitting the fair,
Alone and happy as today...

VI

The maestro waves his baton,
And languid and sad the music bursts out...

I remember my childhood, that day
I was playing by a garden wall
Throwing at it a ball that had on one side
The crawl of a green dog, and on the other
A blue horse running with a yellow jockey...

The music plays on, and here in my childhood
Suddenly between me and the maestro is a white wall,
The ball goes to and fro, now a green dog,
Now a blue horse with a yellow jockey...

The whole scene is my garden, my childhood
Is everywhere, and the ball is playing music,
A sad vague music strolling in my garden
Dressed in a green dog turning into a yellow jockey...
(How fast the ball spins between me and the musicians...)

I throw it against my childhood and it
Crosses the whole scene around me
Playing with a yellow jockey and a green dog
And a blue horse that appears on top of my garden
Wall... And the music throws balls
At my childhood... And the garden wall is made of conducting
Gestures and confused revolvings of green dogs
And blue horses and yellow jockeys...

And from side to side, from right to left,
From where there are trees and among the branches near the top
With orchestras playing,
To where there are rows of balls in the shop where I bought it
And the shopkeeper smiles among my childhood memories...

And the music stops like a collapsing wall,
The ball rolls over the precipice of my interrupted dreams,

And from a blue horse, the maestro, the yellow jockey turning black,
Expresses thanks, setting the baton down on the flight of a wall, [1]
And bows smiling, with a white ball on his head,
A white ball that disappears down behind his back…

[1] flight of a wall: *fuga dum muro*, just as obscure in the original.

Song

Sylphs are they, gnomes playing?…
Caressed in the pine grove,
Shadows and puffs of wind
In time to music move.

They drift in waves as if
Round roads I do not know,
Or as between the trees
Someone might hide, then show.

What I shall never have
Has this vague, distant shape…
I strain my ears, tears start.
I don't know why I weep.

So slight the melody
I wonder is it real
Or is it only dusk,
The pines and how I feel?

But it stops, as a breeze
Forgets the form woe takes;
Now all the music left
Is what the pine grove makes.

from Way of the Cross [1]

O player on the harp, if I could kiss
Your gesture, but could spare your hands my kisses!
And, as I kissed, go down through the recesses
Of dream, until it stood before my face

Turned to Pure Gesture, the fixed gesture cast
Upon the baleful medal – Christian princes
Kneeling, concealing fratricidal glances
When on its solemn way the litter passed!...

Your gesture snatching, falling in a swoon...
Your gesture in its fullness, a cold moon
Rising, with rush-beds in the dark below...

A cave of stalactites your gesture... I am
Helpless to take it, all that I can do
Is gaze and lose it!... And the rest is dream...

[1] Fourth sonnet of a sequence of fourteen, exploring the 'stations' of a Gnostic approach
to 'God, the Great Ogive at the end of everything'.

The sudden hand of some mysterious ghost

The sudden hand of some mysterious ghost
Between the folds of night and of my sleep
Shakes me and wakes me: in the unfathomed deep
Of night its gesture and its face are lost.

But an old terror buried in my heart
And dragged around, as from a throne descends
To be my lord and master: no commands
Does it give me, nor does it nod or hurt.

And at that moment all my life I find
Looped in a rope from the Unconscious Mind
To some dim hand that leads me to its mark:

I find that I am no one but a shade
Whose face I cannot see but am afraid
And I am in a void like the cold dark.

Christmas

A god is born and others die. What is
Has neither come nor gone, but error moves.
Today we have exchanged eternities
And what is past no novelty improves.

Blind knowledge ploughs away at useless soil
And crazy faith dreams through its liturgy.
A new god is a word and that is all.
Don't seek, don't trust, for all is mystery.

Light, short, sweet

Light, short, sweet,
A bird's notes greet
The air on which the day
Makes its way.
I listen, they are gone:
Only because I did, it seems,
The bird moved on.

Never, though
The dawn should glow
Or day touch slopes with gold,
Could I hold
Any pleasure that might
Last longer than the absence, loss,
Before delight.

Poor old music!

Poor old music! How
I wish I knew why
The pleasure you bring
Floods my idle eye.

I've heard you before.
Was it you I heard
In my childhood, has
A memory stirred?

How wildly I seek
That time! I don't know:
Was I happy then?
I was, long ago.

Blank sun of useless days

Blank sun of useless days
Now calm, now full of toil,
Cheer at least the hands
Though out of reach the soul!

And let the hand at least,
Brushing a neighbour skin,
With kindly outward warmth
Conceal the chill within!

Lord, now that pain is ours
And the weakness it involves,
Give us at least the strength
To keep it to ourselves!

Sleep upon my breast

Sleep upon my breast,
And dream there of dreaming…
In your eyes I read
A lascivious scheming.
Sleep where life is but a dream
And love is but seeming.

All is nothing, dream –
Or so it pretends.
Space is dark and numb.
Sleep: as sleep descends,
Teach your heart to smile the smiles
Where memory ends.

In your eyes I read
Apathy within
One who knows the nothingness
That is life, joy, pain.

Far off, in moonlight

Far off, in moonlight,
On the waves a sail
Serenely passing:
What does it reveal?

I don't know, but I
Turn away from me,
And I have a dream
Which I cannot see.

What anguish grips me?
What love none explains?
The sail passes by
And the night remains.

Poor reaper, she is singing, singing

Poor reaper, she is singing, singing,
Convinced perhaps that life is good;
And as she reaps, her song is ringing
With glad, inglorious widowhood.

It ripples like a bird's song, rolls
Across air like a step scrubbed clean,
And there are loops in the sweet toils
Of sound she weaves around, between.

Hearing her makes me glad and sad,
For in her voice is field and strife,
And her song rings as though she had
More cause for singing than has life.

Sing, sing, let reason play no part!
My feeling self is lost in thought.
Pour out into my listening heart
Your voice so wavering, untaught!

Ah, to be you and still be I!
With your glad unself-consciousness
And I self-conscious still! O sky!
O field! O song! How hard the press

Of knowledge, sense that life will fade!
Come and possess my very heart!
Bring my soul back to your slight shade
And bear me off when you depart!

His Mother's Little Boy

On the plain left alone
Where the warm breeze now softens,
With bullets in his brain –
Two, once and once again –
He lies there dead, and stiffens.

His tunic is bloodstained.
With arms outstretched he lies,
Pale, blond, his forces drained,
Staring exhausted, blind
Towards the long-lost skies.

So young! how young he came!
(Well now, how old was he?)
An only son, the name
Mum gave him still the same –
'His mother's little boy'.

From his pocket has slipped
A small cigarette case –
A gift from mum. It kept
Intact there as it slept.
But he is no more use.

From the next pocket splayed,
Its tip still there to flick,
A handkerchief with braid,
Still white… From the old maid
Who wore it round her neck.

At home the prayer still floats:
'Come back soon, well, to me!'
(O nets the Empire knots!)
He lies there dead, and rots,
His mother's little boy.

Seascape

Blessed who see the wave
Of farewell handkerchiefs!
Happy are they who grieve…
I suffer with no griefs.

It hurts me just to think,
For thinking brings the pain,
Orphan of dreams that sink
With the ebb-tide again…

To me, already full
Of fruitless agonies,
Never from dock to sail,
Blows in the tang of days.

A Little Music

A little music, ah, enough
To make sure this uncertainty
Within my soul is taken off
To bring some calm that cannot be!

A little music from the cittern, [1]
Guitar, [2] accordion, hurdy-gurdy [3] …
A voice that strays from what is written…
A dream invisible, unsteady…

A little to escape from life!
Jota [4] or *fado*, to be part
Of the last dance's swirling strife…
And let me never feel my heart!

[1] cittern: *guitarra*, a plucked instrument with six double strings.
[2] guitar: *viola*, cf Spanish *vihuela*. These two instruments accompany the singer of the *fado*, the traditional Portuguese 'fate' song.
[3] hurdy-gurdy: *realejo*, an instrument whose six strings are scraped by an inner wheel turned with a handle.
[4] *jota*: a quick Spanish dance with castanets.

After the Fair

They wander down the road
Singing what no mind rules –
The final hope that lasts
Till the Creation cools.
Nothing at all they mean.
Mummers they are and fools.

They walk in ones and twos
Beneath a springtime moon
In which their sunken dreams
Will never be made known,
And by no act of will
They sing words to a tune.

Lackeys whose myth is dead,
Alone, still lyrical,
Their voice contains no cry,
Hardly indeed a call
Spurned by the infinite
That knows us not at all.

The stars give me a pain

The stars give me a pain
Twinkling all this time,
All this time…
Shall I say it again?

Will there be no fatigue
For things,
For all things,
As for an arm or leg?

A weariness from whiling
The time away,
Just the time away,
The sad time shining, smiling…

Will everything not find
In God's garden
Not death, but beyond,

Another sort of end,
Or an underlying burden –
Something of this kind,
Say, a pardon?

I look at the dumb lake

I look at the dumb lake
Ruffled by moving air,
Not knowing if I think of all
Or all is unaware.

The lake says nothing, air
Stirs but does not touch me.
I do not know if I am glad
Nor if I wish to be.

The ripples tremble, smile
Upon the sleeping wave.
Why have I fashioned out of dreams
The only life I have?

She surprises just by being

She surprises just by being.
She is tall, a smoky gold
And at the mere thought of seeing
Her green body I unfold.

Her tall breasts appear two hills
(If she should be lying down)
Whose outline the morning fills
And there is no need of dawn.

At her white arm's end her hand
Comes to rest with palm spread wide
Where in hatched relief the land
Forms the salient of her side.

As inviting as a boat,
Like a fruit she glistens sweet.
God, when shall I be afloat?
Hunger, when am I to eat?

The Final Incantation

'I have repeated now the ancient spell
But the great Goddess from my sight has gone.
I have repeated, when the full wind fell,
The prayers wherein a fruitful self is furled:
The abyss has given me and heaven has shown
Nothing. The wind whirls, I am all alone,
All slumbers in the chaos of the world.

'Time was when I had mastery of the bramble
And from the ground my sibyl's chant would rear
Presences from those scattered, would assemble
What slumbered in the natural forms of things.
Time was when my voice summoned, loud and clear,
Fairies and elves: I called, they would appear
And all the forest filled with burgeonings.

'My wand, with which I could address at will
Things that exist whose souls are essences,
Acknowledges no more what I am still:
Now, if I draw a circle, nothing moves,
The wind from elsewhere murmurs long-lost sighs,
And moonbeams that beyond the thickets rise
Reveal me as nothing more than paths or groves.

'Now the gift fails me they once loved me for;
No more am I the shape of destiny
To those who, seeking it, sought me. My shore
The sea of arms no more floods with its wave,
Nor does the sun I greeted welcome me,
Nor am I lost in magic ecstasy
By moonlight at the mouth of the deep cave.

'Already now the sacred powers of hell
Slumbering in a godless, aimless dream
Are fully matched with things corporeal,
Deaf to my voice that calls their names abroad.
Music has shut itself off from my hymn
And now my starry fury has gone dim
And my groomed body is no more a god.

'Deities deep down in the gloomy chasm
That I have called upon so often, pale
With love that held me rabid in its spasm,

Today before me stand, although uncalled.
As when I did not love them I would hail,
Unloving now I have them, but know well
They will devour the self that I have sold.

'Yet you, O Sun, whose gold was once my prey,
And you, O Moon, whose silver I converted,
If beauty has been given all away
That I could have so often on demand,
At least let my exhausted self be parted –
The self that is essential be deserted
And soul and self in not my body stand!

'And may my final magic now convert me
Into my statue – sinew, bone and vein!
Die who I am, but who made me and hurt me,
The nameless presence born perpetually,
Flesh of my abstract love dragging its chain,
Be it my death wherein I live again:
Such as I was, being nothing, let me be!'

Cat playing in the street

Cat playing in the street
As if it were your bed,
I envy you your fate
For fate is never said.

Good slave to those grim laws
That govern stones and us,
Pure urges guide your paws,
You feel without a fuss.

You are glad to be so,
Your own nonentity.
I see my absence, know
The self that is not me.

No: don't say a thing!

No: don't say a thing!
The imagined word
From your covered mouth
Is already heard.

This heard is better
Than what you would say.
What you are does not
Flower by phrase or day.

Better than yourself,
Don't say a thing: be!
Naked body's grace
Veiled for all to see.

Death is a bend in the road

Death is a bend in the road,
Dying is just being missed.
I listen and hear you gone
Existing as I exist.

The earth is made of heaven.
Deception has no heir.
No one has ever been lost.
All's true, and a way somewhere.

Autopsychography

The poet is a fake.
His faking seems so real
That he will fake the ache
Which he can really feel.

And those who read his cries
Feel in the paper tears
Not two aches that are his
But one that is not theirs.

And so round in its ring
Giving the mind a game
Goes this train on a string
And the heart is its name.

This

They say I fake or lie
All I write. Not a bit.
It is simply that I
Feel with my mind and wit.
No heart comes into it.

All that I dream or suffer,
That hurts, hastens my end,
Is like a ledge above a
Beauty that lies beyond.
To this I am constrained.

And this is why I write
Of what is not to heel,
Free of my private plight,
Obsessed with the unreal.
Feel? Let the reader feel!

Between sleep and dream

Between sleep and dream,
Between me and my mind
Is what I think I am,
Flows a river without end.

Elsewhere it first unravels,
By shores of many kinds,
Upon those various travels
Where all the river winds.

It comes where I have docked,
The house I am today.
It goes if I reflect;
I wake, it has gone away.

And who I feel and dies
In this self-to-self bond
Sleeps where the river flows –
This river without end.

In this world where we forget

In this world where we forget,
We are shades of who we are
And our real signs in that
Other, our souls' habitat,
Are wry face and gesture here.

All is night, confusion reigns
In what here among us is
Scattered smoke and vague outlines
From the light that dimly shines
In the life that gives us eyes.

But someone, some time, can lift
His gaze clear and will perceive
In the shades that move and shift
What in that world is the drift
Of the sign that makes it live.

And then he will find the sense
Of what sets his face awry,
Turning to his flesh gone hence,
As an image grasped for once,
Insights of the gazing eye.

They, as shades of yearning flesh,
Will lie to that marvellous
Truth they feel bound by the lash
Which now fells them with a crash
To the ground of time and space.

For a moment

For a moment,
Upon my arm,
In a movement
Less of thought than
Of weariness,
You laid your hand
And withdrew it.
Did I feel that
Or didn't I?

I don't know. But
I have, still feel
Some memory,
Steady, solid,
Of you laying
Your hand that had
Felt what it did
Not understand,
But so lightly!…

This is nothing,
But on a road
Such as life is
There is something
Not understood…

Do I know if,
When your hand felt
Itself lying
Upon my arm
And a little
Upon my heart,
There was no new
Rhythm in space?

As if you, not
Intending to,
Touched off in me
Without a word
Some mystery,
Sudden, divine,
That you did not

Know existed.

Likewise the breeze
In the branches
Without knowing
Muttered something
Vague but happy.

Freedom

Oh what fun
To leave a job undone,
A book that must be read
On the shelf instead!
Reading is a bore,
Study even more,
The sun shines
Without immortal lines,
The river flows, smaller or greater,
Without an *imprimatur*,
And the breeze,
So early by nature,
Takes its time with the trees…

Books are sheets of paper inked.
Study is something that leaves indistinct
The distinction between nothing and no thing.

How much nicer, when the fog hangs low,
To await the once and future king, [1]
Whether he comes or no!

What's great is poetry, goodness and the dance…
But above all things, children most entrance,
With flowers, song, moonlight, sun that goes astray
Only when life it warmed it burns away.

What most pleases
Is Christ Jesus,
Who had no knowledge of finance
Nor, it is said, a library…

[1] the once and future king: Sebastian. See note to 'Dom Sebastian, King of Portugal' (p 26)

At the Tomb of Christian Rosencreutz [1]

We had not yet seen the corpse of our prudent wise Father. That is why we removed the altar to one side. Then we could raise a strong sheet of yellow metal, and there lay a fair and famous body, whole and undecayed... and it had in its hand a small parchment book, written in gold, entitled T., which after the Bible is our highest treasure and must not be readily submitted to the censure of the world.

Fama Fraternitatis Roseae Crucis

I

When we are wakened from this sleep of life
And shall know what we are and what that fall
Into the Body was, that dropping off
Into the Night that barricades our Soul,

Shall we learn then the whole of the concealed
Truth about everything that is and flows?
No: in the free Soul it is not revealed...
Nor housed in God who has created us.

God is Man of another God, a greater:
He also has a Fall, Adam Supreme;
He also was, as once was our Creator,

Created, and to him the Truth has died...
Beyond, the Abyss, His Spirit, denies it Him;
The World, His Body, has it not this side.

II

But long before that was the Word, here lost
When the Infinite Light, already quelled,
From Chaos, ground of Being, was upheld
In Shade, and the absent Word was overcast.

But if the Soul feels wrong in form, as Shade
Within her is at last the vision granted
Of the Word of this World, human, anointed,
The Perfect Rose, within God crucified.

[1] Christian Rosencreutz: legendary founder of the Brotherhood of the Rosy Cross, a seventeenth-century German secret society which as the Rosicrucian movement was to attract (among others) Satie, Yeats and Pessoa. A form of Gnosticism like Freemasonry, it claims that the God who became man is inferior to the Being who communicates with its followers.

And then we who are lords of Heaven's threshold
May go in search beyond God to behold
The Master's Secret and the deepest Good;

Wakened from here, but from ourselves too, we
Shall in Christ's present blood at last be free
From all that dies to God, from this World's brood.

III

But here, alas, unreal we blunder, here
We sleep off what we are, and though the truth
Comes to us in our dreams, finally clear,
Because it is in dream we see a wraith.

Shades seeking bodies, once within our reach
How can they show us their reality?
With hands of shade, what is it we Shades touch?
Our touch is but an absence, vacancy.

Who frees us from this Soul, its bolt and bar?
Unseeing, we can hear beyond the hall
Of being: but how, here, fling wide the door?

Laid out before us, in false death at rest
With the closed Book in place upon his breast,
Our Rosecrossed Father knows and will not tell.

To the blind and the deaf

To the blind and the deaf
I leave my bounded soul:
I want to feel all things
In all ways possible.

From heights of consciousness
I survey earth and sky:
Nothing I see is mine
To my innocent eye.

But with such care I look
And into them disperse
Myself, that with each thought
I have become diverse;

And just as things dispersed
Are splinters of the real
I break my soul in bits
And each by name I call;

And if I see my soul
From other points of view,
I wonder if this brings
A chance to judge anew.

Ah, so much like the earth,
The sea, the boundless sky!
The self-creator errs;
Not mine this various I.

If things are splinters of
The knowing universe,
Let bits of me be me,
Unfocused and diverse.

If I feel so removed
And not at home to me,
How is it that my soul
Came finally to be?

This way I fit myself
Into God's cosmic frame.
God has diversity:
Diversities I am,

Thus imitating God
Who when he made the world
Creamed off the infinite
And unity withheld.

The moon (the English say)

The moon (the English say)
Is made out of green cheese.
A thousand times you may
Think it, an idea flees.

It was this, this again,
This idea that would spare
My soul the nagging pain
Of... could it be desire?

I only want my way
Thus: to think as I feel...
The moon (the English say)
Is blue once in a while.

ALBERTO CAEIRO

CONTENTS

from The Keeper of Flocks

2. *My gaze is clear as a sunflower*

My gaze is clear as a sunflower,
It is my habit to walk along roads
Looking right and left,
And from time to time looking back...
And what I see at any moment
Is something I have never seen before,

And I can notice very well...
I can know the essential wonder
A child knows if at birth
It noticed it was actually being born...
I feel myself born at any moment
To the eternal newness of the World...

I believe in the world like a marigold,
Because I see it. But I don't think about it
Because to think is to not understand...
The World was not made for us to think about it
(To think is to have a pain in the eyes)
But for us to look at it and agree...

I have no philosophy: I have feelings...
If I speak of Nature it is not because I know what it is,
But because I love it, and this is why:
Whoever loves never knows what he loves
Nor why he loves, nor what it is to love...

To love is eternal innocence
And the only innocence is not to think...

5. *There is enough metaphysics*

There is enough metaphysics in not thinking about anything.

What do I think of the world?
Who knows what I think of the world?
If I fell ill I would think about it.

What idea do I have of things?
What opinion do I have about causes and effects?

What have I considered about God and the soul
And about the creation of the World?
I don't know. For me, thinking about it is shutting my eyes
And not thinking. It is drawing my curtains
(Except that I have none).

The mystery of things? Who knows what mystery is?
The only mystery is having someone who thinks about mystery.
Whoever is in the sun and shuts his eyes
Begins not to know what the sun is
And to think many things full of heat.
But he opens his eyes and sees the sun,
And he can no longer think about anything
Because the sunlight is worth more than the thoughts
Of all the philosophers and all the poets.
The sunlight does not know what it is doing
And so it does no wrong but is ordinary and good.

Metaphysics? What metaphysics do these trees have?
That of being green and bushy and of having branches
And of yielding fruit in their season, which does not make us think–
Who don't know how to notice them.
But what better metaphysics than theirs –
That of not knowing what they live for
Nor knowing that they don't know?

'Inner constitution of things' ...
'Inner sense of the Universe' ...
That is all wrong, that is all meaningless.
It is incredible that such things can be thought about.
It is like thinking about reasons and ends
When the start of morning sheds light, and round the sides of trees
A vague glittering gold banishes the dark.

Thinking about the inner sense of things
Is even worse than thinking about health
Or taking a glass of water to a spring.
The only inner sense of things
Is that they have no inner sense whatever.

I don't believe in God because I have never seen him.
If he wanted me to believe in him,
He would doubtless come and talk with me
And step in through my door
Saying *Here I am!*

(This may be ridiculous to the ears
Of one who, by not knowing what it is to look at things,
Does not understand one who speaks of them
In the way of speaking that noticing them teaches.)

But if God is the flowers and the trees
And the hills and the sun and the moonlight,
Then I believe in him,
Then I believe in him all the time,
And all my life is a prayer and a Mass,
And a communion with the eyes and through the ears.

But if God is the trees and the flowers
And the hills and the moonlight and the sun,
Why do I call him God?
I'll call him flowers and trees and hills and sun and moonlight;
For if he made himself for me to see him,
Sun and moonlight and flowers and trees and hills,
If he appears to me as trees and hills
And moonlight and sun and flowers,
It is because he wants me to know him
As I know trees and hills and flowers and moonlight and sun.

And so I obey him
(What more do I know of God than God knows of himself?)
I obey him by living, spontaneously,
As one who opens his eyes and sees,
And I call him moonlight and sun and flowers and trees and hills,
And I love him without thinking about him,
And I think of him by seeing and hearing
And I walk with him all the time.

7. *From my village I see as much*

From my village I see as much as from the earth can be seen of the
    Universe...
So my village is as big as any other earth,
For I am the size of what I see
And not the size of how tall I am...

In cities life is smaller
Than here in my house on this hilltop.
In the city the big houses lock away the view,
They hide the horizon, push our gaze far from all the sky,
They make us small because they remove what our eyes can give us
And make us poor because our only wealth is to see.

9. *I am a keeper of flocks*

I am a keeper of flocks.
The flock is my thoughts
And my thoughts are all sensations.
I think with my eyes and with my ears
And with my hands and feet
And with my nose and mouth.

To think a flower is to see it and smell it
And to eat a fruit is to know its taste.

So when on a hot day
I feel sad from enjoying it so much,
And I stretch out in the grass
And shut my hot eyes,
I feel all my body basking in the real,
I know the truth and I am happy.

14. *I don't bother with rhymes*

I don't bother with rhymes. Seldom
Are there two trees alike, one beside another.
I think and write as flowers blush
But express myself less perfectly
Because I lack the divine simplicity
To be all on the outside only.

I look and am moved,
Moved by the water flowing when the ground slopes,
And my poetry is natural as the wind rising...

20. *The Tagus is more beautiful*

The Tagus [1] is more beautiful than the river which flows through my village,
But the Tagus is not more beautiful than the river which flows through my vill
Because the Tagus is not the river which flows through my village.

The Tagus has big vessels
And still upon it sails
For those who see in all things what is not there
The memory of ships.

The Tagus comes down from Spain
And the Tagus flows into the sea off Portugal.
Everyone knows that.
But few know about my village river
Or whence it goes
Or whence it comes.
And so, because it belongs to fewer people,
My village river is freer and greater.

Via the Tagus you can see the World.
Beyond the Tagus lies America
And the fortune of those who find it.
No one has ever thought of what lies beyond
My village river.

My village river prompts no thoughts.
Who stands beside it merely stands beside it.

[1] Tagus: the river at whose estuary Lisbon stands.

21. *If I could crunch up the whole earth*

If I could crunch up the whole earth
And savour it,
I would be happier for a moment…
But I don't always want to be happy.
We have to be unhappy now and then
So that we can be natural…

It is not all sunny days,
And rain, when it is very short, is prayed for.
So I take unhappiness with happiness

Naturally, as one who is not puzzled
That there are mountains and plains
And there are cliffs and grass...

What we have to be is natural and calm to ourselves
Whether happy or unhappy,
To feel like one who looks,
To think like one who walks,
And when we are dying, to remember that day dies,
And that the sunset is beautiful and beautiful the night that is left...
So is it and so be it...

24. *What we see of things is things*

What we see of things is things.
Why would we see something if there were something else?
Why would seeing and hearing be there to deceive us
When seeing and hearing are seeing and hearing?

What matters is knowing how to see,
Knowing how to see without stopping to think,
Knowing how to see when it is obvious,
And neither thinking when it is obvious
Nor seeing when it is thinkable.

But that (alas for us whose souls are in full dress!),
That requires profound study,
An apprenticeship in unlearning
And an isolation in freedom from that convent
Whose poets say that stars are eternal nuns
And flowers convicts of a single day,
But where after all the stars are only stars
And the flowers only flowers,
Being therefore, as we call them, stars and flowers.

28. *Today I read nearly two pages*

Today I read nearly two pages
Of a book by a mystical poet,
And I laughed like one who has wept a lot.

Mystical poets are sick philosophers,
And philosophers are madmen.

For mystical poets say that flowers feel
And they say that stones have souls
And that rivers have ecstasies by moonlight.

But flowers, if they could feel, would not be flowers,
They would be people;
And if stones had souls they would be living things, they would not be
    stones;
And if rivers had ecstasies by moonlight,
Rivers would be sick men.

One has to be ignorant of flowers and stones and rivers
In order to speak of their feelings.
To speak of the souls of stones, of flowers, of rivers,
Is to speak of oneself and one's delusions.
Thank God that stones are only stones,
And that rivers are nothing but rivers,
And that flowers are merely flowers.
As for me, I write the prose of my poetry
And I rest content,
For I know that I understand Nature from without;
And I don't understand it from within
Because Nature has no within;
Otherwise it would not be Nature.

32. Yesterday afternoon a townsman

Yesterday afternoon a townsman
Spoke at the door of the inn.
He spoke with me as well.

He spoke of justice and the struggle for justice
And of the suffering workers,
And of unremitting toil, and of the hungry,
And of the rich, who just turn their backs.

And, looking at me, he saw tears in my eyes
And he smiled approval, judging that I felt
The hatred he felt, and the compassion
He said he felt.

(But I was hardly listening.
What do men matter to me
And what they suffer or suppose they suffer?
Let them be like me – they will not suffer.
All the world's trouble comes from our mattering to one another,
Whether to do good, or to do evil.
Our souls and the sky and the earth are enough for us.
To want more is to lose this, and to be unhappy.)

What I was thinking about
When the people's friend was speaking
(And it moved me to tears),
Was how the distant tinkle of cowbells
As evening drew on
Was not like the bells of a tiny chapel
Call to Mass flowers and streams
And simple souls like mine.

(God be praised that I am not good,
And have the natural selfishness of flowers
And rivers that follow their courses
Preoccupied without knowing
Only with blooming and flowing.
The one mission in the World
Is this – to exist clearly,
And to know how to do it without thinking about it.)

And the man had fallen silent, watching the sunset.
But what does the sunset mean to one who hates and loves?

39. *The mystery of things, where is it?*

The mystery of things, where is it?
Where is it that does not appear
At least showing us what mystery is?
What does the river know of it and what does the tree?
And I, who am no more than they, what do I know of it?
Whenever I look at things and think what men think of them,
I laugh like a brook babbling cool over a pebble.
For the only hidden sense of things
Is that they have no hidden sense at all,
Is stranger than all strangenesses,

Than the dreams of all the poets
And the thoughts of all the philosophers,
That things are really what they seem
And there is nothing to understand.

Yes, this is what my senses have learned by themselves:
Things do not mean: they exist.
Things are the only hidden sense of things.

43. Sooner the flight of a bird

Sooner the flight of a bird, passing and leaving no trace,
Than the passing of an animal, remembered by the ground.
The bird passes and forgets, and so should it be.
The animal, where it is no more and so is useless,
Shows it once was, which is no use.

Memory is a betrayal of Nature,
Because yesterday's Nature is not Nature.
What was is nothing, and to remember is to see nothing.

Pass, bird, pass, and teach me to pass!

47. One exceedingly clear day

One exceedingly clear day
That prompted a wish to have worked hard
So as not to work at all then,
I glimpsed, like a road through trees,
What may be the Great Secret,
That Great Mystery of which false poets speak.

I saw that there is no Nature,
That Nature does not exist,
That there are hills, valleys, plains,
That there are trees, flowers, grasses,
That there are rivers and stones,
But that there is no whole to which all that belongs,
That a real, true oneness
Is a disease of our ideas.

Nature is parts without a whole.
That may be the so-called mystery they speak of.

That was what without pausing to reflect
I guessed right must be the truth
They all go for and do not find,
And only I, because I did not go for it, have found.

The amazing reality of things

The amazing reality of things
Is my everyday discovery.
Everything is what it is,
And it is hard to explain to anyone how glad that makes me,
And how it is enough for me.

To exist is enough to be fulfilled.

I have written enough poems.
I shall write many more, of course.
Every poem tells me this,
And all my poems are different
Because everything that is is a way of saying this.

Sometimes I start looking at a stone.
I don't start wondering whether it feels.
I don't lose myself calling it my sister,
But I enjoy it for being a stone,
I enjoy it because it does not feel anything,
I enjoy it because it has no kinship whatever with me.

Other times I hear the wind passing,
And I find that just to hear the wind passing is worth the trouble of being
    born.

I don't know what others will think on reading this;
But I find this must be all right because I think it unhindered,
With no idea of other people hearing me think it;
For I think it without thoughts,
For I tell it the way my words tell it.

Some time they will call me a materialist poet,
And I admired myself because I did not imagine

I could be called anything.
I am not even a poet: I see.
If what I write has any value, I don't have it:
The value lies there, in my poetry.
It is all utterly independent of my will.

If I die young

If I die young,
Without being able to publish any book,
Without seeing how my poetry looks in print,
I ask anyone who might worry on my account
Not to worry.
If that is how it has turned out, that is how it is.

Even if my poetry is never printed,
There its beauty will lie, if it has any.
But it cannot be beautiful and remain unprinted,
For roots may be underground
But flowers bloom in the open free and for all to see.
It must be so perforce. Nothing can stop it.

If I die very young, let them hear this:
I was never more than a child at play.
I was heathen as the sun and water,
Of a universal religion only men do not have.
I was happy because I did not ask for anything,
Nor sought for anything,
Nor found that there was any more explanation
Than that the word explanation is meaningless.

I craved only to stand in the sun or rain –
In the sun when it was sunny
And in the rain when it was raining
(And never anything else),
To feel heat and cold and wind,
And to go no further.

Once I loved, thought they loved me,
But I was not loved.
I was not loved for the one great reason:
I did not have to be.

I consoled myself by returning to the sun and rain,
And sitting down again at my door.
The fields, when all is said, are not as green for those who are loved
As for those who are not.
To feel is to be distracted.

If, after I die

If, after I die, they should want to write my biography,
There is nothing simpler.
I have only two dates – that of my birth and that of my death.
Between the one and the other all the days are mine.

I am easy to define.
I lived like one damned.
I loved things with no sentimentality whatever.
I never had a wish I could not realise, for I never went blind.
Even hearing was never for me anything but an accompaniment to seeing.
I understood that things are real and all of them different from one
    another;
I understood this with my eyes, never with my thoughts.
To understand this with my thoughts would be to find them all alike.

One day I fell asleep like some child.
I closed my eyes and slept.
Anyway, I was the only Nature poet.

RICARDO REIS

CONTENTS

ODES

ODES

Crown me with roses

Crown me with roses,
Crown me really
    With roses –
Roses that fade
On brows to fade
    So soon!
Crown me with roses
And with brief leaves.
    Enough.

Come and sit down with me, Lydia

Come and sit down with me, Lydia, on the bank of the river.
Quietly let us watch it flowing and learn
That life is passing, and we are not holding hands.
    (Let us hold hands.)

Then let us think, as grown up children, that life
Passes and does not stay, nothing stops or ever turns back,
It goes towards a sea very far away, towards where Fate is,
    Further away than the gods.

Let us stop holding hands, for it is not worth tiring ourselves.
Whether we enjoy or not, we pass with the river.
Better to know how to pass silently
    And without great disquiet.

Without loves, or hates, or passions that raise the voice,
Or envies that set the eyes in motion too,
Or cares, for if it had them the river would still flow,
    Would still go to meet the sea.

Let us love calmly, thinking that we could,
If we would, exchange kisses and embraces and caresses,
But that it is better to sit beside each other
    Hearing the river flow and seeing it.

Let us gather flowers, and you, take hold of them, leave them
On your bosom, and let their perfume sweeten the moment –

This moment when quietly we believe in nothing,
     Innocent pagans of decadence.

At least, if dark comes before, you will remember me after
Without the memory of me burning or striking or moving you,
For we never hold hands, or kiss,
     Nor were we more than children.

And if before me you bear the penny to the dark boatman,
I shall have nothing to suffer remembering you.
You will be sweet to my memory remembering you thus – on the river-
  bank,
     A sad pagan with flowers in your lap.

The roses in the gardens of Adonis

The roses in the gardens of Adonis,
Those fleeting roses, Lydia, I love,
     Which on the day they are born,
     Upon the same day die.
To them the light is everlasting, for
After the sun's birth they are born, and fade
     Before Apollo leaves
     His visible career.
Likewise let us make of our life *one day*,
Willingly, Lydia, oblivious
     That night precedes, succeeds
     The little time we last.

Everything in its season has its season

Everything in its season has its season.
In wintertime the groves are not in bloom,
     Nor in the days of spring
     Are the fields white with frost.
The night as it draws in is not the time,
Lydia, for the heat day asked of us.
     Let us with greater quiet
     Love our uncertain life.
Snug at the fireside, weary not from work

But because now is the hour of weariness,
  Let us not raise our voices
  Above a whispered word,
And let our uttered reminiscences
Come at odd moments and be broken off
  (The sun's dark going is
  No use to us for more).
Little by little let us call to mind
The past and stories told us in the past
  Become now stories of
  Stories that speak to us
Of flowers that in our childhood long ago
We gathered with another consciousness
  And with another kind
  Of outlook on the world.
Thus at the fireside, Lydia, as though
Gods of the hearth, there in eternity,
  As one who dresses up
  Let us put on old times
In that disquiet which taking a rest
Brings to our lives when all we do is think
  Of what we were, and there
  Is only night outside.

From our resemblance to the immortal gods

From our resemblance to the immortal gods
  For our good let us take
Our sense that we are exiled deities
  Having our hold on Life
By some original authority
  Of the same age as Jove.

Arrogant in our lordship of ourselves,
  Let's make the most of things
As of the villa which the gods grant us
  To forget summer in.

No effort in a more tormented form
  Is worth our while for making
The most of the dark river's vague existence
  And its death-dealing stream.

Just as above the gods' heads Destiny
    Is calm and beyond prayer,
Above our own heads now let us raise up
    A voluntary fate
That when it shall oppress us we may be
    That which oppresses us,
And when we go into the night within
    We go on our own feet.

This is our only liberty

This is our only liberty the gods
    Grant – to submit ourselves
To their dominion over our free will.
    This is more worth our while
For only in the illusion of liberty
    Does liberty exist.

No other trick do gods, above whose head
    Dangles eternal fate,
Resort to for the ancient certainty
    Held for their peace of mind
That life for them is both divine and free.

    Behaving like the gods,
Unfree as they who dwell upon Olympus,
    As one who in the sand
Builds castles to amaze those who look on,
    Let us so build our life
And then the gods will learn to give us thanks
    For being as they are.

The ancient rhythm of unsandalled feet

The ancient rhythm of unsandalled feet,
That rhythm still repeated by the nymphs
    When in the grove they beat
    The music of the dance,
Remember as you tread the bright white beach
Made darker by the encroaching spume; to you

Children who do not yet
Care to take care, the loud
Carol replies while like a lofty bough
Gilding the blue sky's curve Apollo bends
And the perpetual tide
Turns with its ebb and flow.

I have heard tell

I have heard tell that once when Persia was
At war – I don't know which –
As the invading City burnt its way
And all the women screamed,
There were two players at a game of chess
Who went on with their game.

Cool in the shade of spreading branches they
Stared at their ancient board,
And by the side of each, awaiting their
Moments of greater ease
When one had made a move and waited now
For his opponent's move,
A pitcher full of wine would soberly
Refresh the player's thirst.

Houses were burnt, and brought to rack and ruin
Was every arch and wall,
Women were raped and then propped up against
Collapsing masonry
To be run through with spears, their children were
Pools of blood in the streets...
But where they were, the city close at hand
And its noise far away,
The players at the game of chess were still
Playing their game of chess.

Although the desert wind brought messages
To them of screams and cries,
And on reflection they knew in their souls
For certain that their wives
And all their tender daughters had been raped
So near and yet so far,

Although that moment when they realised
    A fleeting shadow passed
Over their brows preoccupied and vague,
    In no time their calm eyes
Turned their devoted concentration back
    Towards the old chess board.

When the ivory king is under threat
    What can the flesh and blood
Of sisters, mothers, children mean to them?
    When the rook cannot cover
The move of the white queen as she retreats,
    The sack has little meaning;
And when the hand full of self-confidence
    Checks the opponent's king
The soul is hardly troubled that out there
    Sons are about to die.

Even if suddenly above the wall
    Rises the furious face
Of an invading warrior, and soon
    Bloodily there must fall
The solemn player at his game of chess,
    The moment just before
(Is still given up to working out a move
    To be made hours from then)
Is still devoted to the favourite game
    Of the uncaring great.

Let cities fall, let peoples suffer, let
    Freedom and life be lost,
Inherited possessions quietly burn
    And let them be destroyed,
But when war interrupts the games, then let
    The king be out of check
And the ivory pawn furthest ahead
    Ready to take the rook.

My brothers in our love of Epicurus
    And in our understanding
Better of one another than of him
    Let us learn from the tale
Of the calm players at their game of chess
    How best to spend our lives.

Let all that's serious mean not much to us,
      What is grave weigh not much,
And let the natural instinctive drive
      Yield to the useless joy
(Under the peaceful shadow of the grove)
      Of playing a good game.

What we take with us from this useless life
      Is worth as much if it
Is glory, fame or love, knowledge or life,
      As if it were no more
Than the remembrance of a game well played
      And of a competition
      Won by a better player.

Like a rich burden glory weighs us down
      And like the fever fame,
Love wearies, being serious and searching,
      And knowledge never finds,
And life goes on and hurts because it knows…
      Meanwhile the game of chess
Takes the whole soul, but being a waste it weighs
      Little and comes to nothing.

Ah! beneath shades that love but do not need us,
      With a pitcher of wine
Beside us, busy only with the useless
      Task of the game of chess,
Although the game be no more than a dream
      With no partner to play,
Let us be like the Persians of this tale,
      And while outside, be it near
Or far off, war and fatherland and life
      Call on us, let us leave
Their call to go unheard, each one of us
      Beneath the friendly shades
Dreaming, with each for partners, and the chess
      The fact they do not care.

I prefer roses to my country

I prefer roses to my country, love,
  Magnolias mean more
  To me than glory and virtue.
As long as life does not tire me, I'll let
  Life pass me by as long
  As I remain the same.
What does he care who cares no more that one
  Should lose, another win,
  If dawn still sheds its beams,
If every year with the return of spring
  The trees burst into leaf
  That falls when autumn comes?
As for the rest, the other things that men
  Add to life, what do they
  Contribute to my soul?
Nothing but a desire for unconcern
  And an uncomplicated
  Trust in the fleeting hour.

You, Christ, I do not hate

You, Christ, I do not hate or estimate
Less than the other gods preceding you
  In mankind's memory.
Not more nor less are you, but another god.

You missed the Pantheon. Because you came
Take up your place within the Pantheon,
  But beware lest you try
To seize from other gods what is their due!

Your sad face fills with sympathy towards
The barren grief of old humanity:
  New beauty it has brought,
Yes, to the old uncertain Pantheon.

But let your faithful not exalt you above
Other and earlier gods who dated back
  By being Saturn's sons
Nearer the equal origin of things;

And may they gather better memories
Of chaos, the beginning, and of Night
      Where the gods are no more
Than the stars subject to the whims of Fate!

You are but one eternal god too many.
It is not you but yours I hate, O Christ –
      Our Pantheon that rules
      On our uncertain life.

No greater and no less than the new gods
Your sombre form so full of suffering
      Brought something missing to
      The number of the gods.

So reign as peer of others on Olympus,
Or, should you wish it, here on the sad earth
      Go, wipe away the tears
      Of suffering mankind.

But let your stupid worshippers not come
Blocking in your name the eternal worship
      Of greater presences
      Or partners of your own.

Yes, it is those I hate from the deep core
Of my believing breast and will not follow,
      Those superstitious laymen
      In knowledge of the gods.

The bee that on the wing hovers above

The bee that on the wing hovers above
The bright-hued flower that settles on it, scarcely
      Distinguishable from
      That which it cannot see,
Since Cecrops [1] has not changed. He only who
Lives a life with a being that knows itself
      Grows old, is other than
      The kind by which he lives.
This is the same as what is different. We
Only – O time, O soul, O life, O death! –
      To have more life than life
      Itself, buy it and die.

[1] Cecrops: mythical founder of Athens who introduced agriculture.

The flower you are

The flower you are, not which you give, I want,
For you deny me what I do not ask.
        There will be time for your
        Denial after your gift.
Flower, be my flower! If you are greedily
Plucked by the fateful sphinx's hand, for ever
        A silly shade you will
        Roam, seeking what is not.

What a short season is the longest life

What a short season is the longest life
And youth within it! Ah me, Chloe, Chloe,
        If I don't love or drink,
        Nor without wishing brood,
The merciless law leans on me, the unwilling
Hour brings me pain, the time that never stops,
        And my ears catch the noise
        The rushes make along
The hidden shore where the cold irises
Shoot from the lower sod, and the mainstream
        Does not know where day is,
        A whisper full of groans.

Ashen already over my vain brow

Ashen already over my vain brow
The hair of that young man whom I have lost.
        My eyes are not so bright.
My mouth no longer has a right to kisses.
If you still love me, don't love for love's sake,
        Cuckolding me with me.

In what a flood of grief and bitterness

In what a flood of grief and bitterness
Our narrow life is overwhelmed! How much
     Miserable misfortune
     Grinds us to reign supreme!
Happy the brute beast that upon green fields
Grazes, not knowing its own name, and goes
     To death like going home;
     The scholar too, absorbed
In knowledge, lifted by stern paltry life
Beyond our own like smoke that raises its
     Arms to be lost in a
     Heaven that does not exist.

To no avail now do your hands beseech

To no avail now do your hands beseech,
Nor do your lips convince now they are still
     And stifled underground
     With wet earth laid on them.
Only perhaps the smile with which you loved
Embalms you out of reach, in memories
     Raises you as you were,
     Today a putrid hive.
The useless name which your dead body wore,
Living, on earth, as it were a soul, does not
     Remember. The ode grave,
     Anonymous, a smile.

Whatever stops is death

Whatever stops is death, and that death is
Ours if for our sake it has stopped. That bush
     Withers, and with it goes
     A little of my life.
I am a part of everything I see
And if it passes, I pass. Memory
     Does not distinguish what
     I saw from what I was.

Lydia, when our autumn comes along

Lydia, when our autumn comes along
With winter in its pocket, let us spare
A thought, not for the spring to come, for that
      Belongs to someone else,
Nor for the summer, which will kill us off,
But for that which remains of what is passing –
The present yellow which the leaves live now
      And turns them otherwise.

Not only he who hates or envies us

Not only he who hates or envies us
Limits us, weighs us down: who loves us too
      He limits us no less.
May the gods grant that I, stripped bare of all
Attachments, may with nothing know the cold
      Liberty of the heights.
He who wants little, has all; who wants nothing
Is free; who has not, does not crave, that man
      Is equal to the gods.

You would be great?

You would be great? Be whole: of what you are
      Play nothing up nor down.
Be all in everything and put your most
      Into the least you do.
So the moon shines entire in every lake
      Because it lives above.

My only wish is that the gods forget me

My only wish is that the gods forget me.
I shall be free, not in nor out of luck,
    As the wind that is life
    To immaterial air.
Hatred and love alike seek us, and both,
Either in its own fashion, weigh us down.
    He who by gods is granted
    Nothing, has liberty.

ÁLVARO DE CAMPOS

CONTENTS

Opiary [1]

Before the opium, then my soul grows faint.
On feeling life it rallies but soon fails
And I seek in the opium that consoles
An Orient eastward of the Orient.

This life on board is bound one day to hit me.
There are whole days of fever in my head
And though I search till I might well be dead
I can no longer find a spring to fit me.

Paradox-bound, galactically unable,
Folded in cloth of gold I live my life,
A wave where self-respect tips in a trough
And even joys are ganglions on my trouble.

Thanks to a mechanism made of dooms,
A gear whose meshes fly round out of true,
I pass between visions of scaffolds to
A garden where flowers hover with no stems.

I stagger through an inner life all threaded
With traceries of lace and lacquered stuff.
I seem to be at home, holding the knife
With which old John the Baptist was beheaded.

Atoning for a crime hid in a trunk
An ancestor committed who was dainty,
I have my nerves strung up, twenty by twenty,
And into opium like a pit I've sunk.

When morphine touches with its slumber, I
Merge with the heartbeat of transparencies
And in a night where diamonds crowd the skies
I see the moon rise like my Destiny.

I, who was always a bad student, now
Do nothing more than watch the ship that slides
Along the Suez Canal and how it guides
My life, a lump of camphor in dawn's glow.

The days I once made use of are a wreck.
I've worked towards no more than weariness
That is today a kind of arm whose press

[1] Opiary: *opiário*. A coinage, the word seems to mean 'opium addict'.

Chokes and protects me, wound around my neck.

And I have been a child too, like the rest of 'em
I was born somewhere deep in Portugal
And I have known some English people, all
Of whom said I know English like the best of 'em.

I enjoyed getting poems and short stories
Published by Plon and in *Mercure de France*;[2]
But that life should go on like this? No chance,
If on this trip no wind gave rise to worries!

Life aboard ship is not a laughing matter,
Although there are diversions now and then:
I talk with Germans, Swedes and Englishmen
But my world-weariness does not get better.

I find it is not worth while to have been
Out East, to have seen the Indies and Cathay.
The earth is all alike, one petty way
To live and there are none to choose between.

This is why I take opium. It cheers.
The Moment ailed me: I am convalescent.
I live on the ground floor of thought – not pleasant
When seeing Life go by bores me to tears.

I smoke. I tire. Oh for an earth, I say,
Where so much east was not already west!
Why did I visit Indies that exist
If all the Indies are the soul in me?

I am unlucky in the rights I hold.
My legacy was stolen by the gipsies.
Even when I am close to death, perhaps is
Nowhere to shelter me from my own cold.

I've studied engineering, more or less.
I've lived in Scotland, been to Ireland too.[3]
My heart is now a poor old granny who
Goes begging at the gates of Happiness.

Iron ship, don't make Port Said a port of call!
Turn right, though I don't know what lies in front.

[2] Plon… *Mercure de France*: a Paris publisher and literary journal.
[3] Scotland… Ireland: Pessoa, who never visited the British Isles, is speaking as Álvaro de Campos.

I spend days in the smoke-room like the count –
A French *escroc*, [4] fresh from a funeral.

Back now in Europe, discontent and sure
To be a poet of Somnambolism, [5]
I am for King but not Catholicism
And would enjoy having a share of power.

I'd enjoy having credits, hard cash there,
And being someone, even someone dull.
Today, here, I am nothing after all
More than, aboard some ship, a passenger.

I have no personality, no ways.
More noteworthy than me is that ship's steward
Who sports the high-flown manner of a laird
Straight from a Scottish moor on fasting days.

I cannot settle anywhere, am based
Outside my country. I am ill and weak.
The purser is a crook. He saw me speak
To the Swedish woman… and he guessed the rest.

One day I cause a scandal here on board,
Only to give them something to discuss.
In life I cannot, and am at a loss
When now and then my rage runs overboard.

I spend the whole day smoking, tippling glasses,
Drugs from America that trip you up,
And me already drunk without a drop!
They'd give my nerves a better brain than roses.

I write these lines. It seems impossible
That even having talent does me harm!
The fact remains that this life is a farm
That horrifies the sensitive of soul.

The English triumph over any trial.
No other nation like them can keep Calm,
Cool and Collected. Here they number some
Twenty, of whom one manages a smile.

---

[4] *escroc*: French 'crook'.
[5] Somnambolism: combining somnambulism and Symbolism?

I belong to a class of Portuguese
Who, after India was discovered, stayed
Idle. Of death there's nothing to be said.
I have reflected on this many days.

To hell with life, the fact that people have it!
My bedside book, I have no taste for that.
The Orient sickens me. It is a mat
People roll up, it has no charm to save it.

I sink perforce in opium. To require
That I should live a life of virtue calls
On strength I do not have. These decent souls
Who sleep and eat at the appointed hour,

The devil take them! But no, that is spite,
For these nerves in the end will just unmake me.
Oh, that there is no vessel that will take me
Where I shall long for nothing out of sight!

Now! I grow weary in the same old way.
I need another opium strong enough
To drop out into dreams, be finished off
And laid out by them on a bed of clay.

Fever! If what I have is not a fever,
I don't know how the feverish can feel.
The essential fact remains that I am ill.
Thus, friends, I have accomplished my endeavour.

The night has come. Already the first post
Has sounded, it is time to dress for dinner.
Social life too! Spot on! And marching in a
Column till people's collars are unloosed!

Because it will end badly and there must be
(Ho!) blood and a revolver there to bring
To an end this disquiet I am suffering
For there is no specific remedy.

Who looks at me must find me commonplace,
Me and my life... Well now! a little boy...
Even my eyeglass will identify
Me as a member of a widespread race.

How many souls will live who have been brought,
As I have, into line, like me a mystic!
How many underneath that characteristic
Garb do no feel the dread which is my lot?

If at least on the outside I could be
As interesting as I am within!
I dive into the Maelstrom, spin and spin
More. Doing nothing is the death of me.

A good-for-nothing. But that suits me well!
If only other people were reviled
There I, though out at elbows, might be hailed
A hero, mad, accurst or beautiful!

I have an urge to lift my hands up to
My mouth and bite them through until they hurt –
A novel occupation to divert
The others, who are such good men and true.

The absurd, like a flower of the India
I never met in India, is born
Inside my brain fed up with being outworn.
God, change my life or else take it away…

Lord, leave me in this chair where I am sat
Till they come with a box to put me in.
I was born for the role of mandarin,
Except I lack the quiet, the tea, the mat.

How I would love to drop from here one day
To the grave through a trapdoor that slammed shut!
For blond tobacco I have some repute.
I've done no more than smoke my life away.

And what I want is faith, peace, after all,
Not this confusion every sense produces.
God, put a stop to it! Open the sluices –
Enough of farces played out in my soul!

In the Suez Canal, on board [6]

---

[6] *In the Suez Canal…*: Pessoa was never there, but Campos clearly was; cf *London* at the end of 'Triumphal Ode'.

Triumphal Ode

In the painful glare of the factory's big electric lights
I have a fever and I write.
I write gnashing my teeth, a wild beast for its beauty,
For its beauty quite unknown to the ancients.

O wheels, O gears, *r-r-r-r-r* going on for ever!
Strong, controlled spasm of mechanisms in fury!
In fury outside and inside me,
Through all my nerves withered outside,
Through all the nipples outside everything I feel with!
I have dry lips, O great modern noises,
From hearing you too close,
And my head burns from wanting you to sing with excessive
Expression of all my sensations,
With a contemporary excess of you, O machines!

Feverish and looking at motors as at some tropical Nature –
Great human tropics of iron and fire and force –
I sing, and I sing the present, and the past and the future as well.
For the present is all the past and all the future
And there are Plato and Virgil within the machines and the electric lights
Only because there were old times and Virgil and Plato were human,
And bits of Alexander the Great from perhaps the fiftieth century,
Atoms that will get a fever for the brain of the hundredth-century
    Squirrel,
Go along these transmission belts and these pistons and these flywheels,
Roaring, grinding, whispering, gurgling, unrelenting,
Excessively caressing my body with one caress of the soul.

Ah, to be able to express all of myself as a motor expresses itself!
To be complete as a machine!
To be able to go through life triumphant as a latest-model car!
To be able at least to penetrate myself physically with all that,
To rip all of myself fully open, to become absorbent
To all the perfumes of oils and heats and coals
Of this stupendous, black, artificial, insatiable flora!
Brotherhood with all the dynamics!
Indiscriminate fury of being an active part
Of iron rumbling and a cosmopolitan
Of strenuous trains,
Of the cargo-carrier toil of ships,
Of the lustful, slow rotation of cranes,

Of the disciplined tumult of factories,
And the whispering, monotonous near-silence of transmission belts!

Productive European hours, wedged
Between mechanism and useful business!
Big cities stopping by in cafés,
In cafés – cases of noisy idleness
Crystallising and precipitating
Rumours and gestures of the Useful
And wheels, the cogwheels and bearings of the Progressive!
New, soulless Minerva of quays and platforms!
New enthusiasms for the stature of the Moment!
Keels of smiling iron plates resting in docks,
Or high and dry on the inclined planes of ports!
International, transatlantic, Canadian Pacific activity!
Lights and feverish wastes of time in bars, in hotels,
At Longchamps and Derbies and Ascots,
And in Piccadillies and Avenues de l'Opéra that come
Inside my soul!

Hi there, streets, hi there, squares, hello, *la foule*! [1]
Everything that passes, everything that stops at shop windows!
Merchants; vagrants, dapper *escrocs*;
Obvious members of aristocratic clubs;
Squalid doubtful figures; family men vaguely happy
And fatherly even in the stream of gold running across the waistcoat
From pocket to pocket!
Everything that passes, everything that passes and never passes!
Overemphasised presence of *cocottes*, [2]
Interesting commonplace (and who knows the inside?)
Of middle-class women, mother and daughter mostly,
Walking in the street, going somewhere;
The mincing grace of homosexuals cruising;
And everyone with simple elegance strolling and showing off
And after all having a soul in there!

(Ah, how I would love to be the *souteneur* [3] of it all!)

The marvellous beauty of political corruptions,
Delicious financial and diplomatic scandals,

[1] *la foule*: French 'the crowd'.
[2] *cocottes*: French 'tarts'.
[3] *souteneur*: French 'pimp'.

Political attacks in the streets,
And now and then the comet of a regicide
Lighting with Freak and Fanfare the usual clear
Skies of everyday Civilisation!

Newspaper denials,
Insincerely sincere political articles,
Cheque-book journalism, big-time crimes –
Two columns going over the page!
The fresh smell of printer's ink!
Posters put up recently, still wet!
Yellow *vients-de-paraître* [4] with white wrappers!
How I love you all, all, all,
How I love you in every way,
With my eyes and my ears and my sense of smell
And of touch (what feeling you means to me!)
And with my intelligence like antennae you set quivering!
Ah, how all my senses lust for you!

Fertilisers, steam threshing machines, advances in agriculture!
Agricultural chemistry, and business almost a science!
O showcases of travelling salesmen,
Of travelling salesmen, knights-errant of Industry,
Human extensions of factories and quiet offices!

O farms in shop windows! O mannequins! O latest fashions!
O useless articles everyone wants to buy!
Hey there, big stores with various departments!
Hey there, illuminated signs winking on and off!
Hey there, everything that today is built of, that makes today different
     from yesterday!
Aha, reinforced cement, concrete, from cement, new processes!
Advances in gloriously death-dealing weaponry!
Armour, guns, machine-guns, submarines, aeroplanes!
I love you all, everything, like a wild beast.
I love you carnivorously,
Perversely, curling my eyes
Round you, O big, commonplace, useful, useless things,
O thoroughly modern things,
O contemporaries of mine, the present and nearest form
Of the immediate system of the Universe!
New Revelation, metallic, dynamic, of God!

---

[4] *vients-de-paraître*: literally 'just-outs', though French would express it otherwise.

O factories, O laboratories, O music halls, O Luna Parks,
O battleships, O bridges, O floating docks –
In my turbulent, glowing mind
I possess you like a beautiful woman,
Utterly I possess you like a beautiful unloved woman
Met by chance and found fascinating.

Hullo, façades of big shops!
Hullo, lifts of tall buildings!
Hullo, cabinet reshuffles!
Parliament, politics, chancellors of exchequers,
Cookers of the books!
(A budget is as natural as a tree
And a parliament as beautiful as a butterfly).

Hail, interest in everything in life,
For everything is life, from the diamonds in shop windows
To the night the mysterious bridge between stars
And the ancient solemn sea lapping shores
And being mercifully the same
As it was when Plato was really Plato
In his real presence and in the flesh like the soul within
And he spoke with Aristotle, who was not to be a disciple of his.

I could die cut to pieces by a motor
With the feeling of delicious surrender of a woman possessed.
Let them throw me into furnaces!
Let them put me under trains!
Let them flog me aboard ships!
Masochism by mechanisms!
Sadism of anything modern and me and hubbub!

Gee up, jockey who won the Derby,
To sink my teeth in your two-toned cap!

(To be so tall that I could not go in through any door!
Ah, looking is for me a sexual perversion!)

Hail, hail, hail, cathedrals!
Let me break my head on your corners,

And be carried off the street all bloody
With no one knowing who I am!

O trams, cable cars, undergrounds,
Brush past me till I have a spasm!
Ha! Ha! Ha – ooh!

Laugh full in my face,
O cars packed with merrymakers and…
O everyday throngs neither happy nor sad in the streets,
Nameless motley river where I can bathe as I please!
Ah, what complex lives, what things there among the houses of it all!
Ah, to know all their lives, their money troubles,
Domestic upsets, unsuspected vices,
The thoughts each keeps to himself on his own in his room
And the gestures he makes when no one can see!
Not to know it all is to be ignorant of everything, O rage,
O rage that like a fever and a lust and a hunger
Makes my face thin and sometimes makes my hands shake
Till I clench my fists foolishly right in the middle of crowds
In the jostling streets!

Ah, and ordinary dirty people who always look the same,
Who swear as a matter of course,
Whose sons shoplift from grocers
And whose eight-year-old daughters – and I find this beautiful and I love
     it! –
Masturbate decent-looking men in staircase wells.
The rabble who walk along scaffolding to go home
Along alleys almost unreally narrow and stinking,
Wonderful human people who live like dogs,
Who are below all moral systems,
For whom no religion has been devised,
No art created,
No politics meant for them!
How I love you all for being as you are,
Nor immoral from being so lowly, neither good nor evil,
Beyond the reach of all progress,
Wonderful fauna on the bottom of life's sea!

(At the water-wheel in my back yard
The donkey walks round and round and round,
And the mystery of the world is the same size.
Wipe off the sweat with your arm, discontented labourer.
The sunlight smothers the silence of the spheres
And we are all going to die,
O pinewoods gloomy at dusk,
Pinewoods where my childhood was something else
From what I am today…)

But, ah, once more the constant rage of machines!

Once more the obsession in motion of buses,
And once more the fury to be going at the same time inside all trains
In all parts of the world,
To be saying goodbye aboard all ships,
Which at this time are carrying iron or moving away from docks.
O iron, O steel, O aluminium, O sheets of corrugated iron!
O quays, O ports, O trains, O cranes, O tugs!

Hail, great train disasters!
Hail, collapses of galleries in mines!
Hail, delightful shipwrecks of big transatlantic liners!
Hullo, revolutions here, there, yonder,
Constitutional changes, wars, treaties, invasions,
Uproar, injustices, acts of violence, and perhaps the end shortly,
The great invasion of Europe by yellow barbarians,
And another Sun on the new Horizon!

What does all this matter, but what does all this matter
To the glistening red noise of the age,
The cruel, delicious noise of today's civilisation?
All that blots out everything except the Moment,
The Moment with naked burning trunk like a stoker,
The Moment stridently loud and mechanical,
The Moment dynamic, a passage for all the Bacchantes
Of iron and bronze and the drunkenness of metals.

Ahoy, trains, ahoy, bridges, ahoy, hotels at dinnertime,
Ahoy, tools of all kinds, iron, crude, the smallest,
Precision instruments, tools for grinding, for digging,
Mills, drills, machines that spin round!

Ahoy! ahoy! ahoy!
Ahoy, electricity, diseased nerves of Matter!
Ahoy, wireless, metal sympathy of the Unconscious!
Ahoy, tunnels, ahoy, canals, Panama, Kiel, Suez!
Ahoy, all the past within the present!
Ahoy, all the future already within us! Ahoy!
Ahoy! ahoy! ahoy!
Fruits of iron and usefulness of the cosmopolitan factory-tree!
Ahoy! ahoy! ahoy, ahoy-oy-oy!
I don't know I exist on the inside. I turn, I spin, I mill round.
They couple me to all trains.
They hoist me on all quays.

I turn within the propellers of all ships.
Ahoy! ahoy-oy ahoy!
Ahoy! I am mechanical heat and electricity!

Ahoy! and rails and engine-rooms and Europe!
Ahoy and hurrah for all of me and everything, machines for work, ahoy!
To leap with everything over everything! Up!

Up, up, up and over, up!
Hi there! Hi ho! Ho-o-o-o-o!
Z-z-z-z-z-z-z-z-z-z-z!

Ah, that I'm not everyone and everywhere!

London

Lisbon Revisited (1926) [1]

Nothing attaches me to anything.
I want fifty things at the same time.
I yearn with the anguish of hunger for meat
For I don't know what –
Definitely for the indefinite…
I sleep restlessly, and live in the restless dream
Of a restless sleeper, half dreaming.

They have closed to me all abstract and necessary doors.
They have drawn curtains from all hypotheses I might see in the street.
In the alley once found there is no door with the number they gave me,

I woke to the same life I had fallen asleep for.
Even the armies I dreamed of suffered defeat.
Even my dreams felt false in the dreaming.
Even the life only wished for satisfies me – even that life…

I understand by fits and starts;
I write between spells of weariness;
And a boredom with boredom itself casts me ashore.

I don't know what fate or future attends my rudderless anguish;
I don't know what islands of the impossible South await my shipwreck;
Or what palm groves of literature will give me at least one verse.

[1] Lisbon Revisited: original title in English. The fact that there is an earlier poem with the same title (dated 1923, not translated here) may explain the apparent tautology of 'Once more I see you again'. (Pessoa himself never left Lisbon after 1905.)

No, I don't know this, nor anything else, nor anything at all...
And, deep in my spirit, where I dream what I dreamt,
In the hinterland of the soul, where I remember unbidden,
(And the past is a natural fog of false tears),
On the highways and byways of distant forests
Where I supposed I was,
The last remnants of the final illusion
Flee unprotected,
The armies I dreamed of, routed without having been,
My cohorts yet to exist, collapsed in God.
Once more I see you again,
City of my childhood dreadfully lost...
Sad, cheerful city, once more I dream here...
I? But am I the same who lived here, and came back here,
And returned back here, and back,
And returned afresh back here?

Or are we all the selves that was here or were,
A row of being-beads strung on a memory-thread,
A row of dreams of me by someone outside me?

Once more I see you again,
With my heart more distant, my soul less mine.

Once more I see you again – Lisbon and the Tagus and everything –
A useless passer-by to you and me,
A foreigner here as everywhere,
One of those things in life as in the soul,
A ghost wandering in halls of recollection,
To the noise of mice and creaking floorboards
In the accursed castle of having to live...

Once more I see you again,
A shade passing across shades and flashing
For a moment in a strange sombre light
And gliding into night as the prow of a boat is lost
On water moving out of earshot...

Once more I see you again,
But, ah, I don't see myself again!
The magic mirror is broken in which I saw myself the same,
And in each fateful fragment I see only a scrap of myself –
A scrap of you and of me!...

Tobacco Shop

I am nothing.
I shall never be anything.
I cannot wish to be anything.
Apart from that, I have in me all the world's dreams.
Windows of my room,
Of my room of one of millions in the world that no one knows who it is
(And if they knew who it is, what would they know?),
You look out on the mystery of a street crossed constantly by people,
On a street inaccessible to all thoughts,
Real, impossibly real, certain, unknowably certain,
With the mystery of things underlying rocks and creatures,
With death making walls damp and men's hair white,
With Destiny driving the cart of everything along the road of nothing.

Today I am defeated, as if I knew the truth.
Today I am lucid, as if I were about to die,
And had no more brotherhood with things
Than a farewell, with this house and this side of the street turning
Into a line of carriages in a train, and a whistled departure
From inside my head,
And a jolt to my nerves and a creaking of bones as it goes.

Today I am perplexed, like one who has thought and found and forgotten.
Today I am divided between the loyalty I owe
To the Tobacco Shop across the street, like something real outside,
And to the feeling that everything is a dream, like something real within.

I have failed in everything.
As I have fulfilled no purpose, perhaps everything was nothing.
The apprenticeship they gave me,
I slipped out of it through the window at the back of the house.
I went as far as the country with great purposes,
But there I met only grasses and trees,
And when there were people they were all alike.
I leave the window, feel myself in a chair. What am I to think about?

What do I know of what I shall be, I who don't know what I am?
To be what I think? But I think I am so much!
And there are so many who think they are the same that there cannot be so many

Genius? At this moment
A hundred thousand brains dream of being geniuses like me,
And history will single out – who knows? – not one,

Nor will there be anything but dung from so many future conquests.
No, I don't believe in myself.
In all the madhouses there are crazy fools with so many certainties!
I who have no certainty, am I more certain or less?
No, nor of myself…
In how many garrets and non-garrets of the world
Are not at this time geniuses-to-themselves dreaming?
How many high, noble, clear aspirations –
Yes, truly high and noble and clear –
And who knows if they can be realised,
Will ever see the light of reality or get heard about?
The world is for whoever is born to conquer it
And not for who dreams that he can conquer it, however right he may be.
I have dreamed more than Napoleon achieved.
I have crammed into my hypothetical breast more humanity than Christ did.
I have made philosophies in secret that no Kant wrote.
But I am, and perhaps shall always be, the one in the garret,
Although I don't live in it;
I shall always be *one who was not born for that*;
I shall always be just *one who had qualities*;
I shall always be one who expected them to open the door by a wall with no door
And sang the song of the Infinite in a chicken-coop,
And heard the voice of God in a covered well.
Believe in myself? No, nor in anything.
Let Nature pour over my burning head
Its sunlight, its rain, the wind that catches my hair,
And let the rest come if it will or must, or not come.
Weak-hearted slaves of the stars,
We conquer all the world before we get out of bed;
But we wake and it is dark,
We get up and it is unfamiliar,
We leave home and it is the whole earth,
Plus the solar system and the Milky Way and the Undefined.

(Eat chocolates, little girl;
Eat chocolates!
Look, there is no more metaphysics in the world than chocolates.
Look, all religions teach no more than the sweetshop does.
Eat, grubby little girl, eat!
If only I could eat chocolates with the same truth as you eat!
But I think and, as I pull off the silver paper that is tin foil,
I throw it all on the ground, as I have thrown life.)

But at least from the bitterness of what I shall never be
Remains the scribble of this poetry,
A porch leading to the Impossible.
But at least I devote to myself a contempt without tears,
Noble at least in the grand gesture with which I cast off
The dirty laundry I am, with no list, into the course of things,
And I stay at home with no shirt.

(You who console, who don't exist and so console,
Whether a Greek goddess imagined as a statue that might be alive,
Or a Roman lady impossibly noble and fateful,
Or a princess of troubadours, most gracious and glamorous,
Or an eighteenth-century marchioness, distant in a low-cut dress,
Or a famous *cocotte* from the time of our fathers,
Or something or other modern – I can't quite imagine what –
All, whatever it is, that you may be, if it can inspire, let it!
My heart is an empty bucket.
As those who call up spirits call up spirits I call up
Myself and there is nothing there.
I go to the window and see the street as an absolute clarity.
I see the shops, I see the pavements, I see passing cars,
I see living beings in clothes in each other's way,
I see dogs that also exist,
And all this weighs on me like being condemned to exile,
And all this is foreign, like everything.)

I have lived, studied, loved, even believed,
And today there is no beggar I don't envy just for not being me.

I look at each one's rags and sores and falsehood,
And I think: perhaps you never lived or studied or loved or believed
(For it is possible to make reality of all that and make nothing of it);
Perhaps you have hardly existed, like a lizard whose tail is cut off
And it is a tail restlessly short of the lizard.

I have made of myself what I did not know,
And what I could make of myself I did not make.
The disguise I put on was wrong.
They called my bluff straight away and I did not come clean, and lost myself.
When I wanted to take off the mask
It was stuck to my face.
When I took it off and looked in the mirror
I had aged.
I was drunk, I could no longer put on the disguise I had not taken off.

I threw out the mask and slept in the cloakroom
Like a dog tolerated by the management
Because it is harmless
And I am writing this history to prove that I am sublime.
Musical essence of my useless poetry,
Would I could meet you as something I made,
And not be stuck opposite the Tobacco Shop opposite,

Trampling underfoot the consciousness of being in existence,
Like a carpet a drunkard trips over
Or a doormat the gipsies had stolen and was worthless!

But the Tobacconist has come to the door and stands at the door.
I look at him with the discomfort of an ill-turned head
And with the discomfort of a misunderstood soul.
He will die and I shall die.
He will leave the shop-sign, and I shall leave poetry.
In time the shop-sign too will die, and the poetry too.
After a time the street where the shop-sign was will die,
And the language in which the poetry had been written.
Then the spinning planet will die on which all that took place.
On other satellites of other systems something like people
Will go on making things like poetry and living beneath things like shop-signs,
Always one thing opposite another,
Always one thing as useless as another,
Always the impossible as stupid as the real,
Always the basic mystery as certain as the mystery-sleep of the surface,
Always that or always another thing or neither one thing nor another.

But a man has gone into the Tobacco Shop (to buy tobacco?),
And the plausible reality has suddenly broken over me.
I half rise, energetic, convinced, human,
And I am intending to write this poetry in which I say the reverse.

I light a cigarette as I think about writing it
And I savour in the cigarette liberation from all thought.
I follow the smoke like a path I might take,
And I enjoy, at a sensitive and suitable moment,
Liberation from all speculation
And the awareness that metaphysics is a consequence of being out of sorts
Then I lie back in my chair
And carry on smoking.
While Destiny allows me, I shall carry on smoking.
(If I married the daughter of my washerwoman

I might be happy.)
Seeing this, I get up from the chair. I go to the window.

The man has come out of the Tobacco Shop (putting change in his trousers
    pocket?).
Ah, I know him: it is Stevens without metaphysics.
(The Tobacconist has come to the door.)
As by a divine instinct Stevens has turned and spotted me.
He has waved goodbye to me, I have shouted *Goodbye, Stevens*! and the
    universe
Has rebuilt itself for me without ideal or hope, and the Tobacconist has
    smiled.

Putting it off

The day after tomorrow, yes, only the day after tomorrow...
I shall spend tomorrow thinking about the day after tomorrow,
And so it will be possible; but today no.
No, nothing today; today I cannot.
The muddled persistence of my objective subjectivity,
The sleep of my real life, inserted,
The expected endless weariness,
A weariness of worlds to catch a tram...
This kind of soul...
                                    Only the day after tomorrow...
Today I want to prepare myself,
I want to prepare myself to think tomorrow about the next day...
That is the one that counts.
I already have a plan worked out; but no, today I am working out no plans...
Tomorrow is the day for plans.
Tomorrow I shall sit down at my desk to conquer the world;
But I shall only conquer the world the day after tomorrow...
I feel like weeping,
I feel like weeping a lot suddenly, inside...

No, don't let them want to know any more, it's a secret, I won't tell.
Only the day after tomorrow...
When I was a child the Sunday circus amused me all week.
Today all that amuses me is the Sunday circus of all the week of my
    childhood...
The day after tomorrow I shall be different,

My life will triumph,
All my real qualities as an intelligent, well-read, practical man
Will be summoned by an edict...
But by an edict tomorrow...
Today I want to sleep, I shall draw it up tomorrow...
As for today, what performance would childhood repeat for me?
Even for me to buy the tickets tomorrow,
For the day after tomorrow is surely when the performance is...
Before, no...
The day after tomorrow I shall adopt the public pose I shall study tomorrow.
The day after tomorrow I shall finally be what today I can never be.
Only the day after tomorrow...
I feel sleepy as a stray dog feels cold.
I feel very sleepy.
Tomorrow I shall tell you the words, or the day after tomorrow...
Yes, perhaps only the day after tomorrow...

The future...
Yes, the future...

Chance

In the chance of the street the chance of the blonde girl,
But no, it is not her.

The other was in the other street, in the other town, and I was someone
    else.

I am suddenly lost in the immediate vision,
Another time I am in the other town, in the other street,
And the other girl goes by.

What a great advantage to recall without compromise!
Now I am sorry I have never seen the other girl,
And I am sorry I have not after all so much as looked her way.

What a great adventure to wear your soul turned inside out!
At least poetry gets written.
Poetry gets written, you pass for mad, and then for a genius, probably,
Probably, or even improbably,
A marvel among celebrities!

I was saying that at least poetry gets written...

But that was regarding a girl,
A blonde girl,
But which one?

There was one I saw long ago in another town,
In another sort of street;
And there was the one I saw long ago in another town
In another sort of street;
For all memories are the same memory,
Everything that was is the same death,
Yesterday, today, who knows about tomorrow?

A passer-by looks my way for moment puzzled.
Could I be making poetry in gestures and faces?
Maybe... The blonde girl?
It is the same one after all...
Everything is the same after all...

Only I, somehow, am not the same, and that is the same too after all.

Note

My soul has broken like an empty vase.
It has fallen exceedingly downstairs,
Fallen from the hands of the careless maid,
Fallen, smashed into more pieces than there was china in the vase.

Nonsense? Impossible? Who knows?
I have more sensations than I had when I felt my old self.
I am a scattering of shards on a doormat to be shaken.

I made a noise on landing like a vase breaking.
The gods that there are lean over the banister,
And stare at the shards their maid has made of me.

Don't let them be angry with her.
They are tolerant with her.
What was I but an empty vase?

They look at the shards, foolishly conscious,
But self-conscious, not conscious of them.

They look and smile,
Smile tolerantly at the maid who could not help it.

The great stairway stretches, carpeted with stars.
A shard glitters, turned shiny side out, among the planets.
My work? My chief soul? My life?
A shard.
And the gods look at it especially, for they don't know why it is still there.

De la Musique

Ah, gradually, among the ancient trees,
Her figure looms and I stop thinking...

Gradually, from my anguish I see myself looming...

The two figures meet in the lakeside clearing...

... The two figures dreamt of,
For this was but a ray of moonlight and a sorrow of mine,
And something else assumed,
And what comes of existing...

Honestly, did the two figures meet
In the lakeside clearing?

        (... But if they don't exist?...)

... In the lakeside clearing?...

Birthday

When they used to celebrate my birthday
I was happy and nobody was dead.
In the old house, even my birthday was a centuries-old tradition
And everyone's merriment and mine was in tune with something
    religious.
When they used to celebrate my birthday
I enjoyed the great good health of not receiving anything,
Of being intelligent in the eyes of the family
And of not having the expectations, I no longer know how to have
    expectations.
When I came to look at life, I had lost the sense of life.

Yes, what I supposed myself to be,
What I was at heart and in kinship,

What I was from suburban parties,
What I was from being loved and being a little boy,
What I was – oh, good Lord! – what only today I know I was...
At what a distance!...
(I cannot find it...)
When they used to celebrate my birthday!

What I am today is like damp in the alley behind the house,
Sprouting on the walls...
What I am today (and the house of those who loved me trembles through
     my tears),
What I am today is their having sold the house,
Is their having all died,
Is my outliving myself like a spent match...
When they used to celebrate my birthday...
How I loved that time like a person!
The soul's physical desire to meet itself there again,
Through a journey both metaphysical and carnal,
Like a duality of I towards me...
To eat the past as a hungry man eats bread, with no time to get butter on
     his teeth!

I see it all again with a clarity that blinds me to what is here...
The table laid with more places, with better patterns on the crockery, with
     more glasses,
The sideboard with many things – sweets, fruit, the rest in shadow under
     the shelf –
The old aunts, the different cousins, and it was all for my sake,
When they used to celebrate my birthday...

Stop, my heart!
Don't think! Leave thinking to my head!
O Lord, Lord, Lord!
Today I no longer have birthdays.
I go on.
My days pile up.
I shall be old when I am.
Nothing more.
The madness of not having carried the stolen past in my pocket!...

When they used to celebrate my birthday!...

Great are the deserts

Great are the deserts, and all is desert.
They are not a few tons of stones or bricks erected
Concealing the soil, the so-called soil that is all.
Great are the deserts and the desert souls great –
Desert because nothing passes through them but themselves,
Great because from there all is seen, and all has died.

Great are the deserts, my soul!
Great are the deserts.

I have not drawn a ticket for life,
I have missed the door of feeling,
There is no will or opportunity I have not wasted.
Today all I have left, on the eve of a journey,
With my open suitcase still waiting to be packed,
Sitting in the chair together with shirts that don't fit,
Today all I have left (apart from the discomfort of sitting thus)
Is this knowledge:
Great are the deserts and all is desert.
Great is life, and it is not worth being alive.

I pack the suitcase better with my eyes thinking about packing
Than with packing done by factitious hands (I think that is the word).
I light the cigarette to put off the journey,
To put off all journeys,
To put off the entire universe.

Come back tomorrow, reality!
That will do for today, folks!
Hang on, absolute present!
Better not to be than to be thus.

Let them buy chocolates for the child I have succeeded by mistake,
And let them take down the shop-sign because tomorrow is endless.

But I must pack the suitcase,
I must perforce pack the suitcase,
The suitcase.
I cannot carry the shirts in hypothesis or the suitcase in reason.
Yes, all my life I have had to pack the suitcase.
But all my life too I have remained seated on the corner of the pile of shirts,
Ruminating, like an ox that has failed to be Apis,[1] destiny.

I must pack the suitcase of being.
I must exist packing suitcases.
The cigarette ash falls on the shirt on top of the mound.
I look aside, observe I was lying down.
I only know I must pack the suitcase,
And that the deserts are great and all is desert,
And some parable with regard to this, but I have already forgotten it.

I suddenly get up, am all the Caesars.
I am finally going to pack the suitcase.
Damn, I have to pack it and shut it;
I have to see it taken from here,
I have to exist independently of it.

Great are the deserts and all is desert,
If I am not mistaken, of course.
Poor human soul with an oasis only in the desert next door!

Better to pack the suitcase.
The end.

¹ Apis: the sacred Bull of Memphis.

I have a bad cold

I have a bad cold,
And everybody knows that bad colds
Upset all the system of the universe,
Make us furious with life
And make us sneeze to the point of metaphysics.
I have wasted the whole day blowing my nose.
My head aches vaguely.
A sad condition for a minor poet!
Today I really am a minor poet.
What I used to be was a wish; it has gone.

Goodbye for ever, fairy queen!
Your wings were of sunlight, and I am walking here.
I shall not be well unless I go to bed.
I was never well without lying down on the universe.

Excusez un peu … What a bad physical cold!
I need truth and aspirin.

Ah, a Sonnet…

My heart is a mad admiral who has
abandoned the profession of the sea
and paces up and down at home, his days
spent in slow rituals of memory…

And as he paces there (I also shift
here in my chair, at the mere thought of it)
the abandoned sea from focus does not drift
when idleness tires muscles fighting fit.

Oh, there are yearnings in the arms and legs
and yearnings in the brain beyond them both
and mighty rages stirred up from the dregs.

But – this is rich! – it was without defences
I spoke… so where the devil was I with
an admiral instead of with my senses?…

Typing

Alone in my engineer's cubicle, I draw up the plan,
Sign the project, cut off here,
Far even from who I am.

Next door, in dully sinister accompaniment,
The noisy clacking of typewriters.
How sick I am of life!
How lowering this routine!
What a come-down to be like this!

Long ago, when I was someone else, there were castles and knights
(Pictures, perhaps, in some childhood book),
Long ago, when I was true to my dream,
There were great Northern landscapes overdone with snow,
There were great Southern palm groves flush with green.

Long ago.

Next door, in dully sinister accompaniment,
The noisy clacking of typewriters.

We all have two lives:
The true, the one we dream of in childhood
And go on dreaming of as adults in a substratum of mist;
The false, the one we live when we live with others,
The practical, the useful,
The one where we end up by being put in a coffin.

In the other there are no coffins, no deaths,
Only childhood pictures:
Big coloured books to look at but not to read;
Big pages of colours to remember later.
In the other we are us,
In the other we are alive;
In this we shall die, which is what living means;
This moment, by feeling sick, I live in the other…

But next door, in dully sinister accompaniment,
The voice rises, the noisy clacking of typewriters.

On Sunday I shall walk through the gardens

On Sunday I shall walk through the gardens in the person of others,
Content with my anonymity.
On Sunday I shall be happy – them, them…
On Sunday…
Today is Thursday in a week that has no Sunday…
Not a Sunday.
Never a Sunday.
But there will always be someone in the gardens this coming Sunday.
That is how life passes,
Subtle for whoever feels,
More or less for whoever thinks:
There will always be someone in the gardens on Sunday,
Not on our Sunday,
Not on my Sunday,
Not on Sunday…
But there will always be others in the gardens and on Sunday!

He passed me, came after me

He passed me, came after me in a downtown street –
That shabby man, a professional beggar who looks one in the face,
Who takes to me and I take to him;
And reciprocally, in a grand, overflowing gesture I gave him all I had
(Except of course for what was in the pocket where I carry more money:
I am no fool nor a hard-working Russian novelist,
And romanticism, yes, but easy does it...)

I feel a sympathy for all those people,
Especially when they don't deserve sympathy.
Yes, I too am a tramp and a beggar,
And I too am through my own fault.
To be a tramp and a beggar is not to be a tramp and a beggar:
It is to be off the social ladder,
It is to be not adaptable to the norms of life,
The real or emotional norms of life –
To be not a High Court Judge, someone with a steady job, a whore,
To be not of little worth, an exploited worker,
To be not ill with an incurable illness,
To be not thirsty for justice or a cavalry captain,
To be not – in a word – those social persons of storytellers
Who have their fill of literature because they are right to weep tears,
And revolt against social life because they are right to assume that.

No: anything but to be right!
Anything but to bother with mankind!
Anything but to give way to humanitarianism!
What is the use of a sensation if there is an external reason for it?

Yes, to be a tramp or a beggar as I am
Is not to be a tramp or a beggar, which is usual:
It is to be cut off in the soul, and this is what it is to be a tramp,
It is having to beg the days to pass and leave us, and this is what it is to be a
    beggar.

Anything else is stupid like a Dostoyevsky or a Gorky.
Anything else is to be hungry or not to have to dress.
And, though this happens, this happens to so many people
That it is not worth the trouble to take trouble with people to whom this
    happens.

I am a tramp and a beggar in earnest, that is, in the metaphorical sense,
And I am rolling about in great self-pity.

Pity Álvaro de Campos!
So cut off from life! So run down in sensations!
Pity him, sunk in the armchair of his melancholy!
Pity him, who with (genuine) tears in his eyes,
Has today given, in a grand, liberal, Muscovite gesture,
All he had, from the pocket in which he had little, to that
Poor man who was not poor, whose eyes were professionally sad.
Pity Álvaro de Campos, whom no one bothers with!
Pity him who is in so much trouble with himself!

And, yes, pity him!
Pity him more than many who are tramps and tramp,
Who are beggars and beg,
For the human soul is an abyss.

I know. Pity him!

What is the good of my being able to revolt at a meeting inside my soul!
But even I am no fool!
I have no defence for being able to have social opinions.
I even have no defence at all: I am lucid.
Don't let them try to change my mind: I am lucid.

I have said: I am lucid.
Nothing aesthetic about my heart: I am lucid.
Shit! I am lucid.

Martial Ode

Numberless waterless river – only people and things,
Dreadfully waterless!

Drums are beating far away in my ear,
And I don't know whether I see the river or hear the drums,
As if I could not hear and see at the same time!

Helahoho! helahoho!

The sewing machine of a poor widow bayoneted to death...
She was sewing late with nothing in mind...
The table where the old folk were playing,

All jumbled together, all jumbled together with bodies, with blood,
All a single river, a single wave, a single drawn out horror.

Helahoho! helahoho!

I dug out the tin train of the child trampled in the middle of the road,
And I wept like all the mothers of the world over the horror of life.
My pantheist feet stumbled on the sewing machine of the widow they
    bayoneted
And that poor instrument of peace put a spear into my heart.

Yes, I was to blame for it all, I was the soldier – all of them –
Who killed, raped, burnt and smashed,
I and my shame and my remorse with a misshapen shadow
Walked all over the world like Ahasuerus, [1]
But after my steps rang steps the size of the infinite.

And a physical dread of meeting God makes me suddenly shut my eyes.
An absurd Christ atoning for all the crimes and all the acts of violence,
My cross is inside me, rigid, scalding, smashing
And everything hurts in my soul as vast as a Universe.

I snatched the poor toy from the child's hands and beat him.
His eyes frightened by my son I may have and whom they will also kill
Begged me without knowing how for all pity towards everyone.

From the old woman's room I snatched the picture of the boy and
    tore it up,
She, full of fear, wept and did nothing…
I suddenly felt that she was my mother and down my spine the breath of
    God passed.

I smashed the poor widow's sewing machine.
She wept in a corner with no thought for the sewing machine.
Will there be another world where I shall have a daughter who will be
    widowed and to whom this will happen?

As captain I ordered the shaking peasants to be shot,
I left the daughters of all the fathers tied to trees to be raped.
Now I saw that it was within my heart that it all happened,
And it all scalds and chokes and I cannot stir without it all being the same.
May God have pity on me who had it on nobody!

[1] Ahasuerus: biblical tyrant, husband of Esther.

Tripe Oporto

One day in a restaurant outside space and time
They served me love as cold tripe.
I courteously told the emissary from the kitchen
That I preferred it hot,
That tripe (and it was tripe Oporto) is never eaten cold.

They got impatient with me.
You can never be right, not in a restaurant.
I did not eat it, I did not ask for anything else, I paid the bill
And fell to walking up and down the street.

Who knows what this means?
I don't know, and it happened to me...

(I know full well that in everyone's childhood there was a garden,
Private or public, or the man's next door.
I know full well that our play was its owner,
And that sorrow belongs to today.)

I know that many times over,
But if I asked for love, why did they bring me
Tripe Oporto cold?
It is not a dish that can be eaten cold,
But they brought it to me cold.
I did not complain, but it was cold,
It can never be eaten cold, but it came cold.

Poem in a Straight Line

I never knew who had been beaten up.
All those I know have been champions in everything.

And I, so often shabby, so often dirty, so often worthless,
I so often an irresponsible parasite,
Unforgivably foul,
I who so often could not be bothered to take a bath,
I who so often have been ridiculous, foolish,
Who have wrapped my feet publicly in the carpets of protocol,
Who have been grotesque, paltry, deferential and arrogant,
Who have borne insults and kept quiet,
Who when I have not kept quiet have been more ridiculous still:

I who have been comical to waiters,
I who have felt the winks of errand boys,
I who have caused financial embarrassments, asked for a loan without
    paying,
I who when the punch-up was due have lain low
To dodge the likelihood of being punched up;
I who have borne the affliction of laughable trifles,
I confirm I have no equal there in all this in the world.

Everyone I know who talks to me
Never behaved ridiculously, never bore an insult,
Was never anything but a prince – all of them princes – in life…

If only I could hear someone's human voice
Confessing not a sin but a disgrace;
Telling not an act of violence but one of cowardice!
No, they are all the Ideal, if I hear them and they talk to me.
Who is there in this wide world to confess to me that he has once been
    worthless?
O princes, my brothers,

Damn it, I am sick of demigods!
Where are there people in the world?

Then is it only me who is worthless and wrong on this earth?

Woman might not have loved them,
They may have been betrayed – but ridiculous never!
And I who have been ridiculous without being betrayed,
How can I talk with my betters without faltering?
I who have been worthless, literally worthless,
Worthless in the sense of paltry and disgraceful in worthlessness.

Summer Holidays

The quiet of night, on summer holidays high up;
The quiet, how it deepens
The scattered barking of watch-dogs in the night;
The silence, how it is emphasised,
Because not a thing is humming or murmuring in the dark…

Ah, the oppression of all this!
It oppresses like being happy!
What an idyllic life, if another person had it
With the monotonous hum or murmur of nothing
Under the sky freckled with stars,
With the barking of dogs dusting the quiet of it all!

I came here for a rest,
But I forgot to leave myself there at home.
I have brought with me the essential thorn of consciousness,
The vague nausea, the uncertain sickness of feeling my old self.

Always this unease bitten off in chunks
Like poor brown bread that crumbles as it falls.
Always this discomfort taken in evil gulps
Like a drunkard's wine when it does not stop nausea.
Always, always, always
This defect of circulation in one's own soul,
This swooning of the senses,
This...

Your slender hands, a little pale, a little mine,
Were calm that day in your lap while you sat,
As and where another woman's scissors and thimble would be.
You mused, looking at me as though I were space.
I recall, to have something to think about, without thinking.
Suddenly, with a half-sigh, you interrupted what you were being.
You looked hard at me and said:
'I'm sorry every day isn't like this' –
Like this, like that day which had been nothing...
Ah, you did not know,
Happily you did not know
That the sorrow is that every day is like this, like this;
That the trouble is that, happy or unhappy,
The soul enjoys or suffers the inner boredom of it all,
Consciously or unconsciously,
Thinking or about to think –

I remember photographically your hands at rest,
Softly outstretched.
I remember, at this moment, more of them than of you.
What will become of you?
I know that, in the formidable somewhere of life,
You have married. I believe you are a mother. You must be happy.
Why should you not be?

Only out of wickedness…
Yes, it would be unfair…
Unfair?

(It was a sunny day in the country and I was dozing, smiling.)
… … …
Life…
White or red, it is the same: it makes you throw up.

Drawing by José de Almada Negreiros, done from memory
on returning from Pessoa's funeral

INDEX OF ORIGINAL TITLES
AND FIRST LINES

1: 'O Lisbon, my home'. Rossio Square in Pessoa's time.

2–4: Pessoa's father and his mother at the time of their marriage. Both were well-connected, cultivated and artistic. Pessoa the first-born remained close to his mother and childhood became a remembered Eden.

5–6: (1893–1905) Pessoa was five when his father died. Two years later, his mother married a Portuguese diplomat appointed consul to the British colony of Natal. Pessoa's new family in Durban came to include two brothers and a sister. He attended Durban School, a small school with a distinguished staff. Pessoa proved a precocious, ardent scholar.

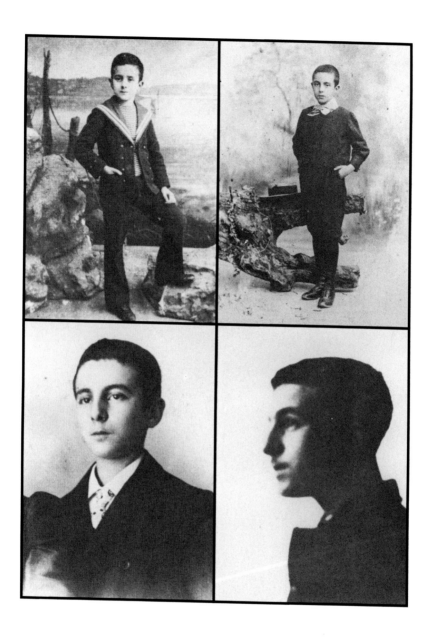

7–10: The growing Pessoa: aged 7, 10, 13 and 17 at which time he left Durban, alone, to go to Lisbon, for higher education.

11: (1908) Pessoa aged 20. By then he had abandoned Lisbon University – riven with student riots – preferring to educate himself more seriously, alone.

12: (1913) Throughout his life Pessoa behaved and dressed with a 'British' restraint. Here, at the start of his literary career, he is seen with the editor of *O Teatro* for which he wrote dramatic criticism.

13: (1910) In 1908 the King of Portugal, Dom Carlos I, and the Crown Prince were assassinated. The heir, King Dom Manuel II, abdicated in 1910 and a Republic was declared. In the years of political turmoil that followed, the young Pessoa became ardently patriotic, fertile in the schemes for his country's good.

32: (1935) The domed wooden trunk in which Pessoa kept whatever he wrote, pieces long and short, complete or sketchy, diary entries, notes and fragments. After his death 25,574 items were inventoried. They are still being sorted and published, volume after volume.

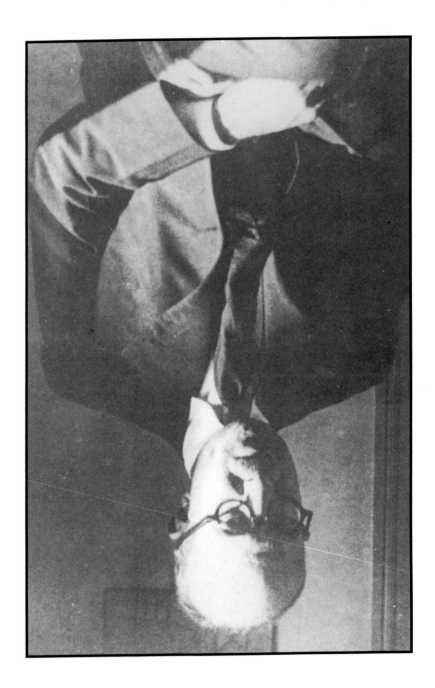

31: (1935) The last portrait.

29: (c. 1931) At Martinhos in the Arcade: Pessoa, in his prime.
30: (1935) At Martinhos in the Arcade: Pessoa, in his last months.

28: (1935) Pessoa is here seen with his step-brother Luís, (who was visiting Lisbon on his honeymoon), his step-sister Henriqueta, her husband and daughter. Pessoa remained in affectionate contact with his relations.

27: (1928) In his later years Pessoa was recognised by some eminent men of letters as the master of 'first modernism' in Portugal; a few, indeed, recognized his genius.

Although Pessoa's published books were few, 205 of his poems & 132 prose works appeared in magazines and journals during his lifetime

Fernando Pessoa,
em flagrante delitro.

25: (c. 1929) Pessoa gave a young, admiring poet this photograph; he was
Ophélia's nephew. She asked for a copy which Pessoa endorsed *in flagrante
delitro*. Their attachment revived for some months, before fading again into
an affection that lasted till his death.

24: (c. 1927) António Botto, poet, aesthete, homosexual – Pessoa published his work and defended his right to be heard, as he did that of other individuals and associations threatened by public or police harassment.

23: (c. 1926) A purposeful Pessoa, striding out in the Chiado.

22: (c. 1923) A diffident Pessoa, with one of his regular employers, probably pursuing his trade as translator with a visiting client and his wife.

21: (1920) Ophélia Queiroz – secretary in a firm for which Pessoa acted as freelance foreign correspondent and translator. She was 19, intelligent and cultivated, when she and Pessoa shared, for several months, a sentimental attachment.

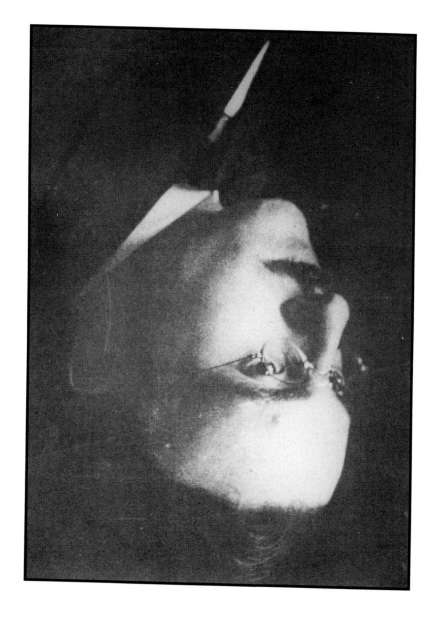

20: (1916) Pessoa, aged 27, at the time of *Orpheu.*

18: Mário de Sá-Carneiro – gifted modernist poet and novelist to whom Pessoa was devoted. Intimate friends, they corresponded freely, contributed to *Orpheu 1*, co-edited *Orpheu 2*, icon of Portuguese modernism. Sá-Carneiro's suicide, aged 26, in Paris, deeply affected Pessoa.

19: Aunt Anica – Pessoa was very fond of her and came to share her interest in the occult.

16: Almada Negreiros – brilliant artist, writer, publicist, *animateur* of modernist 'events', close associate of Pessoa in the production of *Orpheu* and of other publications produced *pour épater le bourgeois*.

17: Armando Côrtes-Rodrigues – Azorean poet and Pessoa's confidant throughout his working life, to whom Pessoa revealed his deeper beliefs and more serious poetic intents.

14: (c. 1921) For meetings of every kind the cafés of Lisbon were the natural resort. Here Pessoa is seen with friends in a favourite haunt: Martinhos in the Arcade.
15: A self-portrait by Pessoa's friend, Almada Negreiros, at a celebrated literary meeting place: Brasileira in the Chiado.

LIFE AND TIMES

L.C.TAYLOR

INTRODUCTION

THE CHRONOLOGICAL OUTLINE OF PESSOA'S LIFE WHICH follows has been divided into fourteen three-year sections. The division is arbitrary but convenient: a year-by-year chronology limps along and gives undue importance to the precise date (when it is known) of each event in a life not notable for incident; three-year stretches less frequently interrupt the description of developments which may continue for several years.

Inconveniently for this chronology, Pessoa was born on the 13 June, almost exactly halfway through the year. Hence, successive three-year stages cover his life from, say, fourteen and a half to seventeen and a half, and so on. The recurrent halves give an appearance of finicalness, but a restriction to whole numbers causes overlap; narrative confusion results.

Each three-year cycle of Pessoa's life is preceded by brief reference to then-current events and artistic achievements. In this way, a reader may see how some other artists reacted to the influences and events in the turbulent times through which Pessoa lived. In youth, he experienced that relative stability and unity in moral and artistic attitudes typical of the late Victorian 'Establishment'; in maturity, he suffered the violent and contradictory extremes of early 'modernism'. The first decade of the new century brought a refreshing rain of change; the First World War a tempest.

Such is, of course, a hazardous generalization, applicable at best only to Europe and North America. The contextual settings provided here to Pessoa's life are Eurocentric: indeed, they emphasize what occurred in Portugal, Britain, America, and France. The reasons for this narrowness of focus are twofold: first, given the constraints of space, selection has had to be ruthless; second, Pessoa had particular access to Portuguese, English, American and French cultures from his mastery of the relevant languages. The bias in selection has also reflected Pessoa's interests: principally literature, philosophy and religion, history and politics and, professionally, commerce. In sum, the selection of events and works made here aims to provide the reader with a sketch of the contemporary context of which Pessoa was likely to have been most aware. The named political and artistic constellations – those nearer often more visible – formed the skies of *his* world, not *the* world.

The information categories used are these:

● *In PORTUGAL*   ■ *ELSEWHERE: public events/social and technical change/science and technology/scholarship and philosophy/literary arts/musical arts/visual arts/other.*

THE LIFE AND TIMES OF PESSOA

■ ELSEWHERE: William II becomes German Emperor. Brazil becomes a Republic / Eiffel Tower / Röntgen – X rays / Rimbaud *Les Illuminations*. Zola *La Bête Humaine*. Ibsen *Hedda Gabler*. Tolstoy *Kreutzer Sonata* / Fauré *Requiem*. Strauss *Don Juan*. Borodin *Prince Igor* / Van Gogh at Arles (suicide 1890). School of Pont-Aven

● PORTUGAL: Death of King Dom Luís; accession of Dom Carlos (1889). In the 'Scramble for Africa' British and Portuguese ambitions clash: an ultimatum from Britain (Portugal's oldest ally) forces Portuguese withdrawal. Mass protests follow. Anglo-Portuguese agreements in the Congo and Zambesi / Antero de Quental *Tendências gerais de Filosofia... do Sec xix*. Eça de Queirós *Os Maias*. Bulhão Pato *Sátiras, Canções e Idílios*. Fialho de Almeida *Os Gatos*. D João da Câmara *Meia-Noite*

Pessoa from birth to 2½ years

◆ FERNANDO ANTÓNIO NOGUEIRA PESSOA WAS BORN in Lisbon on the 13 June 1888.

His mother came from the Azores, where her family had an estate on the island of Terceira. Her father, a magistrate, sent her to Lisbon for much of her education. A cultivated woman, she was well-read, spoke fluent French, wrote verse in Portuguese, and played the piano. When Pessoa was born she was 26.

Pessoa's grandfather on the paternal side was a general, and the family had military traditions; Pessoa's father, however, worked as a civil servant in the Ministry of Justice. His passion was music – he wrote musical criticism regularly for the major Lisbon daily newspaper *Diário de Notícias*. At the time of Pessoa's birth, he was 28.

The family lived in a fashionable quarter in the centre of Lisbon, overlooking the Opera House of S. Carlos.

'*The village where I was born was São Carlos Square, now Directorate Square, and the house where I was born was the one where subsequently (on the second floor; I was born on the fourth floor) the Republican Directorate was established. (Note: the house seems doomed to notoriety, but perhaps the fourth floor will yield better results than the second).*' [Letter to Gaspar Simões, 11 December 1931]

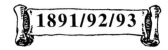

1891/92/93

■ Franco-Russian Alliance. Panama scandal in France. Nansen reaches the North Pole / Bradley *Appearance and Reality* / Verlaine *Bonheur.* Huysman *Là-bas.* Hardy *Tess of the D'Urbervilles.* Wilde *Portrait of Dorian Gray.* Maeterlinck *Pelléas et Mélisande* / Mahler *Symphony no. 1.* Tchaikovsky *Nutcracker Suite.* Verdi *Falstaff.* Dvorak *Symphony no. 5* / Monet *Les Nymphéas.* Cézanne *The Card Players.*

● Further Anglo-Portuguese agreements in Central Africa. *Communist Manifesto* published in Portugal / Oliveira Martins *Os Filhos de D João I* and *Vida de Nun Álvares* / Guerra Junqueiro *Finis Patriae* and *Os Simples.* Trinidade Coelho *Os Meus Amores.* Alberto de Oliveira *Poesias.* Abel Botelho *O Barão de Lavos.* António Nobre *Só.* Fialho de Almeida *O País das Uvas.* João de Deus *Campo de Flores*

Pessoa aged 2½ – 5½

◆ IN JANUARY OF 1893 A BROTHER, JORGE, WAS BORN to Pessoa. That July, when Pessoa had just turned five, his father died of tuberculosis.

The family – mother, two sons, paternal grandmother Dionísia, and two maidservants of long standing – moved to a less grand apartment.

1894/95/96

■ Japan declares war on China. Armenian massacres. Jameson raid. Dreyfus affair in France / Lumière – cinematography. Marconi – wireless telegraphy. Nobel Institute established / Marx *Das Capital vol 3.* Freud *Studies in Hysteria.* Bergson *Matter and Memory* / Mallarmé *Vers et Prose.* Hardy *Jude the Obscure.* Wells *The Time Machine.* Jarry *Ubu Roi.* Chekov *The Seagull.* Housman *A Shropshire Lad.* Tagore *Citra* / Puccini *La Bohème.* Debussy *Prélude à l'Après-midi d'un Faune*

● Revolt in Mozambique (1894) suppressed the following year / First cinematographic show in Lisbon; first films made in Lisbon / Camilo Pessanha goes to Macao. Eugénio de Castro *Silva* and *Belkiss.* Bulhão Pato *Memórias.* Guerra Junqueiro *Pátria.* Raúl Brandão *História de um Palhaço.* Foundation of the 'Decadent' revue *Renascença* / The celebrated mediaeval painting attributed to Nuno Gonçalves discovered in a Lisbon church

Pessoa aged 5½ – 8½

◆ IN JANUARY 1894, PESSOA'S INFANT BROTHER JORGE died. In the same year Pessoa started inventing 'heteronyms' – characters in the 'intimate theatre of the self':

'Ever since I was a small child I felt driven to create a fictitious world around me and to surround myself with friends and acquaintances who never existed [...] Ever since I have known myself as being that to which I refer as "I", I can remember having imagined with great precision of mind, various unreal figures – as far as appearance, movements, characters and life history were concerned – who were so very visible to me and who were as much my own, as the things which we, abusively perhaps, call real life [...] In this way I can recall what seems to me to have been my first heteronym or – more precisely – my first non-existent acquaintance – a certain Chevalier de Pas – when I was only six years old, for whom I wrote letters, by him to myself, and whose image, not entirely faint, still touches on that part of my affection that can be described as nostalgia.' [Letter to Adolfo Casais Monteiro, 13 January 1935]

In 1895 his mother became engaged to Commander João Miguel Rosa, at that time newly appointed Portuguese consul in Durban, capital of the British colony of Natal. The prospect of having to leave Lisbon led to Pessoa writing his first poem, a quatrain dedicated to his mother: he loved his native land, Portugal, but loved his mother most. The marriage took place by proxy in Lisbon in December 1895, and in January 1896, Pessoa, his mother and an accompanying great-uncle sailed for Durban. In October 1896 his step-sister Madalena Henriqueta was born.

'The earliest literary food of my childhood was in the numerous novels of mystery and of horrible adventure. Those books, which are called boys' books and deal with exciting experiences, I cared little for. With a healthy and natural life I was out of sympathy. My craving was not for the probable, but for the incredible, not even the impossible by degree, but for the impossible by nature. My childhood was quiet [...] my education was good. But since I have consciousness of myself, I have perceived in myself an inborn tendency to mystification, to artistic lying. Add to this a great love of the spiritual, of the mysterious, of the obscure, which, after all, was but a form and a variation of that other characteristic of mine, and my personality is, to intuition, complete.' [Undated fragment]

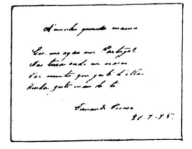

Sailing for Durban ...occasioned Pessoa's first poem, to his mother.

1897/98/99

■ Greece and Turkey at war. Spanish-American war. Anglo-French Fashoda incident in Africa. Boer War. Battle of Omdurman in the Sudan. Cape to Cairo railway. Germany begins Berlin-Baghdad railway / Holt – caterpillar tractor / Edison – electric light; sound recording. Bayer – aspirin / Curie – radium / Veblen *Theory of a Leisure Class* / Tolstoy *Resurrection*. James *The Turn of the Screw*. Conrad *The Nigger of the 'Narcissus'*. Rostand *Cyrano de Bergerac* / Ravel *Pavane pour une Infante Défunte*. Elgar *Enigma Variations*. Sibelius *Symphony no. 1* / Rodin *The Kiss* and *Victor Hugo*. Gauguin *Nevermore*. Rousseau *Sleeping gypsy girl*. Nablis movement / Mackintosh School of Art, Glasgow. Gaudi *Church of Sagrada Familia*

● First manifestations of Carbonária Portuguesa – an anarchist movement. Plague in Oporto / António Feijó *Ilha dos Amores*. José Duro *Fel*. Augusto Gil *Versos*. Teixeira de Pascoaes *Sempre* and *Terra Proibida*. Teixeira Gomes *Inventário de Junho*

Pessoa aged 8½ – 11½

◆ ON HIS ARRIVAL IN DURBAN, PESSOA WAS SENT TO A convent school run by Irish nuns where he stayed for three years of primary schooling. In April 1899 he moved on to the Durban High School.

'I've never suffered any nostalgia for my childhood; in truth, I've never felt the slightest nostalgia. I am, by nature, in the strict sense of the word, a futurist. I'm not by nature pessimistic, nor given to retrospection… From the past I regret only the passing of those I have loved; but that's not a matter of longing for the times when I loved them; only a longing for those people: I would like them to be alive today, of the age they would be today if they were alive.' [Letter to Gaspar Simões, 11 November 1931]

In 1899 one of Pessoa's most persistent heteronyms appeared: the Scot, 'Alexander Search'. Pessoa duly invented a biography for this Scottish

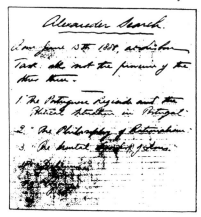

'Alexander Search': the young Pessoa plans his works…the adult Pessoa receives his mail.

engineer, gave him an older brother, cast his horoscope, wrote works in his name. When Pessoa returned to Lisbon in 1905, he had mock visiting cards printed in the name of 'Alexander Search', friends addressed letters to him, and to him were attributed many of Pessoa's poems and prose works in English.

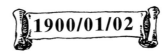

1900/01/02

■ Theodore Roosevelt President of USA. Relief of Mafeking in Africa. Anglo-Japanese Treaty. Boxer rising in China. Queen Victoria dies / Construction of Panama Canal begins. Trans-Siberian railway completed. Wireless telegraphy links Europe-USA / Planck – quantum theory and laws of radiation. De Vries – mutation theory / Freud *The Interpretation of Dreams* and *Psychopathology of Everyday Life.* Croce *Estetica.* Evans *Minoan* excavations. James *Varieties of Religious Experience* / Kipling *Kim.* Mann *Buddenbrooks.* Gide *L'Immoraliste.* Conrad *Lord Jim.* Strindberg *The Dance of Death.* Chekov *Uncle Vanya* and *The Three Sisters* / Debussy *Pelléas et Mélisande.* Puccini *Tosca.* Delius *Appalachia* / Munch *Girls on the Bridge.* Sickert *St Mark's, Venice.* Cézanne *La Nature morte aux Oignons.* Renoir *Le Nu au Soleil* / Frank Lloyd Wright-The Willets' House. Mackintosh – Chair

● State bankruptcy declared (1902) / Eça de Queirós *A Ilustre Casa de Ramires* and *A Cidade e as Serras.* Gomes Leal *Fim do Mundo* and *A Mulher de Luto.* Júlio Dantas *A Severa* and *A Ceia dos Cardeais.* Carlos Malheiro Dias *Os Teles de Albergaria* and *A Paixão do Maria de Céu.* Afonso Lopes Vieira *O Poeta Saudade.* António Nobre *Despedidas*

Pessoa aged 11½ – 14½

◆ IN JANUARY 1900 PESSOA'S STEP-BROTHER LUÍS MIGUEL was born.

Pessoa went to the Durban High School for three years until 1901, getting excellent reports and various school prizes. The headmaster, W.H. Nichols, was a classicist and humanist, widely read in English Literature, who doubtless encouraged and influenced the precocious Pessoa. At this time Pessoa became acquainted with many English classics, acquiring a deep and lasting interest in Shakespeare, and a lifelong delight in *The Pickwick Papers.*

'*In my childhood and early adolescence there was for me – raised and living in English lands – one supreme and enveloping book – Dickens' Pickwick Papers. Still, today... I read and re-read the book as if there were nothing else worth remembering.*' [Letter to José Osório de Oliveira, 1932]

'*Mr Pickwick belongs to the sacred figures of the world's history. Do not, please, claim that he has never existed: the same thing happens to most of the world's sacred figures, and they have been living presences to a vast number of wretches in need of consolation. So, if a mystic can claim a personal acquaintance and a clear vision of the Christ, a human can claim personal acquaintance and a clear vision of Mr Pickwick.'* [Undated fragment]

Pessoa's life-long friend
Pickwick: by Phiz; by Seymour.

In June 1901 Pessoa passed his Higher Certificate with distinction. Soon after, the family returned to Lisbon for an extended period of leave. A year later, Pessoa returned on his own to Durban, to prepare himself – with the help of night classes at the Commercial School – for the Cape University Matriculation Exam.

'It was a good thing for me and for my family that I stayed at home until I was fifteen, where I could live in my usual quiet, reserved way. After that I was sent off far from home to continue my education, and there the new being that I feared stirred in me and took on human form.' [Undated fragment]

1903/04/05

■ Russo-Japanese war. Anglo-French Entente Cordiale. Bloody Sunday in St Petersburg/ Wright Brothers – first powered flight. Photo-electric cell / Einstein – radiation theory / Moore – *Principia Ethica*. Weber *Protestantism and the Capitalist Spirit* / Pirandello *Il Fu Maltia Pascal*. Shaw *Man and Superman*. Barrie *Peter Pan*. Butler *The Way of All Flesh*. Chekov *The Cherry Orchard*. Abbey Theatre founded in Dublin (Yeats, Synge, O'Casey) / Strauss *Salome*. Janáček *Jenofa*. Puccini *Madame Butterfly* / Picasso *Boy with Pipe*. Rousseau *The Wedding* – Fauvism. Cézanne *Mont Sainte Victoire*. Klimt *Judith and Holofernes*

● Visits to Portugal of Edward VII of Britain, Alfonse XIII of Spain, William II of Germany, and President Loubet of France / Telephone system introduced in Lisbon / Teixeira de Pascoaes *Jesus e Pan*. Raúl Brandão *A Farsa*. Guerra Junqueiro *A Oração à Luz*. Carolina Michaelis de Vasconcelos edits *Cancioneiro da Ajuda* (Portuguese traditional poetry). Sampaio Bruno *O Encoberto*. António Patrício *Oceano*. Afonso Lopes Vieira *O Encoberto*. Teixeira Gomes *Sabina Freire*. Wenceslau de Morais *Serões no Japão*

Pessoa aged 14½ – 17½

◆ DESPITE HAVING TO PREPARE LARGELY ON HIS OWN, Pessoa managed, in 1903, to pass the university matriculation exam. Although English was his second language, he was awarded – among 899 candidates – the Queen Victoria Memorial Prize for the best English Essay.

He returned to the Durban High School for sixth-form studies; these covered the first year of the University course. His diary records extensive reading in Portuguese, French and various Classical authors, but above all in this period, in English, including works by several authors who influenced him or with whom he later recognized affinities: Shakespeare, of course, Milton, Byron, the Romantic poets – especially Shelley and Keats – Tennyson, Carlyle, and Browning (whose dramatic reconstructions in *Men and Women* may well have interested the inventor of heteronyms). Among American writers he enjoyed Poe and, later, came to admire Whitman ('[...] *he is the epitome of modern times. His power of expression is consummate, like Shakespeare's*'). The library which Pessoa took from flat to flat throughout his life, and which is now housed in the Casa Pessoa, consists for the most part of books in English. In 1904 Pessoa duly passed the Intermediate Examination in Arts at the Cape University, with credit.

At this time he wrote numerous poems in English and tried his hand at writing novels and detective fiction. New heteronyms appeared – Robert Anon, M.H.F. Lecher and others. His principal French heteronym, Jean Seul, wrote occasional poems throughout Pessoa's life, the last in 1933.

'*[...] This tendency to create another world within me, identical to this one but with different people, has never left my mind. This tendency went through various phases among which the following is one from when I had already become of age. A witty remark which had been burgeoning within me, would seem to me, for one reason or another, completely alien to that which I am or suppose I am. I would say it spontaneously, as if it had come from a certain friend of mine whose name I would invent, on whose life history I would expand and whose physical appearance – face, stature, dress and mien – I would immediately see before me. And it was in this way that I invented and spread around various friends and acquaintances who had never existed but whom I still today, almost thirty years later, am able to hear, feel and see. I repeat: whom I can hear, feel, see... and I miss them [...]*' [Letter to Adolfo Casais Monteiro, 13 January 1935]

Altogether during his life he created some 72 *dramatis personae* in 'the intimate theatre of the self', some little more than a name, others vividly alive and themselves creative.

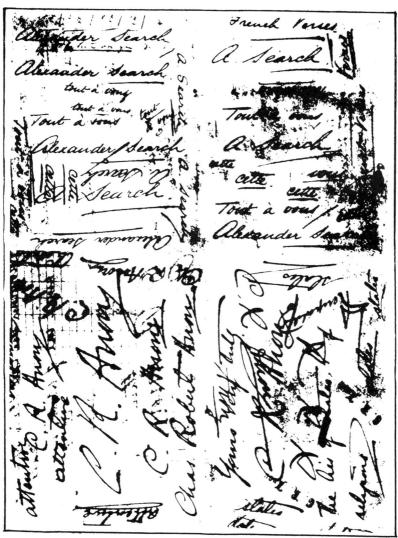

The boy Pessoa practises signatures for his heteronyms.

It was decided that Pessoa should return to Lisbon for university education. He sailed, alone, in August 1905, just turned seventeen. In Lisbon he stayed first with a great-aunt, and then with his mother's sister, Anica and her family. The adolescent Pessoa wrote:

'I have no one to confide in. My family understand not a thing. I can't worry my friends with such matters. In truth, I haven't any intimate friend [...] I'm too timid to confide my anguish to others. A truly intimate friend is one of my ideals, a daily dream, though I'm sure I'll never find one [...] But enough of that. Mistresses or fiancées, I have neither – that's another of my ideas, though when I look deeply into that possibility, I find a vacuum, nothing else. Impossible dream! Poor me! Poor Alastor! O Shelley, how I understand you. Would I be able to confide in my mother? How I wish she were near me. Perhaps I wouldn't be able to confide even in her, but her presence would lighten my suffering. I feel abandoned, like a ship foundering in the midst of the sea. And what indeed am I if not shipwrecked? I can count on no one but myself. What reliance can I place on these lines I write? None. When I re-read them, I realize they are pretentious, that I write them as though for some literary journal. I've even tried to polish up some of them. The fact remains, however, that I suffer. A man clothed in silk may suffer as much as one dressed in a sack or covered in rags. Enough.'
[Undated note]

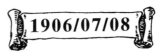

1906/07/08

■ Meeting of first Duma in St Petersburg. Triple alliance formed (Russia-France-Britain). Annexation of Bosnia-Herzegovina by Austro-Hungary / Boy Scouts founded / Pavlov – Study of Reflexes / James *Pragmatism* Bergson *L'Évolution* / Gorki *Mother*. Galsworthy *The Man of Property*. Bennett *The Old Wives' Tale*. Forster *A Room with a View*. Grahame *Wind in the Willows*. France *L'Île des Pingouins*. Adams *The Education of Henry Adams* / Strauss *Elektra*. Abeniz *Iberia*. Villa Lobos *Cánticos Sertanejos*. Debussy *La Mer*. Schönberg *Pieces for piano – opus 11* (basis of Atonality) / 'Discovery' of African art. Braque; Picasso *Les Demoiselles d'Avignon* – Cubism. Chagall *Le Paysan*. Epstein *Figures* / Otto Wagner *Principles of Modern Architecture*. Frank Lloyd Wright – Unity Temple. Ruth St Denis – modern dance

● Left-wing riots in Lisbon. *Coup d'état* by João Franco who becomes dictator, with support of the king. Major military operations in Angola. King Carlos I and the Crown Prince Luis Filipe assassinated (1908); Manuel II becomes king / Manuel Laranjeira *Pessimismo Nacional* / Teixeira de Pascoaes *Vida Etérea* and *As Sombras*. Raúl Brandão *Os Pobres*. Gomes Leal *Mefistófeles em Lisboa*. Luís de Magalhães *Os Cantos do Estio e do Outono*. Alberto Osório de Castro (in Timor) *Flores de Coral*

Pessoa aged 17½ – 20½

◆ IN OCTOBER 1906 PESSOA'S FAMILY RETURNED TO Lisbon on leave and took a flat where Pessoa went to live with them.

There his step-sister, Maria Clara, died in December. Early in 1907 the family went back to Durban and Pessoa went to live with his paternal grandmother Dionísia, by then subject to fits of insanity.

'One of my mental complications – more terrible than words can express – is a fear of madness, which is already in itself a part of madness.' [Note dated 30 October 1908]

During his family's leave in Lisbon, Pessoa had enrolled at the University of Lisbon. The University was the scene of student riots against measures of the dictator João Franco. After a few months Pessoa quit, preferring to study on his own.

'During what I may call my third adolescence, passed here in Lisbon, I lived with Greek and German philosophers and with the French decadents, whose effects were briskly swept from my spirit by Swedish drill and by reading 'Dégénérance' by Nordau.' [Letter to José Osório de Oliveira, 1932]

He continued to write poetry – during the first four years after his return to Lisbon (in 1905) in English, not Portuguese. 107 English poems have survived.

In August 1907, grandmother Dionísia died, leaving Pessoa a small legacy. With a cousin, Pessoa tried to set up a small printing and publishing business, the 'Imprensa Ibis'. Within a few months it failed.

Pessoa now lived alone. He was offered jobs but these would have meant full-time occupation at an employer's disposal. Instead, he began to work, freelance, as a commercial foreign correspondent, a job of some standing which, in time, brought him into contact with leading international companies, for whom he translated and wrote letters in English and French. This, for the rest of his days, provided a sufficient income – at first only marginally so – and left him time for his own writing. In his early years he accepted (and doubtless needed to accept) occasional foreign commissions – in 1911 to translate into Portuguese an American Anthology of Universal Writers, for a Brazilian publisher; in 1914 to collect and translate 300 Portuguese proverbs, for an English publisher. And so on.

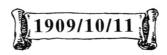

1909/10/11

■ George V king in Britain. Revolution in Mexico. Blériot flies the Channel. Peary reaches the North Pole, Amundsen the South Pole / Model T Ford. The scandalous Argentine tango sweeps USA and Europe. Marinetti *Futurist Manifesto*. Freud founds The International Society for Psychoanalysis / Rutherford – theory of Atomic structure / Whitehead and Russell *Principia Mathematica* / Rilke *Duino Elegies*. Cavafy *Ithaca* / Strauss *Elektra* and *Roskenkavalier*. Mahler *Das Lied von der Erde*.

Stravinsky *Firebird*. Diaghilev's Ballet Russe in Paris. Schönberg *Harmonielehre* / Blaue Reiter group exhibition in Munich. Modigliani in Paris. Matisse *La Dance*. Utrillo *Church at Châtillon*. De Chirico *The Enigma of the Clock Tower*. Morandi, Carrà – Metaphysical painting

● Liberal junta organizes mass demonstrations; (1910) Revolution – Manuel II abdicates; Republic declared. Teófilo Braga becomes president. Separation of Church and State; expulsion of religious orders; suppression of theological faculties; legalisation of civil marriage and divorce. Abolition of titles of nobility. New National Assembly. Monarchist riots – creation of a Republican Guard. Reform of primary education; new Lisbon and Oporto universities founded / Teixeira de Pascoaes *Senhora da Noite* and *Marânus*; he starts the journal *A Águia* and the movement 'Renascença Portuguesa'. Jaime Cortesão *A Morte da Águia*. Augusto Gil *Luar de Janeiro*. António Patrício *O Fim* and *Serão Inquieto*. Teixeira Gomes *Gente Singular*. Afonso Lopes Vieira *Canções do Vento e do Sol*

A PROCLAMAÇÃO DA REPUBLICA

Pessoa aged 20½ – 23½

◆ THIS PERIOD IN PESSOA'S LIFE WAS MARKED LESS BY writing than by reading – in his own growing collection of books and in public libraries, notably the National Library and the Academy of Sciences. He became thoroughly familiar with French symbolists – Baudelaire, Verlaine, Rimbaud, Larforgue and Maeterlinck.

By good fortune Pessoa's step-father's uncle, Henrique Rosa, was *sympathique* – an ex-general of wide culture in both science and literature, who wrote poems (Pessoa later published some of his sonnets), eccentric and self-sufficient. Perhaps with his advice, Pessoa read extensively in nineteenth-century and turn-of-the-century Portuguese poets: Antero de Quental, Almeida Garrett, Cesário Verde, António Nobre and – still alive then – Gomes Leal. By 1912, Pessoa was exceptionally well read in English, French and Portuguese literature and had absorbed most of the influences or became acquainted with most of the affinities which contributed to his subsequent poetic development.

Pessoa continued writing poetry, chiefly in English – poems up to 1909 are generally assigned to 'Alexander Search', thereafter to 'Fernando Pessoa' himself – but sometimes now in Portuguese (such as the six sonnets 'In Search of Beauty'). He also began his undramatic 'drama' *Faust* in 1908, on the five acts of which he continued to work intermittently until 1933.

The feeble showing of the government in response to the British ultimatum about Africa, the assassination of the king and his heir, with the subsequent overthrow of the monarchy, made this a period of patriotic and revolutionary fervour, which Pessoa shared.

'My intense patriotic suffering, my intense desire of bettering the condition of Portugal provoke in me [...] a thousand plans which, even if one man could realise them, he had to have one characteristic which in me is purely negative – the power of will. But I suffer – on the very limit of madness, I swear it – as if I could do all and was unable to do it, by deficiency of will. [...] Besides my patriotic projects – writing of Portugal Republic *– to provoke a revolution here, writing of Portuguese pamphlets, editing of older national literary works, creation of a magazine, of a scientific review, etc. – other plans, consuming me with the necessity of being soon carried out (...) combine to produce an excess of impulse that paralyses my will. The suffering that this produces I know not if it can be described as on this side of insanity. Add to all this other reasons still for suffering, some physical, others mental, [...] complications, money difficulties – join this all to my fundamentally unbalanced temperament and you may be able to suspect what my suffering is.'* [Undated fragment, in English]

Identifying deeply with Portugal, increasingly writing his poems in Portuguese, Pessoa, once returned to his native land, never again left it. Indeed, except for two visits to the nearby Alentejo region, he stayed in Lisbon and the small towns in its purlieus where friends or relatives lived.

'The only person I've ever come across animated by the true spirit of the voyager was a boy in an office where I was once employed. This youth made a collection of travel folders about towns, countries, shipping lines. He hoarded maps – some torn out of newspapers, others he had asked for wherever he could; he had cut out from magazines pictures of landscapes, drawings of exotic costumes, photographs of small boats and great liners. He used to go to the tourist agencies and – on behalf of some company, invented or real, even the one he worked for – ask for brochures about travels in Italy, brochures about voyages in India, brochures about available connections between Portugal and Australia...

'He was not only the greatest traveller I've ever known, because most true; he was also one of the happiest people it has been my fortune to know.' [From *The Book of Disquietude*]

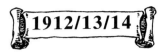

■ Titanic sinks. Panama Canal opens. First and Second Balkan Wars –
Turkey in Europe reduced to Istanbul. German-Turkish Alliance.
Assassination of King George of Greece. Sun Yat Sen – China declared a
republic. Assassination of Archduke Ferdinand at Sarajevo; First World
War begins / Cellophane. Stainless steel / Einstein *General Theory of
Relativity* / Freud *Totem and Taboo.* Jung *Theory of the Collective
Unconscious* / Proust *Un Amour de Swann.* Lawrence *Sons and Lovers.*
Mann *Death in Venice.* Kafka *Metamorphosis.* Pirandello *Se Non Cosi.*
Appollinaire *Alcools.* Pound – theory of Imagism in poetry; (Eliot, Pound
etc) – Manifesto of Vorticism in *Blast* / Ravel *Daphnis et Chloe.* Stravinsky
Rite of Spring. Scriabin *Prometheus.* De Falla *La Vida Breve.* Debussy –
'Orphism' / Matisse *French window at Colliovre.* Kokoschka *The storm.*
Chagall *The Newspaper-seller.* Kandinsky – 'The Spiritual in Art'.
Duchamp exhibits first 'ready-made' – a bicycle wheel

● (1912) 77,000 people emigrate from Portugal. Monarchist factions
unite. Left-wing riots suppressed. Military action in Angola. Amnesty for
Monarchists. Riots against the cost of living / Mário de Sá-Carneiro
Princípio, Amizade, Dispersão and *A Confissão de Lúcio.* Manuel
Laranjeira *Comigo.* Teixeira de Pascoaes *Regresso ao Paraíso* and *Elegias*
and *Verbo Escuro.* Afonso Duarte *Cancioneiro das Pedras* and *Tragédia
do Sol Posto.* Raúl Brandão *O Doido e a Morte.* Aquilino Ribeiro *Jardim
das Tormentas.* Mario Beirão *O Último Lusíada.* João Lúcio *Na Asa do
Sonho*

Pessoa aged 23½ – 26½

◆ FROM NOVEMBER 1912 – PESSOA, WHO HAD BEEN LIV-
ing alone, went to live instead with his aunt Anica, of whom he was fond,
and her young family. Among her interests were spiritualism, astrology
and other manifestations of the occult, which later became important to
Pessoa.

April 1912 marked Pessoa's début as a writer of critical and polemic
articles. He had become a member of the newly-formed 'Portuguese
Renaissance' movement and the April issue of its journal *A Águia* ('The
Eagle') included the first of two parts of his 'New Portuguese poetry sociologically considered'. This was followed, at the end of the year, by the
three parts of 'New Portuguese poetry psychologically considered'. These
pieces succeeded in provoking the hostility of the artistic Establishment in
the leading journals and newspapers. In 1913 Pessoa also began writing
regular drama criticism for *O Teatro,* and *A Águia* published some poems
and his 'static play' *The Mariner.*

This was an exciting time for the young Lisbon intellectuals of the day
and Pessoa was a lively part of it. He frequently gathered with other young
writers and artists in cafés like Martinho in the then Largo Camões, or
Martinho 'in the Arcade', or The Brasileira in the Chiado. Modernist jour-

Pessoa's debut in print: an article in *À Aguia*; dramatic criticism in *O Teatro*.

nals sprang up, usually lasted an issue or two, died, and were replaced by others. Pessoa's intelligence, lucidity and sensitivity led to his being greatly in demand for editing the works of other writers – so did his lack of egotism, for throughout his life he promoted the appearance of the work of others, even when that meant the omission of his own. Almost all the poetry and prose by Pessoa which was published during his lifetime – in all some 430 pieces – appeared in papers and journals, often in ephemeral, small-circulation issues.

'Movements' too – whether patriotic, political, moral, artistic or literary – were many and brief. Pessoa contributed *Paulism* (exemplified in his poem 'Pauis' [Quagmires]) and *Intersectionism*. Then, among the other modernist writers, he met a like-minded poet Mário de Sá-Carneiro, and in due season, they invented *Sensationalism*. In October 1912 Sá-Carneiro left for the Sorbonne in Paris and a frequent correspondence followed between the two of them.

In a letter to Sá-Carneiro, dated February 1913, Pessoa describes his state of mental and creative turmoil at this time.

'*At present I'm going through one of those crises which they usually call, in agriculture, crises of over-abundance. Ideas come into my mind so fast, so abundantly that I have to carry a notebook, and even then the number of pages I fill is so great that I get lost, because there are too many, and other pages I can't decipher because I wrote them too fast. That I lose ideas is an acute torture for me, and the ideas then pursue me, obscurely changed, to torture me more [...] You can't imagine what sort of turmoil went on in my poor head as I walked down the Rua d'Arsenal: verses in English, in Portuguese, reflections, ideas, projects, fragments about which I understand nothing except that they exist, letters with neither beginnings nor endings, critical flashes, metaphysical murmurs... A whole literature, my dear Mário, which comes from a mist, passes through a mist, vanishes into a mist...'* [Letter to Mário de Sá-Carneiro, 1 February 1913]

A month later, a diary entry describes the constituents of a Pessoan day:

'To the Baixa towards one o'clock in the afternoon. I went to the two Lavado offices and at the one in the Rue Augusta I was given a letter to write. At Mayer's office I wrote almost the whole of a letter to Sá-Carneiro. Then I went to the Almada Negreiros exhibition, and on to help – asked to do so by João Correia de Oliveira – with editing O Ocidente. A day of total, mortal depression – Stayed home for the evening. I finished a letter for 'Natal' (replying to the one which described the immortal event) – A letter from Álvaro Pinto, about a subscription to support Gomes Leal.' [Diary, 20 March 1913]

The combination of an excess of fleeting ideas and a state of mind inhibiting more sustained composition may account for his starting his *Book of Disquietude*, which was to become a life-long depository of pieces long and short. The first of them, 'In the Forest of Estrangement', was published in a journal in 1913. In 1914 he wrote the first draft of his long poem in English *Antinous*.

In 1914 Sá-Carneiro returned from Paris, with the artists Amadeo de Souza-Cardoso and Santa Rita Pintor (who brought with him a copy in French of Marinetti's *Futurist Manifesto*). At about this time, wishing to play a trick on Sá-Carneiro, Pessoa tells how he tried to invent 'a pastoral poet of a complicated type' with a view to passing him off as a real person – the future 'Alberto Caeiro' in embryo; and he had somewhat earlier had the idea of writing some poems 'of a pagan type' – such as he later attributed to 'Ricardo Reis'.

Then on 8 March 1914 (as he later recollected), feeling suddenly inspired, he took a sheet of paper, and, going to a tall chest of drawers in his room, began to write, as was his habit, standing up.

'And I wrote thirty-odd poems in one go, in a kind of trance whose nature I cannot define. It was the triumphant day of my life, and it would be impossible to experience such a one again. I began with a little "O Guardador de Rebandos" (The Keeper of Flocks). What followed was the appearance of someone in me, to whom I at once gave the name "Alberto Caeiro". Forgive the absurdity of this sentence: my Master had appeared inside me. That was my immediate sensation. So much so that once those thirty-odd poems were written, I picked up another sheet of paper and wrote, again without a break,

The chest on which Pessoa, in a burst of creativity, wrote the first poems of his principal heteronyms, including 'The Keeper of Sheep' by Caeiro.

the six poems that constitute the "Chuva Oblíqua" (Oblique Rain) by Fernando Pessoa. Immediately and totally. It was the return from "Fernando Pessoa / Alberto Caeiro" to "Fernando Pessoa" himself. Or rather the reaction of "Fernando Pessoa" against his inexistence as "Alberto Caeiro".

'With Alberto Caeiro come into being, I went about discovering for him – instinctively and unconsciously – some disciples. I dragged out the latent Ricardo Reis from his false paganism, found his name and made him coherent, because at that stage I could already see him. And suddenly, in antithesis to the appearance of Ricardo Reis, a new individual burst impetuously onto the scene. In one fell swoop, at the typewriter, without hesitation or correction, there appeared the "Ode Triumphal" by Álvaro de Campos – the Ode of that name and the man with the name he now has.

'I created, therefore, an inexistent coterie. I sorted out the influences and the relationships, listened, inside myself, to the debates and the difference in criteria, and in all of this, it seemed to me that I, the creator of it all, had the lesser presence. It seemed that it all happened independently of me. And so it seems to me still [...] [Letter to Adolfo Casais Monteiro, 13 January 1935]

Pessoa later defined his 'heteronyms':

'A pseudonymic work is, except for the name with which it is signed, the work of an author writing as himself; a heteronymic work is by an author writing outside his own personality: it is the work of a complete individuality made up by him, just as the utterances of some character in a drama

ity made up by him, just as the utterances of some character in a drama would be.' [Article in *Presença*, 1928]

A week after the letter quoted *in extensis* above, Pessoa wrote again to Monteiro remarking: *'Behind the involuntary masks of the poet, the thinker and whatever else, I am essentially a* dramatist*'*. Caeiro, Reis, and Campos, Pessoa's three main poetic heteronyms, had lives, histories, characters, styles and thoughts of their own; their poetic works therefore *'must be considered distinct from that of their author'*. And, indeed, the public persona known as 'Fernando Pessoa' was in some respects a heteronym too. *'No artist should have only one personality. On the contrary, he should have several, each one from like states of mind which would discard the fiction that personality is one only and indivisible.'* On that March day in 1914, Pessoa had found his voice, by finding voices.

In the autumn of 1914, a series of meetings of young writers and artists, including Pessoa and Sá-Carneiro, at the beer-hall Jansen and elsewhere, led to plans for a new journal which would exhibit work in modernist idioms, syntax, imagery and styles.

In November 1914, Pessoa's aunt Anica, and her family, moved to Switzerland. Pessoa once more lived on his own. At this time, deeply depressed, he wrote 'broken and incoherent pieces'. *'My state of mind compels me to work hard against my will on* The Book of Disquietude. *But it's all fragments, fragments, fragments.'* Of its 'author', Bernardo Soares, Pessoa wrote: *'He's a semi-heteronym, because his personality although not my own, doesn't differ from my own, but is a mere mutilation of it.'*

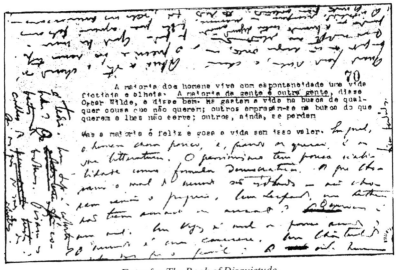

Entry for *The Book of Disquietude*.

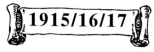

1915/16/17

■ Battles of Verdun (700,000 dead), Ypres, Somme, Gallipoli, Passendale. Easter Rising in Dublin. USA enters war. Tsar abdicates. February and October revolutions in Russia / Machine guns, tanks, poison gas, air-raids / Lenin *State and Revolution*. Spengler *Decline of the West*. Fraser *The Golden Bough*. Freud *Introduction to Psychoanalysis*. Jung *The Unconscious* / Eliot *Prufrock*. Yeats *The Wild Swans at Coole*. Joyce *Portrait of the Artist as a Young Man* / Sibelius *Symphony no 5*. Poulenc *Mouvements Perpétuels*. Satie *Parade* / Mondrian *Composition no 10* – Neo-plasticism. Arp's reliefs and collages. First 'constructivist' works in Moscow. Klee's 'Lettrique' paintings. First Dadaist exhibition, Zurich / Griffith *Birth of a Nation* and *Intolerance*. Original Dixieland Jazz Band in New York

● Riots in several parts of the country. (1916) Confiscation of German boats in Portuguese waters – handed over for use by Britain. (1917) Germany declares war on Portugal; Portuguese battalions to Western Front. Military *coup d'état* by Sidónio Pais, president and dictator. Three general strikes. Madeira bombarded by German navy. Reconciliation with the Vatican / Teixeira de Pascoaes *A Arte de Ser Português*. Almada Negreiros *Manifesto Anti-Dantas*. António Sérgio *Considerações Histórico-pedagógicas* / Raúl Brandão *Húmus*. Almada Negreiros *A Engomadeira*. Mario Beirão *Lusitânia*. Alfonso Lopes Vieira *Ilha de Brumas*

✦ *Pessoa aged 26½ – 29½*

◆ WITH SÁ-CARNEIRO BACK IN PARIS, THE CORRES-pondence between the two friends resumed and achieved an unusual intimacy, tinged with that literary introspection natural to young writers:

'I am writing to you today out of sentimental necessity, a tormented anxiousness to talk to you. As can be deduced from this I do not have anything to say to you. Only this – that today I am in the depth of a depression which has no depth. The absurdity of the sentence itself will speak for me [...]

'In the garden, which I can glimpse through the silent windows of my solitary confinement, the swings have all been thrown above the branches from where they hang, and they are all twisted around very high. And thus, not even the idea of my running away can have swings in my imagination, in order to forget the hour.

'This is more or less, but without style, my state of mind at the moment. Like the mourning maiden of 'O Marinheiro' [The Sailor] my eyes are burning for having thought of crying. I ache through life — little by little in gulps, at intervals. All this is printed in very small print in a book of which the paper cover is coming unstitched.

'If I were not writing to you, I would have to pledge that this letter is sincere and that the things of a hysterical nexus which are to be found there emerged spontaneously from what I feel. But you will certainly feel that this

unperformable tragedy is as real as a coat-hanger or a tea-cup, its reality being full of the here and now, taking place in my soul in the same way as leaves are green.

'It was for this reason that the Prince did not come to reign. This sentence is entirely absurd. But at this moment I feel that absurd sentences produce a great desire to cry.

'It may be that if today I do not post this letter, tomorrow, re-reading it, I will spend time copying it on the typewriter in order to insert sentences and grimaces from it into the 'Livro do Desassossego' [Book of Disquietude]. *But this will not remove anything from the sincerity with which I write this letter, nor from the harrowing inevitability with which I feel it [...]* [Letter to Mário de Sá-Carneiro, 14 March 1916]

The break-through for Portuguese modernism: *Orpheu 2*, cover and contents page.

Early in 1915 appeared the first edition of the planned modernist journal, *Orpheu*. It included Álvaro de Campos's 'Triumphal Ode' and work by Sá-Carneiro, Negreiros and Souza-Cardoso. The journal was greeted with derision. The editor resigned. Sá-Carneiro and Pessoa edited the second issue in June, which included Pessoa's 'Oblique Rain' and Campos's 'Maritime Ode'. (Roy Campbell described this as 'the loudest poem ever written': Campos was then at his most Whitmanesque; he changed greatly in later years.)

The newspaper *A Capital* ran a long, hostile article about *Orpheu* on its front page. Álvaro de Campos vigorously replied, but in a manner which caused strain between Pessoa and his friends. Sá-Carneiro returned to Paris: his father disapproved strongly of his son's involvement with

Orpheu and Sá-Carneiro wrote to Pessoa to say that lack of funds made bringing out the proposed third issue impractical.

In December 1916 Pessoa's much-loved mother suffered a stroke in Durban. Pessoa wrote to Sá-Carneiro:

'For some months my mother's severe illness has depressed me. She has suffered what is prosaically called a stroke — the whole of her left side has been paralysed. She's getting better, according to the letters I get, but so slowly, so hesitantly, that I can't rid myself of a chilling doubt on the subject. This anguish, bodily present in me, deranges me. To that is added the suffering that you – without intending it – have caused me by your terrible crisis. I don't think you realize how deep my friendship is for you, how much I'm attached to you. The fact is that your great crisis has become my great crisis, and I have felt it not just from your letters but by some sort of telepathic 'projection', as they say, of your suffering.' [Letter to Sá-Carneiro, dated 26 April 1916]

On the same day this letter was written, Sá-Carneiro in Paris wrote a last note to Pessoa: 'A big, big good-bye from your poor Mário de Sá-Carneiro' and committed suicide. In subsequent years, Pessoa devoted time and effort to editing and publishing his friend's poems, and eighteen years later wrote a moving sonnet in his memory. Pessoa changed address frequently – three times in as many months. He prepared the proposed *Orpheu 3* on his own, but publication proved impossible.

Orpheu: Negreiros depicts its effect on the cultural 'Establishment'.

Almada Negreiros and Amadeu de Souza-Cardoso (who now shared a studio with Modiliagni in Paris) mounted an exhibition in Lisbon. Negreiros – brilliant as a publicist, actor, impressario of 'happenings', as

well as being a painter and writer – held a Futurist Conference and issued
in 1916 the 'Manifesto Anti-Dantas' — a vehement attack on Portugal's
artistic Establishment, and an explosive, futurist appeal to the 'twentieth-
century generation'. In November 1917 the one and only issue of *Portugal
Futurista* was published, which included poems by Pessoa in his own name
and an 'Ultimatum' by Álvaro de Campos. *Portugal Futurista* was, of
course, partly issued 'pour épater le bourgeois'. (Some of its contributors,
in those hirsute days, shaved not just their faces but heads and eyebrows
too.) A scandalous article by Negreiros in the journal led to the immediate
confiscation of the whole issue by the police.

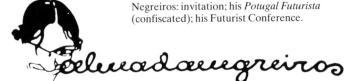

Negreiros: invitation; his *Potugal Futurista*
(confiscated); his Futurist Conference.

PORTUGAL
FUTURISTA
———
Santa Rita Pintor – José de
Almada-Negreiros – Amadeo de
Souza-Cardoso
Appollinaire
Mario de Sá-Carneiro – Fernando
Pessoa – Raul Leal – Alvaro de
Campos
Blaise Cendrars.

Although Pessoa was active in the noisy public activities of young
artists and writers, he had begun privately to write poetry of an original
and quieter kind which, when later published, became part of his main and
distinctive *oeuvre*. Early in 1915 he wrote to a friend and fellow poet:

*'For a long time – ever since I promised you this letter – I've wanted to
talk to you, at an intimate, fraternal level, about my 'case', about the psychological crisis I've been going through for some time. Despite my reserve, I
feel the need to talk to someone, you I think – because you alone among
those I know, have a conception of me which corresponds to my fundamental spirituality. If you are able in some degree to understand me, it is because,*

like me, you are essentially religious: the others who are part of my literary circle, however superior they may be as artists, do not count in the same way as fellow 'souls'; no one has that same awareness – it is my daily companion – of the terrible importance of Life, an awareness which inhibits the creation of 'art for art's sake' and imposes a duty to oneself and to humanity [...]'

The letter continued with an explanation that poems by Caeiro, Reis and Campos, though written dramatically were

'... sincere (in my serious sense of the word) just as what King Lear says is sincere, although he is not Shakespeare, but a creation of his. I mean by insincere those things that are done to astonish people, and also those things which... do not contain a basic metaphysical idea i.e. are not inspired by a sense of the gravity and mystery of Life. For that reason, all I have written in the name of Caeiro, Reis and Campos is serious. In each of them I placed a profound conception of life, a serious involvement with the mysterious importance of Existence.' [Letter to Armando Côrtes-Rodrigues, 19 January 1915]

In the letter Pessoa dismissed his previous involvement with the public as playing the fool.

At this time, in 1915, Pessoa was very hard up. He worked (in the sense of working for money) within self-imposed limits and, as a peripatetic free-lance writer or translator of business letters in English and French, doubt-less suffered the uncertainties of employment and payment experienced by all freelancers. With the war, commerce was disrupted; and some of his business sponsors may have frowned upon his artistic activities and his appearances in print – so bizarre a contrast to his normally restrained and decorous manner. Later, in June 1915, he had to write to Armando Côrtes-Rodrigues again:

'These are violent and afflicting circumstances. Could you lend me five escudos until the first of next month (1st of July)? It is most urgent I assure you. Repayment will be prompt and certain on the date above mentioned, if not before, which could happen, although I do not promise it. If only you could do this! You would help me out in circumstances in which I have no one to turn to. It would be a matter of a few days; nor would I – bearing in mind what you have already explained to me with regard to your situation – trick you, or tell you I would pay you on a certain day, if it were impossible for me to do so [...] Please try and help me out, will you? Only over these next five or six days. I am sure you will manage it.' [Letter to Armando Côrtes-Rodrigues, 23 June 1915]

Two years later, however, in 1917, Pessoa was doing sufficiently well to establish, with two friends, a commercial office where they could receive commissions for their business translation work.

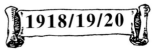

1918/19/20

■ Balfour declaration on Palestine. Execution of the Tsar and his family. Armistice. Treaty of Versailles. Epidemic of Spanish 'flu – more than 100,000 die. Weimar Republic. Mussolini founds Fascist party. League of Nations. Civil war in Ireland – partition. White Russian and Allied armies invade Russia. France occupies the Ruhr. Hitler announces his programme / Prohibition in USA. Alcock and Brown – first flight across Atlantic. Marconi opens in Britain the world's first broadcasting station / Morgan – chromosome theory of heredity / Freud *Beyond the Pleasure Principle*. Keynes *The Economic Consequences of the Peace* / Valéry *Le Cimetière Marin*. Pound *Cantos*. Strachey *Eminent Victorians*. Gide *La Symphonie Pastorale*. Lewis *Main Street* / Bartók *Bluebeard's Castle*. Stravinsky *Pulchinella*. 'Les Six' / Malevitch *White on white*. Picasso *Pierrot and Harlequin*. Gris *Guitar, Book and Newspaper*. Spencer *The Last Supper*. Matisse *The Odalisque*. Modigliani *Reclining Nude*. Brancusi *Bird in Space* / Gropius – Bauhaus

● Sidónio Pais declares a state of siege. General strike. Pais assassinated. Monarchist risings suppressed. Transport strike. Portuguese unions form CGT, with journal *Avanti!*. Further riots and strikes – state of siege declared in Oporto / Alfredo Guisado *Ânfora*. Aquilino Ribeiro *A Via Sinuosa* and *Terras do Demo*. António Patrício *Pedro o Crú* and *Dinis e Isabel*. Florbela Espanca *Livro de Mágoas*. António Sérgio *Ensaios*. Camilo Pessanha *Clepsidra*. Almada Negreiros *Histoire du Portugal par Coeur*

Pessoa aged 29½ – 32½

◆ IN APRIL 1918 SANTA RITA PINTOR, TALENTED PAINTer and *Orpheu* supporter, committed suicide in Paris, leaving a note that all his work should be destroyed. In October, Amadeo de Souza-Cardoso, regarded by Pessoa as 'the most celebrated painter of the Portuguese avant-garde', another *Orpheu* contributor, died in the Spanish influenza epidemic.

Pessoa published some poems in English in booklet form: *Antinous* and *35 Sonnets*. Both books were reviewed by *The Times* and *The Glasgow Herald*. He also wrote, though not for publication then, the 'Poemas Inconjuntos' of Alberto Caeiro. Following the assassination at the end of 1989 of Sidónio Pais, the ruler of Portugal whom Pessoa admired, he wrote 'How to organize Portugal', 'Public Opinion' and a poem 'In memory of President Sidónio Pais' for the journal *Acção*.

In October 1918, Pessoa's step-father died in Pretoria. Early in 1920, Pessoa's mother, his two step-brothers and his sister returned to Portugal. Pessoa rejoined his family in a Lisbon apartment. (His brothers soon migrated to London. His sister married an army officer and continued to live in or near Lisbon.)

In 1920 Pessoa's poem in English 'Meantime' was published in the *Atheneum*. Under the pseudonym 'A.A. Crosse' he began writing in *The Times*. He composed a series of epitaphs in English. Portuguese poems of his appeared in *Ressurreição*.

Pessoa's published
poems in English:
Antinous and *English
Poems*.

In March 1920 Pessoa got to know Ophélia Queiroz, a secretary in one of the companies for which he wrote commercial correspondence in English and French. She was nineteen, of good family, intelligent and cultivated. She gently joined in the 'game' of his heteronyms, addressing letters to Alexander Search and declaring a dislike for Álvaro de Campos who was jealous of her sentimental affair with Pessoa. She and Pessoa met frequently and exchanged numerous notes and letters. In October, however, Pessoa suffered a severe bout of depression (contemplating recourse to a nursing home) and in November he broke off the relationship with Ophélia. His last letter to her concluded with these paragraphs:

'*[...] I ask you not to do as ordinary people do, who are always vile: don't turn away when I pass near you, and remember me without malice. Let us be to one another like childhood friends who loved one another when they were young and who, even when they become adults and know other loves, follow other paths, keep always, in a corner of their hearts, the deep memory of their old, inconsequent affection.*

'*Such "other loves" and "other paths" are for you, my little Ophélia, not for me. My destiny is to follow another Law, the existence of which you know nothing of, in submission more and more to Masters who neither relent nor pardon.*

'*You have no need to understand all that. It is enough that you should retain a tender memory of me, as I, unalterably, shall of you.*' [Letter to Ophélia, 29 November 1920]

They were to renew their relationship nine years later.

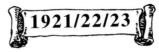

1921/22/23

■ Washington Conference on Disarmament. Mussolini's March on Rome. USSR formed – Lenin's 'New Economic Policy'. Fascist *coup d'état* in Spain by Primo de Riveira. Kemal Ataturk becomes president in Turkey. Ultra-inflation in Germany. Tutankhamen's tomb discovered / Insulin. Sheet steel / Rutherford and Chadwick disintegrate the elements / Lukacs *History of Class Consciousness.* Wittgenstein *Tractatus Logico-Philosophicus* / Joyce *Ulysses.* Eliot *The Waste Land.* Pirandello *Six Characters in Search of an Author.* Hesse *Siddhartha.* Svevo *The Conscience of Zeno.* Borges *Fervour in Buenos Aires* / Prokofiev *Love of Three Oranges.* Stravinsky *Los Noces.* Walton *Façade.* Honegger *King David* / Mondrian *Composition in Blue.* Picasso *The Three Musicians, Two women running on the beach.* Braque *Still life with guitar.* Spencer *The Resurrection* / Le Corbusier's theory of modern architecture / Chaplin *The Kid*

● Portuguese Communist Party founded – Portuguese edition of Lenin's *State and Revolution.* Organized assassination of several Republican leaders. Military revolt in Lisbon put down. The writer Teixeira Gomes elected president. Salazar elected a Deputy; expounds his economic policy. Violent riots in many places against rising prices. Portuguese aviators fly from Lisbon to Rio de Janeiro / Almada Negreiros *A Invenção do Dia Claro* / António Sérgio and others found the journal *Seara Nova.* António Botto *Canções* and *Motivos de Beleza.* Alfredo Cortez *Zilda.* António Ferro *Leviana.* José Pacheco and others found the journal *Contemporânea.* António Feijó *Sol de Inverno.* Aquilino Ribeiro *Estrada de Santiago.* Mario Beirão *Pastorais.* Afonso Lopes Vieira *Amadis de Gaula.* Florbela Espanca *Livro de Soror Saudade.* Raúl Brandão *Os Pescadores* and *O Gebo e a Sombra*

Pessoa aged 32½ – 35½

◆ IN 1921 PESSOA FOUNDED A PUBLISHING HOUSE 'OLISIPO'. Early publications included his own *English Poems 1, 2 and 3* and Almada Negreiros's *A Invenção do Dia Claro* [Invention on a cloudless day].

Trademark of Pessoa's publishing house 'Olisipo'.

Soon Pessoa and his publishing house were involved in literary battles. Repeatedly, Pessoa took up the cause of writers of quality whose freedom to publish was threatened by state intolerance, police intervention, public philistinism or organized opposition. Pessoa wrote articles defending António Botto, poet, aesthete and homosexual, against accusations of immorality. Having invoked the case of the ancient Greeks, he continued:

'... *There is a central idea which, without being either metaphysical or moral, takes the place, in the works of an aesthete, of metaphysical and moral ideas. The aesthete replaces the idea of the truth and the idea of the good with the idea of beauty, and so confers on beauty the weight both of a metaphysic and a morality. The celebrated 'Conclusion' of* The Renaissance *by Pater, the greatest of European aesthetes, is a supreme example of this attitude.'*[1] [Article in *Contemporânea* no 3 1922]

·ANTONIO·BOTTO·

CANÇÕES

SEGVNDA·EDIÇÃO
MVITo·AVGMENTADA
COM·VM·RETRATO·D
AVCTOR·PALAVRAS
DE·TEIXEIRA·DE·PAS·
COAES·E·NOVAS·RE-
FERENCIAS·POR·JAY-
ME·DE·BALSEMÃO
1922

ANTHOLOGIA DE
POEMAS PORTU·
GUEZES MODER·
NOS POR ANTO·
NIO BOTTO E
FERNANDO
PESSOA

1929

An opponent at all attempts at literary suppression, Pessoa published works by António Botto...and collaborated with him.

Olisipo published in 1922 Botto's *Canções* (attacked as 'literatura de Sodoma') and in the following year Raul Leal's *Sodoma Divinizada* which resulted in organized protests by the League of Students. Both booklets were confiscated by the police. Shortly afterwards António Ferro's *Mar Alto* was also seized. Álvaro de Campos wrote a vigorous pamphlet denouncing police and public intolerance, and Pessoa wrote the introduction to Botto's next work *Motivos de Beleza*.

[1] The adolescent Pessoa was taught by three masters from late Victorian Oxford. By then Jowett and others had displaced 'Oxford Movement', High Church sentiment with a new ethos, its spring ancient Greece, its deity Plato. Sensory delight followed by analytic discrimination, *aesthēsis*, was the way to insight into the Good as well as into the Beautiful. With Pater, aesthetic epicureanism became an ardent pursuit, and included a chaste response to youthful grace, so that 'Platonic' *paederestia* was again perceived as a means of spiritual procreancy, and a refreshing element in education. In the tutorial atmosphere of the Durban High School's small sixth form, Pessoa presumably learnt, from the classicist T.H. Blakemore and his Oxford colleagues, the tenets of Oxford Hellenism, which infuse the Odes of 'Ricardo Reis'. Of neo-pagan Hellenism, Oscar Wilde – supreme in 'Greats' among his Oxford generation – was at first the epitome, later the catastrophe.

A new, remarkably stylish and well-produced journal *Contemporânea*, which had printed Pessoa's contributions to the Botto/Leal/Ferro furore, also published his short fiction 'O Banqueiro Anarquista' [The Anarchist Banker] and, between 1922 and 1926, nineteen of his poems. Pessoa prepared unpublished poems by Sá-Carneiro for the same journal.

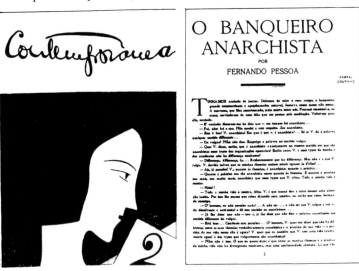

Contemporanea published many poems by Pessoa...and his short story 'The Anarchist Banker'.

'*This letter has no other purpose than writing to you – to write to you to say any old thing, simply to speak to you, even if only by writing... How I regret – more and more – the old times of* Orpheu, *of 'Paulism', of 'Insectionism' and all the rest that belongs to the past. Despite the enormous influence* Orpheu *continues to exert, beyond our imaginings, everything diminishes morally and intellectually [...] Have you seen* Contemporânea? *It has, in some sort, succeeded* Orpheu. *But what a difference! What difference! Certainly it contains things here and there which recall the past; the rest, the overall design... Write to me, write to me as often as you can... [...]*'
[Letter to Armando Côrtes-Rodrigues, 4 August 1923]

By now Pessoa wrote fluently, producing poetry and prose remarkable in quality and diversity. In his youth and young manhood he had read an extraordinary range of literature – in Classical languages, Portuguese, French and English; now writing preoccupied him. An undated fragment may belong to – it seems appropriate to – this period:

'*I have outgrown the habit of reading. I no longer read anything except occasional newspapers, light literature and casual books technical to any matter I may be studying and in which simple reasoning may be insufficient.*

The definite type of literature I have almost dropped. I could read it for learning or for pleasure. But I have nothing to learn, and the pleasure to be drawn from books is of a type that can with profit be substituted by that which the contact with nature and the observation of life can directly give me. I am now in full possession of the fundamental laws of literary art. Shakespeare can no longer teach me to be subtle, nor Milton to be complete. My intellect has attained a pliancy and a reach that enable me to assume any emotion I desire and enter at will into any state of mind. For that which it is ever an effort and an anguish to strive for, completeness, no book at all can be an aid. This does not mean that I have shaken off the tyranny of the literary art. I have but assumed it only under submission to myself. I have one book ever by me – Pickwick Papers. [...] All my books are books of reference. I read Shakespeare only in relation to 'the Shakespeare Problem': the rest I know already. I have found out that reading is a slavish sort of dreaming. If I must dream, why not my own dreams?' [Undated note, in English]

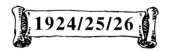

1924/25/26

■ Expulsion of Trotsky; Stalin in power. First labour government in Belgium. French evacuate Ruhr and Rhineland. General Strike in Britain / Baird – first transmission of television, in Britain. Chanel – 'modern woman' / Milliken – cosmic rays / Hitler *Mein Kampf* / Shaw *St Joan*. Mann *The Magic Mountain*. Forster *A Passage to India*. e.e. cummings *xvi poems*. Scott Fitzgerald *The Great Gatsby*. Gide *Les Faux Monnayeurs*. Kafka *The Castle*. Montherlant *Les Bestiaires* / Gershwin *Rhapsody in Blue*. Puccini *Turandot*. Hindemith *Des Marienleben*. Bloch *Concerto Grosso*. Aaron Copland *Symphony no 1*. Berg *Wozzeck*. Honegger *Judith* / Picasso *Three Dancers*. Roualt *The Apprentice*. Moore *Reclining Figure*. Epstein *Rima*. Léger *Les Ballets Méchaniques*. Man Ray's 'Rayograph'. Breton's first Surrealist manifesto / Eisenstein *Battleship Potemkin*. Lang *Metropolis*. Chaplin *The Gold Rush*

Chanel established the 'modern woman'; Negreiros sketched her Portuguese manifestation.

● Teixeira Gomes resigns; Bernardino Machado elected president.
Strikes in Lisbon and elsewhere. (1926) Military coup: General Gomes da
Costa dismisses president, dissolves Assembly etc. Vast national debt /
First radio transmission. Motor cars widespread / First volume of Raul
Proença *Guia de Portugal* / António Patrício *D. João e a Máscaras.*
Teixeira de Pascoaes *Elegia do Amor* and *Sonetos.* Raúl Brandão *O
Avejão.* A Cortez *À la Fé.* Vitorino Nemésio *Paço do Milhafre* and
Varanda de Pilatos. José Régio *Poemas de Deus e do Diabo.* Almada
Negreiros *Nome de Guerra.* António Ferro *Teatro Novo* and *A Amadora
dos Fenómenos.* Eça de Queirós *A Capital, O Conde de Abranhos* and
Alves & Ca. Cabral do Nasciemento *Descaminho*

Pessoa aged 35½ – 38½

◆ IN 1924, PESSOA'S CULTURED AND SUPPORTIVE GREAT-
uncle, General Henrique Rosa died; in 1925 so did his beloved mother.

*'Letters to people I have no particular wish to talk to: such I write willing-
ly. But to my mother, for example, I always wrote grudgingly, precisely
because I loved her too much.'* [Letter to Ophélia, 23 March 1920]

Two journals which Pessoa helped found and edit: for literature...and for commerce.

In 1924 Pessoa and the painter Ruy Vaz founded a review *Athena.*
Among its ambitions was to encourage a 'return to order' after the years of
avant-garde turbulence. Consequently it was a suitable place for the
appearance of the Odes of Ricardo Reis and the poems of Alberto Caeiro;
however, Álvaro de Campos also contributed – an essay 'Apontamentos
para uma estética nao aristotélica' (Notes towards a non-Aristotlean aesthetic). *Athena* expired after its fifth monthly issue.

In 1926 Pessoa and his brother-in-law founded, and jointly edited,
Revista de Contabilidade e Comércio, a revue of commercial and political

events to which Pessoa contributed numerous articles, both about contemporary affairs and, drawing on his professional experience, about business.

'Commerce, however put down in our own times by utopians, is none the less one of the two essential social activities of any civilized society: the other we call culture.' [*Revista de Contabilidade e Comércio* no 3, 1926]

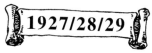

1927/28/29

■ First Five Year Plan in USSR. Workers' revolt in China; Chiang Kai-shek in power. Socialist riots in Austria. Wall St crash / Votes for women in Britain. Graf Zepplin. Lindberg flies the Atlantic solo / Heisenberg – quantum mechanics. Fleming – penicillin / Dunne *An Experiment in Time* / Kafka *The Trial.* Cocteau *Orphée* and *Les Enfants Terribles.* Moravia *Gli Indifferenti.* Faulkner *The Sound and the Fury.* Lawrence *Lady Chatterley's Lover.* Hemingway *A Farewell to Arms.* Woolf *To the Lighthouse* / Ravel *Bolero.* Brecht and Weill *Threepenny Opera* / Miró *Dutch Interior.* Chagall *Marriage of the Cock and the Harlequin.* Dali *Les Désirs.* Magritte *Ceci n'est pas une pipe.* Giacometti *Seated Woman.* Museum of Modern Art opened in New York / Brunel *Un Chien Andalou.* Disney – Mickey Mouse. First sound movie – *The Jazz Singer.* Duke Ellington's Cotton Club Orchestra. Louis Armstrong's Hot Five

● Revolts against the government suppressed by General Carmona. CGT suppressed. Attempted assassinations. (1928) Carmona becomes president. Oliviera Salazar becomes Minister of Finance with wide powers. Budgetary reform and great austerity: external debt much reduced. Religious Orders allowed to return / José Régio and others launch the journal *Presença.* António Botto *Dandismo.* António Pedro *Distância.* Miguel Torga *Ansiedade.* Afonso Casais Monteiro *Confusão.* Ferreira de Castro *Emigrantes.* José Régio *Biografia.* Eça de Queirós *Cartas Inéditas de Fradique Mendes.* Afonso Duarte *Os Sete Poemas Líricos* / Pardal Monteiro founds the journal *Arquitectura* and launches the project for an Instituto Superior Técnico de Lisboa. Leitão de Barros films *Nazaré praia de pescadores*

Pessoa aged 38½ – 41½

◆ IN 1926 STATE BANKRUPTCY HAD LED TO THE OVER-throw of the First Republic, by Marshal Gomes da Costa. In 1927 there were virulent outbreaks: the risings were suppressed, the Confederation of Trades Unions dissolved and militant syndicalists arrested.

Pessoa wrote a pamphlet in 1927 on the Interregnum – 'a defence and justification of the military dictatorship in Portugal'; however, by the time the pamphlet was published, in 1928, the situation had changed. Salazar (once Professor of Economics at Coimbra University) had briefly been a member of the military junta in 1926, being appointed to put the country's dire finances in order; he resigned when the powers he demanded were not given him. He was re-appointed in 1928, and immediately began to put in place the legislative and institutional framework of what was to become the 'Estado Novo', the corporate state of which he later became the ruler. Pessoa reflected on the pamphlet *O Interregno* he had written:

'... *When I wrote that other pamphlet, towards the end of 1927, we were far from the 'Estado Novo' and the New Constitution, although we were already, without realizing it, in the first phase of Salazar. At the time there was indeed an Interregnum, that is to say the Dictatorship was a transitory period. With the vote on the New Constitution, however, it was transformed into a régime, the Interregnum was over. It matters little, if at all, whether we consider the 'Estado Novo' bad. It exists. The Interregnum is finished [...] I don't want to get drawn into discussions of the New Constitution and the Corporate State; I accept them both as disciplines; I keep myself clear of them because I don't agree with them...*' [Fragment for a projected booklet, 'The Interregnum and its Consequences', 1932]

Pessoa's pamphlet arguing the need for the 1928 military interregnum.
Presença supported Pessoa's work enthusiastically.

In 1927 the poet and novelist José Régio started a new journal, the Coimbra-based *Presença*, which was to prove long-lasting and influential. In the second issue José Régio wrote of Pessoa as the master among the new generation of Portuguese poets. Over the years, numerous poems by Pessoa and his heteronyms were first published in this journal.

In 1927, in collaboration with António Botto, Pessoa published an anthology of modern Portuguese poets; and with Botto and others started a short-lived journal *Solução Editora*.

In 1928 he drafted parts of what became *Mensagem* (Message) – not published until 1934; and wrote *Tabacaria* – not published until 1933.

In 1929, Ophélia saw a photograph Pessoa had given her nephew, the poet Carlos Queiroz, which showed Pessoa in an occupation becoming increasingly frequent – drinking at a bar in a café. She asked for a copy, which Pessoa sent, via her nephew, with the inscription: *In flagrante delitro*. Their sentimental relationship was rekindled.

João Gaspar Simões, later Pessoa's biographer, wrote in *Presença* the first critical study of Pessoa's poetry.

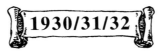

1930/31/32

■ Gandhi begins civil disobedience campaign in India. Britain abandons the gold standard. Nazis become largest party in Reichstag. Franklin Roosevelt becomes president of USA. Japan invades Manchuria and occupies Shanghai. President Doumer of France assassinated. Mosley founds British League of Fascists / Nylon. Perspex. Photoflash bulbs / Urey – heavy water. Chadwick – neutrons. Domgk – sulphamides / Freud *Civilization and its Discontents*. Read *The Significance of Art* / Auden *Poems*. Faulkner *As I Lay Dying*. Caldwell *Tobacco Road*. Artaud's Theatre of Cruelty / Messiaen *Offrandes Oubliées*. Shostakovich *Lady Macbeth of Minsk*. Janáček *The House of the Dead*. Rachmaninoff banned as a decadent in USSR. Martha Graham – School of Modern Dance / Mondrian *Composition with Red, Yellow and Blue*. Dali *Persistence of Memory*. Bonnard *The Breakfast Room*. Epstein *Genesis*. Calder's first mobiles / Clair *À nous la liberté*. Sternberg *The Blue Angel*

● Revolts in Lisbon and Madeira against the dictatorship. (1932) Salazar becomes 'Prime Minister' and further enlarges his powers. Creation of Propaganda Ministry – Marinetti, the 'Futurist', officially welcomed to Lisbon. National Union Party (neo-fascist) founded / Edmundo de Bettencourt *O Momento e a Legenda*. Ferreira de Castro *A Selva*. Aquilino Ribeiro *O Homem que matou o Diabo*, *Batalha Sem Fim* and *As Três Mulheres de Sansão*. Florbela Espanca *Charneca em Flor*. António Pedro *Máquina de Vidro*. Teixeira de Pascoaes *O Pobre Tolo*. João Gaspar Simões *O Mistério da Poesia* and *Elói ou Romance Numa Cabeça*. Saúl Dias *...mais e mais...* Assis Esperança *Dilúvio*. Miguel Torga *Abismo*. José Rodrigues Miguéis *Páscoa Feliz* / First Salão dos Independentes in Lisbon / Manuel de Oliveira films *Douro faina fluvial*. Leitão de Barros *A Severa* (first Portuguese sound film)

Pessoa aged 41½ – 44½

◆ JORGE DE SENA HAS LEFT A DESCRIPTION OF THE mature Pessoa:

'In private life, as I saw him and as all of his family, friends, acquaintances can or did testify, he could be a delightful man, full of charm and good humour, a humour that was very British […] But this role was also that of a heteronym, which saved him from intimacy with anyone while allowing him to take a modest part in the normal feast of daily life. Certainly

there was a kind of frightening cold – something of the terrifying cold that you feel sometimes when reading him – emanating from Pessoa for those not admitted to the inner sanctum.'

Pessoa searched constantly for evidence of the transcendental reality beyond mere appearances, and this led him to an interest in the occult. A similar interest animated many other contemporary artists such as – to cite exemplars from one other culture – Yeats, Epstein, Delius and Augustus John. Traditional religious faith had been severely diminished by scientific reductionism, by rationalism, by the ardent and widespread pursuit of material wealth. Some intellectuals and artists searched for reassurance in still traditional cultures – in the arts and religions of India, in the newly-appreciated 'primitive' art of Africa; others tried to escape the isolation of self-consciousness by using hallucinogenic drugs, like mescalin; yet others turned to magic, ritual and the hopeful darkness of the occult.

Spiritualism flourished: in domestic setting (such as that of Pessoa's aunt Anica) Tarot cards and Ouija boards appeared, and mediums found a ready welcome. Astrology aroused interest (in 1916 Pessoa contemplated setting up as an astrologer, and he frequently cast horoscopes); 'secret' societies prospered (Pessoa was interested in Freemasonry, in the Cabbala and the Rosicrucians); new, arcane theologies attracted many adherents – such as Theosophy (Pessoa translated both Amy Besant and C.W. Leadbeater); a contemporary shaman or magus like Ouspensky, Gurdjieff or Aleister Crowley could attract a considerable following. (In 1930 Aleister Crowley came to Portugal, visited Pessoa, gave lectures, and dramatically 'disappeared' into the 'Boca do Inferno' on the Cascais coast near Lisbon. In 1931 Pessoa translated Crowley's 'Hymn to Pan' for *Presença*). A similar interest in the mysterious and obscure – and his usual concern for artists who suffered philistine opposition – led Pessoa to publish the poems of a displaced Ukrainian Jew in Lisbon, Eliezer Kanenezky, a guru of 'Naturalism'. (Pessoa wrote a preface to the book.)

Throughout this period, Pessoa's three poetic heteronyms, Caeiro, Reis and Campos, were particularly productive.

The renewal of Pessoa's liaison with Ophélia in 1929 continued until 1931 – her last letter to him was dated 29 March. She has left a description of Pessoa at this time:

'Fernando was different. Not just physically – he'd put on weight – but above all in his manner. Always on edge, he was obsessed by his work. He said often that he could never make me happy because of the time absorbed by it. One day he said to me, "I sleep very little, with pen and paper on my beside table. I wake up at night and write – I have to write and that would be tiresome, for 'Baby' wouldn't get her proper sleep." At the same time he feared he could not provide me with my accustomed standard of living. He

was determined not to work every day: he needed to keep time for his own work, which was his life. He was content to have just the necessities to live on: to the rest, he was indifferent. He was neither ambitious nor vain. He was straightforward and faithful. He said to me: "Don't describe me to anyone as a poet. At most say that I write verses".'

In 1932 Pessoa applied for a permanent position – the only time he did so. The job – a sinecure unlikely to intrude upon his writing – was that of Librarian at the Archive-Museum in Cascais. He was unsuccessful.

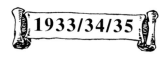

1933/34/35

■ Hitler becomes Chancellor – Musil, Freud, Brecht etc in exile; Bauhaus closed; anti-Semitic laws – concentration camps. Reichstag fire. 'Night of the Long Knives' in Munich. Hitler and Mussolini meet. Saar restored to Germany. Mussolini invades Ethiopia. Stalin eliminates opponents. The Slump – New Deal in USA. Mao Tse-Tung's Long March. First detergent. DDT / Marconi – microwaves. Watt – radar. Juliot and Curie – radioactivity. Fermi measures speed of electrons / Jung *Modern Man in Search of a Soul*. Eddington *The Expanding Universe*. Benedict *Patterns of Culture*. Toynbee *A Study of History*. Webb *Soviet Communism – a new civilization* / Huxley *Brave New World*. Remarque *All Quiet on the Western Front*. Malraux *La Condition Humaine*. Neruda *Residencia en la Terra*. Miller *Tropic of Cancer*. Lorca *Yerma*. Eliot *Murder in the Cathedral*. Canetti *Lie Blendung* / Gershwin *Porgy and Bess*. Berg *Lulu*. Rachmaninov *Rhapsody on a Theme of Paganini*. Balanchine – School of American ballet / Epstein *Ecee Homo*. Miró *Circo*. Marini *Horse and Rider* / Aalto – TB Sanatorium at Paimio. Vigo *Zero de Conduite*. Schoedsack and Cooper *King Kong*.

● (1933) A new constitution establishes the corporate state, 'Estado Novo', which remains in force for 41 years. 140 political prisoners exiled to Azores; 35 university professors dismissed; Freemasons suppressed. Strikes in various factories / António Ferro *Salazar* / Ferreira de Castro *Eternidade* and *Terra Fria*. Joaquim Paço d'Arcos *Herói Derradeiro*. Aquilino Ribeiro *Maria Benigna* and *Quando ao Gavião Cai a Pena*. João Gaspar Simões *Amores Infelizes*. António Botto *Ciúme*. Alfredo Cortez *Gladiadores* and *Horto Fechado e Outros Poemas*. Vitorino Nemésio (in French) *La Voyelle Promise*. Teixeira Gomes *Novelas Eróticas*. Carlos Queirós *Desaparecido*

Pessoa aged 44½ – 47½

◆ IN 1933, PESSOA WENT THROUGH A SERIOUS PERIOD of depression but produced numerous poems, mostly in his own name, many of which appeared in *Presença*, including 'Autopsiographia', the briefest and most penetrating of reflections on the poet's craft.

AUTOPSICOGRAFIA

O poeta é um fingidor.
Finge tão completamente
Que chega a fingir que é dor
A dor que deveras sente.

E os que lêem o que escreve,
Na dor lida sentem bem,
Não as duas que êle teve,
Mas só a que êles não têm.

E assim nas calhas de roda
Gira, a entreter a razão,
Esse comboio de corda
Que se chama o coração.

FERNANDO PESSOA

9

In *Presença* appeared such celebrated poems as 'Autopsiographia'.

In 1933, *Presença* published the remarkable 'Tabacaria' [Tobacco shop] by Álvaro de Campos (chastened since the Whitmanesque days of the 'Triumphal Ode', the 'Maritime Ode', and the 'Ultimatum'). Unlike Caeiro and Reis who had died – the one in 1915, the other in 1919 (though each published 'posthumously') – Campos lived as long as Pessoa. Whereas 'Fernando Pessoa' continued with intellectual experiments and adventures, Campos increasingly became oppressed by the absurdity and anguish of it all; in 'Tabacaria' he sounded positively existentialist.

presença
fôlha de arte e crítica
coimbra, julho, 1933

TaBaCaRia

Não sou nada.
Nunca serei nada.
Não posso querer ser nada.
Aparte isso, tenho em mim todos os sonhos do mundo.

Janelas do meu quarto,
Do meu quarto de um dos milhões do mundo que ninguém
                                                      sabe quem é
(E se soubessem quem é, o que saberiam ?),
Dais para o mistério de uma rua cruzada constantemente
                                                      por gente,
Para uma rua inacessível a todos os pensamentos,
Real, impossivelmente real, certa, desconhecidamente certa,
Com o mistério das coisas por baixo das pedras e dos sêres,
Com a morte a pôr humidade nas paredes e cabelos brancos
                                                      nos homens,
Com o Destino a conduzir a carroça de tudo pela estrada de
                                                      nada.

Estou hoje vencido, como se soubesse a verdade.
Estou hoje lúcido, como se estivesse para morrer,

Saio da janela, sento-me numa cadeira. Em que hei-de
                                                      pensar ?

Que sei eu do que serei, eu que não sei o que sou ?
Ser o que penso ? Mas penso ser tanta coisa !
E há tantos que pensam ser a mesma coisa que não pode
                                                      haver tantos !

Génio ? Neste momento
Cem mil cérebros se concebem em sonho génios como eu,
E a história não marcará, quem sabe ?, nem um,
Nem haverá senão estrume de tantas conquistas futuras.
Não, não creio em mim.
Em todos os manicómios há doidos malucos com tantas cer-
                                                      tezas !
Eu, que não tenho nenhuma certeza, sou mais certo ou
                                                      menos certo ?

Não, nem em mim...
Em quantas mansardas e não-mansardas do mundo
Não estão nesta hora génios-para-si-mesmos sonhando ?
Quantas aspirações altas e nobres e lúcidas —
Sim, verdadeiramente altas e nobres e lúcidas —,

In 1933 also Pessoa wrote an Introduction to Augusto Ferreira Gomes' *O Quinto Império*. Pessoa shared with its author a strange form of Portuguese patriotism – *Sebastianism* – which has persisted through Portuguese history. Sebastianism is a form of the Second Coming – but secular, local, particular. When total disaster overtakes a leader of whom much is hoped, disbelief generates legends of survival, of resurrection; finally, with the passage of time, prophecies arise that he will come again and judgement will follow: those now proud will be abased, those now suppressed exalted, and a better order of things restored. Such was the essence of Sebastianism. The British at least should understand it: King Arthur was their Sebastian, their 'once and future king'. Arthur disappeared in battle, leading the romanized Britons against barbarous Germanic invaders; so Sebastian disappeared in the carnage of Alcacer-Quibir, leading the last crusade against the Moors. Hopes, then myths, of the lost leaders consoled suppressed peoples: in mediaeval times, Arthur – now surrounded with knights – became the resort of the Celtic imagination during English occupation; Sebastianism took root during the 'Babylonian Captivity' of Portugal by Spain and grew during the succeeding centuries of Portugal's relative decline in Europe. Then Arthurian images and rhetoric suddenly revived in Victorian times, animating public – and public school – life: to the British had been assigned a special Imperial mission under God, a chivalrous, civilizing 'dominion over palm and pine'. Sebastianism remained fixed on a remoter future. It assigned to the Portuguese a special mission – an echo of the great days of the Discoveries – as the natural connection between the races of the world; these would join at last in international brotherhood. The idealists of Sebastianism, like Pessoa, looked toward a Fifth Empire that was not a worldly empire by conquest or economic dominance, but a Portuguese-inspired Camelot of willing minds and spirits. As Pessoa put it in 1923, 'We have already conquered the Sea: it remains for us to conquer the Sky, leaving the Earth to others.'

A similar afflatus inspired *Mensagem* (Message), published in 1934, the only *book* of poetry in Portuguese by Pessoa published in his lifetime. The powerful and moving poems it contains deal with themes from Portugal's great past and with hopes for its future. Pessoa entered *Mensagem* for the Antero de Quental prizes. These were awarded in two categories, a larger prize for longer poems, a smaller prize for shorter poems. *Mensagem* qualified by length only for the latter category, but its unusual quality resulted in a substantial increase in the amount of the prize.

In the spring of 1935, Pessoa's step-brother, Luis Miguel, whom he hadn't seen for fifteen years, visited him in Lisbon. Pessoa planned a return visit to London the following year. He remained always in close

Do livro *"MENSAGEM"*
de *FERNANDO PESSOA*

transcrevem-se **3** poemas com
3 ilustrações Inedilas de **ALMADA**

1.

O INFANTE

Deus quer, o homem sonha, a obra nasce.
Deus quiz que a terra fosse toda uma,
Que o mar unisse, já não separasse.
Sagrou te, e foste desvendando a espuma,

E a orla branca foi de ilha em continente.
Clareou, correndo, até ao fim do mundo,
E viu-se a terra inteira, de repente,
Surgir, redonda, do azul profundo.

Quem te sagrou creou-te portuguez.
Do mar e nós em ti nos deu signal.
Cumpriu se o Mar, e o Imperio se desfez.
Senhor, falta cumprir-se Portugal!

2.

O MOSTRENGO

O mostrengo que está no fim do mar
Na noite de breu ergueu-se a voar;
A' roda da nau voou trez vezes,
Voou trez vezes a chiar,
E disse: «Quem é que ousou entrar
Nas minhas cavernas que não desvendo,
Meus tectos negros do fim do mundo?»
E o homem do leme disse, tremendo.
«El-Rei D. João Segundo!»

«De quem são as velas onde me roço?
De quem as quilhas que vejo e ouço?»
Disse o mostrengo, e rodou trez vezes.
Trez vezes rodou immundo e grosso,
«Quem vem poder o que só eu posso,
Que moro onde nunca ninguem me visse
E escorro os medos do mar sem fundo?»
E o homem do leme tremeu, e disse,
«El-Rei D. João Segundo!»

Trez vezes do leme as mãos ergueu,
Trez vezes ao leme as reprendeu,
E disse no fim de temer trez vezes,
«Aqui ao leme sou mais do que eu:
Sou um Povo que quer o mar que é teu;
E mais que o mostrengo, que me a alma teme
E roda nas trevas do fim do mundo,
Manda a vontade, que me ata ao leme,
De El-Rei D. João Segundo!»

3.

PRECE

Senhor, a noite veio e a alma é vil.
Tanta foi a tormenta e a vontade!
Restam-... ... no silencio hostil,
O mar universal e a saudade.

Mas a chamma, que a vida em nós creou,
Se ainda ha vida ainda não é finda.
O frio morto em cinzas a occultou:
A mão do vento pode erguel-a ainda.

Dá o sopro, a aragem — ou desgraça ou ancia—,
Com que a chamma do exforço se remoça,
E outra vez conquistemos a Distancia —
Do mar ou outra, mas que seja nossa!

Excerpts from Pessoa's only book of Portuguese poems, *Mensagem*, appeared in
Diário de Lisboa, with illustrations by Negreiros.

contact with his step-sister and her family in Lisbon. A customary greeting arrived for him on his birthday, on 13 June 1935 – a telegram from Ophélia.

Pessoa wrote a newspaper article protesting at the proposal of the National Assembly to prohibit all secret societies – a ban aimed especially at the Freemasons. In a new journal *Sudoeste* ('South-west'), edited by Almada Negreiros, he wrote a piece '*We, the men of* Orpheu' concluding '*Orpheu is finished*. Orpheu *lives on*'. *Orpheu* had already become, it has remained, the icon of Portuguese modernism.

In 1935 Pessoa wrote a long letter in answer to some enquiries from Adolfo Casais Monteiro about the genesis of his heteronyms and about his occult interests. To questions from other literary colleagues, he wrote about his plans for putting his papers in publishable order.

Those voluminous papers... a wooden trunk overflowing with more than 25,000 items, long and short, complete and fragmentary... have allowed myth-makers to attach to Pessoa the Romantic image of the neglected artist, *à la Bohème*. Here was a great poet, solitary, poor, unrecognized, careless of fame, able to publish only one slim volume of verse (the English poems, published, were 'prentice stuff) whose literary remains established – after his death, of course – that he was a genius.

The truth, as always with Pessoa, is more original and more complex. Solitary he was not, in any ordinary sense: his café companions were many; he had a few friends he could write to with warmth and candour; his parents had been supportive and his relatives maintained affectionate contact. He remained unmarried, but then he was solitary by nature – a gregarious 'loner', driven to live alone by the demands of his avocation as a poet and from the realization – especially acute in his case – that (as we might now conceive) all men inhabit a sort of space-suit, and live, as they must die, alone. Poor? Once established as a 'foreign correspondent', a job with considerable *cachet*, he had enough for his modest needs (and latterly, for a rather immodest amount of smoking and drinking); it was, after all, his deliberate choice not to work at the behest of others more than two days a week. Nor was he unrecognized: some three hundred of his poems – including all the greatest – and a hundred and thirty-two prose pieces were published in journals and newspapers during his life-time, and some critics, few but eminent, had saluted him as the master of 'first modernism' in Portugal. He was not careless of fame – but believed that due acknowledgement could come only from posterity. His 'Erostratus' expounds, in cool analysis, that, during his lifetime, a genius can be recognized only for whatever lesser qualities he has in common with other writers – such subsidiary talents as, say, wit or skill in narration and versification or an ability to comment amusingly on the passing scene. At such a level, a Jonson will

out-glitter a Shakespeare, Walter Scott a Keats, Robert Bridges a Gerard
Manley Hopkins. Those qualities that come to distinguish a genius: a wide-
ranging empathy, say, or 'negative capacity'; or an acute sense of what lies
beneath the transitory and particular; an ability to conceive and execute
work of a coherent kind on a substantial scale; intellectual stamina; something in his writing that is strange, uncanny, inscrutable; a peculiar, distinctive 'voice' – these and similar characteristics found in men of genius make
them *less* comfortably à la mode with the reading public of their day, *less*
likely to appeal to fashionable critics, *less* appealing to their own than to
the next and future generations. Pessoa had no illusions about receiving
prompt acclaim. Due recognition, *in time*, mattered greatly to him; contemporary celebrity certainly did not:

'*Sometimes I think about celebrated men and then I feel all the bane of
celebrity. Celebrity is a plebianism. It wounds any person of sensitivity. It is a
plebianism in that, by exposing a person to public gaze, to the common view,
it forces a sensitive person to share the same position as those who behave
scandalously in the street, or gesticulate and talk loudly in a public place. The
man who becomes a celebrity no longer has any privacy... the walls surrounding his private life are turned to glass; his clothes acquire a certain
excess; his slightest actions – even the most ludicrously human – which he
should want to keep invisible, become, beneath the magnifying glass of
celebrity, little exhibitions which soil the soul or weary it. You have to be really coarse to live at ease with celebrity. And, beside its plebian character,
celebrity is a contradiction: whereas it gives the impression of valuing and
supporting a person, it actually devalues and enfeebles him. The unknown
man of genius can relish the voluptuous contrast between his obscurity and
his genius; when he reckons he could be celebrated if he so wished, he is mea-
suring his value against the one true yardstick – himself. Once recognized
publicly, however, he no longer possesses the power to return to obscurity.
Celebrity is irreparable. Like time, the machine can't be put into reverse.*'

Raul Leal, a literary friend of Pessoa and *Orpheu* collaborator, who
shared Pessoa's occult interests, tells us that in 1935 Pessoa believed he
had two more years to live. The horoscope cast by Pessoa for himself made
that certain. [1] Pessoa expected to use the time to arrange his work for publication – a task that would have taxed the most determined and ruthless of
men, and must have daunted someone so hesitant, so aware of every alternative, so costive of every line he wrote. In the event, death overtook him.

---

[1] Raul Leal wrote that Pessoa had shown him the horoscope. Leal studied
it and realized, he says, that Pessoa had cast it wrong. Leal hadn't the heart
to tell Pessoa so. *Se non è vero, è ben trovato.*

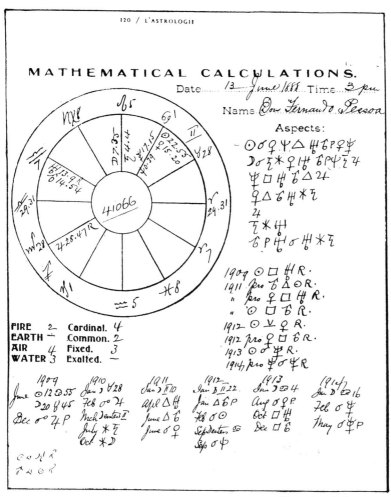

Pessoa's auto-horoscope.

On 28 November Pessoa was taken to hospital. Cirrhosis of the liver was diagnosed. He died two days later, attended by his personal doctor (a cousin) and two friends. His last words, written in English, were *I know not what tomorrow will bring.*

He was buried on 2 December in the vault of his grandmother Dionísia.

Miguel Torga – the doyen of contemporary Portuguese letters, (a doctor by profession) then a young man, wrote in his journal:

'Fernando Pessoa is dead. As soon as I heard the news in the paper, I closed my surgery and plunged into the mountains. There, with the pines and the rocks, I wept for the death of the greatest poet of our times, whom Portugal watched pass by in his coffin, on his way to immortality, without even asking who he was.'

THE BOOK OF DISQUIETUDE

A Sampler

selected by **P.J. KAVANAGH**

translated by **RICHARD ZENITH**

A sampler from THE BOOK OF DISQUIETUDE[1]

From the Introduction by Richard Zenith

FERNANDO ANTÓNIO NOGUEIRA PESSOA WAS BORN IN 1888, spent much of his childhood in Durban, South Africa, and returned to his native Lisbon when he was seventeen. He hardly ever left the city again. He led a quiet existence as a writer of foreign correspondence for business firms, had a limited social life and virtually no love life. He published four volumes of poetry, three of which were in English, and regularly contributed to magazines, but his literary genius went largely unrecognized until after his death in 1935. Pessoa was convinced of his own genius, however, and he lived for the sake of his writing. Although he was in no hurry to publish, he had grandiose plans for Portuguese and English editions of his complete works, and he seems to have held on to just about everything he wrote. His legacy consisted of a large trunk full of poetry, prose, philosophy, criticism, translations, linguistic theory, horoscopes and assorted other texts, variously typed, handwritten or illegibly scrawled in Portuguese, English and French. He wrote in notebooks, on loose sheets, on the backs of letters, advertisements and handbills, on stationery from the firms he worked for and from the cafés he frequented, on envelopes, on paper scraps, and in between the lines of his own earlier texts.

Pessoa was meticulous and left his universe of papers in a definite if

---

[1] For most of his adult life, Pessoa wrote pieces, some complete, some fragmentary, intended for *The Book of Disquietude* – 'in preparation', as he described it in a literary journal which published some early pieces – a preparation overtaken by death. No one knows exactly which pieces in what order Pessoa would have used to comprise his enigmatic masterpiece.

Richard Zenith, an American scholar living in Lisbon, worked through the Pessoa archives to compile, and then to translate, the most abundant version of 'The Book' in any language (Carcanet, 1991). Printed here is part of the Introduction by Zenith to his version, which gives a vivid picture of the travails of piecing together so strange a work from so unique a writer.

The Introduction refers by folio numbers to particular passages among the 520 numbered folios in the full text. Of the whole work, only a small sample – selected by P.J. Kavanagh – can be included here; consequently many of the folios numbered in the Introduction will not be found in this sampler. We have left in all the folio numbers, however, for some readers may be stimulated to pursue the passages referred to, in the complete edition.

The numbered sections of *The Book of Disquietude* are generally represented in this secion by brief, self-contained extracts – samples for this sampler.

enigmatic order, but over the years, as people sifted through the contents of the legendary trunk, pulling out and publishing things here and there, what had been a labyrinth became a jungle, and a not insignificant number of manuscripts were lost or stolen. The trunk's contents began to be catalogued in 1968, but in a general and unreliable way, so that the researcher of 'E3', the Pessoa archives, had better approach them in the spirit of an archaeologist.

Many have lamented the dishevelled state of Pessoa's *oeuvre*, much of which is still unpublished, but it is hard to imagine a logical order for the 27,543 documents that constitute his archives. The poet of many faces presumably knew his way around the labyrinth he inhabited, but would it make sense to anyone else? 'Whatever I feel, in the true substance with which I feel it,' Pessoa wrote in a fragment destined for *The Book of Disquietude*, 'is absolutely incommunicable; and the more profoundly I feel it, the more incommunicable it is. So in order to transmit to someone else what I feel, I must translate my feelings into his language... [W]hat I must finally do is convert my feelings into a typical human feeling, even if it means perverting the true nature of what I felt' (f.265). This is the essential activity of art, according to the same fragment. Throughout most of his life, beginning even with the childhood personae called by names such as Dr Pancrácio and David Merrick, Pessoa scrupulously denatured and reformulated what he felt in order to make it into communicable art, and so he probably would not mind too much that the pieces he left have been (dis)arranged into a new order. A new order represents a new opportunity to make what he felt communicable, to get to the bottom of... of what? This is where the author's disquietude begins, and perhaps also where it ends. 'We are two abysses – a well staring at the sky' (f.11). And the two reflected and became four, then eight, sixteen, and so on. Pessoa is famous for three poetic heteronyms – Alberto Caeiro, Álvaro de Campos and Ricardo Reis – but there were at least seventy-two 'dramatis personae' in Pessoa's theatre of himself, which lives on (the way it always lived) in the mass of hopelessly disconnected, interconnecting texts now housed in the National Library of Lisbon.

Pessoa would no doubt smile, in the afterworld he did not have faith enough to believe in or even to disbelieve in, if he knew that the very first item in the very first envelope of his thoroughly reshuffled and catalogued papers bears the heading *A[lavaro] de C[ampos] (?) or B[ook] of D[isquietude] (or something else altogether)* – like a warning at the gates that everything beyond them will be subject to doubt, the mere stroke of a pen making all the difference. 'Be plural like the universe!' wrote Pessoa with a flourish on a scrap of paper in Envelope 20, and he set the example, multiplying himself into Campos, Caeiro, Reis, the Search brothers, António

Mora, Bernardo Soares and many others, but none of the stars in his universe were fixed. They had their individuated personalities and their own biographies, but they could not help but be fluid and overlapping entities, for they were all Fernando Pessoa, or they were what he was not, which in the cosmos of Pessoa comes down to the same thing. 'Art is a substitute for acting or living,' we are told in the text that belongs either to 'A. de C.' to 'B. of D.' or to 'something else altogether'. And the same voice continues: 'What we don't have, or don't attempt, or don't obtain, can be possessed through dreams, and these are what we use to make art.' Not only the words of this text (f.234), but the very fact that Pessoa hesitated over where it should go, are good grounds for including it in *The Book of Disquietude*, whose essential heart is hesitation. The vacillating protagonist, Bernardo Soares, shies away from doing or trying to do, and it causes him anxiety just to think of performing a simple act like buying bananas from a street vendor (f.62). He dreams instead, but he is a special kind of dreamer. Bernardo Soares does not merely dream so as to pass the time or to escape life temporarily; he uses his dreams to *possess* what he lacks in life, and with these dreamed realities he fabricates his art, a *permanent* refuge, from which he escapes back to reality only when circumstances oblige him. And the concrete manifestation of his art is nothing more or less than this 'factless autobiography' (f.12) entitled *The Book of Disquietude*. Soares' project is essentially a scaled-down version of Pessoa's, and within the trunk of multifarious writings we now know as the Pessoa archives, *The Book of Disquietude* is like a smaller trunk, full of long and short, divergent and frequently contradictory fragments written throughout Pessoa's adult life. *The Book* is a depository not only for Bernardo Soares' 'lucid diary' (f.211) and 'haphazard musings' (f.14) but for Fernando Pessoa's prose poems, literary fragments and occasional writings that had no other home.

2

The Book of Disquietude is Pessoa's magnum opus which he never succeeded in finishing and which, had he forced it into a finished state, would be vastly less grand than the scattered, impossibly ambitious work he left us. I have called it a depository, but it was a depository for gems, both polished and rough-hewn, the first of which was called *In the Forest of Estrangement* (f.295), published in 1913 under the name of Fernando Pessoa and identified as 'from *The Book of Disquietude*, in preparation'. It was the first creative prose text published by Pessoa, just one year before the 'birth' of Caeiro, Campos and Reis (who were given retroactive birth dates: 1889, 1890 and 1887, respectively). The nature of *The Book* changed gradually and drastically during the next two decades, being the quintessential testimony of Pessoa's journey in self-fragmentation. Conceived before the three major heteronyms, it also outlived two of them. The last dated poem of Alberto Caeiro is from 1930; the last of Ricardo Reis, from 1933; Álvaro de Campos, the heteronym closest to Pessoa and closest in sprit to the narrator of *The Book of Disquietude*, accompanied his creator until the end, as *The Book* surely did, although its last dated fragment is from 1934. Bernardo Soares, the main but not exclusive narrator of the book was so close to Pessoa – closer even than Campos – that he couldn't be considered an autonomous heteronym. 'He's a semiheteronym,' Pessoa wrote in the last year of his life, 'because his personality, although not my own, doesn't differ from my own but is a mere mutilation of it.'

Originally a short story writer, Bernardo Soares probably came into existence before 1920. We do not know exactly when he assumed fictional authorship of *The Book of Disquietude*, but he was definitely responsible for its final and most prolific phase, from 1929 on. The fragments of this period are often dated, rarely have titles, and are written in refined but direct prose. The 'author' calls these predominantly existential and aesthetic reflections his 'Confessions' (f.12), and there is much here that would no doubt be in Pessoa's autobiography, had he written one. Soares, like Pessoa, lives a non-life, shunning the outer world, which he finds sordid and petty beside his dreams. Like Pessoa, Soares never goes anywhere, for he can journey to the infinite in a ride across town on the tram (f.177). 'If I were to travel,' he says, 'I'd find a poor copy of what I've already seen without taking one step' (f.141). Life, Soares insists, is whatever we conceive it to be, and in one of his truly euphoric moments (f.42) he repeats over and over a line from Caeiro, like a jubilant refrain: 'I'm the size of what I see!' And in another passage (f.105) he headily affirms that in dreams he has been any number of Caesars, all of them more glorious than the real one.

And yet he admits that, while often happy and often cheerful, he is always sad (f.37). Life catches up with him. Forced to deal at least minimally with the real world, he is no longer able to maintain the illusion: he remembers that his dreams are only dreams, 'an attic made out to be an empire' (f.486). In the real world Soares acutely feels his useless and even abject condition as a nondescript assistant bookkeeper for a fabric warehouse. He realizes that he is a victim of personal circumstances, his mother having died when he was only a child (in Pessoa's case it was his father); he is a victim of the times, for he was born into a generation that had lost faith in God (f.1) as well as in science and social progress (f.312); he is a victim of the forces of heredity (f.291); and he is even a victim of the day's weather (f.443). But the main cause of his disquietude is consciousness. He could be happy as a human animal (f.451) if it were not for his consciousness, which oppresses him like an infinite cell (f.39). Because it is infinite, there's no escaping it! Consciousness has replaced whatever real substance the bookkeeper might have had. He no longer has feelings, just the consciousness of feelings. He is his own shadow, having sold his body to the devil (f.512). That is why he longs to be a figure in a painting (f.89) or to be the lover of a woman on a Chinese teacup (f.402). Then he would at least have substance, even if only in two dimensions. Since he has only his own hazy self and empty dreams, he tries to convert them into art. 'I am the selfsame prose I write,' says Soares (f.196), and he repeatedly makes the point that what he writes, however bad, is at any rate something tangible.

In all of this Bernardo Soares sounds a lot like Pessoa himself, but we should not equate the two. Soares was something less than his creator. He was a mutilated Pessoa, a Pessoa with missing parts. Soares had little personality and no sense of humour; Pessoa was endowed with large measures of both. Pessoa was shy but never self-deprecating, and indeed he had no reason to be. Like his semiheteronym, Pessoa was an office worker in Lisbon's old commercial district, and for a time he regularly took his meals at a certain corner of Douradores Street, the site of Soares' rented room and of Vasques & Co., the place where he worked. But whereas Soares was condemned to the drudgery of filling in ledgers with the prices and quantities of fabric sold, Pessoa had a relatively prestigious job writing business letters, usually in English or French, for various international firms. He came and went pretty much as he wanted, never being obliged to work set hours. As for their respective inner lives, Soares takes his progenitor's for a model: 'I've created various personalities within. [...] I've so externalized myself on the inside that I don't exist there except externally. I'm the living stage where various actors act out various plays' (f.308). But we have no evidence that these various actors really (or *un*really, I should say) existed in Bernardo Soares. We have only his word to go on. Pessoa, as we know, gave literary substance to dozens of derivative personalities, not least among them being the disquieted assistant bookkeeper.

3

If Bernardo Soares does not measure up to the full Pessoa, neither are his diary writings the sum total of *Disquietude*, to which he was after all a johnny-come-lately. *The Book of Disquietude* was various books (yet ultimately one book), with various authors (yet ultimately one author), and even the word *disquietude* changes meaning as time passes. In its initial stage, the book consisted largely of symbolist texts that bore titles and were attributed to Pessoa himself or to Vicente Guedes, a literary persona discussed below[1]. Pessoa left about half a dozen lists of titles that were to

---

[1] 'Discussed below' – in a part of the Introduction not included here.

be included in this embryonic *Disquietude*. Here is a typical one:

B. of D.
1. Introduction
2. In the Forest of Estrangement
3. Rainy Landscape
4. Oblique Rain
5. Funeral March for King Ludwig II of Bavaria
6. Diary
7. Symphony of a Restless Night
8. Morning
9. Triangular Dream
10. Our Lady of S[orrows?] (?)
11.
12.

Texts have been found for most but not all of these titles, which may be because the texts were never written. Pessoa had that habit. His archives are full of titles for non-existent poems, stories, treatises and entire books. Had he even halfway realized all his literary projects, the tomes would fill a good-sized library. *The Book of Disquietude* is emblematic of the capricious author's difficulty. He begins his project by writing texts that attempt to elucidate a psychic state or mood through florid descriptions of weather and landscape, through idealized visions of sexless women (see 'In Praise of Sterile Women', f.369, or 'Our Lady of Silence', f.422), through childhood evocations, and through medieval imagery – kings, queens, cortèges, castles. The underlying psyche belongs to Pessoa, but it is abstracted. The writing is impersonal, the narrative voice ethereal, and the word *disquietude* refers not so much to an existential trouble in man as to the restlessness and uncertainty everywhere present and now distilled in the rhetorical narrator. But the force of another disquietude – more intimate and profound – gradually prevails, and the book takes unexpected turns. Already towards the end of 1914, Pessoa writes to Armando Côrtes-Rodrigues, an Azorean poet: 'My state of mind compels me to work hard, against my will, on *The Book of Disquietude*. But it's all fragments, fragments, fragments.' The manuscript copies of these fragments are full of blank spaces where words or phrases or whole paragraphs were to be inserted later, and some of the fragments were no more than outlines or notations for future texts that were never written. Pessoa realized that the project had got out of hand (if in fact he ever firmly grasped it), for in another letter to Côrtes-Rodrigues he writes that *The Book*, which he calls 'that pathological production', is going 'complexly and tortuously forward', as if of its own accord.

And so Pessoa let the book go, scribbling *B. of D.* at the head of sundry texts, sometimes as an afterthought, or with a question mark expressing doubt. *The Book of Disquietude* – forever tentative, indefinite, and in transition – is one of those rare works in which *forme* and *fond* perfectly reflect each other. Always with the intention of revising and assembling the fragments, but never with the courage or patience to take up the task, Pessoa kept adding material, and the parameters of the amorphous work kept expanding. Besides the symbolist and diary texts, Pessoa included maxims, philosophical speculations, aesthetic credos, sociological observations, and literary criticism. He even put the *B. of D.* trademark on the copy of a letter to his mother (AP-4 in the Appendix). We may view *The Book of Disquietude* as a lifelong sketchbook of loose pages containing the essential artist in all of his heteronymic variety (and especially in the 'sensationist' Álvaro de Campos – see f.133 or f.161). Or we may read it as the traveller's journal (f.1), a 'book of random impressions' (f.486), Pessoa's faithful companion throughout his literary odyssey that never left Lisbon.

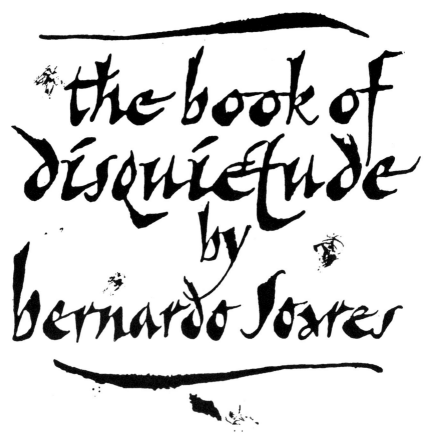

the book of disquietude by bernardo soares

[1] I WAS BORN IN A TIME WHEN THE MAJORITY OF YOUNG PEOPLE had lost faith in God, for the same reason their elders had had it – without knowing why. And then, since the human spirit naturally tends towards judgements based on feeling instead of reason, most of these young people chose Humanity to replace God. I, however, am the sort of person who's always on the fringe of what he belongs to, seeing not only the multitude he's a part of but also the wide open spaces around it. That's why I didn't give up God as completely as they did, and I never accepted Humanity. I reasoned that God, while improbable, might exist, in which case he should be worshipped; whereas Humanity, being a mere biological idea and signifying nothing more than the animal species we belong to, was no more deserving of worship than any other animal species. The cult of Humanity, with its rites of Freedom and Equality, always struck me as a revival of those ancient cults in which gods were like animals or had animal heads.

[46] The beauty of a nude body is only appreciated by peoples that use clothing. Chastity is important for sensuality like resistance for energy.

[84] 6 May 1930. Metaphysics has always struck me as a prolonged form of latent insanity. If we knew the truth, we'd see it; everything else is systems and trappings. If we think, the world's inscrutability is enough for us; to want to understand it is to be less than persons, since to be a person is to know that it can't be understood.

I'm handed faith like a sealed package on a strange-looking platter and am expected to accept it without opening it. I'm handed science, like a knife on a plate, to cut the folios of a book whose pages are blank. I'm handed doubt, like dust inside a box – but why give me a box if all it contains is dust?

I write because I don't know, and I employ the lofty, alien terms for Truth according to what the emotion requires. If the emotion is clear-cut and fatal, then I naturally speak of the Gods, thereby framing it in a consciousness of the world's multiplicity. If the emotion is profound, then I naturally speak of God, thereby placing it in a single consciousness. If the emotion is a thought, I naturally speak of Destiny, thereby shoving it up against the wall.

Sometimes the mere rhythm of a sentence will require the Gods and not God; other times the two words 'the Gods' will impose themselves so that I must verbally change universe; still other times what will matter are the needs or an inner rhyme, a switch in metre or a burst of emotion, and polytheism or monotheism will adjust accordingly. The Gods are contingent on style.

[103] *Aesthetics of Abdication.* To conform is to submit, and to conquer is to conform, to be conquered. Thus every victory is a vulgarity. The conqueror inevitably loses all the qualities of disappointment that led him to the fight that brought victory. He is satisfied, and only those who conform – who lack the mentality of the conqueror – are satisfied. The conqueror can only be one who never achieves his end. Only the man forever dispirited is strong. The best and most regal course is to abdicate. The supreme empire is that of the emperor who abdicates from all normal life and from other men, the preservation of his supremacy not weighing on him like a load of jewels.

[107] 'I want you only for my dream,' they tell the beloved women in verses they don't send – I mean they who dare not tell her anything. This 'I want you only for my dream' is a verse from an old poem of mine. I note this with a smile, and I don't even comment on the smile.

[108] To act is to rest.

[113]   Every man of today, unless he has the moral stature and intellectu-al profile of a rustic or a pygmy, loves with romantic love when he loves. Romantic love is a rarefied product of century after century of Christian influence; and everything about its substance and development can be explained to the unenlightened by comparing it to a suit, or some other outfit, fabricated by the soul or the imagination, clothing those whom the mind thinks it fits, when they chance to come along.

But every suit, since it isn't eternal, lasts as long as it lasts; and soon, under the fraying outfit of the ideal we've formed, there emerges the real body of the human person we dress in it.

[143]   *Maxims* To have sure and definite opinions, instincts, passions, and a steady and familiar character – all of this leads to the horrendous conversion of our soul into a fact, materializing it into something external. Life is a sweet, fluid state of ignorance about things and about ourselves. (It's the only lifestyle appropriate and stimulating to a wise man.)

To know how to stand constantly between ourselves and external things is the highest degree of wisdom and prudence.

Our personality should be inscrutable, even to ourselves. That is why we must always dream, being sure to include ourselves in our dreams so that we won't be able to have opinions about ourselves.

And we must especially prevent our personality from being invaded by others. All outside interest in us is a flagrant disrespect. What saves the common greeting 'How are you?' from being an unforgivable vulgarity is its generally utter emptiness and lack of all sincerity.

To love is to tire of being alone: it is therefore a cowardice, a betrayal of ourselves. (It's exceedingly important that we not love).

To give good advice is to insult the faculty of erring that God gave to others. And we should hope, in our own interest, that the acts of others be more and more unlike our own. It makes sense only to *ask* for advice from others, for thus we can be sure – on doing just the opposite – that we are absolutely ourselves, in absolute disaccord with all Otherness.

The only advantage of studying is to take delight in what others haven't said.

Art is an isolation. Every artists should seek to isolate others, to fill their souls with a desire to be alone. The supreme triumph for an artist is when his readers, after reading his words, prefer to have them and not read them. It's not because this is what happens to celebrated artists, but because it really is the greatest tribute (...)

[149]   These considerations came to me after reading a newspaper article about the great and multi-faceted life of a celebrity – an American million-aire who had been everything. He'd achieved all he'd set out to do –

money, love, friendship, devotion, travels, collections. Money can't buy everything, but the great magnetism by which money is acquired can indeed acquire almost everything.

As I set the paper down on the restaurant table, I was already reflecting on how the same thing, taking a smaller compass, could be said about the firm's sales representative, more or less my acquaintance, who's eating lunch at the table in the back corner, as he does every day. All that the millionaire had, this man has – in smaller measure, to be sure, but consonant with his stature. Both men have had equal success, and there's not even a difference in terms of fame, because there too the difference in environments establishes their identity. There's no one in the world who doesn't know the name of the American millionaire, but there's no one in Lisbon's commercial district who doesn't know the name of the man eating lunch in the corner.

These men, then, have obtained all that their hand could by reaching forth their arm. The difference between them was the length of their arm; they were identical in other respects. I've never been able to envy this sort of person. I've always felt that virtue lay in obtaining what was out of one's reach, in living where one isn't present, in being more alive after death than during life, in realizing, finally, something difficult, something absurd, in conquering – like an obstacle – the world's very reality.

[150] Some have a great dream in life and fall short of it. Others have no dream, and also fall short of it.

[153] How often I've heard people say the same old phrase that symbolizes all of the absurdity, all of the nothingness, all of the spoken ignorance of their lives. It's the phrase they use in reference to any material pleasure: 'This is what we take away from life...'

Take where? take how? take why? It would be sad to wake them out of their darkness with a question like that... Only a materialist can utter such a phrase, because everyone who utters such a phrase is a materialist, even if unconsciously. What does he plan to take from life, and how? Where will he take his pork chops and red wine and lady friend? To what heaven that he doesn't believe in? To what land where he'll only take the rottenness that was the latent essence of his entire life? I can think if no phrase that's more tragic and more patently revealing of human humanity. Thus the plants would speak if they were able to know that they enjoy the sun. Thus animals would speak about their somnambulant pleasures, were their power of self-expression not inferior to man's. And perhaps even I, on writing these words with a vague impression that they might endure, imagine that my memory of having written them is what I 'take away from life.' And just as a common corpse is lowered into the common ground, so the equally useless corpse of the prose I wrote will be lowered into common oblivion. A man's pork chops, his wine, his lady friend – who am I to make fun of them?

Brothers in our common ignorance, different expressions of the same blood, diverse forms of the same heredity – which of us can deny the other? A wife can be denied but not mother, not father, not brother.

[157]   I'm always amazed when I finish something. Amazed and distressed. My perfectionist instinct should inhibit me from finishing; it should inhibit me from even beginning. But I get distracted and begin doing something. What I achieve is not the product of an act of my will but of my will's surrender. I begin because I don't have the strength to think; I finish because I don't have the courage to quit. This book is my cowardice.

If I very often interrupt a thought with a scenic description that in some way fits into the real or imagined scheme of my impressions, it's because the scenery is a door through which I flee from my awareness of my creative impotence. In the middle of the conversations with myself that form the words of this book, I have the sudden need to talk to someone else, and so I direct myself to the light which hovers, as now, over roof-tops that glow as if they were damp, or to the urban hillside with its tall, gently swaying trees that seem strangely close and on the verge of silently collapsing, or to the steep houses that overlap like placards and whose windows are like letters where the dying sun gilds the humid glue.

Why do I write, if I can write no better? But what would become of me if I didn't write what I'm capable of, however inferior my attempt may be to what I am? I'm a plebeian of ambition, because I try to fulfil it; like someone afraid of a dark room, I'm afraid to be silent. I'm like those who prize the medal more than the effort, and savour the glory of the fur-lined cape.

For me, to write is to disdain myself, and yet I can't quit writing. Writing is like the drug that I abhor and take, the addiction that I disdain and depend on. There are necessary poisons, and some are extremely subtle, composed of ingredients from the soul, herbs collected from among the ruins of dreams, black poppies found next to graves [...], the long leaves of obscene trees that sway their branches on the audible banks of the soul's infernal rivers.

To write is to lose myself, yes, but everyone loses himself, because everything is lost. I, however, lose myself without any joy – not like the river going into the sea for which it was secretly born, but like the puddle left on the beach by the high tide, its stranded water never returning to the ocean but merely sinking into the sand.

[163]   Twice in my adolescence – which I feel so remotely it seems like something I read somewhere or like a personal narrative I was told – I

enjoyed the humiliating grief of being in love. From my present vantage point, looking back to that past which I'm unable to designate as remote or recent, I think it was good that this experience of disillusion happened to me so early.

Nothing happened, except in what I felt. Outwardly speaking, legions of men have suffered the same torments. But (...)

All too early, through a simultaneous and mutual experience of my sensibility and my mind, I came by the notion that the life of the imagination, however morbid it might seem, is nevertheless the life that suits temperaments like my own. The fictions of my imagination may weary me, but they neither grieve nor humiliate. With lovers who are impossible, false smiles, deceitful affection and shrewd caresses are also impossible. Such lovers never forsake us, nor will they ever cease to exist.

Our soul's great anxieties are always cosmic cataclysms. Whenever we experience them, the sun veers wildly around us and the stars are shaken. In every feeling soul Destiny will sooner or later pay out an apocalypse of anxiety – a pouring out of all skies and worlds over its disconsolation.

To feel oneself superior and to be treated by Destiny as utterly and incurably inferior – who in such a plight can boast of being a man?

If one day I were given a flash of expressive power so great that it concentrated all art in me, then I would write a eulogy to sleep. I know no greater pleasure in life than that of being able to sleep. The total extinguishing of life and the soul, the complete banishment of all beings and people, the night with neither memory nor illusion, the absence of past and future, (...)

[166]   Government is based on two things: restraint and deception. The problem with glittering moral terms is that they neither restrain nor deceive. At most they intoxicate, which is something else again.

If there's one thing I hate, it's a reformer. A reformer is a man who sees the world's superficial ills and sets out to cure them by aggravating the more basic ills. A doctor tries to bring a sick body into conformity with a normal, healthy body, but we don't know what's healthy or sick in the social sphere.

I consider humanity to be merely one of Nature's latest schools of decorative painting, I don't fundamentally distinguish a man from a tree, and I naturally prefer that which is more decorative, that which interests my thinking eyes. If the tree is more interesting to me than the man, I'm sorrier to see the tree felled than to see the man die. There are departing sunsets that grieve me more than the deaths of children. In everything I have no feeling, in order that I can feel.

[177]   Wise is the man who monotonizes his existence, for then each

minor incident seems like a marvel. A hunter of lions feels no adventure past the third lion.

[180] *1st Article* The generation that I belong to was born into a world divested of supports for those with a heart as well as a brain. The destructive work of previous generations left us a world that offered no security in the religious sphere, no stability in the everyday sphere, and no tranquility in the political sphere. We were born right into the midst of metaphysical anguish, moral anxiety and political disquietude. Inebriated with external formulas and the abstract processes of reason and science, the generations that preceded us did away with the foundations of the Christian faith, for their Biblical criticism – moving from textual to mythological criticism – reduced the gospels and the earlier sacred writings of the Jews to a doubtful heap of myths, legends and mere literature; and their scientific criticism gradually revealed the mistakes and ingenuous notions of the gospels' primitive 'science'. At the same time, the spirit of free inquiry brought all metaphysical problems out into the open, and with them all the religious problems that had to do with metaphysics. Inebriated with a hazy notion they called 'positivism', these generations criticized all morality and scrutinized all rules of life, and all that remained from the clash of doctrines was certainty of none of them and grief over there being no certainty. A society so undisciplined in its cultural foundations could obviously not help but be a political victim of its own chaos, and so it was that we woke up to a world eager for social novelties, and it gleefully set out to conquer a freedom that no one could identify and a progress that no one had defined.

But while the sloppy criticism of our fathers bequeathed us the impossibility of being Christians, it didn't bequeath us an acceptance of the impossibility; while it bequeathed us a disbelief in established moral formulas, it didn't bequeath us an indifference to morality and to the rules of human co-existence; while it left the political problem in doubt, it didn't leave our spirit indifferent to how this problem might be solved. Our fathers wreaked destruction with joy, for they lived in a time that still reflected the solidity of the past. It was the very thing they destroyed that gave strength to society and thus made it possible for them to destroy without noticing that the building was cracking. We inherited the destruction and its results.

Today the world belongs only to the stupid, the insensitive and the agitated. Today the right to live and triumph is achieved by almost the same behaviour that leads to internment in a mental institution: inability to think, amorality, and hyperactivity.

[198] There are people who truly suffer for not having been able to live with Mr Pickwick in real life and to have shaken Mr Wardle's hand. I'm one of those. I've wept literal tears over that novel, for not having lived in that time and with those people, real people.

[213] 18 September 1931 Just as, whether we know it or not, we all have a metaphysics, so too, whether we like it or not, we all have a morality. I have a very simple morality – not to do good or evil to anyone. Not to do evil, because it seems only fair that others enjoy the same right I demand for myself – not to be disturbed – and also because I think that natural evils are enough for the world. We in this world are all living on board a ship that is sailing from one unknown port to another; we should treat one another with a traveller's cordiality. Not to do good, because I don't know what good is, nor even if I do it when I think I do. How do I know what evils I generate if I give a beggar money? How do I know what evils I produce if I teach or instruct? Being in doubt, I refrain. And besides, in a certain way I think that to help or clarify is to commit the evil of interfering in the lives of others. Kindness depends on a whim of our mood: we have no right to make others the victims of our whims, regardless of how human or caring they may be. Good deeds are impositions; that's why I categorically abhor them.

    If, for moral reasons, I don't do good unto others, neither do I expect others to do good unto me. If I get sick, what most horrifies me is to oblige someone to take care of me, something I'd loathe doing for another. I've never visited a sick friend. And whenever I've been sick and had visitors, it has always struck me as a bother, an insult, an inexcusable violation of my resolute privacy. I don't like people to give me things, for I feel that they're obligating me to give in return – to them or to others, or to whomever.

    I'm highly sociable in a highly negative way. I'm inoffensiveness incarnate. But I'm no more than this, I don't want to be more than this, I can't be more than this...

    I consider myself fortunate that I no longer have family, as it relieves me of the obligation of loving someone, which I'd surely find burdensome. Any nostalgia I feel is literary. I remember my childhood with tears, but they're rhythmic tears, in which prose is already being formed. I remember childhood as an external thing and by way of external things; I remember only external things. It's not the stillness of evenings in the country that endears me to the childhood I spent there, it's the way the table was set for tea, it's the way the furniture was arranged in the room, it's the faces and physical gestures of the people. I feel nostalgia for scenes. Thus someone else's childhood can move me as much as my own; both are purely visual phenomena from a past I'm unable to fathom, and my perception of them is literary. They move me, yes, but because I see them, not because I remember them.

    I've never loved anyone. The most that I've loved are my sensations –

states of conscious seeing, impressions of an alert hearing, and aromas through which the humility of the outside world speaks to me of things from the past (easily remembered by their smells), giving me a reality and an emotion that goes beyond the simple fact of the bread being baked inside the bakery, as on that remote afternoon when I was coming from the funeral of my uncle, the one who really loved me, and I experienced a kind of sweet relief, I don't know why.

This is my morality, or metaphysics, or me: Passer-by of everything, even of my own soul, belonging to nothing, desiring nothing, being nothing – abstract centre of impersonal sensations, a fallen sentient mirror, reflecting the world's diversity. I don't know if I'm happy this way. Nor do I care.

[214]   The only noble destiny for a writer who publishes is to be denied a celebrity that he deserves. But the truly noble destiny is that of the writer who doesn't publish. Not who doesn't write, for then he wouldn't be a writer. I speak of the writer who because of his nature writes, and because of his spiritual disposition doesn't show what he writes.

[217]   To have opening opinions is to sell out to yourself. Not to have opinions is to exist. To have all opinions is to be a poet.

[218]   My God, my God, who am I watching? How many am I? Who is I? What is this gap between me and me?

[248]   To be a retired major seems to me ideal. It's a shame one can't have eternally been nothing but a retired major.
    The thirst for wholeness left me in this state of useless bitterness.
    The tragic futility of life.
    My curiosity – kindred spirit to the skylarks.
    The treacherous anxiety of sunsets; the dawn's timid shroud.
    Let's sit down here. From here we can see more of the sky. The vast expanse of these starry heights is consoling. Looking at them, we're not so grieved by life; the slight wave of a small fan passes across our life-wearied face.

[250]   The active life has always struck me as the least comfortable of suicides.

[255]   I've never found any convincing arguments except for inertia. Over time I became increasingly dominated by a sullen awareness of my inertia and my role as an abdicator. Seeking out modes of inertia, pledging to flee all effort and exertion and social responsibility – this is the substance from which I carved the mental statue of my existence.

[259]   More than once, while leisurely strolling the streets in the after-

noon, my soul has been suddenly and violently struck by the bizarre presence of organization in things. It's not so much natural things that so powerfully cause this sensation in me; it's rather the signs, the layout of the streets, the people dressed up and talking, the various jobs, the newspapers, the logic of everything. Or rather, it's the fact that signs, ordered streets, jobs, men and society exist, everything fitting together and going forward and opening up paths...

I've never understood how anyone who has ever considered the tremendous fact of this universal watch mechanism can deny the watchmaker, in whom not even Voltaire disbelieved. I understand why, in light of certain aspects that have apparently deviated from a plan (and it was necessary to know the plan to know the aspects had deviated), one might attribute an element of imperfection to this supreme intelligence. I understand this, although I don't accept it. I also understand why, in light of the evil in the world, one might not acknowledge that the creating intelligence is infinitely good. I understand this, although again I don't accept it. But to deny the existence of this intelligence, i.e. of God, strikes me as one of those idiocies which sometimes afflict, in a single point of the intelligence, men who in all other points may be superior – those, for example, who systematically make mistakes in adding and subtracting, or those who (considering now the intelligence of the sensibility) cannot feel music, or painting, or poetry.

I've said that I don't accept the rationale for the imperfect watchmaker, or for one who is not benign. I reject the rationale for the imperfect watchmaker because those features of government and the organization of the world that strike us as flawed or nonsensical cannot validly be considered as such until we know the plan. We plainly see there's a plan in everything; we see certain things that strikes us as nonsensical, but we should remember that if there's a reason for everything, then there must also be a reason for these specific things. We see the reason but not the plan; how then can we say that certain things are outside the plan, when we don't know what the plan is? Just as a poet of subtle rhythms can insert an a-rhythmic verse for rhythmic ends, i.e. for the very end he seems to be forsaking (and a critic who's more rectilinear than rhythmic is liable to say that the verse is in error), so the Creator can insert things that our narrow reasoning considers a-rhythmic into the majestic flow of his metaphysical rhythm.

As for the rationale behind the idea of an unbenign watchmaker, I agree that it's a harder argument to refute, but only apparently. We could say that we don't really know what evil is, thus are not able to affirm if something is bad or good. A pain, however, even if for our ultimate good, is obviously bad in itself, and this is enough to prove the existence of evil in the world. A toothache is enough to make one disbelieve in the goodness of the Creator. The basic error in this argument seems to lie in our complete ignorance of God's plan, and our equal ignorance of what, as an intelligent person, the Intellectual Infinite might be. The existence of evil is one thing; the reason for its existence is another. The distinction may be subtle to the point of seeming sophistic, but it's without a doubt valid. The existence of evil cannot be denied, but one can deny that the existence of evil is evil. I admit that the problem persists, but it persists because our imperfection persists.

[275] To have already read *Pickwick Papers* is one of the great tragedies of my life. (I can't go back and read it for the first time.)

[280] An opinion is a vulgarity, even when it's not sincere. Every sincerity is an intolerance. There are no sincere liberal minds. There are, for that matter, no liberal minds.

[301] Disdain everything, but in such a way that your disdain doesn't touch you. Don't think you're superior because you disdain. This is the key to the art of noble disdain.

[307] I'm riding on a tram and, as usual, am closely observing all the details of the people around me. For me these details are things, voices, phrases. Taking the dress of the girl riding in front of me, I break it down into the fabric from which it's made and the work that went into making it (such that I see a dress and not just fabric), and the delicate embroidery that trims the collar decomposes under my scrutiny into the silk thread with which it was embroidered and the work it took to embroider it. And immediately, as in a textbook of basic economics, factories and jobs unfold before me: the factory where the cloth was made; the factory where the darker-coloured silk was spun to trim with twisting flourishes its place around the neck; the factories' divisions, the machines, the workers, the seamstresses. My inwardly-turned eyes penetrate into the offices, where I see the managers trying to stay calm, and I peek into the account books where everything is recorded. But that's not all: I see beyond to the private lives of those who live their social lives in these factories and offices... All the world unrolls before my eyes merely because there is in front of me – on the nape of a dark-skinned neck whose other side has I don't know what face – a regularly irregular dark-green fringe on a light-green dress.

The social side of life lies entirely before my eyes.

And beyond this I sense the loves, the secrecies and the souls of all who laboured so that the woman in front of me in the tram would wear, around her mortal neck, the sinuous banality of a dark-green silk trim dress on a less dark green cloth.

I get dizzy. The seats in the tram, made of a thin but tough woven straw, take me to distant places and proliferate within me in the form of industries, workers, their houses, lives, realities, everything.

I get off the tram exhausted and dazed. I've just lived all of life.

[312]   I belong to a generation which inherited disbelief in the Christian faith and created in itself a disbelief in all other faiths. Our fathers still had the believing impulse, which they transferred from Christianity to other forms of illusion. Some were champions of social equality, others were wholly enamoured of beauty, still others had faith in science and its achievements, and there were some who became even more Christian, resorting to various Easts and Wests in their search for other religious forms that would entertain their otherwise hollow consciousness of merely living.

We lost all of this. We were born with none of these consolations. Each civilization follows the particular line of a religion that represents it; resorting to other religions, it loses the one it had, and ultimately loses them all.

We lost the one, and all the others with it.

And so we were left, each man to himself, in the desolation of feeling ourselves live. A ship seems to be an object whose end is to sail, but no, its finality is to reach a port. We found ourselves sailing, without any idea of the port at which we ought to arrive. Thus we reproduced a painful version of the Argonauts' adventurous formula: to sail is what's necessary, not to live.

[328]   For the time being, since we live in society, the only duty of the superiors is to reduce to a minimum their participation in the life of the tribe.

They shouldn't read the newspapers, for example, or should only read them to find out what anecdotal and unimportant things are happening. You can't imagine the delight I get from the provincial news round-up. The very names make doors to the indefinite open up in me.

The most honourable stance for a superior man is to not know who his country's chief of state is, or whether he lives under a monarchy or a republic.

His attitude should be to position his soul in such a way that passing events and things don't touch him. If he doesn't do this, then he'll have to take an interest in others so as to look out for himself.

[329]   Those of us who aren't homosexuals wish we had the courage to be. Our distaste for action inevitably feminizes us. We missed our true calling as housewives and idle chatelaines on account of a sexual mix-up in our current incarnation. Although we don't believe this at all, our blood enjoys the irony of our acting within as if we did.

[332] I feel more kinship and intimacy with certain characters described in books and certain images I've seen in prints than I feel with many so-called real people, who are of that metaphysical futility known as flesh and bone. And 'flesh and bone' in fact describes them rather well: they're like chunks of meat exposed on the marble counter of a butcher's, dead things bleeding like lives, legs and cutlets of Destiny.

I'm not ashamed of feeling this way, as I've discovered that's how every-one feels. Behind people's mutual contempt and the indifference that allows them to kill each other like assassins who don't really feel they're killing, or like soldiers who don't think about what they're doing, is that no one pays heed to the seemingly abstruse fact that the people around them are also living souls.

On certain days, at certain moments, brought to me by I don't know what breeze and opened to me by the opening of I don't know what door, I suddenly feel that the corner grocer is a thinking entity, that the shop assis-tant, who at this moment is bent over a sack of potatoes next to the entrance, is truly a soul capable of suffering.

When I was told yesterday that the employee of the tobacco shop had committed suicide, it seemed like a lie. Poor man, he also existed! We had forgotten this, all of us, all who knew him in the same way as all those who never met him. Tomorrow we'll forget him even better. But he evidently had a soul, for he killed himself. Passion? Anxiety? Undoubtedly... But for me, as for the whole of humanity, there's only the memory of a dumb smile and a shabby sports coat that hung unevenly from the shoulders. That's all that remains to me of this man who felt so much he killed himself for feeling, since what else does one kill himself for? Once, as I was buying cigarettes from him, it occurred to me that he would go bald early. It turns out he didn't have time enough to go bald. That's one of the memories I have of him. What other one can I have if even this one is not of him but of one of my thoughts?

I suddenly behold the corpse in the coffin where they placed him, in the strange grave where they must have lowered him. And it dawns on me that the cashier of the tobacco shop, crooked coat and all, was in a certain way the whole of humanity.

[411] The countryside is where we are not. There, and there alone, are real trees and real shade.

[412] The slight inebriation of a mild fever, when a soft and penetrating discomfort is cold in our aching bones and warm in our eyes, under our throbbing temples – I adore this discomfort like a slave his beloved master. It gives me that feeble, quivering passivity in which I glimpse visions, turn corners of ideas and founder among interpolations of feelings.

To think, to feel and to want become a single confused thing. Beliefs, sensations, imagined things and real things are all mixed up, like the contents of various drawers when overturned on to the floor.

[414] *Millimetres (sensations of slight things)* The present is ancient, for everything that ever existed was present, and so I'm fond of things (because they belong to the present) like an antique dealer, and I have the wrath of a superseded collector for anyone who replaces my mistaken notions about things with plausible and even indisputable, scientifically based arguments.

The various points which a butterfly successively occupies in space are various things which, to my amazed eyes, remain visible in space. My recollections are so alive that (...)

But it is only subtle sensations, and of the slightest things, that I live intensely. Perhaps this is due to my love of the futile. Or maybe it's because of my attention to detail. But I'm inclined to believe – I can't say I know, as I never analyse these things – that it's because slight things, having absolutely no social or practical importance, are for that very reason absolutely free of sordid associations with reality. What is slightest smacks to me of unreality. The useless is beautiful because it's less real than the useful, which continues and prolongs, while the marvellously futile and gloriously minuscule stay where they are and as they are, living freely and independently. The useless and the futile open up intervals of humble stasis in our real lives. What dreams and amorous delights are stirred in my soul by the mere insignificant existence of a needle pinned to a ribbon! A pity for those who don't realize the importance this has!

Among the sensations which penetratingly grieve us to the point of becoming agreeable, the disquietude of the mysterious is one of the most extensive and complex. And the sense of mystery is never more evident than in the contemplation of tiny things which, because they don't move, are perfectly translucent, allowing mystery to show through them. It's harder to feel mystery when contemplating a battle – and yet to consider the absurdity of there being people and societies and conflicts between them is what can most unfurl the victory flag of mystery within our minds – than when contemplating a small stone on the road which, triggering no other idea beyond that of existence, must in due course trigger – if we continue to contemplate it – the idea of the mystery of its existence.

Blessed be the instants and the millimetres and the shadows of tiny things, even more humble than the things themselves! Instants (...) Millimetres – how astonished I am by their audacity in existing side by side and so close together on a tape-measure. Sometimes I suffer and delight in these things. And I feel stupidly proud.

I'm a diffusely impressionable photographic plate. All of the details are disproportionately engraved on me and form a whole. I only attend to myself. For me the outer world is always a manifest form of sensation. I never forget that I feel.

[473]   The aristocrat is he who never forgets that he's never alone; that's why etiquette and decorum are the privilege of aristocracies. Let's internalize the aristocrat. Let's take him out of his gardens and drawing-rooms and place him in our soul and in our consciousness of existing. Let's always act toward ourselves with decorum and good manners, with studied and for-other-people gestures.

[490]   We are ultimately indifferent to the truth or falseness of all religions, of all philosophies, and of all the uselessly verifiable hypotheses which we call sciences. Nor are we really worried about the destiny of so-called humanity, or about what as a whole it does or doesn't suffer. Charity, yes, for our 'neighbour', as the Gospel says, and not for man, of whom it says nothing. And we are all like this to some extent. How much does a massacre in China really weigh on even the most noble of us? It will cause more grief, even to the most sensitively imaginative, to see a child in the street get slapped for no apparent reason.

[508]   Whoever has read the pages of this book will by now surely have concluded that I'm a dreamer. And he will have concluded wrongly. I lack the money to be a dreamer.

TWO POSTHUMOUS INTERVIEWS

ANTONIO TABUCCHI :
A conversation in the Autumn of 1935
Translated by John Byrne

JOSÉ BLANCO :
'Fernando Pessoa, Europe & the Portuguese Discoveries'
Translated by Janet Louth

ANTONIO TABUCCHI :
A Conversation in the Autumn of 1935

I N THOSE LATTER DAYS IT WOULD HAPPEN TO HIM frequently, not always but in certain seasons, autumn for example: the particular yellow of the leaves, each one different, each one in its own way, seemed to him to trace in the air an equation, something perfect and eternal, like Newton's binomial theory, but of an instantaneous eternity, solid and organic.

He would pick up a fallen leaf in the garden of S. Pedro de Alcantara and put it in his pocket as if it held the dead essence of mathematics. He would catch the tram going down to the Cais do Sodre, get off in front of the statue of Camões and, trying to remain unnoticed, cross the Chiado as if behind a curtain, peeping out at life – that's how it would feel, a green curtain, an ochre curtain, the sun outlining his silhouette on the pavement – the shadow of a shadow, he thought – and would proceed to the small bar where over a glass of brandy there might appear the formal equilibrium of a Venus de Milo, perfectly poised over the barrels. Ah, being alive, what equilibrium! And what weariness. Things too, it was clear, felt the same weariness. And maybe the same desire for absolution, a damp, nocturnal cloak which would absolve those beings who, wrapped in their clothes, pass each other by. And the dogs, too, which also exist.[1]

He was sleeping badly, troubled by nightmares. That monstrous ear, the whispered temptation of St Anthony, Van Gogh's ear, the ear of an unknown Master, inside him, listening to him. The owner of the bar was looking at him curiously, as if he wanted to draw his portrait. Some idea, a portrait. Perhaps it was an obsession but he thought that everybody was looking at him as if they wanted to draw his portrait, even the owner of the bar with his intellectual air and beard. They were all looking at him and he felt them everywhere: behind him, at the table nearby, at the traffic lights, by the road signs, among the clouds at sunset, among the many-coloured house fronts.

He paid for his brandy and slowly followed the Rua Augusta as far as the Terreiro do Paco. The square was deserted. He went into the phone box and dialled a number in Agrigento in Sicily.

'Yes,' said a voice, 'Luigi Pirandello speaking.'

---

[1] The 'dogs which also exist' and, later, 'unmetaphysical Esteves' are allusions to Pessoa's poem 'Tobacco shop'.

'*Good evening, Pirandello, Fernando Pessoa here.*'

'It's a great pleasure to hear you,' said Pirandello. 'Where are you speaking from?'

'*From a phone box in Lisbon.*'

'Impossible.'

'*No, it's not impossible, believe me; I do have some minor powers.*'

'And to what do I owe the pleasure of your call?'

'*I wanted to talk to you, this being the last autumn of my life.*'

'How do you know?'

'*I have cast my horoscope.*'

'I shall die in 1936,' said Pirandello. 'Every Sunday morning I am at home to my characters: it was Madam Pace who told me so.'

'*I'm beginning to be everywhere, all over the place,*' said Pessoa, '*it's a funny feeling, I don't know if it's already the prologue to death or to another kind of life; perhaps the same thing is happening to you.*'

'Yes, much the same sort of thing is happening to me too, in effect. I'm here in Agrigento and I'm there in Lisbon with you, but it's hard for any-one else to understand.'

'*Oh, but the world is full of unmetaphysical Esteves, my dear Pirandello. And of minor masters, too. Can you imagine, I know one who wanted to make me take off my mask. My mask, my God, my mask.*'

'It's difficult to be multiple: so many souls do not fit in one body. As I've told you, I set a timetable for my visits but my characters get impatient, they crowd round my door and often invade my room in an unruly fashion, besieging me, demanding explanations, knowing that I shall shortly die. And you, how do you deal with this problem?'

'*I don't know,*' said Pessoa. '*What happens to me is quite the opposite: it is I who go looking for my personalities. I try to drag them in by their coats and make them turn towards me so that I know who they are. I am an author in search of my characters. A few months ago I wrote a letter to a friend of mine, trying to impose some sort of system on all these spectres. Of course I told him a string of lies, you know how these things are, poetics a posteriori...*'

'If I have to be sincere, the same thing happens to me. It is I who seek out my characters. First comes the work and only then come the theories about it, as someone once said. It's a useless, selfish task which generally leads to false conclusions.'

'*It's a shame that you could only stay such a short time in Lisbon; I would have liked to have known you better.*'

'Have you published anything since we last saw each other?'

'*Just a little book, a small volume. It is called* Mensagem – "*Message*"– *in Italian "Messagio".*'

'And what is it about, this "messagio"?'

*'It is hard to say: it is really rather ambitious, though the attempt is proba-
bly grander than the outcome. Sometimes I feel like one of those fairground
toys – do you know those little wooden bicycles which you can buy at country fairs, each with a motto painted on it for the instruction of children? Or
perhaps the child is me. But it does not matter; the world is so full of obscurity that we cannot see what is close to us. Now I must leave you, my powers
are failing and the line is getting weaker. Goodbye, dear Pirandello, we shall
certainly see each other at some future date.'*

'Until I see you again, my dear Pessoa.'

He hung up and left the phone box. Night had fallen in a moment; over the
phone box hung the sickle moon, just as it appears in paintings.

Above & on page 195: Bronze Medallions by Martius Correia

188

JOSÉ BLANCO :
Fernando Pessoa, Europe and the Portuguese Discoveries

I THINK THIS IS THE SECOND TIME FERNANDO PESSOA has granted a posthumous interview. The only other, as far as I know, was given by telephone to Antonio Tabucchi, who published it later, in 1988. Touched by the homage paid him by Europalia at this vast European gathering, in which Portugal has the chief part, Pessoa has agreed my request.[1] This time the interview is taking place live by means of the special frequency channel that links Brussels to the poets' heaven. (Unfortunately I did not manage to persuade the engineer Álvaro de Campos to take part. He would certainly have had some very interesting things to say about the subjects we are going to tackle.)

Good morning, Mr Pessoa. I think you can hear me and so we can begin.

Today your works are recognized throughout the world as among the most important of the century. You are considered one of the great modern masters – what more can be said? However, some people still doubt your 'sincerity'. They persist in thinking that, at bottom, you are nothing but a 'feigner' – a trickster – the skilful inventor of clever intellectual games meant to mystify your fellow men.

In this connection I should like to ask my first question: is there any real feeling or any sincerity in your work? In other words: did you have a fundamental aim to which you devoted your short time in this world?

My intense patriotic suffering, my intense desire of bettering the condition of Portugal provoked in me – how to express with what warmth, with what intensity, with what sincerity! – a thousand plans which, even if one man could realize them, he had to have one characteristic which in me is purely negative – the power of will. No one suspected my patriotic love, intenser than that of everyone I met, of everyone I knew. The warmth, the intensity – tender, revolted and eager – of [my patriotism] I shall never express. [1]

That is what you felt in 1908. You were only 20 years old then; you were a young man who had lived abroad and had rediscovered his deepest roots in Portugal. Didn't this initial youthful fervour, the sincerity of which

---

[1] This 'interview' was first read at the 'Europalia Festival – Portugal' in Brussels, 1991. All the words of Pessoa have been compiled from his own works – sources are given at the end of this piece. Álvaro de Campos had composed in 'Ultimatum' a violent manifesto against 'European mandarins' – hence the reference to him on this occasion.

seems beyond question, grow weaker in the course of your life?

Anything that is literary trifling, pure art, began to seem more and more hollow and repulsive when measured against my deepest feelings and my growing awareness of the terrible religious mission that every man of genius receives from God with that genius. To have some effect on humanity and contribute to the progress of civilization with all my might became the one serious overwhelming purpose of my life. [2]

The concept of patriotism, which had always played a greater or lesser part in my scheme of things, grew within me; and I never thought of producing anything without the intention of exalting the name of Portugal through everything I might do. The reason is that I took art and life very seriously. When one looks at the melancholy and mysterious spectacle of the world through religious eyes, that is the only possible attitude consonant with one's own sense of duty. [3]

You have spoken about your life. It looks as if public opinion has come to believe firmly that it was very like that of the unpretentious office clerk whom you called Bernardo Soares: modest, dull and disappointing. Do you think the interpretation of your biographers is correct?

Some of the old navigators had a proud motto: 'Sailing is necessary: living is not.' I made the spirit of that saying my own, adapting it to my own situation: 'Living is not necessary; what is necessary is to create.' I didn't reckon on enjoying my life; I didn't even think of it. I wanted it to be great, even if my body and soul were to be the fuel to feed the fire. I wanted it to be the life of all humanity, even if that meant giving up the idea that it was mine. [4]

And what, among such grave concerns, was the place of the works of those others whose names you used – Alberio Caeiro, Ricardo Reis and Álvaro de Campos? Some people persist in seeing in them nothing but a playful device, skilful and striking, which, moreover, began, on your own admission, as a trick you wanted to play on your friend Mário de Sá-Carneiro.

I created and lived a whole literature, which is sincere because it is felt, and which forms a current capable of exerting a good influence on people. I class as insincere things done to cause astonishment, and also – and pay attention for this is important – those which are not based on a fundamental metaphysical idea, that is to say, those where there is not even the slightest breath of a notion of the gravity and mystery of life. So everything I wrote under the names of Caeiro, Reis and Álvaro de Campos is serious. In all three I introduced a profound view of life, different in each, but in all of them a concern for the mysterious importance of the simple fact of existence. [5]

For my part, I am quite ready to accept what you say – though with all due respect I think it judicious, with regard to certain aspects of your work, to maintain an attitude of prudence, in response to the paradoxical and unforeseeable facets of your character. But clarify a point for me: are you not worried that modern critics may find your declarations of patriotism not to their liking? Patriotism is not really fashionable nowadays...

Patriotic feeling is one of the commonest things in all literatures. It is in fact the constructive sublimation of hatred, as necessary to existence as love – another common theme in all literatures. [6]

We'll come back to the question of your patriotism in a little while. In 1919, with some of your friends, you thought up the idea of publishing a Portuguese review aimed solely at foreigners, which would appear in French and English alternately. Like so many others, this idea was never put into action. What was your aim at that time?

We wanted to hurl our lack of reverence for Europe in its face; to show it that, as good Portuguese, we were men who 'do not consent'; that cosmopolitan geniuses, 'universally renowned' thinkers and other such trash inspired in us neither respect nor even attention.

It was arranged for the first number of the review to break the tradition of servility which rests heavily on the life of the Portuguese. It was possible that once the idea became a reality it would prove to be fruitless and that the anticipated success would come to nothing. In any case, we should have given an example of disrespect towards the European idols; we should at least have said what we thought of them, which was something. [7]

So the review would have been a practical illustration of the principles defended by the engineer Álvaro de Campos two years earlier in his 'Ultimatum', where he cried out: 'Is there anyone in Europe who has an inkling of where the New World is to be found?'

For God's sake! Men whose forefathers discovered new seas and new lands can quite well take the risk of finding out that there is no talent to be discovered among the international bureaucrats who claim the monopoly of intelligence. [8] I was thinking of writing a long piece, at once destructive and constructive, with the title 'First Epistle of the Bœotians', the Bœotians being the inhabitants of Europe in general. We were the non-Bœotians – that goes without saying. [9]

Besides this sort of thing, which is certainly stimulating but somewhat negative, would the review have had a constructive purpose?

Broadly speaking, our object was simply this: the creation of a Portuguese culture. We were not looking for (or rather I thought we ought not to be looking for) a Portuguese Weltanschauung, in the narrow sense of a 'Germanic culture' made Portuguese, but in the ancient Hellenic sense of a universal Portuguese culture. To create a way of thinking, an intellectual attitude, about which it could be said that, although universal, it could have come only from Portugal. [10]

Greece, always Greece at the root of your thinking...

Only two nations – the Greece of times past and the Portugal of tomorrow – have received from the gods the gift of being not only themselves but all the others too. I should like to draw your attention to the fact, which is more than just geographical, that Lisbon and Athens are on almost the same latitude. [11]

Today, in the Europe of 1991, regionalism and nationalism are very much on the agenda. What did they mean to you in 1919 – that is to say, more than seventy years ago?

Regionalism is a fatty degeneration of nationalism, and so is nationalism. And as nationalism is anti-Portuguese (it is only any good in the south, for the Latin and Iberian peoples), regionalism in Portugal is a disease of something that does not exist. Loving our country is not the same as loving our garden. And we might cavil at this notion of a garden. My Lisbon garden is simultaneously in Lisbon, in Portugal and in Europe. The good regionalist loves it because it is in Europe. But when I get to this kind of regionalism I am already a Portuguese and am no longer thinking about my garden. (All this is no less true because of the fact that my garden is entirely metaphorical. God and even the universe are also metaphors.) [12]

And if I were to ask you to sum up, in one of your famous paradoxical syntheses, what it is to be a Portuguese today in Europe, what would you say?

To be a Portuguese, in the proper sense of the word, is to be European without the discourtesy of nationality. [13]

The Great Discoveries are – as they will be above all in 1992 and the following years – one of the great topics of the day, especially in Spain and Portugal. To use the happy formula of our mutual friend Eduardo Lourenço, who is also here, the Discoveries are 'this kind of identity card that every Portuguese carries in the inside pocket of his soul'. Weighing his words carefully (which was not his habit), Álvaro de Campos once wrote that the truly great act in the history of Portugal, 'that long, careful, scientific time of the Discoveries', was 'the great cosmopolitan act of History'. Don't you find that a bit overstated?

I have had enough of the long injustice done us by all the histories of Europe, and I am fed up with it. [14]

Our Discoveries are a work whose special meaning has not yet been grasped by contemporary sociological intuition, partly because sociology does not yet exist, and partly because what does exist of it has been produced by the Jesuitical bias of the French, by the gross lack of historical intuition of the Germans and by the insular ignorance of the English. [15] What constitutes the value of the Discoveries of the Portuguese is not the Discoveries in themselves, but the system. Portugal was the first to systematize the discovery and revelation of the world. Sociologically the Discoveries (of the Spanish, the French, the English or anyone else) are therefore all Portuguese. Historically they are what they are, but history is nothing but the store of facts or pseudo-facts on which sociology works. [16]

And what about the great navigators who were not Portuguese – Columbus (the Galician, as you called him) and the Englishman Cabot, for example.

You can forget about Columbus and Cabot. Columbus is sociologically Portuguese, because the Discoveries were a Portuguese initiative, just like their scientific conception and the construction of the whole as a fact of civilization, and as a result everyone who has contributed to them has for that very reason become Portuguese. [17]

The one you admire most of all is Prince Henry the Navigator, in whom you saw, in *Mensagem*, 'The only emperor who holds, in truth/The world's globe in his hand.'

In all the history books, when they talk about the Discoveries, the authors always cite two or three names around which they twist a poor triumphal wreath in honour of the explorers. These three names are Columbus, Vasco da Gama and Magellan. Now there is one thing of which sociologists can be certain, which is that the great name in connection with the Discoveries is that of Prince Henry the Navigator, one of the greatest creators of civilization the world has ever known; Columbus, da Gama and Magellan are his agents. [18]

If the creators of civilization have one thing in common, it is the failure to recognize the importance of what they are creating. Prince Henry the Navigator was the most systematic of all the creators of civilization, but he did not see what a marvel he was creating – the entire modern transatlantic civilization, which nevertheless had appalling consequences, such as the existence of the United States. [19]

I was beginning to wonder why I had not yet heard one of your usual quips... This passionate enthusiasm for the Discoveries led you, in 1922, to publish the poems 'Portuguese Sea' that you included in *Mensagem* in 1934. Don't you think it was, so to speak, superfluous, as Camões had already written the definitive work on the subject, *The Lusiads*?

Our only period of creation was devoted to creating a world. We did not have time to think about it. Camões himself was only what he forgot to do. The Lusiads is a great work, but it was never really written. In a literary sense Portugal's past was still to come. Prince Henry the Navigator, Albuquerque and the other demi-gods of our glory were still waiting for their poet. Camões was too close to them to be able to dream them. When you are on the slopes of the Himalayas, the Himalayas are only the slopes of the Himalayas. But from a distance, or in the memory, or in the imagination, the Himalayas gain their full height, or even a bit more. [20]

In 1938, only four years after the publication of *Mensagem*, Hernâni Cidade – who was one of the most penetrating of Camões' interpreters – wrote that your book certainly deserved its title, as it was a message of faith in an ideal of 'future universal solidarity' of which Portugal would be the instrument. Much closer to us, Eduardo Lourenço considers that your questioning of Portugal involves a deflection of the usual meaning of patriotism, and that *Mensagem* is an anti-*Lusiads*, an elegiac epic in the self-induced disintegration of the historical particularity of the Portuguese, the sublime suicide of the personality at a time when impersonality was truly universal and fraternal. Do you agree?

There are three social realities – the Individual, the Nation and Humanity. Everything else is factitious. The Nation may be a social reality, but it is not a material reality: it is a trunk rather than a root. The Individual and Humanity are places, the Nation is the path which leads from one to the other. Unless we degenerate, it is easy to feel that it is by means of patriotic fraternity that we shall gradually rise to fraternity with all men.

It follows that the more intensely patriotic we are – as long as we know how – the more intensely we shall be preparing ourselves, with those who are with us, for a future resolution for humanity, which we ought always to consider desirable, even if God makes it impossible. [21]

So you still believe in the future of Portugal and the Portuguese?

Our future is to be everything. Who, if he is Portuguese, can live within the restraints of a single personality, a single nation, a single faith? We have already conquered the Sea, we still have to conquer Heaven, leaving Earth to the Others, to those who are eternally Other, Others by birth, to the Europeans who are not Europeans because they are not Portuguese. To be everything, in every way, because truth does not exist if it lacks anything! [22]

Yet some people have gone further in the interpretation of *Mensagem*. Onésimo de Almeida maintains that the myth you put forward there, even though it is cloaked in hermetic elements, is a rational creation. He says that you, believing, like Carlyle, that the poet is the greatest of heroes and a driving force in the civilizing process of a people, have made a conscious decision to adapt to the Portuguese situation the myth of the general strike put forward by Georges Sorel. It does not matter to you that the Fifth Empire is in fact unattainable: the important thing is to set in motion, by means of the myth, a dynamic process favourable to acts of redemption.

There is only one sort of propaganda capable of raising a nation's morale – the building up or renewal and then the spread of a great national myth. Humanity instinctively hates the truth, because this same instinct tells it that there is no truth, or that the truth is out of reach. The world is conduct-ed by means of lies; anyone who wants to arouse or lead it has to lie outra-geously, and he will be even more successful if he lies to himself and persuades himself of the truth of the lie he has invented. Fortunately we have the Sebastianist myth, which has deep roots in the past and in the souls of the Portuguese. So our task was easier; we did not have to create a myth, it was enough to renew it. If this were done by each one of us individually and within himself, the dream would easily spread in whatever we said or wrote, and the right atmosphere would then be created for all the others to breathe it like us. Then there would arise, in the soul of the Nation, the unforeseeable phenomenon that would engender the New Discoveries, the New World, the Fifth Empire. King Sebastian would be back. [23]

It seems to me that that gives credibility to the comment of Patrick Quillier, when he compares you, *mutatis mutandis*, to President Kennedy when he designated 'new frontiers' to his country at the beginning of the 1960s. Of course, the 'new frontiers' you talk about in *Mensagem* are not physical or technological – we are not talking about getting to the moon...

The future social structure of the Portuguese race will be something at once religious and political, democratic and aristocratic, linked to the pre-sent formula of civilization and to another, new one. This formula must dis-tance itself from Christianity, and from Catholicism in particular, in matters of religion; from modern democracy in all its guises in matters of politics; from the radical commercialism and materialism of modern life in matters of civilization in general.

And our great race will set off in search of a new India which has no spa-cial existence, in ships made from the stuff of dreams. And its true destiny, its supreme destiny, of which the work of the navigators was only the dim earthly prelude, will be realized providentially. [24]

The time granted to us for this interview is coming to an end and I should like to ask you one last question. If you had managed to publish the *Book of Disquietude* in your lifetime and had suggested to Bernardo Soares that he should dedicate it to Prince Henry the Navigator, that emble-matic figure you so much admire, how would you see that dedication?

Sir, your ships never made a more important voyage than that accom-plished by my thought in the course of this book. Your initiative, Sir, led to the discovery of the Real World; mine will lead to the discovery of the Intellectual World. I too have finally arrived at the furthest void, at the intan-gible edge of the limit of being, at the uncertain door of the remote abyss of the World. I passed through that door, Sir. I sailed, Sir, on that sea. I con-templated, Sir, that invisible abyss. Invoking your Portuguese name, I lay this work of supreme Discovery before you, the creator of the Argonauts. [25]

'Supreme Discovery', you said. So there is no contradiction between *Mensagem* and the *Book of Disquietude*. On the contrary, there is in all your work an essential coherence, for, from beginning to end, the breath of adventure blows over it, that interior adventure that you have persistently tried to transform so that it is not just individual but Portuguese, not Portuguese but European, and not European but universal. Fifty-six years after leaving this world you seem to have managed it.

Thank you, Mr Pessoa. I'll leave you to return to your celestial café table and get on with your never-ending writing. By the way: if you see him, give my good wishes to the engineer Álvaro de Campos.

The texts of Pessoa's 'answers' above were taken from vols. II and III of Pessoa's *Obra Poética e em Prosa* organized by António Quadros (Oporto: Lello & Irmão, 1986), as follows: (1) II, p. 78; (2) II, pp. 176-177; (3) II, p. 177; (5) II, p. 178; (6) II, p 304; (7) II, p. 218; (8) II, pp. 218-219; (9) II, p. 223; (10) II, p. 220; (11-12-13) III, p. 702; (14) III, p. 954; (15) III, p. 989; (16) III, p. 944; (17) III, pp. 953-954; (18) III, pp. 989-990; (19) II, p. 1304; (20) III, pp. 702-703; (21) II, pp.1341-1342; (22) III, pp. 703-704; (23) III, p. 710; (24) II, pp. 1194-1195. Text (4) was published for the first time by Maria Aliete Galhoz in Pessoa's *Obra Poética* (Rio de Janeiro: Aguilar, 1960). Text (25) was taken from Teresa Sobral Cunha's version of *Livro do Desassossego*, vol. I, p. 214 (Lisbon: Prescença, 1990).

PROSE

Selected by
Eugenio Lisboa, Helder Macedo & L.C. Taylor
Translated by
Bernard McGuirk & Maria Manuel Lisboa

CONTENTS

EDITORIAL CONVENTIONS USED IN THE PROSE SECTION:

Most of the texts of Pessoa's prose have been taken from three source books which, for the sake of brevity, have been abbreviated to initials, as follows:

PDE = Fernando Pessoa. Páginas de Doutrina Estética, selecção, prefácio e notas de Jorge de Sena, Editorial Inquérito, Lisboa 1946
PIAI = Fernando Pessoa. Páginas Íntimas e de Auto-Interpretação. Textos estabelecidos e prefaciados por Georg Rudolf Lind e Jacinto do Prado Coelho, Edições Ática, Lisboa 1966
PETCL= Fernando Pessoa. Páginas de Estética e de Teoria e Crítica Literárias. Textos estabelecidos e prefaciados por Georg Rudolf Lind e Jacinto do Prado Coelho, Edições Ática, Lisbos 1967

Sources other than above are given in full.

Most of the texts were written by Pessoa in Portuguese and have here been translated; quite a few, however, Pessoa wrote in English. These are indicated by a heading: [*Original in English*].
    Some titles are Pessoa's own and these are shown in roman type; other titles, provided by the editors, are set in italic type.

Pessoa's texts are often incomplete, with alternatives he intended to consider, or gaps he meant to fill, or discontinuities and doubts left for future revision. Such uncertainties in the source materials are indicated by *round* brackets. Interventions by the present editors – for example, cuts to shorten a text for this edition – are shown in *square* brackets.

ON HIMSELF

A tendency to mystification   [Original in English]

THE EARLIEST LITERARY FOOD OF MY CHILDHOOD
was in the numerous novels of mystery and of horrible adventure. These
books, which are called boys' books and deal with exciting experiences I
cared little for. With a healthy and natural life I was out of sympathy. My
craving was not for the probable, but for the incredible, not even for the
impossible by the degree, but for the impossible by nature.

My childhood was quiet (...), my education was good. But since I have
consciousness of myself, I have perceived in myself an inborn tendency to
mystification, to artistic lying. Add to this a great love of the spiritual, of
the mysterious, of the obscure, which, after all, was but a form and a variation of that other characteristic of mine, and my personality is, to intuition,
complete.   [source: PIAI]

No soul more loving, or lonely   [Original in English]

NO SOUL MORE LOVING OR TENDER THAN MINE HAS
ever existed, no soul so full of kindness, of pity, of all the things of tenderness and of love. Yet no soul is so lonely as mine – not lonely, be it noted,
from exterior, but from interior circumstances. I mean this: together with
my great tenderness and kindness an element of an entirely opposite kind
entered into my character, an element of sadness, of self-centredness, of
selfishness therefore, whose effect is two-fold: to warp and hinder the
development and full *internal* play of those other qualities, and to hinder,
by affecting the will depressingly, their full *external* play, their manifestation. I shall analyse this, one day I shall examine better, discriminate, the
elements of my character, for my curiosity of all things, linked to my
curiosity for myself and for my own character, leads to one attempt to
understand my personality.   [Dated 30.10.08. Source: PIAI]

A spirit of hesitancy and doubt   [Original in English]

IT IS NECESSARY NOW THAT I SHOULD TELL WHAT
manner of man I am. My name, it matters not, nor any other outward
detail particular to me. Of my character aught must be said.

The whole constitution of my spirit is one of hesitancy and of doubt.
Nothing is or can be positive to me; all things oscillate round me, and I with
them, an uncertainty unto myself. All for me is incoherence and change.
All is mystery and all is meaning. *All things are 'unknown' symbolic of the
Unknown.* Consequently horror, mystery, over-intelligent fear.

By my own natural tendencies, by the surroundings of my earliest life, by the influence of studies undertaken under the impulse of them (these very tendencies), by all this I am of the internal species of character, self-centred, mute, not self-sufficing but self-lost. All my life has been one of passiveness and of dream. All my character consists in the hatred, in the horror of, in the incapacity pervading all that is me, physically and mentally, for decisive acts, for definite thoughts. I had never a resolution born of a self-command, never an external betraying of a conscious will. My writings were none of them finished; new thoughts intruded ever, extraordinary, inexcludable associations of ideas bearing infinity for term. I cannot prevent my thought's hatred of finish; about a single thing ten thousand thoughts, and ten thousand inter-associations of these ten thousand thoughts arise, and I have no will to eliminate or to arrest these, nor to gather them into one central thought, where their unimportant but associated details may be lost. They pass in me; they are not my thoughts, but thoughts that pass through me. I do not ponder, I dream; I am not inspired, I rave. I can paint, but I have never painted; I can compose music, but I have never composed. Strange conceptions in three arts, lovely strokes of imagining caress my brain; but I let them slumber there till they die, for I have not power to give them their body, to make them things of the world outside.

My character of mind is such that I hate the beginnings and the ends of things, for they are definite points. The idea of a solution being found for problems the highest, the noblest, of science, of philosophy, afflicts me; that aught might be determined of God or of the world horrorizes me. That things of most moment should be accomplished, that men should one day all be happy, that a solution might be found to the ills of society, even in its conception maddens me. Yet I am not evil nor cruel; I am mad and that as it is difficult to conceive.

Though I have been a reader voracious and ardent, yet I remember no book that I have read, so far were my reading states of my own mind, dreams of my own, nay, provocations of dreams. My very memory of events, of external things is vague, more than incoherent. I shudder to think how little I have in mind of what my past life has been. I, the man who holds that to-day is a dream, am less than a thing of to-day.

[*source*: PIAI]

Fear of Insanity   [*Original in English*]

ONE OF MY MENTAL COMPLICATIONS – HORRIBLE beyond words – is a fear of insanity, which itself is insanity. I am partly in that state betrayed as his by Rollinat in the opening poem (I think) of his '*Névroses*'. Impulses, criminal some, insane others, reaching, amid my agony, a horrible tendency to action, a terrible *muscularity*, felt in the muscles, I mean – these are common with me and the horror of them and of their intensity – greater than ever now both in number and in intensity – cannot be described.   [Dated 30.10.08. *Source*: PIAI]

My inner sense predominates   [*Original in English*]

I WAS A POET ANIMATED BY PHILOSOPHY, NOT A philosopher with poetic faculties. I loved to admire the beauty of things, to trace in the imperceptible through the minute the poetic soul of the universe.

The poetry of the earth is never dead. We may say that ages gone have been more poetic, but we can say (...)

Poetry is in everything – in land and in sea, in lake and in riverside. It is in the city too – deny it not – it is evident to me here as I sit: there is poetry in this table, in this paper, in this inkstand; there is poetry in the rattling of the cars on the streets, in each minute, common, ridiculous motion of a workman, who the other side of the street is painting the sign-board of a butcher's shop.

Mine inner sense predominates in such a way over my five senses that I see things in this life – I do believe it – in a way different from other men. There is for me – there was – a wealth of meaning in a thing so ridiculous as a door-key, a nail on a wall, a cat's whiskers. There is to me a fulness of spiritual suggestion in a fowl with its chickens strutting across the road. There is to me a meaning deeper than human fears in the smell of sandalwood, in the old tins on a dirt heap, in a match box lying in the gutter, in two dirty papers which, on a windy day, will roll and chase each other down the street. For poetry is astonishment, admiration, as of a being fallen from the skies taking full consciousness of his fall, astonished about things. As of one who knew things in their souls, striving to remember this knowledge, remembering that it was not thus he knew them, not under these forms and these conditions, but remembering nothing more.

[*Source*: PIAI]

Formative reading

LETTER TO JOSÉ OSORIO DE OLIVEIRA, EDITOR[1]. I received your question five minutes ago: 'Which are the books which have

---

[1] The editor of the *Diário de Lisboa* wrote to some leading writers in 1933 asking about their reading. Pessoa's answer was not published until 29 May 1936, after his death.

bathed you in a more intense atmosphere of moral energy, generosity, greatness of soul, idealism?' As you can see, I reply at once. You tell me that it is a question posed by António Sérgio, whom I do not know personally, but for whom I have the highest regard. It is all the more reason to reply speedily; it is not however, a reason for being lucid or explicit, seeing as it is a subject upon which, until now, I have not reflected.

As, however, in all the difficulties of life, it behoves one always to act before thinking, I will answer before I know what I am saying, and the reply will therefore bear the royal stamp of sincerity.

I pose a preliminary question. The terms of the question presuppose that moral energy, generosity, greatness of soul and idealism are abstract persons in my daily life. Unfortunately, or fortunately, they are not. I do not imply I am not acquainted with them, but I do not know them as intimately as I do whimsicality, insincerity and absurdity – sometimes even logical raving, which has been one of my main exteriorizations.

I translate the question, therefore, into the following: 'Which are the books which have most transfigured me in myself into that different person which we all wish to be?' As regards this, I have an answer – the one, instantaneous and unthought out, to which I refer above, and which ought to contain the real one.

In my childhood and early adolescence there was for me, living and being brought up in English lands, a supreme and all-absorbing book – *The Pickwick Papers*, by Dickens; even now, and for that reason, I read and re-read it as though doing no more than remembering.

In my adolescence Shakespeare and Milton dominated my mind, as well as, albeit subsidiaries, those English Romantic poets who are their irregular shadows; among these Shelley was perhaps the one with whose inspiration I most closely interacted.

In what I may call my third adolescence, spent here in Lisbon, I lived in the atmosphere of the Greek and German philosophers, as well as that of the French Decadents, whose impact was swept from my mind by Swedish gymnastics and by the reading of Nordau's *Dégénérescence*.

After this, any book that I read, be it prose or verse, reason or emotion, be it a meditation upon the fourth dimension or a detective novel, it is, in the moment of reading it, the only thing I have read. They all have an overriding importance which disappears the following day.

This reply is entirely sincere. If it apparently contains a trace of paradox, the paradox is not my own: it is I.   [*Source*: PDE]

Enough of reading!   [*Original in English*]

I HAVE OUTGROWN THE HABIT OF READING. I NO LONGER read anything except occasional newspapers, light literature and casual books technical to any matter I may be studying and in which simple reasoning may be insufficient.

The definite type of literature I have almost dropped. I could read it for learning or for pleasure. But I have nothing to learn, and the pleasure to be drawn from books is of a type that can with profit be substituted by that which the contact with nature and the observation of life can directly give me.

I am now in full possession of the fundamental laws of literary art. Shakespeare can no longer teach me to be subtle, nor Milton to be complete. My intellect has attained a pliancy and a reach that enable me to assume any emotion I desire and enter at will into any state of mind. For that which it is ever an effort and an anguish to strive for, completeness, no book at all can be an aid.

This does not mean that I have shaken off the tyranny of the literary art. I have but assumed it only under submission to myself.

I have one book ever by me – *Pickwick Papers*. I have read Mr W.W. Jacobs' books several times over. The decay of the detective story has closed for ever one door I had into modern writing.

I have ceased to be interested in merely clever people – Wells, Chesterton, Shaw. The ideas these people have are such as occur to many non-writers; the construction of their works is wholly a negative quantity.

There was a time when I read only for the use of reading. I now have understood that there are very few useful books, even in such technical matters as I can be interested in.

Sociology is wholesale (...); who can stand this scholasticism in the Byzantium of to-day?

All my books are books of reference. I read Shakespeare only in relation to the *Shakespeare Problem*: the rest I know already.

I have found out that reading is a slavish sort of dreaming. If I must dream, why not my own dreams?   [*Source*: PIAI]

Planning Publication (1)

LETTER TO ADOLFO CASAIS MONTEIRO, 13 JANUARY 1935[1]:

[1] Adolf Casais Monteiro questioned Pessoa about three distinct subjects: (a) his publication plans – dealt with here; (b) the advent of the heteronyms – Pessoa's answer appears in the appropriate section, on p214; (c) Pessoa's beliefs in the occult – see p269.

Many thanks for your letter, to which I will reply immediately and in full. Before actually beginning, I would like to apologise for writing on this rough paper. I have run out of the proper one, it is Sunday and I can find no other. But better bad paper, I believe, than a delay.

First of all, I would like to tell you that I would never perceive 'other reasons' in anything that you might write, in disagreement, about me. I am one of the few Portuguese poets who has not decreed his own infallibility, or who sees any criticism of himself as an act of *lèse*-divinity. In any case, be my mental flaws as they may, I have no trace of a persecution complex. Apart from that, I am sufficiently aware of your intellectual independence, which, if I may say so, I greatly approve of and praise. I never proposed to be Master or Leader – Master because I do not know how to teach, nor whether I would have anything to teach; Leader because I do not even know how to boil an egg. Do not worry, therefore, under any circumstances, with regard to anything you might have to say about me. I do not look for dungeons in penthouses.

I entirely agree with you in saying that my choice of début with a book such as *Mensagem* [Message], was not a happy one. I am, in point of fact, a mystical nationalist, a rational Sebastianist. But I am also, apart from that, and even in opposition to it, many other things. And those things, because of the very nature of the book, are not included in *Mensagem*.

I began my publications with that book for the simple reason that it was the first book which, I know not why, I managed to have organized and ready for press. As it was ready, I was encouraged to publish it: I agreed. Nor did I do it, I am bound to say, with a view to the possibility of the Secretariat prize, although if I had, this would not imply a significant intellectual sin. My book was ready in September, and I actually thought that I was ineligible for the prize, since I was unaware that the deadline for the submission of the book, originally the end of July, had been extended until the end of October. As, however, by the end of October there were already printed copies of *Mensagem*, I submitted the number the Secretariat required. The book fell exactly within the conditions (nationalism) of the competition. I entered it.

When I sometimes considered the order of a future publication of my works, a book such as *Mensagem* never figured as first. I hesitated as to whether I ought to start with a long book of poetry – some 350 pages long – encompassing the various personalities of Fernando Pessoa himself, or whether I ought to open proceedings with a detective story, which I have not yet managed to complete.

I agree with you, I said, in that the choice of first publication of *Mensagem* was not a happy one. But I agree with the fact that it was the best début I could make. Precisely because that facet – in a way secondary

– of my personality had never been sufficiently highlighted in my magazine contributions (except in the case of 'Mar Português' [Portuguese Sea] part of this same book) – precisely because of that it was convenient that it should appear, and now. It coincided, without any planning or premeditation on my part (I am incapable of pragmatic premeditation), with one of the critical moments (in the original sense of the word) of the reshaping of the national subconscious. What I did by chance, and was completed in conversation, was exactly patterned with Square rule and Compasses, by the Great Architect.

(I interrupt here. I am neither insane nor drunk. I am, however, writing off the top of my head, as fast as my typewriter allows, and I draw upon expressions that come to me, without any regard to their literariness. Imagine – and you will be right in doing so, because it is true – that I am simply talking to you.)

I now answer directly your three questions: (1) Future plan for the publication of my works; (2) The genesis of my heteronyms; and (3) Occultism.

Having accomplished, under the circumstances I outlined to you, the publication of *Mensagem*, which is a unilateral manifestation, I intend to proceed as follows. I am now completing an entirely rewritten version of 'Banqueiro Anarquista' [The Anarchist Banker] it should be ready soon, and I intend, as soon as it is, to publish it at once. If I do so, I will immediately translate it into English, and I will try and see whether I can get it published in England. Such as I envisage it, it has European potential. (Don't take this in the sense of an imminent Nobel Prize.) Then – and now I shall actually answer your question, which addresses itself to poetry – I intend, over the summer, to compile that long volume I mentioned, of the short poems of Fernando Pessoa himself, and see whether I can get it published towards the end of the present year. That will very likely be the volume you expect, and it is the one I myself wish to bring out. That one, then, will incorporate all the facets, except the nationalistic one, which *Mensagem* already expressed.

I referred, as you can see, exclusively to Fernando Pessoa. I think nothing about Caeiro, Ricardo Reis or Álvaro de Campos. I can do nothing about their publication except when (see above) I am awarded the Nobel Prize. And however – I think it with sadness – I put into Caeiro all my power of dramatic depersonalization, I put into Ricardo Reis all my mental discipline, clothed in the music which belongs to it, I put in Álvaro de Campos all the emotion which I give neither to myself nor to life. To think, my dear Casais Monteiro, that all these must, in the practicalities of publication, give way to Fernando Pessoa, impure and simple!

I believe I have replied to your first question*. If I omitted something, let me know what. If I am able to answer I will. I have no further plans for the moment. And, knowing as I do what my plans are, and what their outcome tends to be, there are grounds for saying, Praise Be to God!

(source: PDE)

Planning publication (2)

LETTER TO ADOLFO CASAIS MONTEIRO, 20 JANUARY 1935: Many thanks for your letter. I am glad I managed to say something that really interested you. I actually began to doubt I had, due to the hasty and rushed manner in which I wrote to you, in the rhythm of the mental chat I was having with you.

I reply and with equal spontaneity, therefore lack of method and order, to your letter just arrived. But at least I give some sort of answer. I answer the various points in random order.

As regards your study of me, for which I first of all thank you, for the honour it represents: delay it until after I have published the long book gathering the vast orthonymous work of Fernando Pessoa. Barring any unexpected complication, I should have the book ready and in print in October of this year. And then you will have sufficient data: that book, the subsidiary aspect embodied in *Mensagem* [*Message*], and the substantial body, already published, by the heteronyms. With this you will already be able to grasp an 'impression of the whole', supposing, that is, that I have in me something as outlined as a whole.

In all this, I refer simply to the poetry, I am not however constrained to that smile of the world of letters. But, as regards the prose, you already know me, and what is published is enough. By that date, which I indicate as probable for the publication of the longer book 'O Banqueiro Anarquista' (newly re-written and formatted), a detective story (which I am writing and which is not the one to which I referred in my previous letter), and other odd pieces which circumstances may suggest, ought to be published.

Your observation concerning the lack in me of anything that might legitimately be called evolution of any kind is extraordinarily perceptive. There are poems of mine, written when I was twenty, which are the equals in merit – in so far as I can judge – of the ones I am writing at present. I do not write better now, except in as far as my knowledge of the Portuguese language is concerned – a cultural factor, not a poetic one. I write differently. Maybe the solution to this lies in the following.

What I am in essence – behind the involuntary masks of the poet, the thinker, and whatever else there might be – is a playwright. The phenomenon of my depersonalization, to which I alluded in my previous letter, in the explanation of the heteronyms, leads naturally to that definition. That being the case, I do not evolve, I TRAVEL. (A slip towards the capital letters key led to that word being typed in upper case. This is right, therefore I will leave it as it is.) I progressively change personalities, I (here maybe there is evolution) progressively enrich myself in the capacity to create new personalities, new ways of pretending I understand the world, or rather, of pretending one can understand it. Therefore I referred to that progress in me as comparable not to an evolution, but to a voyage: I did not ascend from one level to another; I moved on, on a single plane, from one place to another. It is true that I lost certain simplicities and naïveties from my adolescent poems; that, however, is not evolution, only ageing.

I believe these hasty words have conveyed a glimpse of a clear idea of that in which I agree with you and accept your criterion that there has been no evolution as such in me.

I refer now to the eventuality of the publication of books of mine in a near future. There is no cause for you to worry about difficulties in that sphere. If I really want to publish Caeiro, Ricardo Reis and Álvaro de Campos, I can do so immediately. But in fact I fear the commercial unviability of books of that kind and type. That is the only reason for my hesitation. As for the long poetry volume, that one, like any other, already has a guarantee of publication. If I place more emphasis on that one that on any other, it is because I find greater mental advantages in its publication, and, despite everything, less risk of failure in its publication.

As for the publication of *O Banqueiro Anarquista* [The Anarchist Banker] in English, in that respect, too, I believe, albeit for other reasons, I do not foresee any insurmountable difficulties. If the work carries any potential interest for the English market, the literary agent to whom I intend to send it will place it sooner or later. It will not be necessary to resort to the support of Richard Aldington, a reference for which I nevertheless thank you. Literary agents (to answer now your question as to what they are) are individuals, or firms, who refer books and other writings by authors to publishers or editors of newspapers whom they, more capably than the authors themselves, consider adequate, for a commission of usually ten per cent. With regard to this, I know what I should do and to whom I should go – something rare in me, in point of fact, in any practical circumstance of life.

Fondest regards from your comrade, friend and admirer.   [*Source*: PDE]

Planning publication (3)

LETTER TO GASPAR SIMÕES 28 JULY 1932 [...] I AM BEginning – slowly, since it is not something I can do quickly – to classify and re-read my papers: with a view to publishing towards the end of the present year, one or two books. They will probably both be poetry, since I do not think I will be able to prepare anything else in the near future, by preparing meaning of course having it the way I want it.

Originally, my intention was to begin my publications with three books, in the following order: (1) 'Portugal' [working title for *Mensagem*] of which 'Mar Português' (*Contemporânea*) constitutes the second part; (2) 'The Book of Disquietude' (Bernardo Soares, but subsidiarily, since B.S. is not a heteronym but a literary persona); (3) 'The Complete Poems of Alberto Caeiro' (with the preface by Ricardo Reis, and, as a postface, the 'Notes in Remembrance' by Álvaro de Campos). Later, the following year, there would follow, on its own or with any other book, 'Song-book' (or any other equally unexpressive title), in which I would gather (in Books I to III or I to IV) several of my many loose poems, which besides are by nature unclassifiable except in that unexpressible fashion.

As it happens, however, 'The Book of Disquietude' needs much balancing and revision, so that I cannot decently estimate the time it will take me to do so as much under a year. As for Caeiro, I remain undecided. It also needs some revision, but not much. Apart from that one could say that it is completed, although some of the 'Uncollected Poems' and one or two of the alteration notes to be carried out in the first Guardador de Rebanhos [Keeper of Flocks] are scattered amongst my papers. Once these scattered elements are found, however, the book can be quickly finished. It has one disadvantage – the near impossibility of its success, which entails its publication at the cost of material sacrifice. The material sacrifice will depend, of course, upon my financial situation at that moment. In any case, in the course of this revision and classification of my papers, I am gradually finding, and tidying up, what belongs to Caeiro.

I do not know whether I have ever told you that the heteronyms (according to my last resolution with regard to them) are to be published by me, under my own name (it is already too late, and therefore absurd to think of a perfect disguise). They will constitute a series called 'Ficções de Interlúdio', [Fictions of the Interlude] or anything better which might occur to me. Thus the title of the first volume would be, more or less: 'Fernando Pessoa: Ficções do Interlúdio' – 'Poemas Completos de Alberto Caeiro (1889-1915)'. And the following ones along the same lines, including one, singular but very difficult to write, which contains the aesthetic debate between myself, Ricardo Reis and Álvaro de Campos, and perhaps, still, other heteronyms, since there are still a few others (including an astrologer) yet to appear.

Most probably, in fact, as regards the first book of the heteronyms. I will include in it not only Caeiro and the 'Notas' by Álvaro de Campos, but also some three to five books from the 'Odes' by Ricardo Reis. The volume will therefore contain what is essential for an understanding of the inauguration of the 'school', the works of the Master and a few of the direct disciples, including (in the 'Notas') already some by the other disciple. This involves also a purely material factor, which leads me to decide upon a volume of this nature: if I included only Caeiro and the 'Notas', the book would be neither short (like 'Portugal') nor average length (more or less 300 pages), like 'Cancioneiro'. With the inclusion, which, as I explained, is after all reasonable, of Ricardo Reis, the volume attains a normal length.

My possibly professional intention at the moment is to publish, if I can this year or early next year, 'Portugal' and the 'Cancioneiro'. The former is nearly ready and it is a book which has possibilities of success unlike any of the others. The latter is ready: all that remains is selection and re-arrangement.

As I know that these things do not bore you, and as, in a way, all this constitutes a reply (a rather long one in fact) to your remark regarding my date of publication I have not refrained from writing at length.

Along with everything I have said, I have possibly two or three pamphlets or extended articles to be done or in progress. The likelihood is that although they will be written in Portuguese, I will translate them into English and publish them first (possibly in a magazine) in England. All this, however, is up in the air.

An embrace from your fond friend and admirer.   [*Source*: PDE]

THE HETERONYMS

The Advent of the Heteronyms

LETTER TO ADOLF CASAIS MONTEIRO, 13 JANUARY 1935
[...] I will move on to your question[1] about the genesis of my heteronyms. I will attempt to answer it fully. I begin with the psychiatric part. The origin of my heteronym lies in the deep streak of hysteria which exists in me. I do not know whether I am simply a hysteric, or whether I am more accurately a hysterico-neurasthenic. I incline towards the latter hypothesis, because there are in me phenomena of abulia which do not figure in the archive of symptoms of hysteria itself. Be that as it may, the psychic origin of my heteronyms lies in my organic and constant tendency towards depersonalization and simulation. These phenomena – luckily for myself and for others – were cerebralized in me; that is to say, they do not manifest themselves in my day-to-day life, externally and in my contact with others; they explode inwardly and I experience them entirely within myself. If I were a woman – in women hysterical phenomena erupt in fits and the like – each poem of Álvaro de Campos (the most hysterically hysterical of myself) would scare the neighbours. But I am a man – and in men hysteria assumes mainly mental aspects: therefore everything ends in silence and poetry...

This explains, *tant bien que mal*, the organic origin of my heteronymism. I will now tell you the actual history of my heteronyms. I will begin with those that have died, and of some I no longer remember – those who remain lost in the remote past of my almost forgotten childhood.

Since childhood I have had the tendency to create around me a fictitious world, to surround myself with friends and acquaintances who never existed. (I am not sure, it goes without saying, whether they indeed did not exist, or whether it is I who do not exist. In this, as in all else, we ought not to be dogmatic.) Ever since I have known myself as that which I call me, I recall needing, psychologically, in outline, movements, character and history, various unreal figures who were as visible and as mine, in my eyes, as those things which, possibly abusively, we call real life. This tendency, which came to me ever since I recollect being a self, has always accompanied me, slightly altering the type of music with which it enchants me, but never altering the nature of its spell.

I remember, thus, what seems to me to have been my first heteronym, or rather, my first inexistent acquaintance – a certain Chevalier de Pas when I was about six, on whose behalf I wrote letters to myself, and whose appearance, not entirely hazy, still has a hold on that part of my affections which borders upon *saudade* [nostalgia]. I recall, less clearly, another figure whose name I can no longer remember, also foreign, and who was, in

---

[1] See footnote on p206

some forgotten way, the rival of Chevalier de Pas... Things that happen to all children? Undoubtedly – or perhaps. But I lived them to such an extent that I still live them, since I recollect them with such intensity that an effort is necessary to make me conscious that they were not realities.

This tendency to create around me another world, equal to this one but with other people, never abandoned my imagination. It went through phases, among them the following, in adulthood: a witticism would occur to me, for one reason or another entirely alien to what I am, or what I think I am. I would say it immediately, spontaneously, as belonging to a certain friend of mine, whose name I would invent, whose history I would add, and whose appearance – face, stature, dress and gesture – I immediately saw in front of me. In this way I made and made known several friends and acquaintances who never existed, but even now, thirty years on, I hear, feel, see. I repeat, I hear, feel, see... And I miss them.

(Once I start talking – and typing for me is talking – I find it difficult to stop. Enough of boring you, Casais Monteiro! I will start on the genesis of my literary heteronyms, which is, after all, what you want to know. In any case, the above gives you the history of the mother who gave birth to them.)

Around 1912, if I am not mistaken (and I am probably not too much mistaken), it occurred to me to write some poems of pagan character. I sketched some lines in irregular metre (not in the style of Álvaro de Campos, but in a semi-regular style), and I gave it up. There sketchily appeared, however, in an undefined twilight, a vague portrait of the person who was doing that. (Without my knowledge, Ricardo Reis had been born.)

A year and a half or two years later, it occurred to me one day to play a prank on Sá-Carneiro – to invent a bucolic poet of convoluted character, and introduce him. I cannot remember how, in some kind of reality. I spent a few days elaborating the poet but I achieved nothing. On a day when I had finally given up – it was 8 March 1914 – I drew near a tall chest of drawers, and, taking up pen and paper, I began to write, standing up, as I do whenever possible. And I wrote thirty-odd poems in one go, in a kind of trance whose nature I cannot define. It was the triumphant day of my life, and it would be impossible again to experience such a one. I opened with a title, 'Guardador de Rebanhos' [Keeper of Flocks]. What followed was the appearance of someone in me, to whom I at once gave the name Alberto Caeiro. Forgive the absurdity of this sentence: my master had appeared inside me. That was my immediate sensation. So much so that, once those thirty-odd poems were written, I picked up another sheet of paper and wrote, again uninterruptedly, the six poems which constitute the 'Chuva Oblíqua' [Oblique Rain] by Fernando Pessoa. Immediately and totally... It was the return of Fernando Pessoa/Alberto Caeiro to Fernando Pessoa himself. Or rather, it was the reaction of Fernando Pessoa against his inexistence as Alberto Caeiro.

With Alberto Caeiro come into being, I went about discovering for him – instinctively and unconsciously – some disciples. From his false paganism I dragged out the latent Ricardo Reis, found him a name and adjusted him to himself, because at that stage I could already *see* him. And suddenly, in antithetical derivation to the origin of Ricardo Reis, a new individual burst impetuously on the scene. In one fell swoop, at the typewriter, without any hesitation or correction, there appeared the 'Ode Triunfal' [Triumphal Ode] by Álvaro de Campos – the ode of that name and the man with the name he now has.

I created, therefore, an inexistent *coterie*. I sorted out the influences, traced the friendships, listened, inside myself, to the debates and the differences in criteria, and in all this it seemed to me that I, the creator of it all, was the lesser presence. It seemed that it all happened independently of me. And so it still seems to me. If one day I am able to publish the aesthetic discussion between Ricardo Reis and Álvaro de Campos, you will see how different they are, and how I count for nothing in it.

On the occasion of *Orpheu*'s publication, it was necessary to find some last minute material to fill the required number of pages. I suggested to Sá-Carneiro writing an 'old' poem by Álvaro de Campos – a poem of how Álvaro de Campos would have been before he met Caeiro and fell under his influence. It was in this way I wrote 'Opiário', in which I tried to convey all the latent tendencies of Álvaro de Campos, as they would subsequently burgeon, but still without any trace of contact with his master Caeiro. Of all the poems I have written, it was the most laborious one, in view of the dual power of depersonalization which I had to generate. Still, I think it wasn't bad, and that it conveys Álvaro de Campos in embryo...

I believe I have explained the origin of my heteronyms. If there is still anything concerning which you require more lucid clarification – I am writing fast, and when I write fast I am not clear-sighted – tell me and I will gladly supply it. Oh, and one more thing, a real hysterical complement: while writing certain parts of the 'Notas para recordação do meu Mestre Caeiro' [Notes for the Memoir of my Master Caeiro], by Álvaro de Campos, I have cried real tears. Just so you know who your are dealing with, my dear Casais Monteiro!

A few more notes on the subject... I *see* in front of me, in the colourless but real space of dreams, the faces, the gestures of Caeiro, Ricardo Reis and Álvaro de Campos. I made up their ages and lives. Ricardo Reis was born in 1887 (I don't remember the date and the month, but I have them somewhere), in Porto, he is a doctor and is at present in Brazil. Alberto

Caeiro was born in 1889 and died in 1915; he was born in Lisbon, but he lived almost his entire life in the country. He had no profession and hardly any education. Álvaro de Campos was born in Tavira, on 15 October 1890 (at 1.30 in the afternoon, according to Ferreira Gomes; and he is right, since the horoscope for that hour is correct). As you know, he is a naval engineer (a graduate of Glasgow), but at present he is here in Lisbon, unemployed. Caeiro was of medium height, and, although truly fragile (he died of tuberculosis), he did not seem as fragile as he was. Ricardo Reis is slightly, very slightly shorter, more heavily built, but wiry. Álvaro de Campos is tall (1.75 metres, 2 cms more than me), thin and with a tendency to stoop. All clean-shaven – Caeiro blonde and pale, blue eyes; Reis a sallow dark complexion; Campos somewhere between fair and dark, vaguely the type of the Portuguese Jew, straight hair, however, side parting, eyeglass. Caeiro, as I have said, had hardly any education whatsoever – only primary school; his father and mother died early, and he remained at home, living off a small income. He lived with an old great-aunt. Ricardo Reis, brought up in a Jesuit college, is, as I said, a doctor; he has lived in Brazil since 1919, in self-imposed exile, because he is a monarchist. He is a Latinist through external influences, and a semi-Hellenist through being self-taught. Álvaro de Campos had a normal high school education; then he was sent to Scotland to study engineering, first mechanical and then naval. In one of the vacations he went on a trip to the East, which gave rise to *Opiário*. He was taught Latin by an uncle from the Beiras, who was a priest.

How do I write in the name of these three?... Caeiro out of pure and unexpected inspiration, without knowing or even suspecting that I am about to write. Ricardo Reis after abstract deliberation, suddenly given substance in an ode. Campos when I feel a sudden urge to write, and I know not what. (My semi-heteronym, Bernardo Soares, who actually resembles Álvaro de Campos in many aspects, appears whenever I am tired or sleepy, in order that he may have the traits of reasoning and inhibition slightly suspended; his prose is constantly wandering. He is a semi-heteronym because, while his personality is not my own, it is not different from mine, but merely a mutilated version of it. He is myself but without the same powers of reasoning or of the affections. His prose-style, excluding the haziness which reasoning gives to mine, is the same as this one, and the language is in everything alike; whereas Caeiro wrote bad Portuguese, Campos was not bad but had slips such as saying 'me myself' rather than 'I myself', etc., Reis better than me, but with a purism which I regard as exaggerated. The most difficult thing for me is to write the prose of Reis – still unpublished – or that of Campos. Simulation is easier, even because more spontaneous, in the case of poetry.)

At this point you must be cursing the bad luck which has dropped you, through reading, into a madhouse. In any case, the worst part of all this is the incoherence with which I have written it. I repeat, however: I write as if I were speaking to you, in order that I may write immediately. Otherwise months would elapse without my succeeding in writing anything [...]

[*Source*: PDE]

Caeiro, Reis, and Campos compared

[*Original in English*]

TO WHOM CAN CAEIRO BE COMPARED [...] EVEN IF WE think of him as a man who lives outside civilization (an impossible hypothesis, of course), as a man of an exceptionally clear vision of things, that does not logically produce in our minds a result resembling *The Keeper of Sheep*. The very tenderness for things as mere things which characterizes the type of man we have supposed (posited) does not characterize Caeiro. He sometimes speaks tenderly of things, but he asks our pardon for doing so, explaining that he only speaks so in consideration of our 'stupidity of sense', to make us feel 'the absolutely real existence' of things. Left to himself, he has no tenderness for things, he has hardly any tenderness even for his sensations. Here we touch his great originality, his almost inconceivable objectiveness (objectivity). He sees things with the eyes only, not with the mind. He does not let any thoughts arise when he looks at a flower. Far from seeing sermons in stones, he never even lets himself conceive a stone as beginning a sermon. The only sermon a stone contains for him is that it exists. The only thing a stone tells him is that it has nothing at all to tell him. A state of mind may be conceived resembling this. *But it cannot be conceived in a poet*. This way of looking at a stone may be described as the totally unpoetic way of looking at it. The stupendous fact about Caeiro is that out of this sentiment, or rather, absence of sentiment, he makes poetry. He feels positively what hitherto could not be conceived except as a negative sentiment. Put it to yourselves: what do you think of a stone when you look at it without thinking about it? This comes to this: what do you think of a stone when you don't think about it at all? The question is quite absurd, of course. The strange point about it is that all Caeiro's poetry is based upon that sentiment that you find it impossible to represent to yourself as able to exist. Perhaps I have not been unsuccessful in pointing out the extraordinary nature of Caeiro's inspiration, the phenomenal novelty of his poetry, the astonishing unprecedentedness of his genius, of his whole attitude.

Alberto Caeiro is reported to have regretted the name of 'Sensationism' which a disciple of his – a rather queer disciple, it is true – Mr Álvaro de Campos, gave to his attitude, and to the attitude he created. If Caeiro protested against the word as possibly seeming to indicate a 'school', like Futurism, for instance, he was right, and for two reasons. For the very suggestion of schools and literary movements sounds badly when applied to so uncivilized and natural a kind of poetry. And besides, though he has at least two 'disciples', the fact is that he has had on them an influence equal to that which some poet – Cesário Verde, perhaps – had on him: neither resembles him at all, though, indeed, far more clearly than Cesário Verde's influence in him, his influence may be seen all over their work.

But the fact is – these considerations once put aside – that no name could describe his attitude better. His poetry *is* 'sensationist'. Its basis is the substitution of sensation for thought, not only as a basis of inspiration – which is comprehensible – but as a means of expression, if we may so speak. And, be it added, those two disciples of his, different as they are from him and from each other – are also indeed sensationists. For Dr Ricardo Reis, with his neo-classicism, his actual and real belief in the existence of the pagan deities, is a pure sensationist, though a different kind of sensationist. His attitude towards nature is as aggressive to thought as Caeiro's; he reads no meanings into things. He sees them only, and if he seems to see them differently from Caeiro it is because, though seeing them as unintellectually and unpoetically as Caeiro, he sees them through a definite religious concept of the universe – paganism, pure paganism, and this necessarily alters his very direct way of feeling. But he is a pagan because paganism is *the* sensationist religion. Of course, a pure and integral sensationist like Caeiro has, logically enough, no religion at all, religion not being among the immediate data of pure and direct sensation. But Ricardo Reis has put the logic of his attitude as purely sensationist very clearly. According to him, we not only should bow down to the pure objectivity of things (hence his sensationism proper, and his neo-classicism, for the classic poets were those who commented least, at least directly, upon things), but bow down to the equal objectivity, reality, naturalness of the necessities of our nature, of which the religious sentiment is one. Caeiro is the pure and absolute sensationist who bows down to sensations quâ exterior and admits no more. Ricardo Reis is less absolute; he bows down also to the primitive elements of our own nature, our primitive feelings being as real and natural to him as flowers and trees. He is therefore religious. And, seeing that he is a sensationist, he is a pagan in his religion; which is due, not only to the nature of sensation once conceived of as admitting a religion of some kind, but also to the influence of those classical readings to which his sensationism had inclined him.

Álvaro de Campos – curiously enough – is on the opposite point, entirely opposed to Ricardo Reis. Yet he is not less than the latter a disciple of Caeiro and a sensationist proper. He has accepted from Caeiro not the

essential and objective, but the deducible and subjective part of his attitude. Sensation is all, Caeiro holds, and thought is a disease. By sensation
Caeiro means the sensation of things as they are, without adding to it any
elements from personal thought, convention, sentiment or any other soul-
place. For Campos, sensation is indeed all but not necessarily sensation of
things as they are, but of things as they are felt. So that he takes sensation
subjectively and applies all his efforts, once so thinking, not to develop in
himself the sensation of things as they are, but all sorts of sensations of
things, even of the same thing. To feel is all: it is logical to conclude that the
best is to feel all sorts of things in all sorts of ways, or, as Álvaro de Campos
says himself, 'to feel everything in every way'. So he applies himself to feeling the town as much as he feels the country, the normal as he feels the
abnormal, the bad as he feels the good, the morbid as the healthy. He
never questions, he feels. He is the undisciplined child of sensation. Caeiro
has one discipline: things must be felt as they are. Ricardo Reis has another kind of discipline: things must be felt, not only as they are, but also so as
to fall in with a certain ideal of classic measure and rule. In Álvaro de
Campos things must simply be felt.

But the common origin of these three widely different aspects of the
same theory is patent and manifest.

Caeiro has no ethics except simplicity. Ricardo Reis has a pagan ethics,
half epicurean and half stoic, but a very definite ethics, which gives his
poetry an elevation that Caeiro himself, though, mastership apart, the
greater genius, cannot attain. Álvaro de Campos has no shadow of an
ethics; he is non-moral, if not positively immoral, for, of course, according
to his theory it is natural that he should love the stronger better than the
weak sensations, and the strong sensations are, at least, all selfish and
occasionally the sensations of cruelty and lust. Thus Álvaro de Campos
resembles Whitman most of the three. But he has nothing of Whitman's
camaraderie: he is always apart from the crowd, and when feeling with
them it is very clearly and very confessedly to please himself and give himself brutal sensations. The idea that a child of eight is demoralized (Ode II,
ad finem) is positively pleasant to him, for the idea of that satisfies two
very strong sensations – cruelty and lust. The most Caeiro says that may be
called immoral is that he cares nothing for what men suffer, and that the
existence of sick people is interesting because it is a fact. Ricardo Reis has
nothing of this. He lives in himself, with his pagan faith and his sad epicureanism, but one of his attitudes is precisely not to hurt anyone. He cares
absolutely nothing for others, not even enough to be interested in their
suffering or in their existence. He is moral because he is self-sufficient.

It may be said, comparing these three poets with the three orders of religious spirits, and comparing sensationism for the moment (perhaps

improperly) with a religion, that Ricardo Reis is the normal religious spirit of that faith; Caeiro the pure mystic; Álvaro de Campos the ritualist in excess. For Caeiro loses sight of Nature in nature, loses sight of sensation in sensation, loses sight of things in things. And Campos loses sight of sensation in sensations.

[Source: PIAI]

Alberto Caeiro – Translator's preface[1]

[Original in English]

AT FIRST SIGHT IT SEEMS THAT SOMETHING OF WHITman is present in these poems. I have no information as to Caeiro's knowledge of foreign languages, or of English and of Whitman particularly; yet, on the face of it, and after a very cursory reading of the poems, I suspect the first to have been, at best, very slight, and the second and third nil. However it may be, on close examination there is really no influence of Whitman here. There is at most an occasional coincidence and the coincidence is merely of tone, and more apparent therefore than real. The essential difference is enormous.

The traits common to the two poets are the love of Nature and simplicity, and the astounding acuity of sensation. But, whereas Whitman insistently reads transcendental meanings into Nature, nothing can be further from Caeiro's attitude than that; it is, as a matter of fact, the exact opposite of his attitude. And whereas Whitman's sensations are immensely various and include both natural and artificial, and the metaphysical as well as the physical, Caeiro's persistently exclude even the more 'natural artificial' things and are only metaphysical in that extremely peculiar negative manner which is one of the novelties of his attitude.

Again, Caeiro has a perfectly definite and coherent philosophy. It may not be as coherent in word and phrase as might be wished from a philosopher; but he is not a philosopher, but a poet. It may not be coherent from the outset, but it grows more and more definite as we read on till, in the final poems of the *Keeper of Sheep*, it takes a definite and unmistakable shape. It is a quite perfectly defined absolute objectivism – the completest system of absolute objectivism which we have ever had, either from philosopher or from writer. There is philosophy in Whitman, but it is the philosophy of a poet and not of a thinker; and where there is philosophy it is not of an original cast, the sentiment alone being original. Not so in Caeiro, in whom both thought and feeling are altogether novel.

---

[1] Pessoa aspired to an English edition of the poems of Caeiro (and of Reis and Campos) which he would translate. Here is his sketch for a suitable preface.

Finally, though both are 'sensationists', Caeiro's sensationism is of a type different from Whitman's. The difference, though it seems subtle and difficult to explain, is nevertheless quite clear. It lies chiefly in this: Caeiro seizes on a single subject and sees it *clearly*; even when he seems to see it in a complex way, it will be found that it is but some means to see it all the more clearly. Whitman strives to see, not clearly, but deeply. Caeiro sees only the object, striving to separate it as much as possible from all other objects and from all sensations or ideas not, so to speak, part of the object itself. Whitman does the exact contrary; he strives to link up the object with all others, with many others, with the soul and the Universe and God.

Lastly, the very temperaments of the two poets differ. Even when he thinks, Whitman's thought is a mode of his feeling, or absolutely a mood, in the common decadent sense. Even when Caeiro feels, his feeling is a mode of this thought.

This description of their differences might be prolonged indefinitely. Whitman's violent democratic feeling could be contrasted with Caeiro's abhorrence for any sort of humanitarianism, Whitman's interest in all things human, with Caeiro's indifference to all that men feel, suffer or enjoy.

After all, and all things considered, when we eliminate the superficial resemblance derived from non-rhythmical character of the poetry of both men, and the abstract revolt against civilization, the resemblances between them are exhausted.

Besides, Whitman has really a sense of metrical rhythm; it is of a special kind, but it exists. Caeiro's rhythm is noticeably absent. he is so distinctly intellectual, that the lines have no wave of feeling from which to derive their rhythmical movement.

What after all is Caeiro's value, his message to us, as the phrase goes? It is not difficult to determine. To a world plunged in various kinds of subjectivisms, he brings Absolute Objectivism, more absolute than the pagan objectivists ever had it. To a world over-civilized he brings Absolute Nature back again. To a world merged in humanitarisms, in workers' problems, in ethical societies, in social movements, he brings an absolute contempt for the fate and the life of man, which, if it be thought excessive, is at least natural to him and a magnificent corrective. Wordsworth had opposed natural man to artificial man; 'natural man' is for Caeiro as artificial as anything else except Nature.

Our first impression of Caeiro is that everybody knows what he tells us, that there is therefore no need to say it. But it is the old story of Columbus' egg. If everybody knows this, why has no one said it? If not worth saying, but true, why has every poet said the contrary?   [*Source*: PIAI]

called him 'a materialistic poet'. While unable to find the right words, since my master Caeiro is not definable in any precise words, I told him, however, that the classification was not entirely absurd. And I explained to him, more or less accurately, the nature of classic materialism. Caeiro listened to me with an attentive, pained expression and then said abruptly: 'But in point of fact that is very stupid. That is like priests without religion, and therefore without any excuse.'

I was astonished, and I pointed out to him various similarities between materialism and his own doctrines, excluding his poetry. Caeiro protested:

'But that which you call poetry is everything. It is not even poetry: it is seeing. Those materialistic people are blind. You say that they say that space is infinite. Where did they see that in space?'

And I, disoriented. 'But do you not conceive of space as infinite? Can you not conceive of space as infinite?'

'I conceive of nothing as infinite. How can I conceive of something as infinite?'

'My dear chap, said I. 'Imagine a space. Beyond that space there is more space, beyond that some more, and then more, and more, and more... without end...'

'Why?' said my master Caeiro.

I was in a mental earthquake. 'Suppose it ends,' I shouted. 'What comes after that?'

'If it ends, after that there is nothing,' he replied.

This kind of argument, cumulatively childish and feminine, and therefore unanswerable, knotted my brain for a while.

'But can you conceive that?' I let drop at last.

'Can I conceive what? Something having limits? How else? That which has no limits does not exist. To exist means something else existing, therefore everything must have limits. What is so difficult about conceiving that a thing is a thing, and that it is not always another thing further on?'

At that point I felt in my bones that I was arguing not with another man but with another universe. I made one last attempt, a tangent which I forced myself to feel as legitimate.

'Look here, Caeiro... consider numbers... where do numbers end? Let us take any number – 34, for example. Beyond that we have 35, 36, 37, 38, and so on and so forth, without the possibility of an end. There is no such thing as a number so big that there is not a larger one...'

'But those are only numbers,' protested my master Caeiro. And then he added, gazing at me with formidable infancy: 'What, in point of fact, is 34?'

There are sudden sentences, profound because they come from the depths, which define a man, or rather, through which a man defines himself, without definition. I recollect the one with which Ricardo Reis once defined himself to me. The conversation was about lies, and he said: 'I detest a lie, because it is an inexactitude.' Ricardo Reis in his entirety – past, present, and future – is in this sentence.

My master Caeiro, since he said nothing except what he was, may be defined through any of his sayings, written or spoken, especially after the period which begins from the middle of 'The Keeper of Flocks' onwards. But from all the many sentences which he wrote and which are in print, from among many he said to me and which I may tell or not tell, the one which encapsulates him with greatest simplicity is that which he said to me once, in Lisbon. We were talking about I know not what connected with the relations between each of us and oneself. And I suddenly asked my master Caeiro, 'Are you contented with yourself?' And he replied, 'No: I am contented'. It was like the voice of the Earth, which is everything and no one.

I never saw my master Caeiro unhappy. I do not know whether he was unhappy when he died, or in the preceding days. It would be possible to find out, but the truth is that I never dared ask those who witnessed his death anything about it or how he experienced it.

In any case, it was one of the anguishes of my life – one of the real ones among so many that have been fictitious – that Caeiro should die without me beside him. This is foolish but human, and that is how it is.

I was in England. Even Ricardo Reis himself was not in Lisbon; he was back in Brazil. Fernando Pessoa was, but it was the same as if he were not. Fernando Pessoa feels things but he does not stir himself, not even inside.

Nothing can console me for not having been in Lisbon that day, except that consolation spontaneously afforded me by thinking of my master Caeiro. No one is inconsolable beside the memory of Caeiro, or of his verses; and the very idea of nothingness – the most appalling of all, if considered with sensitivity – has, in the work and memory of my beloved master, something luminous and lofty, like the sun on the snows of unattainable heights.   [*Source*: PDE]

Praise and Criticism of R. Reis

ÁLVARO DE CAMPOS WRITES: OUR RICARDO REIS HAD a lucky inspiration, if indeed he relies upon inspiration, at least apart from explanations, when he reduced his *ars poetica* to six lines.

Not *ars poetica* in general, but his own. I will accept that he may devote his proud mind exclusively to lofty efforts (whatever they may be), although as far as I am concerned, a poetry which limits itself to the confined space characteristic of high peaks, must be narrow. But the connection between such lofty heights and lines of a given number of syllables is less clear to me. And curiously, the poem, lofty heights apart – which is personal and therefore held back by Reis, who keeps it to himself – is full of truth.

The thought is thus soaring and regal:

> *The subjugate sentence seeks it*
> *And enslaved rhythm is its servant.*

With the qualification that thought must be emotion and, again, achieve the loftiness mentioned above, it is indeed true that if emotion is powerfully *conceived*, the sentence which defines it acquires spontaneity, and the rhythm which conveys it arises throughout the sentence. I cannot conceive, however, that any emotions, not even those of Reis, can be universally bound to Sapphic or alchaic odes, or that Reis, be it in the course of begging a lad not to run away from him, be it to say that he is sorry that he must die, must perforce do so in subordinate clauses which are twice as long and twice as short, and in subservient rhythms which cannot accompany the subordinate clauses except in metres of ten syllables in the former, and six syllables in the latter case, with a rhythmical cadence highly disconcerting to the emotions.

I do not condemn Reis, any more than I do any other poet. I really appreciate him, to tell the truth, more than I do many others, much more. His inspiration is narrow and dense, his thought compactly sober, his emotion genuine, if a little too focused upon the compass point called Ricardo Reis. But he is a great poet – on this point I admire him – that is, if there are great poets in this world, outside the silence of their own hearts.

[*Source*: PIAI]

Sketch for 'Tabacaria'[1]

MAN, THE FOOL OF HIS INSPIRATION, CHINESE PUPPET OF his vain anxiety, rebellious and ignoble, slave of the same laws of Chemistry, follows the imperturbable rotation of the Earth its implacable trajectory around a yellow star, without hope, without rest (?), without any comfort other than his illusions of reality and the reality of his illusions. He governs states, institutes laws, starts wars: leaves behind memories of battles, verses, statues and buildings. The Earth will grow cold to no avail. Unaware of all that, unaware (?) from birth, the sun if it once yielded light, will cease to do so: if it bore life, it will beget its own death. Other star and satellite systems will possibly beget new humanities: other kinds of deceptive eternities will nourish other types of souls: other creeds will pass through distant corridors of multiple reality. (?) Alternative Christs will be

---

[1] Pessoa wrote this 'title' on this note. In the ordinary use of the word, the text is not a 'sketch', but a meditation, or philosophical orientation, preceding the writing of that great work

raised to new crosses in vain. Secret new sects will handle the secrets of magic or of the Kabbalah. And that magic will be of another kind, and that Kabbalah will be different. (...)

Only a single one, passive disobedience, without mutinies or smiles, as much slavery as rebellion (...), is the spiritual system which befits the absolute exteriority of our existential bondage.   [Source: PIAI]

Heteronyms: degrees of independence

SOME FIGURES I INSERT IN SHORT STORIES, OR IN THE subtitles of books, and I sign my name to what they say; others I project entirely and I do not sign, except for saying that I created them. The various types of figures are as follows: in those which I detach absolutely, even the style is alien to me and, if the figure so requires it, contrary even to my own; in the figures I subscribe to there is no difference from my own style, with the exception of those inevitable details without which they would be indistinguishable among themselves.

I shall compare some of these figures, in order to show, through illustration, of what those differences consist. The assistant book-keeper Bernardo Soares and the Baron of Teive – are both 'minely' [minhamente] alien figures – they write with the same stylistic substance, the same grammar and the same type and form of character: that is because they write with a style which, good or bad, is my own. I compare the two because they are instances of the same phenomenon – the inadaptation to the reality of life, and, what is more, inadaptation for the same motives and reasons. But, whereas the language is the same in the Baron of Teive [and] in Bernardo Soares, the style differs inasmuch as that of the nobleman is intellectual, devoid of imagery, a little – how shall I put it – stiff and restricted: and that of the citizen is fluid, participating in music and painting, not very architectural. The nobleman thinks clearly, writes clearly, and controls his emotions, if not his feelings; the book-keeper controls neither emotions nor feelings, and when he thinks this takes second place to feelings.

There are, on the other hand, remarkable similarities between Bernardo Soares and Álvaro de Campos. But in Álvaro de Campos there erupts immediately the shoddiness of the language, the looseness of imagery, more intimate and less seemly than that of Soares.

There are accidents in my distinguishing them one from the other which weigh as great burdens in my spiritual discernment – distinguishing a certain musifying composition by Bernardo Soares from one of similar content which is mine.

There are moments in which I do so suddenly, with a perfection which astonishes me; astonishes me without lack of modesty, since, disbelieving as I do in any fragment of human freedom, what takes place inside me astonishes me in the same way that what takes place in others would astonish me – both strangers.

Only a great intuition can act as compass in the wastelands of the soul; only with a sense which utilizes intelligence, but does not resemble it, although in this respect it becomes one with it, can one distinguish these dream figures in their reality one from the other.

◆

In these doublings of personality, or rather, inventions of different personalities, there are two degrees, or types, which will be clear to the reader, if you have followed them, by means of distinct characteristics. In the first degree, the personality distinguishes itself by means of ideas and feelings exclusive to itself, distinct from mine, just as, below that degree, it identifies itself through ideas, expressed in reasoning or argument, which are not my own, or which, if they are, I am not aware of. 'O Banqueiro Anarquista' [The Anarchist Banker] is an example of this lower degree; the 'Livro do Desassossego' [The Book of Disquietude] and the personality of Bernardo Soares are the higher degree.

The reader will notice that, although the 'Livro do Desassossego' [The Book of Disquietude] was published under the name of a certain Bernardo Soares, assistant book-keeper in the city of Lisbon, I did not however include it in these 'Ficções do Interlúdio' [Fictions of the Interlude]. This is because Bernardo Soares, while distinct from me in his ideas, sentiments, ways of seeing and understanding, is indistinguishable from me in his style of exposition. I convey the difference in personality through the style which comes naturally to me, with the exception of the inevitable distinction in special tone, which the very specificity of the emotions necessarily projects.

In the case of the authors of 'Ficções do Interlúdio', it is not only the ideas and the feelings which differ from mine: the technique of composition itself, the very style, differs from mine. In those instances each protagonist is created as essentially different, not just differently thought out. For this reason, poetry is predominant in 'Ficções do Interlúdio'. In prose, it is more difficult to other oneself.

◆

Aristotle divided poetry into lyric, elegiac, epic and dramatic. As is the case with all well-thought out classifications, this particular one is useful and clear; as is the case with all classifications, it is false. The genres cannot be divided with such intimate ease, and, if we analyse carefully what constitutes them, we will ascertain that there is a continuous gradation from lyric to dramatic poetry. Effectively, if we go to the very origins of dramatic poetry – Aeschylus, for example – it would be more accurate to state that what we encounter here is lyric poetry in the mouth of various protagonists.

The first degree of lyric poetry is that in which the poet, having concentrated his feeling, expresses that feeling. If, however, he is a creature of changeable and multifarious feelings, he will express something like a multiplicity of characters, united solely by temperament and style. A stage further, in the poetic continuum, and we encounter the poet who is a creature of various and fictitious feelings, more imaginative than sentimental, experiencing each state of soul through intelligence rather than emotion. This poet will find expression through a multiplicity of characters, united in this case not through temperament and style, since temperament is replaced here by imagination, as is feeling by intelligence, but only through simple style. Yet another stage, in the same continuum of depersonalization, or rather of imagination, and we have the poet who integrates himself to such a degree in each of his various mental states that he undergoes absolute depersonalization, to the extent that, by experiencing analytically that state of soul, he turns it into the expression of another character, and, that being so, style itself tends to vary. Taking the final step along the continuum, we have a poet who is several poets, a dramatic poet writing in lyric poetry. Each group of more similar states of soul will insensibly come to constitute one character, with his own style, with feelings possibly different, even antithetical, to those typical of the poet in his live person. In this way, lyric poetry – or any literary form analogous in substance to lyric poetry – will have been carried towards dramatic poetry, without, however, acquiring the form of drama, neither explicably nor implicitly.

Let us suppose that a supreme case of depersonalization, such as Shakespeare, rather than creating the simple protagonist of Hamlet as part of a drama, created him simply as character, without the drama. He would have written, so to speak, a drama for a single character, a prolonged and analytical monologue. It would not be feasible to seek in that character a definition of the feelings and thoughts of Shakespeare, unless the character were a creative failure, because only the bad playwright reveals himself.

For a temperamental reason of some description, which I do not propose to analyse, and the analysis of which is of no interest, I constructed inside myself various characters different from each other and from me, and to them I attributed various poems which are unlike how I, in my feelings and ideas, would write them.

It is thus that these poems by Caeiro, those of Ricardo Reis and those of Álvaro de Campos must be considered. It is fruitless to search in any of them for ideas or sentiments of mine, since many of them express ideas which I do not accept, feelings I have never experienced. They ought simply to be read as they are, which in any case is how one ought to read.

Here is an example: I wrote with alarm and repugnance poem number eight of 'Guardador de Rebanhos' [The Keeper of Flocks] with its childish blasphemy and its absolute anti-spiritualism. In my own self, the apparently real self with whom I live socially and objectively, I neither resort to blasphemy nor am I anti-spiritual. Alberto Caeiro, however, as I conceived him, does and is both: it is in that way, therefore, that he must write, whether I wish it or not, whether I think like him or not. To deny me the right to do this would be analogous to denying Shakespeare the right to give expression to Lady Macbeth's soul, on the grounds that he, a poet, was neither a woman, nor, to one's knowledge, hysterico-epileptic, or to attribute to him hallucinatory tendencies and an ambition which does not stop at crime. If that is the case with regard to the fictional protagonists in a drama, it is equally true with regard to fictional protagonists without a drama, since this is true because they are fictional, and not because they are integrated in a drama.

It seems pointless to explain something so simple in itself, and so intuitively comprehensible. It so happens, however, that human stupidity is boundless, and human goodness is not remarkable.   [*Source*: PIAI]

POETICS

Limits

TO FEEL IS TO CREATE
To feel is to think without ideas, and therefore to feel is to understand, since the Universe has no ideas.
 – But what does it mean to feel?
 To have opinions is not to feel.
 All our opinions are other people's.
 To think is to want to convey to others that which one thinks one feels.
 One can only convey to others what one thinks.
 What one feels cannot be conveyed. One can only communicate the *value* of what one feels. One can only convey the experience of what one feels. It is not that the reader can feel suffering in common (?) It is enough that he feels in the same way.
 Feeling opens the doors of the prison with which thought locks the soul.
 Clearsightedness should only reach as far as the threshold of the soul. In the very antechambers of feeling explicitness is forbidden.
 To feel is to understand. To think is to err.
 To understand what someone else thinks is to disagree with that person. To understand what someone else feels is to be that person. To be someone else is extremely useful in a metaphysical sense. God is everyone.
 To see, to hear, to smell, to taste, to touch – are the only commandments of God's law. The senses are divine because they represent our link with the Universe, and our link with the Universe God.   [*Source*: PIAI]

Sensation and Art [1]   [*Original in English*]

[...] HAVING SHOWN OUR OWN ORIGINS, AND, CURSORILY, our use of and differences from those origins, I will now more expressly state, as far as that is possible, in a few words what is the central attitude of Sensationism.
 1. The only reality in life is sensation. The only reality in art is consciousness of the sensation.
 2. There is no philosophy, no ethics and no aesthetics even in art, whatever there may be in life. In art there are only sensations and our consciousness of them. Whatever love, joy, pain, may be in life, in art they are only sensations; in themselves, they are worthless to art. God is a sensation of ours (because an idea is a sensation) and in art is used only [as?] the expression of certain sensations – such as reverence, mystery, etc. No artist

[1] Proposed letter to an English publisher.

can believe or disbelieve in God, just as no artist can feel or not-feel love or joy or pain. At the moment he writes he either believes or disbelieves, according to the thought that best enables him to obtain consciousness and give expression to his sensation at that moment. Once that sensation goes, these things become to him, as artist, no more than bodies which the souls of sensations assume to become visible to that inner eye from whose sight he writes down his sensations.

3. Art, fully defined, is the harmonic expression of our consciousness of sensations; that is to say, our sensations must be so expressed that they *create an object which will be a sensation to others*. Art is not, as Bacon said, 'man added to nature'; it is sensation multiplied by consciousness – multiplied, be it well noted.

4. The three principles of art are 1) every sensation should be expressed to the full, that is, the consciousness of every sensation should be sifted to the bottom; 2) the sensation should be so expressed that it has the possibility of evoking – as a halo round a definite central presentation – the greatest possible number of other sensations; 3) the whole thus produced should have the greatest possible resemblance to an organised being, because that is the condition of vitality. I call these three principles 1) that of Sensation, 2) that of Suggestion, 3) that of Construction. This last, the great principle of the Greeks – whose great philosopher did indeed hold the poem to be 'an animal' – has had very careless handling at modern hands. Romanticism has indisciplined the capacity of constructing which, at least, low classicism had. Shakespeare, with his fatal incapacity to visualise organised wholes, has been a fatal influence in this respect (you will remember that Matthew Arnold's classical instinct guided him to an intuition of this). Milton is still the great Master of Building in poetry. Personally, I confess that I tend ever more and more to put Milton above Shakespeare as a poet. But – I must confess – in so far as I am anything (and I try hard not to be the same thing three minutes running, because that is bad aesthetic hygiene) I am a pagan, and I am therefore rather with the pagan artist Milton than with the Christian artist Shakespeare. All this, however is *passim*, and I hope you will excuse its insertion into this place.

I sometimes hold that a poem – I would also say a painting or a statue, but I do not consider sculpture and painting arts, but only perfected artisans' work – is a person, a living human being, belongs in bodily presence and real fleshy existence to another world, into which our imagination throws him, his aspect to us, as we read *him* in this world, being no more than the imperfect shadow of that reality of beauty which is divine elsewhere. I hope some day, after death, I shall meet in their real presences the few children of these I have as yet created and I hope I shall find them beautiful in their dewy immortality. You may perhaps wonder that one who declares himself a pagan should subscribe to these imaginations. I was a pagan, however, two paragraphs above. I am one no longer as I write this. At the end of this letter I hope to be already something else. I carry into practice as far as I can that spiritual disintegration I preach. If I am ever coherent, it is only as an incoherence from incoherence. (...)

[*Source*: PETCL]

Translating poetry   [*Original in English*]

A POEM IS AN INTELLECTUAL IMPRESSION, OR AN IDEA made emotion, communicated to others by means of a rhythm. This rhythm is double in one, like the concave and convex aspects of the same arc: it is made up of a verbal or musical rhythm and of a visual or image rhythm, which concurs inwardly with it. The translation of a poem should therefore conform absolutely (1) to the idea or emotion which constitutes the poem, (2) to the verbal rhythm in which that idea or emotion is expressed; it should conform relatively to the inner or visual rhythm, keeping to the images themselves when it can, but keeping always to the type of image.

It was on this criterion that I based my translations into Portuguese of Poe's 'Annabel Lee' and 'Ulalume', which I translated, not because of their great intrinsic worth, but because they were a standing challenge to translators.   [*Source*: PETCL]

Random Note

ÁLVARO DE CAMPOS WRITES: THE SUPERIOR POET SAYS what he actually feels. The average poet says what he decides to feel. The inferior poet says what he thinks he ought to feel.

None of this is in any way related to sincerity. First of all, no one knows what they truly feel: it is possible to experience relief at the death of a loved one, and to think we are experiencing sorrow, because that is what one ought to feel on such occasions. The majority of people feel conventionally, although with the greatest human sincerity; what they do not feel is with any kind or degree of intellectual sincerity, and that is the one that matters in a poet. So much so that I do not believe that there are, in all the already long history of Poetry, more than some four or five poets who said what they truly, and not merely effectively felt. There are some, very great, who never said it, who were always incapable of saying it. At most there are, in certain poets, moments in which they say what they feel. Wordsworth said it, here and there, Coleridge said it, once or twice; so

'The Rime of the Ancient Mariner' and 'Kubla Khan' are more sincere than the whole of Milton, or even than the whole of Shakespeare. There is just one necessary qualification with regard to Shakespeare: it is that Shakespeare was essentially and structurally factitious; and therefore his constant insincerity becomes almost a constant sincerity, whence his greatness.

When an inferior poet feels, he feels always to order. He may be sincere in his emotions: what does it matter, if he is not so in poetry? There are poets who hurl what they feel into poetry; they have never ascertained that they did not feel it. Camões weeps for the loss of his gentle spirit; and after all, it is Petrach who weeps. If Camões had experienced an emotion truly his, he would have found a new form, new words – anything rather than the sonnet and decasyllabic metre. But he did not: he used decasyllabic metre as he would don mourning in real life.

My master Caeiro was the only truly sincere poet in the world.

[*Source*: PDE]

The culture of a poet

INTELLIGENCE ELABORATES UPON ELEMENTS ORIGINATing from the outside, that is, it works upon data from the senses. These elements fall into three different categories – those which are sensations as such, elements directly from the senses; those which result from the direct transmission of alien sensations and impressions, gathered from social intercourse; and those which are the result of indirect influences, impressions gathered from books, museums, laboratories. The elements directly from the senses are, in themselves, necessarily limited, since each one of us is only himself: he does not see except with his own eyes, does not hear except with his own ears. We do not see or hear well and in depth except when intelligence, amplified by the other two factors or by either of them, amplifies our sensations, with which it insensibly collaborates. We see and hear better – in the sense of more completely and interestingly – the wider and more well-informed the intelligence behind our seeing and hearing. It is for this reason that Blake said quite rightly: 'A fool does not see the same tree as a wise man.' (A fool and a wise man do not see the same tree.)

It follows, therefore, that external data will be all the more complete and suggestive the more that intelligence is constituted by impressions gathered through social intercourse, impressions gathered in books, museums, in laboratories. The sum of the former category of impressions is usually labelled experience, the latter culture. These two elements, direct and indirect, reflect each other: social intercourse may or may not be an important element in mental build-up, depending upon the culture of the society with which intercourse takes place. Culture is the important element – whether it is acquired through reading or studying, or whether it is indirectly taken in through association with those who are in command of it. 'Only a fool,' said Bismarck, 'learns from experience; I have always learned through the experience of others.'

Culture, however, is not an inevitable result; it does not exist if the individual does not possess the capacity for culture, and it exists in the individual, as a result, in proportion to the presence of that capacity. Culture is mental nourishment, and that nourishment, in order to be nutritious, must be assimilated. So that the man to whom we refer as cultured is he who has the capacity to assimilate culture, of transmuting cultural influences in the substance of his spirit, and he who in fact acquires those influences. Moreover, the capacity for culture inevitably leads the individual to seek culture.

There are three types of culture – that which results from erudition, that which results from translated experience, and that which results from the multiplicity of intellectual interests. The first is the result of patient and painstaking study, by the systematic assimilation of the results of that study. The second is the result of the natural speed and depth of the benefit of whatever has been read, seen or heard. The third is the result, as stated previously, of the multiplicity of intellectual interests: none will be profound, none will be dominant, but the variety will broaden the spirit. We will supply examples of all in that they existed in three great poets; we find the first in Milton, who consciously prepared himself for his poetic work – whatever it was to be, since in his youth he did not know what it would be – through the acquisition of Greek, Latin, Hebrew and Italian (all of which he not only read but wrote), and through the study of the classics in the first two languages. We find the second in Shakespeare, someone not well-read or scholarly, but intense and profound with regard to the benefiting from everything he saw and heard, to the point of involuntary simulating an erudition which he truly did not have. We see the third in Goethe, who had neither the erudition of Milton nor the ultra-assimilation of Shakespeare, but whose variety of interests, encompassing all the arts and almost all the sciences, made up in universalism for what it lacked in depth or absorption.

A poet who knows what Gauss' coordinates are has greater probability of writing a good love sonnet than a poet who does not know. Nor does this imply more than superficial paradox. A poet who goes to the trouble of taking an interest in a mathematical abstruseness possesses the instinct of intellectual curiosity, and someone who possesses the instinct of intellectual curiosity surely gathers, in the course of his life's experience, details of love and feeling superior to those which might have been gathered by someone who is only capable of taking an interest in the normal flow of life which affects him – the feeding crib of the trade and the reins of submission. One is livelier than the other at least as poet: hence the subtle relation between Gauss' coordinates and the Amaryllis of the moment.

One is a man who is a poet, the other an animal who writes verses.

[*Source*: PETCL]

Degrees of lyricism in poetry

THE FIRST DEGREE OF LYRIC POETRY IS THAT IN WHICH the poet, of intense and emotional temperament, spontaneously or ponderously expresses that temperament and those emotions. It is the most common type of lyric poet; it is also the least worthy one, as a type. The intensity of emotions stems, in general, from unity of temperament; and therefore this kind of lyric poet is generally monochordic, and his poems revolve around a certain, generally small, number of emotions. Therefore, with regard to this type of poet, it is common to say, because it is accurately remarked, that one is 'a poet of love,' another 'a poet of nostalgia,' a third 'a poet of sadness'.

The second degree of lyric poetry is that in which the poet, because more intellectual or imaginative, or possibly even only because more cultivated, already lacks the simplicity of emotions, or the limitation these entail, which identifies the poet of the first degree. The former will also typically be a lyric poet, in the common sense of the word, but he will no longer be a monochordic poet. His poems will encompass various themes, linked nevertheless by temperament and style. While he is diverse in his types of emotion, he is not in the manner of feeling. Thus a Swinburne, so monochordic in temperament and in style, can nevertheless write with equal skill a love poem, a morbid elegy, a revolutionary poem.

The third degree of lyric poetry is that in which the poet, even more intellectual, begins to depersonalize himself, to feel, not just because he feels, but because he thinks he feels; to feel states of soul which he truly does not possess, simply because he understands them. We are in the antechamber of dramatic poetry, its intimate essence. The temperament of the poet, whichever it might be, is dissolved by intelligence. His work is unified only by style, last bastion of his spiritual unity, of his coexistence with himself. Such is Tennyson, writing both 'Ulysses' and 'The Lady of Shallot', such, and more, is Browning, writing what he called 'dramatic poems,' which are not dialogized, but are monologues revealing various souls, with whom the poet has no identity, claims to have none, and often wishes to have none.

The fourth degree of lyric poetry is that much rarer one, in which the poet, even more intellectual but equally imaginative, embarks upon complete depersonalization. He not only feels, but lives, the states of soul which he does not directly possess. In a large number of souls, he will lapse into dramatic poetry as such, as did Shakespeare, a substantially lyrical poet raised to dramatist through the amazing degree of depersonalization he attained. In either case he will continue to be, albeit dramatically, a lyric poet. That is the case of Browning, etc (*ut supra*). It is no longer even style which defines the unity of the man: only that which is intellectual in the style points to it. It is so in Shakespeare, in whom the unexpected texture of the sentence, the subtlety and complexity of the utterance, are the only thing which links the speech of Hamlet to that of King Lear, that of Falstaff to that of Lady Macbeth. And so it is in Browning through *Men and Women* and the *Dramatic Poems*.

Let us suppose, however, that the poet, still avoiding dramatic poetry, poetry which is externally so, progresses still one stage further in the depersonalization continuum. Certain states of soul, thought and not felt, imaginatively felt and therefore experienced, will tend towards the definition, in his eyes, of a fictitious person who might sincerely feel them (…)

[*Source*: PETCL]

Ambience

ÁLVARO DE CAMPOS WRITES: NO AGE TRANSMITS ITS sensibility to any other: it transmits only the intelligence it had of that sensibility. Through emotion we are ourselves; through intelligence we are other. Intelligence scatters us; therefore, it is because of what scatters us that we survive ourselves. Each age hands down to the ones that follow merely that which it was not.

A god in the pagan sense – that is, in the real sense – is nothing more than the intelligence that a being has of itself, since that intelligence, which it has of itself, is the impersonal and therefore ideal shape of what it is. When we form an intellectual concept of ourselves, we create a god out of ourselves. Only a few, however, form an intellectual concept of themselves, because intelligence is essentially objective. Even among the greatest geniuses, rare were the ones who existed entirely objectively face to face with themselves.

To live is to belong to another. To die is to belong to another. To live and to die are the same thing. But to live is to belong to an *outside* other, and to die is to belong to an *inside* other. The two resemble each other, but life is the outside of death. Therefore life is life and death is death, because the outside is always truer than the inside, which is why the outside is that which is visible.

All true emotion is a lie in the realm of intelligence, because the two are incompatible. All true emotion, therefore, has a false expression. To express oneself is to say what one does not feel.

The horses in the cavalry are what constitutes the cavalry. Without their mounts, the riders would be pedestrians. The place is what constitutes the locality. Being there is being.

To pretend is to know oneself. [*Source*: PDE]

Types of lyric poetry

TO THE THREE SUB-SPECIES OF LYRIC POETRY – HEROIC, elegiac and the lyric itself – the ancients attributed the protection of three muses. Calliope for the first, Erato for the second, and for the third Polymnia.

In good aesthetic rationale we denominate as lyric poetry all that which is neither dramatic nor narrative: and in the type of poetry which we call narrative, we surely ought to include the didactic kind. Lyric poetry may express directly the feelings and emotions of the poet, without wishing to draw from them any general conclusions, or to attribute to them any wider implications than the fact of their being simply emotions and feelings: this is the poetry which is actually or simply lyrical. This is the one over which Polymnia reigns. Lyric poetry may also express not the feelings and emotions of the poets, but rather the notion he has developed of those feelings, or of those of others: this is the true elegiac poetry, which is not necessarily sad, as the common use of the name suggests. This poetry's muse is Erato. Finally, lyric poetry may aim to exalt or humble the person or the acts of another, not so much by commenting upon them, as by elevating or subduing them: this, in its two manifestations, is heroic and satirical poetry. Calliope reigns over these as is her due, even if the ancients did not accord to her regency over satire. [*Source*: PETCL]

CRITICAL STANDPOINTS

Freudianism, and other critical approaches

LETTER DATED 11 DECEMBER 1931 TO GASPAR SIMÕES:
Thank you very much for your letter which I have just received, and for the
cutting from the Malaga newspaper. It does not matter that neither the
book-keeper passage nor the Álvaro de Campos sonnet appeared in number 33 of *Presença*; I am glad that the translation of the 'Hymn to Pan'
appeared. That is the one whose absence would have proved embarrassing
to me. And why should you be angry with my lengthy contribution to
Descobrimento? I am willing to offer equally extensive contributions to
Presença. In each case, however, I have taken into consideration the
nature of the publications. I think it is unfair to send you work which
would take up three of your pages, especially as *Presença* ought to offer
the better part of its more prominent space to younger poets and prose
writers, only slipping in those of my generation out of friendship for us, as
a token of our approval of you, and to fill up blank spaces.

Having dealt with these minor preliminaries by way of answering your
letter, I will now undertake a review of your book – *O Mistério da Poesia*
[*The Mystery of Poetry*]; including one of the pieces on me which you put
in your book, despite my having promised it to you long ago. You must
understand above all that I am going to dash off this review straight onto
the typewriter at which I am sitting, without pause for thought and without
seeking to achieve literature, or to make rounded sentences, or anything
but the spontaneous mechanics of writing. As I do not have your book to
hand, I shall have to allude rather than quote, if and when the need arises.
I warn you of this so you will not discern some ulterior intention on my
part when, in fact, it is only a matter of not having your book with me.

I have for a long while held in high esteem your talent in general and
your critical acumen in particular. Over and above everything else, I want
you to know that this is my basic opinion. Anything which in the course of
this letter may diverge from this statement refers merely to accidents and
details. Proof that what I say of your intelligence is indeed true – though
you may not be in a position to ascertain as much – is my use of the words
'admiration' and 'admirer', words I do not use casually; 'appreciation' is as
far as I tend to go when I cannot, in good conscience, go any further.

In my opinion, *O Mistério da Poesia* signals, in the evolution of your
spirit and of its expression, an intermediary stage between *Temas*
[*Themes*] and a work of yours still to be written. *O Mistério da Poesia* is
essentially – in my opinion, as ever – a transitional work: it is more profound and more confused than *Temas*. You have grown mentally – one
does so until the age of 45 – and you are going through a stage of growing
pains. You feel the need to explain more and in greater depth than you did

in *Temas*, but you have, in part, not yet come to command the means of achieving depth and, in part, you seek to delve into aspects of the human soul which it will never be possible to plummet. Hence – again, in my opinion – all the feverish, hasty, breathless elements, obstructive in the main to the clear-sightedness of some observations, and wholly destructive to that of others.

Quite apart from what I see as simply evidence of personal development, I believe you perhaps allow yourself to be a trifle excessively influenced by the European intellectual milieu, with all its theories claiming to be scientific, with all its talented and skilful exponents proclaiming themselves and being proclaimed as geniuses. I am not accusing you of not *perceiving* this: at your age one never does. I marvel nowadays – I marvel with horror – at what I once admired – sincerely and intelligently – until the age of thirty, in the past and the then-present of international literature. In my case this applied as much to literature as to politics. Nowadays I marvel, with pointless (and therefore unjust) shame, at how much I admired democracy and believed in it, of how sincerely I believed that it was worth making an effort for the sake of that inexistent thing called 'the people', of how genuinely, and without stupidity, I supposed that to the word 'humanity' there attached a corresponding sociological significance, rather than the simple biological correlate of 'human species'.

Among the guides who have drawn you into the relative labyrinth which you have entered, I believe I may single out Freud, taking that to mean Freud and his followers. I regard this as entirely understandable, not only for the general reasons outlined above, but also for the specific one of Freud's being truly a man of genius, the creator of a criterion of the psyche which is both original and appealing, and whose derived transmissible power has enabled it to become an open paranoia of the interpretative kind. The success of Freud in and beyond Europe is, in my opinion, partly a consequence of the originality of the criterion in question; partly of the degree to which it partakes of the strength and narrowness of madness (thus do religions and religious sects come about, the latter including those of political mysticism, such as fascism, communism, and the like); but mainly due to the fact that the criterion is grounded (save for deviations in the case of some followers), in a sexual interpretation. This makes possible the writing, in the guise of scientific texts (which they sometimes are) of wholly obscene books, and the 'interpretation' (in general without any critical rationale) of past and present artists and writers, in ways degrading, in the style of the 'Brasileira do Chiado' café, thus ministering psychic masturbations to the vast onanistic network which seems to make up contemporary civilizing thought.

Understand my meaning: I do not thereby intend even to suggest that this last detail might be the aspect of Freudianism which hypnotically appeals to you. But it was this very point which gave rise to the worldwide fascination with Freudianism, and which therefore publicized the system. It was just the same when Jung achieved notoriety from the non-literary device of attacking the Catholic Church (in which deep down he believed), and the 'bourgeoisie' (of which he was too clearly an adornment), and we, in my generation, came to admire him on literary grounds, even though we did not agree with either of the two factors which had given rise to the very fame for which we read and admired him.

In my opinion, then (always an opinion), Freudianism is an imperfect, narrow, and very useful system. It is imperfect if we expect it to offer us the key (something no system can) to the undefined complexity of the human soul. It is narrow if we assume, on its account, that everything is reducible to sexuality, since nothing is entirely reducible to one single thing, not even in life at the level of atomics. It is extremely useful because it drew psychologists' attention to three most important aspects of the life of the soul and, therefore, to its interpretation: (1) the unconscious and our consequent status as irrational animals; (2) sexuality, whose importance, for various reasons, had been previously underrated or ignored; (3) that which, in my own terminology I will name *translation*, or the transformation of certain psychic elements (not just sexual ones) into others, through the distortion of, or deviation from, the originals, and the possibility of determining the existence of certain qualities or faults through the intermediary of apparently unrelated effects.

Already before I had read anything by or about Freud, even before I had heard of him, I myself had arrived at the conclusion indicated as (1), and at some of the results which I included under sub-section (3). As regards (2), I had made fewer observations, in view of my lack of interest in sexuality, both my own and that of others – the former as a consequence of the minor importance I have always attached to myself, as a physical and social being, and the latter out of reluctance (in my own head) to interfere, albeit merely in interpretative fashion, in the lives of others. I have not read much Freud, nor much concerning the Freudian system and its derivatives; but what I have read has been of extraordinary use – I confess – to sharpen my psychological scalpel and to polish or replace the critical microscope's lenses. I did not need Freud (nor could he, as far as I can ascertain, enlighten me in this respect) to be able to distinguish between conceit and pride, in instances where the two may be confused, through cases which give indirect rise to those attributes. Nor did I need Freud in the sphere of sub-section (2), to recognize simply by means of literary style, the pederast and the onanist, and, within the said category, the practising and psychic onanist respectively. Nor to recognize the three elements constitutive of the style of the pederast, the three elements of that of the onanist (and the divergence, in one case, between the practising and the psychic onanist) – for none of these did I need Freud or the Freudians. But Freud and his followers did enlighten me about many other things with regard not only to this particular area, but the other two also: it had never occurred to me, for example, that tobacco (and I will add 'and alcohol') could be a 'translation' of onanism. After what I read in connection with this, in a brief study by a psychoanalyst, I immediately ascertained that, of the five perfect specimens of onanism which I have known, four neither smoked nor drank, and the fifth, who did smoke abhorred wine.

This subject has forced me into the area of sexuality, but only insofar as it serves as an illustration, as you no doubt understand, and to let you know how much, while I criticize and diverge from it, I acknowledge the hypnotic power of Freudianisms over intelligent beings, in particular if their intelligence is of a critical nature. What I wish to emphasize here is that it seems to me that such a system, and all analogous to it or derivative from it, should be employed by us as stimulants to critical perspicacity, rather than as scientific dogma or as laws of nature. And it seems to me that you have restored to them a little in the manner just described, and were consequently drawn along by much that is pseudo-scientific in many aspects of these systems, much that is conducive to falsification; by much that is daring, in other aspects, and conducive to excessive hastiness; and by much that is abusively sexual in still other aspects and conducive to an automatic debasement, especially vis à vis the public, of the criticized author, so that the explanation, sincerely sought and innocently expounded, results in aggression. Is this because the public is stupid? Indubitably, but that which defines the public as public, its collective nature, for that very reason deprives it of intelligence, which is an individual prerogative. Robert Browning, who was not only a great but also an intellectual and subtle poet, was once confronted with the question of Shakespeare's indisputable homosexuality, so clearly and constantly affirmed in the *Sonnets*. Do you know what was Browning's reply? 'If so the less Shakespeare he!' Thus is the public, my dear Gaspar Simões, even when that public is called Browning, who was not even collective.

In these remarks, the result of a solitary mental chat, and conveyed at the speed of the typewriter, I include the greater part of the adverse criticisms I have to make regarding *O Mistério da Poesia*. They concern, if I may express myself so pompously, one of the methodological aspects of your book. But it also contains some elements of unnecessary haste and of critical precipitateness alien to any question of method. If, by your own admission, you do not possess the necessary biographical elements for an assessment of what might have been Sá-Carneiro's soul, why do you base your conclusions on this lack of data? Are you certain, merely because I say so and insist upon it, that I miss my childhood and that music represents for me – how shall I put it – the natural and fettered medium of my most intimate expression? And note that I mention the text on Sá-Carneiro, which, given its lack of data, is an admirable instance of critical acumen, and the text concerning me which is only flawed in that it is based, as though on truth, on elements which are untrue because I, artistically, can do no other than lie.

Let me be more concrete. Sá-Carneiro's work is entirely permeated by an internal inhumanity, or rather, non-humanity: it has neither human warmth nor human tenderness, with the exception of that which is self-directed. Do you know why? Because he lost his mother when he was two years old, and never experienced maternal love. I have always remarked that the step-children of life lack tenderness, be they artists or mere men; be it that they lacked a mother because she died, or because she failed them out of coldness or distance. There is one distinction: those who lacked a mother because she died (unless they are by nature cold, something Sá-Carneiro was not) turn their tenderness upon themselves, substituting themselves in place of the unknown mother; those who lacked a mother because she was cold lose the tenderness they might have been capable of and (unless they are geniuses of tenderness) become implacable cynics, monstrous offspring of the native love they have been denied.

I will specify further, with regard now to myself. I never missed my childhood; in truth, I have never missed anything. I am, by nature, and in the literal sense of the word, a futurist. I am incapable of experiencing pessimism, or of looking backwards. As far as I am aware, only lack of money (at that very moment) or thunderstorms (while they last) can depress me. Of the past, I only miss bygone persons, whom I have loved; but it is them that I miss, not the time when I loved them: I would want them to be alive now, and as old as they would now be, if they were alive now. All the rest are merely literary poses, intensely experienced by dramatic instinct, whether I sign them as Álvaro de Campos or as Fernando Pessoa. They are sufficiently illustrated, in their tone and truth, by that short poem of mine which begins with 'the church-bell of my home village…'. The church-bell of my home village, Gaspar Simões, is that of the Church of the Martyrs, in the Chiado. The village where I was born was São Carlos' Square, now Directorate Square, and the house where I was born was that where subsequently (on the second floor; I was born on the fourth floor) the Republican Directorate would be established. (Note: the house was doomed to notoriety, but hopefully the fourth floor will yield better results than the second.)

Following these specifications, or whatever they are, I now wish to return (if my capacities allow me, as I am already rather tired) to a methodological point. In my view (here are those words again), the critic's function should confine itself to three points: (1) to study the artist exclusively as artist, and allowing into his analysis no more of the man than is strictly necessary in order to explain the artist; (2) to search out what we may refer to as the central explanation of the artist (lyrical type, dramatic type, lyrical/elegiac type, poetic/dramatic type, etc.); (3) through an understanding of the essential inexplicability of the human soul, to surround these analyses and searches with a tenuous poetic aura of incomprehensibility. This third point perhaps may have a dimension of the diplomatic, but even truth, my dear Gaspar Simões, requires diplomacy.

None of this, I believe, needs clarification, except perhaps for the point I have signalled as (2). I prefer – even if only for the sake of brevity – to explain by means of an example. I choose myself because I am the one immediately at hand. The central point of my personality is that I am a dramatic poet; continually, and in everything I write, I exhibit the intimate exhaltation of the poet and the depersonalization of the playwright. I fly as another – and that is all. From the human viewpoint – which is no business of the critic because it cannot help him any – I am a hystero-neurasthenic with the overriding influence of the hysterical in the sphere of the emotions, and of the neurasthenic in the spheres of intellect and of the will: meticulous as regards one and feebleness as regards the other. As long as the critic bears in mind, however, that I am essentially a dramatic poet, he has the key to my personality, insofar as that can interest him, or anyone else who is not a psychiatrist, something which, conceivably, the critic need not necessarily be. Equipped with this key, he can slowly open all the locks of my writing. He knows that, as a poet, I feel; that, as a dramatic poet, I feel by detaching myself from myself; that, as a dramatist (not poet), I automatically transform what I feel into an expression alien to what I have felt, constructing in the realm of the emotions an inexistent person who might truly have felt it and, as a consequence, might have other connected emotions which I, entirely myself, have forgotten to experience.

I will stop here. I will re-read this letter, make any necessary alterations, and send it to you. Moreover, I am being very earnestly pressed to stop typing by a friend of mine, even more of a drunkard than myself, who has just arrived and does not wish to get drunk alone. Therefore 'I am going to re-read this letter', means that I am going to introduce no alterations with the exception of those mistakes that occurred between myself and the typewriter. If you find that anything is unclear, let me know and I will tell you. And you have not forgotten, of course, that all this was written without any preparation – hurled across the pages with all the rapidity which the typewriter can lend to unfolding thoughts.

No, I have not forgotten that I have not tackled what is possibly misguided in your concept of my emotive understanding of music. I skipped over this detail because it hampered the speed of my exposition and because I know nothing about it. But that desire for music is another of the witticisms of my dramatic spirit. It depends upon time, place, and whichever part of me is inclined to pretend about places and times.

Nor have I forgotten, of course, that somewhere further back in this letter, I wrote something concerning the 'sharpening of the psychological knife', and 'polishing or replacing the critical microscope's lenses'. I remark, with pride, that I have used, while speaking about Freud a phallic image and an ionic image; or thus, doubtlessly, he would perceive it. What he would conclude, I cannot hazard. In any case, to hell with him!

And now, I am definitely tired and thirsty. Forgive the parts in which my expression has failed my ideas, and that in which ideas have plundered upon lies or indecision.

A big hug from your great friend and admirer, Fernando Pessoa.

PS There is one part of your letter to which I neither responded nor referred. The one which deals with the note on *Descobrimento*, about Camilo Pessanha.

I wish merely to refer to the influence which Pessanha might have had on Sá-Carneiro. He had none. On me he did have some influence, because everything influences me; but it is best not to discern Pessanha's influence in everything which, in my verses, is reminiscent of Pessanha; and certain English poetic influences, which I intensely experienced before I even knew of the existence of Pessanha, act in the same way that he does.

But as for Sá-Carneiro... I knew, almost by heart, almost every one of Pessanha's poems, because Carlos Amaro recited them to me several times. I transmitted them to Sá-Carneiro who was naturally enchanted by them. However, I do not perceive them to have influenced Sá-Carneiro in anything. A great admiration does not imply a great influence, or even any influence at all. I have a great admiration for Camões (the epic poet, not the lyrical), but I am not aware of any element of Camões which might have influenced me, even though I am so easily influenced. And this precisely for the same reason which explains the non-influence of Pessanha on Sá-Carneiro. It is because what Camões might have taught me, had already been taught to me by others. The exhaltation and sublimation of the national instinct are phenomena which are essentially impossible to teach: we either naturally possess patriotic feeling, or we do not; we either possess the capacity to exhalt and sublime our feelings, or we do not. (And, apart from this, the patriotic instinct is one of the most common things in all literatures, being, as it is, the constructive sublimation of hatred, which is as necessary to existence as love – the other thing equally shared by all literatures.) And the construction and the scope of the epic poem are to be found in Milton (whom I read before I read *The Lusiads*), to a greater degree than in Camões. Well, Sá-Carneiro had either in himself, or as a consequence of other sources, everything that Pessanha could have given him, when he first heard, as he said, 'of his verses'. This explains, simultaneously, the non-influence and the great admiration.

[*Source*: PDE]

Aesthetics and Ethics

ÁLVARO DE CAMPOS WRITES, 17 OCTOBER 1922[1] : I write to congratulate you on your *Contemporânea* to tell you that I have been writing nothing and to place some qualifications on Fernando Pessoa's article.

I would also have liked to have sent you some contributions. But, as I told you, I am writing nothing. Once upon a time I was a decadent poet; at present I believe that it is I who am decadent and not the poet.

So much for me, who, when all is said and done, am the nearest person to myself. As regards you and your magazine, I miss our *Orpheu*! You carry on surreptitiously, good for you. After all, we are all in the same position. It seems that we alter only with the oscillation of those seeking to retain their balance. I repeat that I congratulate you. I used to think it difficult to achieve with printed matter such a sight for sore eyes in Portugal. I am glad I was wrong. I foresee for *Contemporânea* all the future success which I also wish it.

Now for Fernando's article. In the interval between the first word of this letter and the first word of this paragraph, I have almost forgotten what I wanted to tell you about the article. Perhaps I intended to say exactly what I am about to write. Well, I promised, and I say what I feel at this moment, according to my present state of nerves.

Fernando Pessoa is still sticking to that fixed idea, for which I have so often criticized him, of thinking that things can be proved. Nothing is proven, except in order to achieve the hypocrisy of not stating anything. Reason is a form of timidity – two timidities, perhaps, the second being the embarrassment of keeping quiet.

Aesthetic ideals, my dear José Pacheco, aesthetic ideals! Where did this sentence find its meaning? And what did it discover there, when it found it? There are no ideals, no aesthetics, except in the illusions we build upon

[1] Letter supposedly from Newcastle upon Tyne, to the Editor of *Contemporânea*, José Pacheco

them. The ideal is a myth of action, a stimulant like opium or cocaine: it helps us to be others, but at a price – with the failure to be even who we might have been.

Aesthetics, José Pacheco? There is no beauty, as there is no morality, as there are no formulae except those which define compounds. In the physiochemical tragedy we call Life, those things are like flames, mere signs of combustion.

Beauty began by being an explanation which sexuality offered itself for preferences very probably of magnetic origin. It is all a game of strengths, and with regard to the work of art we do not have to seek 'beauty' or anything which might exist in the enjoyment of that name. In all human or non-human attainment, we seek only two things, strength and the balance of strength – energy and harmony, if you like.

Faced with any work of art – from the art of keeping pigs to that of composing symphonies – I ask only: how much strength? how much more strength? how much tendentious violence? how much tendentious reflective violence, tendentious self-directed violence, the strength of the strength of not changing direction, which is an element of its strength?

The rest is the myth of the Danaids, or any other myth – because all myth is that of the Danaids, and all thought (tell that to Fernando) forever fills a perpetually empty barrel.

I read Botto's book[1] and I like it. I like it because Botto's art is the opposite of mine. If I only liked my art, I would not even like that, because I alter.

And apart from liking it, why do I like it? It is always dangerous to ask, because there might be an answer. But I ask – why do I like it? Is there power, is there balance of power, in the *Canções* [*Songs*]?

I praise in the *Canções* the power I find in them. A power which I do not perceive as in any way connected with ideals or with aesthetics. It is related to immorality. It is absolute immorality, devoid of doubts. Thus they have absolute direction – power, therefore; and there is harmony in not accepting any conditions upon that immorality. Botto tends with tenacious energy towards us all that is immoral; and he has the harmony of not tending towards anything else. I think it is pointless to bring the Greeks into this; it would be all Greek to Fernando if they turned up demanding satisfaction for the aesthetic muddle in which he dropped them. As if the Greeks were ever aestheticians anyway! The Greeks just existed.

Botto's art is essentially immoral. There is not a shred of decency in it.

---

[1] Pessoa, always ardent to uphold the right of artists to be heard, whatever their views, and being an admirer of the poems of António Botto, published *Canções* through his own publishing house, Olisipo, in 1922. Botto was a declared aesthete and homosexual.

And that is a strength because it is a non-hypocrisy, a non-complication. Wilde constantly went off at a tangent. Baudelaire formulated a moral thesis of immorality; he said evil was good because it was bad, and in this way he defined it as good. Botto is stronger: he offers purely immoral reasons for his immorality, because he offers no reasons.

In Botto there is something which is strong and firm: he offers no excuses. And I think, and perhaps I will always be bound to think, that to offer no excuses is better than to be right.

I will say no more. If I carried on I would end up by contradicting myself. That would be abominable, because it might be a way (an inverted one) of being logical. Who knows?

I remember with nostalgia – here in the barren North – our days of *Orpheu*, the old comradeship, everything about Lisbon that I liked, everything about Lisbon that I did not like – everything with the same longing.

I salute you in Constellated Distance. This letter carries my affection for your magazine; it does not carry my friendship for you because you have had that for a long time.

Tell Fernando Pessoa not to be right.

Fondly from your friend and comrade. Álvaro de Campos

[*Source*: PDE]

Notes for a Non-Aristotelian Aesthetic[1]

I

NOWADAYS EVERYONE KNOWS, AFTER KNOWING IT, THAT there are so-called non-Euclidean geometries, geometries, that is, that depart from premises different from those of Euclid, and arrive at different conclusions. Each of these geometries has a logical trajectory: they are independent interpretative systems, independently applicable to reality. This process of multiplying 'true' geometries, thus creating, so to speak, abstractions of several types of the same objective reality, proved fruitful both in and beyond mathematics (Einstein owes a lot to it).

And just as it is possible to devise, as were devised – and as it was useful that it should be the case – non-Euclidean geometries, I do not know what reason could possibly be invoked against the devising, against there being devised, and against the fact that it would be useful to devise, non-Aristotelian aesthetics.

It has been a long time since, without noticing it, I formulated a non-Aristotelian aesthetic. I wish to leave these jottings towards it in parallel,

[1] by Álvaro de Campos

modest or not I don't know, with Riemann's thesis on classic geometry.

I call Aristotelian any aesthetic with claims that the objective point of art is beauty, or rather, producing in others the same impression as derives from the contemplation or experience of beautiful things. For classical art – and its derivatives, romantic, decadent, and the like – beauty is the objective; they merely diverge in the routes they take towards that end, in exactly the same manner as in mathematics it is possible to demonstrate the same theorem in different ways. classical art gave us great and sublime works, which does not mean that the theory of the construction of those works is right, or is the only 'right' theory. In fact, both in theory and in practice, one frequently arrives at a correct result through uncertain or even erroneous processes.

I believe it is possible to formulate an aesthetic based not on the idea of beauty, but on that of *strength* – taking the word strength, of course, in its abstract and scientific sense; because if it were to be taken in the ordinary sense, it would be, in a way, merely a disguised form of beauty. This new aesthetic, while accepting the quality of a large number of classical works – albeit according to criteria which differ from those of the Aristotelians, which naturally was also that of their authors – establishes the possibility of constructing new kinds of artistic works which those who uphold the Aristotelian theory could neither foresee nor accept.

Art, as far as I am concerned, is, *like all activity*, a sign of force, or energy; but, because art is produced by living beings, and is therefore a product of life, the forms of force which manifest themselves in art are the forms of force which manifest themselves in life. But the *élan vital* is dual, integrative and disintegrative – anabolic and catabolic, as physiologists say. Without the coexistence and equilibrium of those two forces life is impossible, since pure integration is the absence of life, and pure disintegration is death. And because these forces are essentially opposed and balance each other out in order for life to exist, while it does so, life is an action accompanied, automatically and intrinsically, by the corresponding reaction. And it is in the automatic nature of the reaction that resides the specific phenomenon of life.

The value of a life, that is, the vitality of an organism, lies in the intensity of its power of reaction. As, however, this reaction is automatic, and balances the action which provokes it, the force of action, or in other words of disintegration, must be equal, or equally great. In order for there to exist intensity or vital value (in the concept of life there is no room for any concept of value other than that of intensity, in other words, degree of life), or vitality, it is essential that these two forces both be intense, but equal, since, if they are not, not only is there no equilibrium, but one of the forces will, moreover, be small, at least in relation to the other. Therefore, vital equilibrium is, not a fact in itself – as the Aristotelians claim in relation to art (let us not forget the point of these notes) – but the abstract result of the intersection of two facts.

And since art comes about because of feeling, and for the purpose of feeling – without which it would be either science or propaganda, – it is based on sensibility. Sensibility, therefore, is the *life* of art. It is within sensibility, therefore, that are found the action and the reaction which constitute the art of living, the disintegration and integration which, in a state of equilibrium, give it life. If the force of integration, in art, came from outside sensibility, it would come *from outside life*; it would be the case not of an automatic or natural reaction, but rather of a mechanical or an artificial one.

How shall we apply to art the vital principle of integration or disintegration? The problem poses no difficulties; as is the case with the majority of problems, it is sufficient, in order to resolve it, to discern clearly what the problem is. Going straight to the fundamental aspect of integration and disintegration, that is, to its manifestation in the so-called inorganic world, we see integration manifesting itself as *cohesion*, disintegration as the *tendency to rupture*, that is, the tendency, due to causes (at this level) almost invariably macroscopically external – in fact perpetually operative, to a greater or lesser degree – towards the cision of the body, its breakage, its ceasing to be the body it is. In the so-called organic world these forces are perpetuated, under a different name, because the form of their manifestation differs.

In sensibility, the principle of cohesion comes from the individual, who is characterized by that sensibility, or rather, by the form of that sensibility, since it is the form – taking this word in its abstract and complete sense – which defines the individualized compound. In sensibility, the principle of rupture is present in many different forces, mostly external ones, which however are reflected in the physical individual through non-sensibility, in other words, of intelligence and will – the former tending to disintegrate sensibility by disturbing it, inserting in it elements (ideas) of a general nature and therefore necessarily antithetical to the individuals, tending to render sensibility human rather than personal; the second tending to disintegrate sensibility by imposing limits upon it, stripping it of all elements which are inappropriate to action itself because they are excessive, or to speedy and perfect action because they are superfluous, tending therefore to render sensibility centrifugal rather than centripetal.

Against all these disruptive tendencies sensibility reacts in order to cohere, and like all *life*, it reacts by means of a special form of cohesion, which is *assimilation*, in other words, the conversion of the elements of alien forces into its own elements, into its own substance.

Thus, contrary to Aristotelian aesthetics, which requires that the individual generalize or humanize his necessarily specific and personal sensibility, in this theory the charted route is the opposite: it is the general which must be made specific, the human which must be individualized, the external which must be rendered internal.

I believe this theory to be more logical – if there is such a thing as logic – than the Aristotelian; I believe it to be the case for the simple reason that, in this theory, art becomes the opposite of science, something which is not the case with Aristotelianism. In Aristotelian aesthetics, as in science, art progresses from the specific to the general; in this theory, art progresses from the general to the specific, in antithesis to science, in which effectively and undoubtedly one goes from the specific to the general. And as science and art are, both intuitively and axiomatically, antithetical activities, so must their modes of manifestation be antithetical, and the theory which purports that those modes are antithetical is more likely to be right than that which purports that they are convergent or analogous.

II

Art is above all a social phenomenon. But in man there are two traits which are directly social, that is, directly connected to his social existence: the spirit of gregariousness, which makes him feel himself to be the same as other men, or similar to them, and therefore draws him to them; and the spirit of individuality or separateness, which leads him to draw away from them, and place himself in opposition to them, as their rival, their enemy, or their half-enemy. Any individual is simultaneously individual and human: different from all others and like all others.

A healthy social existence for the individual is the result of the equilibrium of these two feelings: the healthy social being is defined by an aggressive brotherhood. And if art is a social phenomenon, the social being already includes the gregarious element; it remains to discover where in it is to be found the separatist element. We cannot search for it outside art, because in that case art would include an element alien to itself, and it would be all the less art; we have to search for it inside art – that is, the separatist element must manifest itself also in art, and as art.

This means that, in art, which is above all a social phenomenon, both the gregarious and the separatist spirits must assume the *social form*.

But the separatist, anti-gregarious spirit, has of course two forms: the distancing of others, and the imposition of the individual upon others, the overriding by the individual of others – *isolation* and *dominion*. Of these two, the latter is the true social form, because to isolate oneself means ceasing to be social. Art, therefore, is above all, an attempt *to dominate others*. There are, of course, several ways of dominating, or seeking to dominate others; art is one of them.

So there are two ways of dominating or winning – to captivate and to subjugate. Captivation is the gregarious way of dominating or winning; subjugation is the anti-gregarious way of dominating or winning.

In all superior social activities these two processes prevail, because inevitably there can be no others; and if I refer specifically to the superior social activities, it is because it is they, because they are superior, which imply the idea of dominion. The superior social activities are three – politics, religion and art. In each of these branches of superior social activity one finds the process of captivation and the process of subjugation.

In politics there is democracy, which is the policy of captivation, and dictatorship, which is the policy of subjugation. Every system which depends on pleasing and captivating is democratic – be it the oligarchic or plutocratic captivation of modern democracy, which, deep down, only captivates certain minorities, which include or exclude the real majority; be it the mystical and representative captivation of medieval monarchies, the only true democratic system, therefore, since only the monarchy, through its essentially mystical nature, can captivate majorities and groups, organically mystical in their profound mental life. Any political system which depends upon subordination and subjugation is dictatorial – be it the artificial despotism of the tyrant in command of physical strength, inorganic and unrepresentative, as found in decadent empires and *political* dictatorships; be it in the natural despotism of the tyrant endowed with mental power, organic and representative, concealed messenger, when his hour is at hand, of the unconscious destinies of a people.

In religion there is metaphysics, which is the religion of captivation, since it seeks to insinuate itself through reasoning, and to explain or to prove something is to wish to captivate; and there is religion itself, which is the system of subjugation, because it subjugates through unproved dogma and inexplicable ritual, thus acting directly and supremely upon the confusion of the soul.

As in politics and in religion, so too in art. There is an art which dominates through captivation, and another which dominates through subjugation. The first is art according to Aristotle, the second is art as I see it and uphold it. The first is based upon the idea of *beauty*, because it is based on the concept of pleasing; it is based on *intelligence*, because it is based upon that which, because it is general, is comprehensible and therefore *pleasant*; it is based upon artificial unity, *constructed* and inorganic, and therefore *visible*, like that of a machine, and therefore *enjoyable* and pleasant. The second is naturally based upon the idea of *strength*, because it is based upon that which *subjugates*; it is based upon *sensibility*, because it is sensibility which is specific and personal in those of us who dominate, because, if it were not so, to dominate would mean to lose personality, or, in other words, to be dominated; and it is based upon spontaneous and organic, *natural* unity, which may be felt or not felt, but which can never be seen or visible, because it is not there to be seen.

All art starts with sensibility and is truly based on it. But whereas the Aristotelian artist subordinates his sensibility to his intelligence, in order that he may render that sensibility human and universal, in other words, in order that he may render it accessible and pleasing, and thus enable him to *captivate* others, the non-Aristotelian artist subordinates everything to his sensibility, converts everything into a matter of sensibility, in order that, in rendering his sensibility *abstract* like intelligence (without it ceasing to be sensibility), *emanatory* like will (without however being will), he may become an *abstract, sensitive, emitting source*, forcing others, whether they wish it or not, to feel what he has felt, dominating them through inexplicable force, in the same way that the more powerful athlete dominates the weaker one, in the way the spontaneous dictator subjugates the entire people (because he is 'all' synthesized and therefore stronger than it in its entirety), in the way the founder of religions dogmatically and absurdly converts alien souls into the substance of a doctrine which, deep down, is nothing other than the founder himself.

The true artist is a *dynamogenic* source; the false or Aristotelian artist is a mere piece of transforming apparatus, destined merely to convert the continuous current of his own sensibility into the alternating current of the intelligence of another.

But among the classical, that is, Aristotelian artists, there are true, yes true and false artists; and among the non-Aristotelians, too, there are true artists and mere simulators – because it is not theory that makes an artist, but having been born an artist. What I think and uphold is that every real artist is encompassed by my theory, whether he perceives himself as Aristotelian or not; and every false artist is encompassed by Aristotelian theory, even if he pretends to be non-Aristotelian. This is what remains to be explained and demonstrated.

My aesthetic theory – contrary to Aristotelian theory which rests upon the beauty principle – is based upon the idea of strength. And the idea of beauty can be strength. When the 'idea' of beauty is an 'idea' of sensibility, an *emotion* rather than an idea, a sensitive disposition of temperament, that 'idea' of beauty is power. It is only when it is a simple intellectual idea of beauty that it is not strength.

Thus, the art of the Greeks is great even according to my criterion, and it is so *particularly* according to my criterion. For the Greeks beauty, harmony, proportion, were not concepts of their intellect, but intimate tendencies of their sensibility. That is why they were a people of *aestheticians*.

Seeking, demanding beauty, *all of them*, in *everything*, *always*. That is why they *transmitted* their sensibility into the future world with such violence that we still live subjected to its oppression. Our sensibility, however, is now so different – so much has it been worked over by so many and such prolonged social forces – that we no longer are able to receive that transmission with our sensibility, only with our intelligence. This aesthetic disaster of ours was consummated by the fact that we generally received that emission of Greek sensibility through the Romans and the French. The former, although chronologically near the Greeks, were, and had always been, to such an extent incapable of aesthetic feeling, that they had to resort to intelligence in order to *receive* the Greek aesthetic emission. The latter, narrow in sensibility and pseudo-lively in intellect, capable therefore of 'taste' but not of aesthetic emotion, distorted the already distorted Romanization of Hellenism, elegantly photographed from the Roman painting of a Greek statue. For those capable of grasping it, the distance between *The Iliad* and *The Aeneid* is already great – so great that even translation cannot conceal it; that between a Pindar and a Horace seems infinite. But no lesser is the distance which separates even a two-dimensional Homer like Virgil, or a Pindar in Mercatorial guise like Horace, from the lifeless tedium of a Boileau, of a Corneille, of a Racine, of all the unsurpassable aesthetic rubbish of French 'classicism', that 'classicism' whose posthumous rhetoric still strangles and strips of virtue the admirable transmissory sensibility of Victor Hugo.

But just as for the 'classicists' or pseudo-classicists – the 'Aristotelians' as such – beauty was able to reside not in the inclinations of their sensibility but solely in the preoccupations of their reason, so, for the phoney non-Aristotelians, could force be *an idea of the intelligence* and not a disposition of sensibility. And just as the simple intellectual idea of beauty does not empower one to create beauty, since only sensibility truly creates, because it truly *emits*, similarly also the simple intellectual idea of strength, or of non-beauty, does not empower creativity, any more than the other, the power or the non-beauty which it purports to create. That is why there exist – and in what abundance they exist! – simulators of the art of strength or of non-beauty, who create neither beauty nor non-beauty, because they are positively able to create nothing; who create neither false Aristotelian art, because they do not wish to create it, nor false non-Aristotelian art, because false non-Aristotelian art is impossible. But in all this they involuntarily, and albeit incompetently, give rise to Aristotelian art, because they practice art with their intelligence, not with their sensibility. The majority, if not all the so-called Realists, Naturalists, Symbolists, Futurists, are mere simulators, I will not go so far as to say without talent, but at least, and only in some cases, merely with the talent of simulation. What they write, paint or sculpt may

have some interest, but it is the interest of acrosticism, of single-trace drawings and the like. It is fine, as long as it is not called 'art'.

In any case, up to the present, when for the first time an authentic non-
Aristotelian doctrine of art has appeared, there have been only three true
manifestations of non-Aristotelian art. The first is in the astounding
poems of Walt Whitman; the second is in the more than astounding poems
of my master Caeiro; the third is in the two odes – *Ode Triunfal*
[Triumphal Ode] and *Ode Maritima* [Maritime Ode] – which I published
in *Orpheu*. I do not ask whether this is immodest. I state it as truth.

[*Source*: PDE]

ESOTERICA:
Patriotism/Sebastiansim; the Occult

My intense patriotic suffering   [*Original in English*]

MY INTENSE PATRIOTIC SUFFERING, MY INTENSE DESIRE of bettering the condition of Portugal provoke in me – how to express with what warmth, with what intensity, with what sincerity! – a thousand plans which, even if one man could realise them, he had to have one characteristic which in me is purely negative – the power of will. But I suffer – on the very limit of madness, I swear it – as if I could do all and was unable to do it, by deficiency of will. The suffering is horrible. It holds me constantly, I say, on the limit of madness.

And then ununderstood. No one suspects my patriotic love, intenser than that of everyone I meet, of everyone I know. I do not betray it; how do I then know they have it not? how can I tell their care is not such as mine. Because in some cases, in most, their temperament is entirely different; because, in the other cases they speak in a way which reveals the nonexistence at least of a name patriotism.

The warmth, the intensity – tender, revolted and eager – , of mine I shall never express, (…)

Besides my patriotic projects – writing of *Portugal Republic* – to provoke a revolution here, writing of Portuguese pamphlets, editing of older national literary works, creation of a magazine, of a scientific review, etc. – other plans, consuming me with the necessity of being soon carried out (…) combine to produce an excess of impulse that paralyses my will. The suffering that this produces I know not if it can be described as on this side of insanity.

Add to all this other reasons still for suffering, some physical, others mental, the susceptibility to every small thing that can cause pain (or even that to a normal man could not cause any pain), add this to other things still, complications, money difficulties – join this all to my fundamentally unbalanced temperament and you may be able to *suspect* what my suffering is.

[*Source*: PIAI]

Imperial languages   [*Original in English*]

IF THE POSSESSION OF A GREAT LITERATURE WERE IN itself sufficient to establish, not the mere survival, but the widespread survival of a language, ancient Greek would today be the second language of civilization. But even Latin, which was once this, has not been able to continue being this. To have a hold on a quantitative future, a language must possess something more than a great literature: the possession of a great literature is an advantage more real than actual, it will save a language from death but will nor promote it to life.

The primary condition for a large hold on a future is, in a language, its natural widespreadness, and this depends on the mere physical fact of the number of people who speak it naturally. The secondary condition is its ease in being learnt; if Greek were easy to learn, we would all have Greek today as a second language. The tertiary condition is that the language be as pliant as possible, so that there be in it as full a capacity for expression of all moods as can be, and a consequent capacity to admit, by translation, the reflex of other languages and thus dispense, from the literary standpoint, with the learning of them.

Now, taking not only the present but immediate future, in so far as it may be considered as developing on the embryo conditions of our time, there are only three languages with a popular future – English (which has already a widespread hold), Spanish and Portuguese. They are the languages spoken in America, and in so far as Europe means European civilization, Europe is becoming more and more settled in the Western continent. Such languages as French, German and Italian are never anything but European: they have no imperial power. So long as Europe was the world, they held their own, and even triumphed over the other three, for English was insular and Spanish and Portuguese right at the end. But when the world became the earth, the scene shifted.

It is therefore among these three languages that the future of the future will lie.[1]   [*Source*: *Pessoa Inédito* Lisbon 1993]

A different sort of patriotism

LAST OCTOBER [1935] I PUBLISHED AND DELIBERATELY made available in the bookshops, on the 1st December, a book of poems, constituting effectively a single poem, called *Mensagem* [*Message*]. That book was awarded a prize, under special and for me extremely honourable conditions, by the Ministry of National Propaganda.

Many who read *Mensagem* with appreciation, as well as many who read it with little appreciation or with none, were perplexed and confused by certain things: the structure of the book, the ordering or subjects in it, and mainly the mixture to be found in it, of a nationalist mysticism, usually immeshed wherever it manifests itself among us, with the spirit and the doctrines of Rome, but here with a religiosity, which from this point of view is clearly heretical.

---

[1] Each nation has a language (sometimes more than one) which its resident people use officially. UN statistics list nations along with the size of their populations and their relevant official languages. Among European languages – ranked according to the total populations world wide using them – the order (as Pessoa foresaw) is English, Spanish, Portuguese...

Another phenomenon independent of *Mensagem*, and subsequent to its publication, further increased the perplexity of the various readers. That phenomenon was my article on the subject of *Associações Secretas* [Secret Associations], published in the *Diário de Lisboa*, of 4 February [1935]. That article is an attack against proposed government legislation on the subject of the title, and it is, correspondingly, a full defense of Freemasonry, against which the legislative proposal was intended, and against which the law at present is directed.

The article is patently that of a liberal, of a radical enemy of the Church of Rome, and of someone who extends towards Freemasonry and Freemasons a profoundly fraternal feeling.

An attentive reader of *Mensagem*, whatever his concept of the book's worth, would not be surprised at the anti-Romanism, constantly if negatively emergent in it. An equally attentive reader, but one also acquainted with the understanding or at least the intuition of hermetic matters, would not be surprised at the defence of Freemasonry in the author of a book so abundantly steeped in Templarian and Rosicrucean symbolism. Such a reader would easily conclude that, as the Templar Orders, although they do not exercise political activity, endorse social concepts identical, in their positive and their negative aspects, to that of Freemasonry; and as Rosicruceanism, in its social aspect, revolves around ideas of fraternity and peace (*Pax profunda, frater/* is the Rosicrucean greeting, both for Brothers and for prophanes), the author of such a book would perforce be a liberal, by derivation if not by temperament.

But as a matter of fact, I have always been faithful, by temperament further reinforced by upbringing – my education is entirely English – to the essential principles of liberalism – which are the respect for human dignity and for freedom of mind, or, in other words, individualism and tolerance, or, still in a word, brotherly individualism.

There are three social realities – the Individual, the Nation, and Humanity. All the rest is fiction.

The Family, Religion, and Class, are all fictions. The State is a fiction. Civilization is a fiction.

The individual, Nation and Humanity are realities because they are perfectly defined. They have outline and shape. The individual is supreme reality because he has the material and mental shape – he is a living body and a living soul.

Nation is also a reality because it is defined by territory, or idiom, or historical continuity – one of those elements, or all of them. The contour of the nation is however less defined, more contingent, whether geographically, because borders are not always what they ought to be; or linguistically, because large distances in space separate countries with a common language which naturally ought to constitute a single nation; or historically, because, on the one hand different criteria regarding the national past rupture, or tend to rupture, the national whole, and, on the other hand historical continuity operates differently upon different sectors of the population, different with respect to temperament, customs or culture.

Humanity is another social reality, as strong as the individual, stronger even than the Nation, because more clearly defined than the latter. The individual is, deep down, a biological concept; Humanity is, deep down, a zoological concept – neither more nor less than the animal species constituted by all the animals in human form. One and the other are root realities. The Nation, being as it is a social reality, is not a material one: it is more a stem than a root. The Individual and Humanity are *places*, the Nation the *path* between them. It is through patriotic fraternity, easily felt unless one is degenerate, that one gradually attains sublimation, or will do so, until fraternity with all men is reached.

It follows from this that, the more intensely patriotic we are – as long as we know how to be patriots – the more intensely we will be preparing ourselves, and with us those who are with us, for a future human achievement, which we ought not to cease desiring, even were God to make it impossible. The Nation is the present schooling for the future super-Nation. It behoves us, however, to remember that we are as yet, and will be for centuries, in the schooling stage, and only that.

To be intensely patriotic means three things. First, it is to value in ourselves the individual we are, and to attempt the valuing of our compatriots, in order that the Nation, which is the living sum-total of the individuals which constitute it, and not the pile of rocks and sand which constitute its territory, or the collection of words separated or linked together which constitute its lexicon or its grammar – may take pride in us, who, because she nurtured us, are her sons, and her parents, because we continue creating her. (…)

◆

The true origin of this article lies in a personal event: the fact that there are many – many for someone who knows few – who confessed that they did not understand how, after writing *Mensagem*, a nationalist book of verses, I had come out in defence of Freemasonry in the *Diário de Lisboa*. From that personal and concrete fact I drew the rationale and the substance for this impersonal and abstract article. What an obscure poet or the (slightly less obscure) defender of the Masonic Order does and thinks matters nothing and to no one; but it should matter something to everyone to make clear what was confused, to draw together what was erroneously parted, and that there should be less mist hanging over ideas, even if it is not by means of ideas that one ought to expect Dom Sebastião.

One thing, and one alone worries me: that with this article I may contribute, in any degree, towards the hindering of Portuguese reactionaries in one of their greater and juster pleasures – that of uttering nonsense. I trust, however, in the rock-like solidity of their skulls and in the virtues inherent in that firm and totalitarian faith which they divide, in equal portions, between Our Lady at Fátima and His Grace Dom Duarte Nuno of Bragança.   [*Source*: PIAI]

The Fifth Empire[1]

What do you believe to be the future of the Portuguese race?
THE FIFTH EMPIRE, THE FUTURE OF PORTUGAL – I DON'T believe, I *know* – is already written down, for whoever knows how to read it, in the verses of Bandarra, as well as in the prophecies of Nostradamus. The future is to be universal. What true Portuguese can, for example, live in the sterile straightjacket of Catholicism when, beyond it, he can experience all the varieties of Protestantism, all the beliefs of the Orient, all paganisms, dead and alive, which can be amalgamated, Portuguese fashion, into one Superior Paganism? Not one god should remain alien to us. Let us encompass all the gods. We have already conquered the Sea; it remains for us to conquer the Sky, leaving the Earth for others, those who remain eternally the Others, Others by birth, the Europeans who aren't truly European because they are not Portuguese. Let us be everything, let us include every variant, because truth cannot be the complete truth if things still lie outside it. Let us, then, believe in Superior Paganism, in Supreme Polytheism! Let us be eternally suspicious of each and every god because only all the gods combined comprise Truth itself.   [*Source*: *Portugal, Sebastianismo, Quinto Império* – obras em prosa de Fernando Pessoa ed. António Quadros, Lisbon 1986]

Occult experiences

LETTER TO HIS AUNT ANICA, 24 JUNE 1916: TOWARDS THE end of March (if I'm not mistaken) I began to become a medium. Imagine! Me – who, as you should remember, was always a backward member in the semi-spiritualist séances we used to have, I have suddenly, begun to write automatically. Once, at home, after having been at the Brasileira, I felt the urge, literally, to take a pen and place it on paper. Of course, this wasn't

---

[1] Interview in *Revista Portuguesa* dated 23-24 October 1924

until after I'd become aware of such a compulsion. At the time I was not concentrating; I'd taken up the pen naturally, like someone who had absent-mindedly taken up a pen to scribble. Since this first séance, I've begun to write the signature (which I know well) of 'Manuel Gualdino da Cunha', yet I was far from thinking of Uncle Cunha. Subsequently I wrote other things, without either precision or interest or importance. From time to time I wrote, sometimes deliberately, sometimes feeling obliged to do so. but it was very rare for the 'communications' to make sense. I could make out certain phrases. There was above all one oddity – an irritating tendency for the answer to my questions to be given in *figures*, as well as a tendency to draw. The drawings weren't of particular things but of kabbalistic and freemasonry signs, occult symbols and other items of the same sort that concern me little. This is nothing like your own automatic writing, Aunt Anica, nor that of Maria – a narrative, a series of replies in a coherent language. This is something more imperfect, more mysterious.

I should say that the spirit of Uncle Cunha has never manifested itself in this writing (nor in any other fashion). The present communications are, so to speak, anonymous, and each time I've asked 'who is speaking' I'm driven again to drawings or figures [...]

My 'mediumship' doesn't stop there. I've discovered another kind of mediumship that I've never felt before, except, so to speak, negatively. When Sá-Carneiro was going through his great mental crisis in Paris, which led him to kill himself, *I felt that crisis here*, a sudden depression fell on me from *outside*, one that I couldn't understand at the time. This form of sensitivity hasn't continued at all strongly. However, I am keeping for the last the most interesting detail: it is that I am in course of developing the qualities not only of a medium who writes but also of one who *sees*. I have begun to have what occultists call 'astral visions' or 'etheric vision'. All this is only at an early stage but I've no doubt it is there. It is still imperfect and happens only from time to time but when it does something *definitely* occurs. There are moments, for example, when I've had touches of 'etheric vision' – and when I see the 'magnetic aura' of certain people and, above all, my own, whether in the mirror or, in the darkness, irradiating my hands. This isn't a hallucination because what I saw others have seen, or rather one other who has qualities of the same sort well developed. I succeeded, at a fortunate moment of etheric vision, at the Brasileira in the Chiado one morning, *to see the aura of a person through his clothes and his skin*. That was a fully fledged etheric vision. Shall I possess it fully – that is to say, yet clearer and when I so wish? Astral vision I have more imperfectly. But sometimes in the night I close my eyes and see a series of little pictures, very rapid, very clear (as clear as things seen in daylight). They include strange figures, drawings, symbolic signs, numbers (I have already

seen numbers) etc. And there is – a most curious sensation – sometimes a sudden feeling of being a part of something else. My right arm, for example, begins to rise of its own volition. (Clearly, I could *resist*, but the fact is that I had not wanted to raise my arm at that time). [...]
    Don't think I'm going mad. Not at all: curiously, in terms of *mental equilibrium* I've never been better [...]
    I don't know if you will really think I'm mad. I don't think so. Such things are abnormal but not *unnatural*. I would beg you not to speak of them to anyone. There's no advantage in doing so and plenty of inconveniences (some of which we may not anticipate).
    Au revoir my dear aunt. My best regards to Maria and to Raul. Kisses to little Edward. I embrace you, very, very warmly; your affectionate and grateful nephew, Fernando.
    [*Source: Vida e Obra de Fernando Pessoa* by João Gaspar Simões, Lisbon 1950]

The Heresy of Gnosis

[...] THUS WE SAW THAT CHRISTIANITY CONGLOMERATED elements which are analytically reducible to five, but which as regards their origin, are but three: Jewish monotheism, neoplatonic mysticism and the paganism of Roman decadence (?????). In the conflict with Judaism, the most rigidly Judaic christism flowed back towards its source and was lost. In the conflict between paganism and christism, the former, when it did not become integrated with the latter, entirely perished. In the course of the conflict with neoplatonic mysticism, however, something else happened. By engaging in antesyncretic conflict with christism, this mysticism gave rise to the famous heresy of Gnosis. This heresy never disappeared. Opposed, externally crushed, this sect of occultism became secret, disappeared from historical evidence, but not from life. It is not impossible to find, here and there, evidence of its secret endurance. And that endurance yields aspects of conflict against official christisim, in particular Catholicism. In parallel with official christism, with its various mysticisms and asceticisms and its various magic arts, we can discern the episodical surfacing of a strand which indubitably dates back to the Gnosis (in short to the fusion between the Jewish kabbalah and neoplatonism) and which reveals itself to us now in the guise of the Knights of Malta, or the Knights Templar, now disappearing reappears in the Rosa-Cruz in order fully to re-emerge with Masonry. The Freemasons are the descendants, remotely but through an unsevered tradition, from the esoteric minds which constituted Gnosis. The masonic formulae and rites are clearly Judaic; the concealed substratum of those rites is evidently gnostic. Freemasonry derived from one of the branches of the Rosa-Cruz.

It would appear absurd to quote this christist undercurrent, were it not for the fact that its historical importance, albeit covert, is enormous. It exerted a powerful influence during the Renaissance and the Reformation; its assimilation into the French Revolution has been pointed out. The nature of this matter evidently precludes a precise study of it; but that which comes to light from the interstices of history can leave no doubt about it. The modern revival of systems of the occult, notable in particular through the importation, in English-speaking countries, of so-called esoteric Buddhism, an atrocious amalgamation of savage superstitions, decadent humanitarianism and patched-up gnosticism, brought again to the surface what was left in Europe of the occult tradition of Gnosis.

[*Source*: PIAI]

Occult beliefs

LETTER TO ADOLFO CASAIS MONTEIRO, 13 JANUARY 1935: […] I must still answer your question[1] regarding occultism. You ask me whether I believe in occultism. Formulated in that way the question is unclear; I understand the spirit of it, however, and I will reply to it. I believe in the existence of worlds superior to our own and in the inhabitants of those worlds, in experiences of varying degrees of spirituality, growing in subtlety until a Supreme Being is reached, who presumably created this world. It is possible that there are other Beings, equally Supreme, who may have created other universes, and that those universes coexist with our own, in interpenetrating manner or otherwise. For these reasons, and others still, the External Order of Occultism, that is Freemasonry, avoids (with the exception of Anglo-Saxon Freemasonry) the expression 'God', given its theological and popular implications, and prefers to say 'Great Architect of the Universe', an expression which leaves unresolved the question of whether He is Creator or simply Governor of the world. Given these scales of beings, I do not believe in direct communication with God, but, according to our spiritual honing, we may gradually enter into communication with ever loftier beings. There are three routes towards the occult: the magical route (including practices such as spiritualism, intellectually on a par with witchcraft, which is also magic), a route which is in all senses extremely dangerous; the mystical path, which has no dangers as such, but is uncertain and slow; and the so-called alchemical way, the most difficult and perfect of all, because it implies a transmutation of personality itself which prepares it, without any major risks, rather with

---

[1] See footnote on p206

defences which the other routes do not afford. As to the 'initiation' or absence of it, I can only tell you what may or may not satisfy your question: I do not belong to any Initiating Order. The quotation in the epigraph of my poem, *Eros and Psyche*, from a passage (translated, since the *Ritual* is in Latin) in the Ritual of the Third Degree of the Order of Knights Templar of Portugal, simply indicates – which is a fact – that I have been allowed to leaf through the Rituals of the first three degrees of that Order, extinguished, or dormant, since approximately 1888. If it were not in abeyance, I would not quote the text of the Ritual, since one ought not to quote (while indicating the origin) passages of Rituals still in operation.

I believe, my dear friend, that I have answered, albeit with certain incoherences, your questions. If there are others which you still wish to put to me, do not hesitate. I will reply, according to my ability, the best I can. What may happen, and which I hope you will instantly forgive me, is that I do not reply so speedily.

Fondest regards from the friend who greatly esteems you and admires you,

PS (!!!) 14/1/1935 Apart from the copy which I usually keep for myself when I type, of any letter involving explanations of the nature of these, I am keeping an extra copy, both in case this letter gets lost, and in case you might possibly need it for another purpose. That copy is always at your disposal.

Another thing. It may happen that, for the purpose of any work of yours, or anything else, you may need in the future to quote passages of this letter. You are hereby authorized to do so, *but with one qualification*, and I beg your leave to emphasize this to you. The paragraph on occultism, on page seven of my letter, what is contained in that paragraph cannot be reproduced in print. I believe that in answer to your question, I deliberately stepped somewhat outside the natural limits in this sphere.

This is a private letter, therefore I did not hesitate to do so. Nothing prevents you from reading that paragraph to anyone you see fit, as long as that person also follows the criterion of not reproducing in print the contents of what is written there. I believe I may rely on you for that negative purpose.

I am still in your debt with a long-overdue letter about your last books. I maintain what I believe I told you in my previous letter: when I spend a few days in Estoril (which I believe will now only be possible in February), I will bring that correspondence up to date, because in that respect I am in debt not only to you but also to several other people.

It occurs to me to ask you again something which I asked previously, and to which you did not reply: did you receive my booklets of verses in English, which I sent you some time back? 'For my reference,' as one says in commercial language, I would request you to let me know as soon as possible that you have received this letter. Thank you.   [*Source*: PDE]

WRITERS:
their freedom; their fame

Charles Dickens   [*Original in English*]

MR PICKWICK BELONGS TO THE SACRED FIGURES OF THE
world's history. Do not, please, claim that he has never existed: the same
thing happens to most of the world's sacred figures, and they have been
living presences to a vast number of consoled wretches. So, if a mystic can
claim a personal acquaintance and clear vision of the Christ, a human man
can claim personal acquaintance and a clear vision of Mr Pickwick.

Pickwick, Sam Weller, Dick Swiveller – they have been personal
acquaintances of our happier hours, irremediably lost through some trick
of losing that time and space have nothing to do with. They have lapsed
from us in a diviner way than dying, and we keep their memory with us in a
better manner than remembering. The human trammels of space and time
do not bind them to us, they owe no allegiance to the logic of ages, nor to
the laws of living, nor to the appearances of chance. The garden in us,
where they live secluded, gathers in flowers of all the things that make
mankind copious and pleasant to live with: the hour after dinner when we
are all brothers, the winter morning when we all walk out together, the
feast-days when the riotous things of our imperfection – biologic truths,
political realities, being sincere, striving to know, art for art's sake – lie in
the inexistent other side of the snow-covered hills.

To read Dickens is to obtain a mystic vision – but, though he claims so
often to be Christian, it has nothing to do with the Christian vision of the
world. It is a recasting of the old pagan noise, the old Bacchic joy at the
world being ours, though transiently, at the coexistence and fullness of
men [...]   [*Source*: PETCL]

Shakespeare   [*Original in English*]

THE BASIS OF LYRICAL GENIUS IS HYSTERIA. THE MORE
pure and narrow the lyrical genius, the clearer the hysteria is, as in the case
of Byron and Shelley. But in this case the hysteria is, so to speak, physical;
that is why it is clear.

In the lyrical genius of the grade above this – that which ranges over several types of emotion – the hysteria becomes, so to speak, mental; either
because, as in Victor Hugo, a violent physical health drives it inwards from
physical manifestation or (...)

In the lyrical genius of the highest grade – that which ranges over all
types of emotion, incarnating them in persons and so perpetually deper-
sonalizing itself – the hysteria becomes, so to speak, purely intellectual;
either because physical health is good but vitality deficient (...)

[...] Hysteria takes on different mental forms according to the general temperament with which it happens to coincide (meet). If health be frail in any way, the form of hysteria will be almost physical; and, if the hysteric be a lyric poet, he will sing out of his own emotions, and, the greater number of times, out of a small number of emotions. If health be good or very good, the constitution strong and, except for hysteria, the nerves fairly sane, the operation of hysteria will be purely mental; and the lyric poet produced will be one who will sing of a variety of emotions without going out of himself – either because, like Goethe, who was of this type, he has a variety of emotions, all, however, personal, or because, like Victor Hugo, he is constantly, though uniformly and monotonously, impersonal and fictitious. If, finally, the constitution be neutral, that is to say, neither strong nor weak, as in the case of a frail but not unhealthy man, the operation of hysteria will become vaguely physical and vaguely mental, neither wholly one thing nor the other; the result will be, in the case of the lyric poet, a mixture of the two others – the capacity to *live* in imagination the mental states of hysteria, the power therefore to project them outwards into separate persons, in other and more precise words, the psychological ability which goes to make, but does not essentially make, the dramatist.

(Shakespeare was then 1) by nature, and in youth and early manhood, a hysteric; 2) later and in full manhood a hystero-neurasthenic; 3) at the end of his life a hystero-neurasthenic in a lesser degree; he was also of a frail constitution and of deficient vitality, but not unhealthy. Thus much we have determined already.)

[...] Great as his tragedies are, none of them is greater than the tragedy of his own life. The Gods gave him all great gifts but one; the one they gave not was the power to use those great gifts greatly. He stands forth as the greatest example of genius, pure genius, genius immortal and unavailing. His creative power was shattered into a thousand fragments by the stress and oppression of life. It is but the shreds of itself. *Disjecta membra*, said Carlyle, are what we have of any poet, or of any man. Of no poet or man is this truer than of Shakespeare.

He stands before us, melancholy, witty, at times half insane, never losing his hold on the objective world, ever knowing what he wanted, dreaming ever high purposes and impossible greatnesses, and waking ever to mean ends and low triumphs. This, this was his greatest experience of life; for there is no great experience of life that is not, finally, the calm experience of a disillusion.

His wavering purpose; his unsettled will; his violent and fictitious emotions; his great, formless thoughts; his intuition, the greatest that has ever been, seeing right through a thought and expressing it as if the thought itself spoke, living an alien life down to its blood and flesh and speaking from it as the man himself could never have done; his power of observation, gathering a whole thing into one paramount aspect; his practical ability born of his quick understanding of things...

When the higher faculties of the mind are broken, in abeyance, or sluggish in their operation, the lower ones assume an unwanted force. Thus his practical ability was the one thing that withstood the stress and pressure of life and lack of will. He could amass money who strove in vain to amass the completion of created beauty. (ms.: If we wish to determine whether he was indeed thus, we have to see whether, towards the end of his life, there is not a growth of abruption in practical things.)

He began with two long narrative poems – highly imperfect as narrative wholes, and that is the beginning of his secret – written when he had yet an instinct to write greater than the intellectual impulse for it. With broadening consciousness, he lost his rapidity (...)

[...] Shakespeare was initially more vain than proud; at the end of his life – or, at least, of his writing life – he became more proud than vain. It is easy to conjecture why: he was unappreciated; what appreciation he had was more insulting than to be enjoyed, for where he was rated well he was not rated high, and, thinking and knowing himself (for this he must have done) the greatest genius of his age, he yet saw how whatever appreciation was shown him bulked small in view of the admiration in which Jonson was held, and others smaller than Jonson, and how appreciation no smaller than shown to him was shown to Daniel, to Webster, who knows if even to the Mundays ('our best plotter'), the Heywoods and the Days. His vanity was necessarily shaken by this, if not abolished altogether; and the tendency to depression fatal in a temperament of which neurasthenia is a component must have achieved the transformation.

Pride is the consciousness (right or wrong) of our own worth, vanity the consciousness (right or wrong) of the obviousness of our own worth to others. A man may be proud without being vain, he may be both vain and proud, he may be – for such is human nature – vain without being proud. It is at first sight difficult to understand how we can be conscious of the obviousness of our worth to others, without the consciousness of our worth itself. If human nature were rational, there would be no explanation at all. Yet man lives first an outer, afterwards an inner, life; notion of effect precedes, in the evolution of mind, the notion of the inner cause of effect. Man prefers being rated high for what he is not, to being rated half-high for what he is. This is vanity's working.

As in every man the universal qualities of mankind all exist, in however low a degree of one or another, so all are to some extent proud and to some extent vain.

Pride is, of itself, timid and contractive; vanity bold and expansive. He who is sure (however wrongly) that he will win or conquer, cannot fear. Fear – where it is not a morbid disposition, rooted in neurosis – is no more than want of confidence in ourselves to overcome a danger.

When therefore Shakespeare's vanity gave way to pride, or, better, when the mixture of much vanity and some pride which was initial in him gave way to a mixture of scant vanity and some pride, he was automatically dulled for action, and the neurasthenic element of his character spread like a slow flood over the surface of his hysteria.

The outward intellectual sign of vanity is the tendency to mockery and to the abasement of others. He only can mock and delight in the confusion of others who instinctively feels himself not amenable to similar mockery and abasement. The earlier part of Shakespeare's work is full of 'gulls', of derision of some figures. He takes part with some of his creations against others (...).

This declined towards the end of his written work. Humour supplanted wit. Humour is no more than the consciousness that what is laughable is akin to ourselves. It is born of the opposite of both vanity and pride, that is to say, of humility, of the sense, rational or instinctive, that at bottom we are no more than other men. Humour, if it had a philosophy, would be deterministic. The effect of the pride he had in checking his vanity, the further checks on that vanity from inappreciation and insuccess in higher things liberated more and more Shakespeare's humour.

His very pride could not grow because inappreciation dulls pride itself, if pride be not overweening and temperamental, as it was, for instance, in Milton, who, though not very vain, had nevertheless more vanity than he would have liked to have been aware of. [...]

Only an overweening and temperamental pride can resist constant inappreciation; some doubt must creep into the mind as to whether its sense of its own worth is really valid. The introspective mind has so often seen its Junos turn out to be clouds that it cannot be shaken in the assurance of so naturally misleading a thing as a man's appreciation of himself.

Inappreciation – There are things in Shakespeare which a lower Elizabethan might have written in a happy moment; these were surely appreciated. But these are the lesser part of Shakespeare; if he had written but them, he would have been a man of talent, of great talent perhaps, not, as he essentially was, a man of genius. In so far as he was, not an Elizabethan poet, but Shakespeare, that is to say, in so far as he was what we now admire him essentially for having been, he is sure to have been unappreciated. Those flashes of intuitive expression which in a cluster of words gather the scents of a thousand springs, those sudden epithets that flash down into the abysses of understanding, these, which are our daily astonishment and the reading of which cannot pall their novelty nor sear their freshness, must have fallen flat on contemporary minds, for it is in these that Shakespeare, like genius itself, was above his age. How can an age understand or appreciate what is, by definition, above it? Much of the best he wrote will have been taken for rant, nonsense or madness. We may rest assured that, if we could call up Jonson from the shades and ask him for examples of that (Shakespeare's) want of art (...), we would be surprised to hear him cite, among things which are perchance rant, many of the jewels of Shakespeare's greater verse.

Yet, as there is an intuition of understanding just as there is one of conception, one as rare and as flash-like as the other, once or twice some of the higher spirits of the age must have caught a glimpse of the transcendency. This would be the worse for the appreciation of the author. Nothing so harms a man in the estimation of others than the sense that he may be their better. To the general and constant sense that he is not their superior there is added the occasional suspicion that he may be, and inappreciation, colourless in itself, takes on the hue of envy, for men envy by supposition, who admire only under certainty. Hesitation as to whether a man may be our better is as unnerving as hesitation as to whether something disagreeable may happen to us; we hope not, but we hope uncertainly. And as we thereby fear the more the event we half-fear, in the other case, dislike the more the man we almost admire. In both cases, we dread the possibility of certainty more than the certainty itself.

Whether it is only the sense of inappreciation that plays like a gloom over the darker tragedies of Shakespeare's maturity, it is impossible to ascertain; but it is not likely that such inappreciation should have stood alone in the causation of the melancholy that shows directly in *Hamlet*, that trickles through the phrases of *Othello* and of *King Lear*, that, here and there, twists, as if following the contortion of the suffering mind, the very wording of the supreme expressions of *Antony and Cleopatra*. Inappreciation itself unfolds into several depressive elements. We have first inappreciation itself, secondly the appreciation of lesser men, thirdly the sense that, some effort like that of other men – the learning of one, the connection of another, the chance, whatever it might have been, of a third one, might have conquered the difficulty. But the very genius that causes the initial inappreciation dulls the mind to the activities that could counteract it. The poor and proud man, who knows that he would be less poor if he could but beg or humble himself, suffers no less from his poverty, not only from the better status of men less proud or more fortunate, but also from the impossibility of begging as they or stooping as they to what frees them from a similar poverty. There is then a revolt of the man against his own temperament; doubt sets in towards himself, and, as the poor and proud man may ask himself whether he is not rather unskilled in the things of practice than too proud to descend to them, or whether his pride be not the mask to himself of his incompetence for action.

The inappreciated man of genius may fall into doubt whether his inferiority of practical sense is not an inferiority in itself and not only the negative side of a superiority, the defect of a merit which could not exist without that defect.

Shakespeare's case was patently worse. He had stooped to the same arts as the lesser men that stood higher than he, as the still lesser men that stood as high as he or very little below him. He had done the same hackwork as they, without having been born for that hackwork. He had altered and arranged alien plays, and, whatever he may have thought of that, for it is possible he may have repugned that less than we imagine, being both used to it and integrated in the environment of that activity, he surely cannot have adapted himself to those conditions to the insane extent of thinking he was thereby doing justice to his great genius or in the right place of action for the possibilities of his mind. By doing what lesser men were naturally doing he had become himself, outwardly at least, a lesser man. not only had he not revealed himself by thus stooping to the common drudgery; he had masked himself the more.

For the learning, which was part of Jonson's credit with the public, he had, as we have seen, neither appetence nor patience; possibly he even had not time; and he had not received it in early youth, when it is imposed and not sought. From the establishment of influential connections, a humble condition possibly, a lack of disposition certainly, debarred him. To pushing his way among equals, by the social craft of mutual praise and the like, the pride he had, though not great, was too great, and it would have grown against the attempt, and gathered a fictitious force.

He had possibly triumphed and made his way materially, in so far as money was concerned. That also, though agreeable in itself – whatever its exact degree might have been – must have figured as an ironic comment in the margin of his inappreciation. To fail to be known justly as a poet is not compensated by just success as a shopkeeper.

Shakespeare is the greatest failure in literature, and it is perhaps not too much to suppose that he must have been, to a great extent, aware of it. That vigilant mind could not have deceived itself as to this. The tragedy of his unsuccess was but the greater by the mixture with the comedy of his success.

All these are but modes and shapes of the inappreciation which he felt. But the depression of spirit, the dulling of the will, the sickening of purpose, which the sense of inappreciation caused, must have made themselves felt on other lines than the direct work for which his mind felt itself born. The will which was dulled for writing must have been dulled also for other ways of action. The depression of spirit must have had outlets other than the figure of Hamlet and the phrasing of the greater Tragedies. The sickening of purpose must have discoloured his life, as it paled his poems and his plays. And the joys untasted, the activities uncared for, the tasks avoided and hurried away must have recoiled, in their mental effect, upon the depression that engendered them, and made greater the dispiritedness which was their cause.

To this extent we may justly and confidently go. What else there was, foreign to this, to radicate that depression we cannot now determine; if there were anything. What outward events of an untoward nature can have impinged on that depressed mind, it is useless to try to investigate. This much, however, we may say: that those events must have existed. If they had not, the expression of that dispiritedness would have been, not the verbal and psychological content of the Tragedies, but nothing at all. Depression leads to inaction; the writing of plays is, however, action. It may have been born of three things: 1) the need to write them – the practical need, we mean; 2) the recuperative power of a temperament not organically (only) depressed, reacting, in the intervals of depression, against depression itself; 3) the stress of extreme suffering – not depression, but suffering – acting like a lash on the cowering (?) sadness, driving it into expression as into a lair, into objectivity as into an outlet from self, for, as Goethe said, 'action consoles of all'.

The presence of all three factors can be predicted. The need to write these plays shows the intensity and bitterness of the phrases that voice depression – not quiet, half-peaceful, somewhat indifferent, as in *The Tempest*, but restless, sombre, dully forceful. Nothing depresses more than the necessity to act when there is no desire to act. – The recuperative power of the temperament, the great boon of Shakespeare's hysteria, shows in the fact that there is no lowering, but a heightening, of his genius. That part of that is due to natural growth, need not, and cannot, be denied. But the overcuriousness of expression, the overintelligence that sometimes even dulls the edge of dramatic intuition (as in Laertes' phrases before mad Ophelia) cannot be explained on that line, because these are not peculiarities of growth of genius, but more natural to its youth than to its virile age. They are patently the effort of the intellect to crush out emotion, to cover depression, to oust preoccupation of distress by preoccupation of thought. – But the lash of outward mischance (no one can now say what, or how brought about, and to what degree by the man himself) is very evident in the constant choice of abnormal mental states for the basis of these Tragedies. Only the dramatic mind wincing under the strain of outer evil thus projects itself instinctively into figures which must utter wholly the derangement that is partly its own.   [*Source*: PETCL]

Victor Hugo

[...] THE DIFFICULTY HOWEVER BECOMES SENSIBLY GREATer when we pass from the mere attempt to classify Victor Hugo as a poet to trying to understand him as a mind. He is a philosophical poet – this much is clear from the choice he makes of his themes, from the poems he rises most in, from the whole habitus and trend of his mind, which habitually treats philosophically the simplest themes. He meets a beggar and the beggar becomes *the* beggar for him: he generalises him, distinctly a philosopher's act. He takes the smallest, most everyday objects for his theme and draws from them conclusions widely transcending their apparent scope – and this is philosophical work. But his mind is the reverse of philosophic. He thinks in images not in ideas – that is the first obstacle; and all philosophical thought, properly so called, is – it is hardly necessary to say so – the contrary of that. Every small thought is for him an image; every great thought a vision. He is perpetually at Patmos, too perpetually, if perpetuity admit the saying this. – But he is not only a visioner, he is, besides, confused in his thought, in his vision-thought. He merges accessory images into larger ones, confuses the vision itself by partial metaphors, which rise on the swell of line by line composition.

But this is not all. He is, if not evidêntly, at least overapparently insincere in his philosophical theories: '*Ce que dit la bouche d'ombre*' overwhelms, but does not leave an impression of having been thought through feeling, of having pervaded *qua* theory the whole being of the poet. It gives us an impression analogous to that of Pope's philosophy in the *Essay on Man*: that of having been poetically conceived, not spiritually felt.

To refer to opposites, the contrary impression is given by Wordsworth in the great 'Ode' or in the 'Tintern Abbey' lines: here it seems that a sincere faith does make itself visible in poetry. It was on an intuition of this that Renan called Victor Hugo *cymbale*. This, however, is the product of the non-subjective character of his poetry. It seems to issue from outside the soul, somewhere from the circumference of the mind. What Lowell said of Poe can be applied to Victor Hugo, though in another sense: in Victor Hugo indeed the heart seems to be crushed out by the mind; not, however, as in Poe, by the evident pervadence of the intellect (...), but by some approximate and distant psychic fact – the almost-evident crushing out by the theme of the conviction of the theme.

In Victor Hugo the intellect is not great. But his sensibility is not great, either. The perusal of his poetry leaves in us the impression of a powerful and unfeeling mind. There is something exterior, gestural, in all he writes; the bitter rest hatred [sic] seems calculated as his intensest philosophy seems circum-thought rather than thought. His private life helps in this: no act of his stamps him as possessed of anything resembling sensitiveness. On the contrary, his fundamental coarseness (...) pierces through every cover he or others ever tried to put upon him. (Goethe wrote lyrical poems with greater show of feeling than Hugo. This is of course dramatic power, in part. He may not feel really the state of mind he describes, but he ever thinks himself with feeling it.)   [*Source*: PETCL]

A Warning on the subject of Morality[1]

ÁLVARDO DE CAMPOS WRITES: WHEN THE PUBLIC LEARN-ed that the students of Lisbon, when not shouting obscenities at passing ladies, were committed to preaching morality to the world, it uttered an impatient exclamation. Yes – precisely the exclamation which the reader has just uttered...

To be young is not to be old. To be old is to have opinions. To be young is not to give a damn about opinions. To be young is to allow others to go to hell in peace, together with their opinions, good or bad – good or bad, since we never know which ones we will take to hell with us.

Schoolboy likely lads interfere with writers who do not share their cast of mind in the same way that they interfere with passing ladies. If they don't know why before you tell them, they wouldn't know later, either. If they did, they wouldn't bother either ladies or writers.

Damn! Come on, lads: study, have fun and shut up. If you study sciences, study them; if you study arts, study them; if you study humanities, study them. Amuse yourselves with women if you like women; amuse yourselves otherwise if you prefer. Anything goes, because it doesn't go beyond the body of the one who is amusing himself.

But as for the rest, keep quiet. Keep quiet as silently as possible.

Because there are only two ways of being right. One is to keep quiet, which is the most suitable one for young people. The other is to contradict oneself, but only older people can do that.

Everything else is dreadfully tedious for anyone who just happens to be around. And the society in which we were born is the place where, more than in any other, we just happen to be around.   [*Source*: PDE]

---

[1] The League of Students in Lisbon organised demonstrations against the publication of António Botto's *Canções* and Raul Lent's *Sodoma Divinizada*, declaring them immoral. Both booklets were seized by the police. The text that follows is that of a pamphlet issued by 'Álvaro de Campos', from 'Europe', dated 1923.

The Individuality of Genius[1]

IN ART EVERYTHING IS PERMISSIBLE, AS LONG AS IT IS superior. The ordinary man may not be unpatriotic, because he does not have a mentality above the norm, and therefore he may not have it above the immediate species, which is the nation to which he belongs. The genius may be so. It so happens, ironically, that the great geniuses in general conform to normal feelings: Shakespeare was intensely, even excessively patriotic.

An unpatriotic genius is a phenomenon which I would not call common, but acceptable. An unpatriotic labourer is simply an imbecile.

The man of the species cannot have opinions, because opinion belongs to the individual, and as long as a man belongs in organic manner to a family, a class, anything which may constitute an immediate and live environment, he ceases to be an individual and becomes but one cell among others. Only the nation, because it is an abstract environment, since it belongs partly to the past and partly to the future, does not encumber the individual soul.

The problem of protection for artists, or any problem of similar ilk, does not apply to the man of genius, whose mental life is something apart and generally goes uncomprehended in his lifetime, or, at least, uncomprehended in precisely that which is the genius within him.

Artists, writers who must live off their writing, ought to be protected and defended, and those are never the men of genius. The man of genius is the product of a complex set of circumstances, beginning with hereditary ones, including those of the environment, and concluding with minimal episodes of fate.   [*Source*: PIAI]

'**Erostratus**'[2]   [*Original in English*]

[...] GENIUS IS INSANITY MADE SANE BY DILUTION IN the abstract, like a poison converted into a medicine by mixture. Its proper

---

[1] Sketch for a reply in an interview, 1924.
[2] These paragraphs comprise about two-thirds of those written by Pessoa, from time to time, for a projected essay or booklet given the working title 'Erostratus'. Pessoa neither finished the piece nor finally revised the paragraphs he had written: there are discontinuities between sections, gaps left for additions, alternatives for future decision, occasional words which defy interpretation, and, towards the end, merely notes. Nonetheless, the paragraphs convey the originality and activity of Pessoa's thought, expressed here in his exact and flexible English. They also help to explain why Pessoa, well aware of his worth, was so little concerned about public recognition during his lifetime; any such hope, this cool analysis states, must prove a chimera.

product is abstract novelty – that is to say, a novelty that conforms at bottom to the general laws of human intelligence, and not to the particular laws of mental disease. The essence of genius is inadaptation to environment; that is why genius (unless it be accompanied by talent of wit) is generally uncomprehended of its environment; and I say 'generally' and not 'universally' because much depends on the environment. It is not the same thing to be a genius in ancient Greece and in modern Europe or the modern world.

Shakespeare was unknown as a genius in his time, for the loud though posthumous praises of Ben Jonson are no more than the loud language of the time, devoid of meaning and applied by the same Jonson to men of whom no one today knows anything – that Lord Mounteagle of whom he says that he 'stood the master-mind' (no less) in that time, or the very James I.

Shakespeare was admired in his time as a wit, not as a man of genius. How could he be admired as a man of genius? It was the creator of Falstaff that could be understood; the creator of Hamlet could not be. If the anti-Stratfordian [greges] had ever taken the trouble to notice this, many absurd comparisons with the praise given to Jonson or to other men of their time would have been rendered impossible. Shakespeare is the example of great genius and great wit linked to insufficiency of talent. He is as supreme in the intuition that constitutes genius as in the quickness of strangeness that constitutes wit as he is deficient in the constructiveness and the coordination which constitute talent.

Milton is the example of the union of great genius and great talent. He has the intuition of genius and the formative power of talent. He had no wit; he was, in fact, a pedant. But he had the pedant's firm, though heavy, will.

Wordsworth, for instance, is the example of pure genius, genius unallied to talent or wit. Whereas Shakespeare, however imperfect in the whole some of his works may be, is never tedious and never mean; whereas Milton, however dull he may be, is never low, Wordsworth, when his genius deserts him, falls beneath meanness and below dullness (...)

[...] Wit is common and generally human. If anyone doubt this, he need but buy a copy of *Answers* and read the winning phrases in a contest of wit, which they call *Nuggets*. There quite obscure persons have flashes of wit which, as wit, could be cited to the honour of an acknowledged genius in it.

I have often reflected how wise are the sayings of Goethe in his conversations with Eckermann. But I have also often reflected how many sayings equally wise I have heard in the course of my life, in conversations with people who, however intelligent, were hardly candidates for Goethes.

Again, ideas are common, even brilliant ideas. The world is always over-packed with geniuses of the casual. It is only when the casual becomes the universal by intense concentration on it, by extensive working of it into consequences and conclusions, that right of entry is gained into the mansions of the future.

It is this consideration that does to a great extent stultify, in point of definite survival the critical efforts of an Arnold, of a Lytton Strachey, of an Aldous Huxley. They are all extremely clever; they are all, more or less, impatiently incoherent. There is perhaps more wisdom, or worldly wisdom, as such, in a book by Aldous Huxley than in all Spencer. But Spencer will be remembered, though unread, a thousand years from now; and for Aldous Huxley there will be neither reading nor remembering.

Because we come ever to the central point of all triumph, be it against the adversity of circumstances or the inertia of the future: will, and will only, makes us win. Will only will convert our casual thought into a system and thus give it body; will, and will only, will lift our happy phrase into a doctrine of that happiness. Many men throw out phrases which contain in germ great Kantisms; but only Kants expand the phrases into the greatness of worlds. The greatness of a phrase of Goethe lies in that it is not the phrase itself, but the consequence of genius.

[...] Taking this distinction of human faculties in conjunction with the distinction of human environments, it is at once seen that the two classes fit each other. It is obvious, from the joint analysis of the two classes, that genius involves an adaptation to the abstract environment which is formed by the general rule of mankind, which is common to all nations and to all times; the proper reward of genius is therefore immortality. It is obvious that talent involves an adaptation to the essential elements which, in a particular application or manifestation, make an age or a nation what it is at a certain time; the proper reward of talent is therefore what we have called fame. It is obvious that wit involves an immediate application to the immediate environment; this is shown in the one form of wit which we particularly call wit, for a joke has no point if no point can be seen. (...)

Many men with no great claim even to mere great wit could have made most of Shakespeare's jokes, as jokes. It is in the creation of the figures who make those jokes that genius underlies wit; not what Falstaff says but what Falstaff is is great. The genius made the figure; the wit made it speak. There are, in the great witty stream of French literature, many writers and speakers who have made better wit that Boileau. Boileau has not gone in wit beyond such minor epigrammatists as the Chevalier de Cailly. But the building by talent of witty wholes is outside the power of those greater minors.

[...] The celebrity of nations is, in a certain sense, similar to the celebrity of men. There are nations which are geniuses; there are nations which are talents, and there are nations which are wits.

In that civilization to which we belong, there are three nations which are geniuses – the three nations which have built up the modern world. Their direct greatness has differed, but their recognition by the world has been almost equal in not having been immediate.

Modern civilization is based, back of itself, on three principles – Greek Culture, Roman Order and Christian Morals. Greek Culture means individualistic rationalism, and every time that a European nation has departed from this fundamental element, it has fallen or lost. Roman Order means the concept of the State as Empire, and every time a European nation has lots its sense of this, it has fallen or taken meanness. (...)

After this, modern civilization is based on three elements: nationality, which was created by Italy; universality, which was created by Portugal; and liberty, which was created by England.

These elements, which the genius of three nations created, were spread by the talent of three other nations. Germany, by converting the renascence into the reformation; Spain, by (...), and France, by universalizing the English Revolution. [...]

Travels by sea like those of Drake, Frobisher, Cook and (as the Patent Office says) 'the like' are so insignificant in the sociology of discovery that [...] it were a wiser patriotism with Englishmen to omit all reference to them except as national incidents of a foreign impulse. Politics and not navigation is the English contribution to the substance of civilization. England found the sea only after it was told where it was.

[...] When there is genius without either talent or cleverness, the genius becomes consubstantial with insanity. This is the case of men like Blake. They present a universality; else they would not be geniuses, but mere madmen; but they present, by the very nature of their case, a limited universality, they figure an experience of all times, but common in all times to a very few men in each. These men, being geniuses, become immortal, but they will always be immortal at home, where they will not be seen unless they be visited. A Blake or a Shelley can never appeal to the generality of any age; they have the beauty of rarities rather than the beauty of perfect things. They may become, at one time or another, so long as that time is not theirs, very widely popular, but they will become so only by suggestion, decent coterieness, critical excitement.

[...] One of the most disconcerting phenomena in celebrity is that of what may be called fictitious genius. Genius manifests as an inadaptation to environment. Sometimes, however, there is difference from environment without real inadaptation (…).

The case of Robert Burns, writing in Scots and in songs in a world of English and couplets, is the example of fictitious genius. But the very acceptance by the age warns us off the grass of calling him genius. Such differences cannot be accepted as genius unless they are not genius at all. Blake was different from the same age, and the age did not heed him.

Fictitious genius lives by outward opposition to the age; real genius consists in an inward opposition (…).

When an age aches for something new (if ages ever ache), it wants something old. Burns brought into the eighteenth century a tradition different from the central literary tradition altogether alien to European literature. But he brought a tradition; he brought nothing new. In this manner do we receive a curious impression from the negro songs and negro music that have invaded modern Europe; but those songs are nothing new in themselves. If they were, they would not please us. We know they are not new and love their novelty for that.

[…] If anyone wishes clearly to understand what is meant by the pressure of a known name, he need but figure to himself the following hypothesis. Let him suppose a book of poems, published today, by an unknown poet. Let that book be composed of great poems of great poets. Let it be submitted, in the course of reviewing, to a competent critic who, by some odd chance, might happen to be ignorant of every poem there printed, even though acquainted with every poet represented. Does anyone suppose that the competent critic, even if he had it in his power to write, say, the leading article in *The Times Literary Supplement* (no less would be deserved by such a book), would write anything more than a short notice, in 6-point type, in the bibliographical part of that paper? And the poet would be lucky if he got a notice in the text-pages.

The pressure of a known name does not mean that the critic will think a poem good or bad in function of a known name. But he will give careful attention, word by word and phrase by phrase, to the poem of a reputed poet; he will do nothing of the sort by the absolute stranger. If anyone will take the trouble, as I once did, either to pass off as the work of an unknown poet, or of his own self (this was what I did), the poem of a celebrated poet; or if he will pass off some unknown lines as a celebrated poet, he will discover this very easily. In both cases and for opposite reasons the lines must be good or the test will not be just (…).

[…] The formation of definite fame is analogous to this. An author of real genius has become famous in his time; he has become famous because he has been in some sort of adaptation to his time. That adaptation can be of three sorts; complete (that is to say, in virtue of the substance and entire content of his work), partial (that is to say, by virtue of one part of his work, the other being worthless), and imperfect (that is to say, by virtue of one part of his work, the other being, though great, incomprehensible to his times).

In the reaction which the following age makes against the age before it, each of these types of author is subject to a definite treatment. The one who was completely adapted to his age, yet is nevertheless a genius (in other words, the author in whom genius and intelligence have been intermixed) will be retained as famous, but set down lower than he was. This is the case of Victor Hugo, who is a great poet, and was so considered in his time; he is still considered a great poet, but a lesser one than he was thought.

The one who was partially adapted to his time will be put down much lower; he will survive as a note. Scholars will read him; extracts may revive the accidents of his name. This is the case of men like the lesser lyrists of all times, the better class of passing essayists, the novelists who have good pages and a lost story. The one-poem man, like Blanco White or Felix d'Arvers, is typical of this half-class.

The one whose adaptation was imperfect will obviously survive the other way about, but he will rise in fame. What was of his time will be understood and put second, though retained; what was above his time will take first place. The great example of this is Shakespeare, who was famous in his time as a witty writer and has since become famous as a great tragic writer in whom comedy was a secondary, though a great, aspect of his genius.

[...] There is in genius an obscure element – that obscure element, real but difficult to define, which is called mediumnity when it assumes certain aspects. A case like that of Napoleon makes this clear. Napoleon was the medium of a vast number of tendencies of his age and time; if he had not been such a medium he would not have got hold of that age. He was sent out by it to come in to it, and commanded because it told him to command it.

[...] It may be admitted that genius is unappreciated in its age because it is opposed to that age; but it may be asked why it is appreciated by the times that come after. The universal is opposed to any age, because the characteristics of that age are necessarily particular; why therefore should genius, which deals in universal and permanent values, be more kindly received by one age than by another?

The reason is simple. Each age results from a criticism of the age that preceded it and of the principles which underlie the civilizational life of that age. Whereas one principle underlies each age, or seems to underlie it, criticism of that one principle is varied, and has in common only the fact that it is a criticism of the same thing. In opposing his age, the man of genius implicitly criticizes it, and so implicitly belongs to one or another of the critical currents of the next age. He may himself produce one or another of those currents, like Wordsworth; he may produce none, like Blake, yet live by a parallel attitude to his, risen in that age by no discipleship properly such.

The more universal the genius, the more easily he will be taken up by the very next age, because the deeper will be his implicit criticism of his own. The less universal, within his substantial universality, the more difficult will his way be, unless he happens to hit the sense of one of the main critical currents of the age come after.

[...] For Hamlet is, in a different way than was once thought, the essential figurement of his creator. He is a man too great for himself. Such was Shakespeare, such was Leonardo da Vinci. These men had too much soul for accomplishment. It is not the tragedy of inexpression, but the larger tragedy of too much capacity for expression and too much to express even for that capacity. No man reveals himself because he cannot; but men like Shakespeare and Leonardo do not reveal themselves because they can. They are prefigurements of some greater thing than man and are frustrate on the frontier. They are failures, not because they could have done better, but because they have done better. They have surpassed themselves and lost.

The lesser geniuses are haunted by their genius, and they are mediums who must be imperfect; but these are perfect mediums (...).

To write good prose a man must be a poet because a man must be a poet to write well at all.

[...] Whether the present age is favourable or not to the detection of genius, is a point to be amply understood. No age is favourable, in terms of the case, to the detection of genius. But an age where there are currents and cross-currents of thought and conflicts and cross-conflicts of feeling is apter than a stable and grounded time to appreciate the strange and the untoward. Yet there are difficulties. On the one side, there are too many people writing, drawing and otherwise messing up (passing) art. This establishes confusion. On the other hand, this very multitude of artists makes publicity and self-assertion of the lowest kind the defence against obscurity. The result is that on the confusion produced by great numbers there is superimposed the obstruction deliberately made by coteries, sometimes of one man only. The man of genius has greater possibilities than in the worst darkness of the enlightened ages. He is sure of some public, but he is not sure of being able to meet it. He can reckon on acceptance (var.: recognition), but not on getting it. Like the two natural halves of the loving Platonic soul, the genius and his public seek each other, but, as commonly happens in the other matter, they often never meet. (...)

[...] Posterity, says Faguet, likes only concise writers: *la postérité n'aime que les écrivains concis.* Men will ever read even though with trouble the immediate temporal, for what private interest, so to speak, there may be in it for them. They will always read a five-hundred page novel on their own times, as they will always read a five-hundred page manuscript on the history of their family, or of their neighbours. But the past will appeal to them only by perfection and brevity. [...]

Most of modern literature is written talk, fireside telling with the voice raised, the wrong afflatus, sometimes that sad Letter to Posterity which, as Voltaire said of J.B. Rousseau's poem of the name, will never reach the addressee. We waste in writing the time we should gain in talking, or, mayhap, we do not waste it, but have no one to talk to by voice, or we like an audience too large for the reach of the larynx, and the patience of the far-off listener. Hence our bright and futile novels, our clever and null satires and essays, our dinner-table poems: things often entertaining, frequently superior, always worth doing so long as we do not call them art. But it is true that if we did not think them art we would not do them, little as they are, at all.

The concentrated effort required to produce even a small good poem exceeds the constructive incapacity, the meanness of understanding, the futility of sincerity, the disordered poverty of imagination which characterize our times. When Milton wrote a sonnet, he wrote as if he were to live or die by that sole sonnet. No sonnet should be written in any other spirit. An epigram may be a straw, but it should be the straw at which the dying poet grasps.

Great art is not the work of journalists, whether they write in periodicals or not.

[...] The great novelists, the great artists and the great other things of our time point with pride to their fortunes and to their public. They should at least have the courage to sneer at their past inferiors. Wells should laugh at Fielding and Shaw at Shakespeare; as a matter of fact, Shaw does laugh at Shakespeare.

They have celebrity, such as the time can give; they have the fortune which follows upon that celebrity; they have the honours and the position which follow upon either or both of those. They cannot want immortality. What the Gods give they sell, the Greeks said. And English children are told that they cannot have the cake they eat.

[...] Nothing worth expressing ever remains unexpressed; it is against the nature of things that it should remain so. We think that Coleridge had in him great things he never told the world; yet he told them in the 'Mariner' and 'Kubla Khan', which contain the metaphysics that is not there, the fancies they omit and the speculations nowhere to be found. Coleridge could never have written those poems if there had not been that in him that the poems do not express by what they say, but by the mere fact that they exist.

Each man has very little to express, and the sum of a whole life of feeling and thought can sometimes bear total in an eight-line poem. If Shakespeare had written nothing but Ariel's song to Ferdinand, he would not indeed have been the Shakespeare he was – for he did write more – but there would have been enough of him to show that he was a greater poet than Tennyson. [...]

Variety is the only excuse for abundance. No man should leave twenty different books unless he can write like twenty different men. Victor Hugo's works fill fifty large volumes, yet each volume, each page almost, contain all Victor Hugo. The other pages add up as pages, not as genius. There was in him no productivity, but prolixity. He wasted his time as a genius, however little he may have wasted it as a writer. Goethe's judgment on him remains supreme, early as it was given, and a great lesson to all artists: he should write less and work more, he said. This is, in its distinction between real work, which is non-extended, and fictitious work which takes up space – one of the great critical sayings of the world.

If he can write like twenty different men, he is twenty different men, however that may be, and his twenty books are in order.

[...] It is ideas, as distinct from purposes, that make immortality – ideas as form and not as substance. In art everything is form, and everything includes ideas. It does not matter to the judgment of posterity whether a poem contains materialist or idealist notions; it matters whether these notions are high or not, agreeable in their form – even their mental and abstract form – or disagreeable.

This would seem to make propaganda not injurious to art, so long as there is art. It is indeed not essentially injurious, but, that it may not so be, it is necessary that, against his own purpose and intent, the artist forget the propaganda in the art. It may be that the *Divine Comedy* is intended to be Catholic propaganda – a rather futile thing in Catholic times; but Dante, when he wrote it, forgot all about the propaganda and wrote poetry. The propaganda does no harm to the poetry, for the simple reason that it did not get there. The result is that a third of Dante's commentators consider the *Divine Comedy* heretical, and many of these as purposely so. If the poem can be considered as Catholic and anti-Catholic, the propaganda is certainly not very efficacious. The same applies to the kindred and different poem which stands beside the *Divine Comedy* on the sorting of the ages. Milton wrote it down as his purpose to justify the ways of God to man, and his poem contains two heroes – Satan, who revolts against God, and Adam whom God has punished. He has justified the ways of man to God. His poem has set up an epic for one form of Christianity, and the result is that the author was an Arian, his form of Christianity being the absence of Christianity. (His vast learning and experience of the learnt has put everything into his Christian epic; the only thing left out was Christ. Has anyone ever felt Christian after reading *Paradise Lost*?).

[…] The truth about such men as Shaw and (…) is that they are barbarians. They break in upon civilization with the novelty of not belonging to it, and make as much show as a negro in Scandinavia. Their very blackness is their white mark. The real novelty that endures is one that has taken up all the threads of tradition and weaved them again into a pattern that tradition could not weave them into. The essential ideas of genius are as old as the basis of genius which is the existence of mankind. Each man of genius takes up this old thread-worn garment (…).

The other element of notoriety called fame is being a barbarian. By being a barbarian I mean coming into civilization from outside it; belonging to it by street number but without the soul to understand why streets were made and numbers put to the old tradition of separate doors.

All great poets have belonged to a continuation of the same tradition diversified by temperament. Some have done this by giving their individuality to elaborate learning; this is the case of Virgil (learned in his time), Dante and Milton. Others have done this by gathering within their individuality the totality of observation and experience; this is the case of men like Shakespeare and Walt Whitman. The definite moral characteristic of the first is their seriousness, their high seriousness as Matthew Arnold would have said. The definite moral characteristic of the second is their amorality; both Shakespeare and Whitman were indifferent to moral values except in so far as they were susceptible of being converted by temporary emotion into aesthetic values. Both were paederasts, by the bye. (…)

The essential thing about the barbarian is that he is wholly modern; he is altogether of his times because the race to which he belongs has no civilizational times before. He has no ancestors outside biology. The common trait of Lenin and Shaw, of Wells and (…) When they appeal to something outside themselves, they appeal to things like mankind, which is the common expression for the animal species that has the human form and inexistent outside zoology, or science, which has nothing to do with the human mind except being produced by it, but not for it.

The negro always wears the latest fashions. The cannibal, if he were here, would always order (have) the latest dishes. Both, for obvious reasons, sometimes feel pessimistic.

[...] Blank verse, the one so called is an extremely dull medium to write in. Only the subtlest rhythmical faculty can ward off flatness, and it cannot ward off flatness for a long time. Perfect poems can be written in blank verse, that is to say, poems which can be read with interest and attention, and will fulfil and satisfy; but they must be short – 'Tithonus' or 'Ulysses' or 'Oenone' and the like. When not short, or not sufficiently short, they can hold themselves up only by strong interest, and it is very difficult, except in drama, to carry strong interest along the desert of blank verses. Blank verse is the ideal medium for an unreadable epic poem. All the metrical science of Milton, and it was very great, cannot make of *Paradise Lost* anything but a dull poem. It is dull, and we must not lie to our soul by denying it. One element such a poem may have – quick action, material or mental – and it might escape dullness thereby; action as in Arnold's *Sohrab and Rustum*, which is marvellously readable (...)

In Milton there is very little action, properly such, very little quick action, and the thought is all theological, that is to say, peculiar to a certain kind of metaphysics which does not concern the universality of mankind.

The fact is that the epic poem is a Graeco-Roman survival, or very nearly so.

Only prose, which disengages the aesthetic sense and lets it rest, can carry the attention willingly over great spaces of print. *Pickwick Papers* is bigger, in point of words, than *Paradise Lost*; it is certainly inferior, as values go; but I have read *Pickwick Papers* more times than I can reckon, and I have read *Paradise Lost* only one time and a half, for I failed at the second reading. God overwhelmed me with bad metaphysics and I was literally God-damned.

Anyone who is in any way a poet knows very well how much easier it is to write a good poem (if good poems lie in the man's power) about a woman who interests him very much than about a woman he is deeply in love with. The best sort of love poem is generally written about an abstract woman.

A great emotion is too selfish; it takes into itself all the blood of the spirit, and the congestion leaves the hands too cold to write. Three sorts of emotions produce great poetry – strong but quick emotions, seized upon for art as soon as they have passed, but not before they have passed; strong and deep emotions in their remembrance a long time after; and false emotions, that is to say, emotions felt in the intellect. Not insincerity, yet a translated sincerity, is the basis of all art.

[...] He (the artist) may not be intelligent, but he must be intellectual.
Art is the intellectualization of sensation (feeling) through expression.

The intellectualization is given in, by and through the expression itself. That is why great artists – even great artists in literature, which is the most intellectual of the arts – are so often unintelligent persons.

[...] We shall move from private poets to public anthologies. Tennyson, as a useless whole, occupies nearly a thousand double-column pages. How much Tennyson will occupy [in] the perhaps less than a thousand simple pages of the future complete English Anthology?

One thing that will happen, unless, with the progress of popular education (democracy) we grow progressively less rational, is the careful sifting, generation after generation, of absolute from relative values. One kind of relative value dies by death – the relative value that is absolute in respect of its own age. (We have spoken of it above). But there is another, and a subtler, kind of relative value – it is the relative value which is absolute out of respect of its own age. A man who, in the eighteenth century, happened, by some unknown mental trick, to write something like bad Tennyson or worse Mallarmé, would be an astonishing phenomenon in his time. He would attract our present historical attention by virtue of that extraordinary departure from his times; he would be called a genius and a forerunner, and he would have the concrete right to both titles. But bad Tennyson or worse Mallarmé would become bad Tennyson and worse Mallarmé as soon as there were a Tennyson and a Mallarmé, and the relative value would be flagrantly relative; it would become historical and not poetical. What would be such a man's position? (in the final scheme of celebrity?) He would have done an easy thing when it was difficult – that is all. But a genius is a man who does a difficult thing, even when it is easy.

The central thing about real geniuses is that they are not forerunners. The very instance that the word arouses defines the case: that John the Baptist was Christ's forerunner means that he was unimportant in comparison with Christ.

But all our culture and greater latitude of experience both of culture and of sensation will not lead us to make 'Lycidas' the forerunning of anything, unless that something be worth far less than 'Lycidas'. Shakespeare's phrasing is imitable – it is, indeed, very easy to imitate – but Shakespeare's genius is not.

It is curious to see how many great poets (artists) are implicit in earlier lessers; more curious still to distinguish in what cases there has been a mere forerunning, in what a casual influence. But the essence of a great artist is to be explicit, and what was implicit was only implicit.

There is hardly any, if any, great artist in the world for whom a definite forerunner cannot be found. Each artist has a typical style; yet in almost every case, if not in every one, that typical style was already shadowed in a former artist of no importance. Whether there was a vague influence in the undercurrents of the age, which the first caught vaguely and the second clearly; whether there was a chance inspiration, like an outward thing in the former, which the latter, by direct contact, wakened in his temperamental brain into a definite inner inspiration; whether the two cases were consubstantial – not one of the hypotheses matters, except historically. The genius will be the final product; and he will be as final after as before.

[...] This value of the element of foreignness, so clear in the provincial case of Burns, is evident on higher levels. Much of the glory of Homer, deserved as it is, is due to people who cannot read Greek. His prestige is in part that of a God, because like a God he is both great and half-known. 'How dull Milton is!' said an enthusiast once to me. 'How different from Homer and Virgil!' I exclaimed. And he agreed at once. Yet Milton is no less dull than Homer – except as in so far as we are inevitably keener critics of the more difficult English tensyllable verse than of the easier and more distant Greek hexameter – and he is certainly less dull than Virgil, the monotony of whose verbal care is unalloyed by thought, such as the theology of Milton, which, even where it is dull, is nevertheless metaphysics. The mental vacuity of the great epic poets is sometimes epic in itself.

Some, indeed, escape into lusciousness and pageant, like Spencer, whose *Faerie Queene*, however, no one ever read.

[...] We read epics for the fable, or for the treatment of it, or for the verse.

Epics fundamentally dealing with religion can attain a full splendour only when that religion ceases to be of importance (loses its own importance). We delight in Athene because we are (perhaps precipitately) convinced that she did not exist. *Paradise Lost* is different. No one believes in Adam and Eve, but there are matters of controversy about the Trinity.

Dante has stood greatness better, for in the Protestant countries he is mere fable, and in the Catholic countries there is no religion.

These stunt diers succeed in making death comic and courage disgusting. It needs all our traditional use of respect to pity fools, and vain fools at that. Their end unites (?) suicide without pathos and tragedy without dignity.

It is idle, though perhaps interesting, to discuss what Columbus was, historically; sociologically, he is Portuguese.

Shaw is aware of mankind only as a problem. Chesterton is safer because he knows mankind to be a fact.

The astonishing fact – the only real fact – that things exist, that anything exists, that being is, is the soul of the breath of all the arts. That particular part of romanticism, which it fell to Coleridge best to form, has been called the Renascence of Wonder. But all genius (every idea of genius) is a renascence of wonder. In the soul, to accept is to lose.

A hope in a final – but not too final – justice, the 'God writes straight on crooked lines' of the Portuguese proverb...

... unless by a practical development of Einstein it be possible to relay our talk into the past. But there is a linguistic brake to that: the ancients are spared more than our mere noise. When Caesar begins to have heard Mussolini, he will be no wiser than he now yet has been.

End: The Gods will not tell us, nor will Fate. The Gods are dead and Fate is dumb. [*Source*: PETCL]

COMMENT AND RESPONSE

Pessoa's Place in Literature

GEORGE STEINER : Pessoa is one of the evident giants in modern literature. To read him is to enter fascinating and urgent worlds.

HAROLD BLOOM [*includes Pessoa among the twenty-six writers he discusses as essential to* The Western Canon *of literature (from Dante, Chaucer and Shakespeare... to Tolstoy, Proust and Joyce). He here comments on the influence of Whitman on Borges, Neruda and Pessoa*]: ... the amazing Portuguese poet, Fernando Pessoa (1888-1935), who as a fantastic invention surpasses any creation by Borges [...] Powerful as many of Pessoa's lyrics are, they are only one part of his work; he also invented a series of alternative poets – Alberto Caeiro, Álvaro de Campos, Ricardo Reis among them – and proceeded to write entire volumes of poems for them, or rather *as* them. Two of them – Caeiro and Campos – are great poets, wholly different from each other and from Pessoa, not to mention Reis, who is an interesting minor poet [...] Caeiro is a fascinating attempt to write what cannot be written. At the other limit of expression [...] Pessoa stations the outrageous Campos [...] the thirty-page 'Maritime Ode', Campos's masterwork and one of the major poems of the century [...] The ultimate lesson of Whitman's influence – on Borges, Neruda, Paz and so many more – may be that only an originality as outrageous as Pessoa's could hope to contain it without hazard to the poetic self or selves.

JORGE LUIS BORGES [*A 'letter' to Pessoa, for the commemoration of the fiftieth anniversary of his death, three years before the centenary of his birth*]: It is not the geographical links between us, but the blood of the Borges of Moncorvo and Acevedo which helps me to understand you, Pessoa. It cost you nothing to renounce all schools and dogmas, the self-important posturings, the rhetoric, and the dogged chore of representing a country, a class or an age. No doubt you have never pondered your place in the history of literature. I am quite sure that these sonorous tributes will astonish you — astonish you and yet touch your heart. Today you are *the* poet of Portugal. Inevitably, someone will pronounce the name of Camões. Dates – so beloved of all such celebrations – will not be lacking. You wrote for yourself, not for glory. Together we are going to share your verses; let me be your friend.

JOHN HOLLANDER : If Fernando Pessoa had never existed, Jorge Luis Borges might have had to invent him... This volume has brought a great poet to our attention again. Anybody who cares about poetry, about fictions of identity, about the whole of modernism, must be grateful.

ALBERTO DE LACERDA : I shall venture to say that, given the tragic implacable light which Pessoa throws on identity, on responsibility, poetic and otherwise, on shifting the notion of sincerity from the lyrical impulse to intellectual and psychological honesty, he is not the greatest, but the most emblematic poet of the Twentieth Century, as Baudelaire was for the Nineteenth Century. And he wrote, with a combination of strange passion and alluring detachment, the Intellectual Comedy that Valéry had dreamt of.

CYRIL CONNOLLY : Melancholy, mysterious, mildly paranoid, incontestably Portuguese... Pessoa hived off separate personalities like swarms of bees... I have sought for his shade in those Edwardian cafés in Lisbon which he haunted, for he was Lisbon's Cavafy or Verlaine.

ROMAN JAKOBSON : The name of Fernando Pessoa demands to be listed with those of other great world-class artists born in the 1880s: Stravinsky, Picasso, Joyce, Braque, Khlebnikov, Le Corbusier. Within this Portuguese poet we find, as if condensed, all the most typical characteristics of that remarkable group.

JOEL SERRÃO : Kierkegaard and Pessoa, beyond the circumstances of their individual lives, were above all witnesses – and also the theological, philosophic and poetic incarnations – of the crisis of values current in their time and still seething in our own. This crisis is common to all western countries, though in each it has taken a particular form according to local conditions, to the legacy of the past, to the hopes or despair of the present.

ANDREW HARVEY : Fernando Pessoa, with Rilke and Yeats, dominates twentieth-century poetry. Less visionary than Rilke and less brashly rhetorical than Yeats, he seems in many ways more contemporary in his range of acid bewilderments, his peculiar and plangent mixture of scepticism, anguish and bald detachment.

GABRIEL JOSIPOVICI : When I think of what is most radical in the literature of the past hundred years, of what embodies most clearly the essential spirit of modernism, I think of five grey-suited gentlemen: Constantin Cavafy, Franz Kafka, T.S. Eliot, Fernando Pessoa, Jorge Luis Borges [...] they are the ones who have renewed the language and shown us the way forward.

JEAN-MARIE LE SIDANER : Alone, in a suburban landscape or beside a canal, I've often thought of those office-workers, Kafka, Cavafy and Pessoa.

I too have laboured eight hours a day in dreary places, day-dreaming of power, of voyages, until it was time to go.

And then I would linger in the town, interminably, fashioning my heart of glass.

ROY CAMPBELL : [Pessoa] may claim to be the greatest literary figure of modern times.

ANTONIO TABUCCHI : [*Opening sentences of 'Requiem: a hallucination'*]: I thought: the bloke isn't going to turn up. And then I thought: I can't call him a 'bloke', he's a great poet, perhaps the greatest poet of the twentieth century, he died years ago, I should treat him with respect or, at least, with deference.

ANTONIO TABUCCHI : In nineteenth century fiction, characters had to be described straight off. There were rules for it. But Pessoa and Pirandello play the hunt-the-character game with the reader, and I've learnt from them.

HECTOR BIANCIOTTI : Here was Freud, patiently re-mapping the nature of man; there, Pirandello defining his characters through his metaphor of the broken mirror; Joyce, Svevo, Kafka, Proust, Eliot, all wrestling with their master-works: all over Europe an exuberant burgeoning of genius. But nothing in Portugal or so it seemed, and so in our blindness we long believed. And yet, at that very moment, on the furthest Atlantic shores of our continent, just before the darkness of Salazar's dictatorship engulfed the land, a young man of 26 proudly throws down this challenge to himself: 'What can a man of genius do but make – of himself and by himself – a whole literature?' And he will meet the challenge.

MICHAEL HAMBURGER : [In the poem] *The Tobacco Shop...* Pessoa anticipates not only existentialism but the *nouveau roman* and playwrights like Ionesco.

ANTHONY BURGESS : The once fashionable term 'existential' has been applied to [The Book of Disquietude]... If this is a novel which disdains the traditional movement of the novel, then it belongs to a very European category, though one is hard put to define exactly how... The elegance of the style... is an important component and a very ironic one... We must be given the chance to learn more about [Fernando Pessoa].

LAWRENCE FERLINGHETTI [*Dedication in his* Love in the Days of

Rage]: 'For Fernando Pessoa whose Anarchist Banker prefigured mine'.

MARK STRAND : Fernando Pessoa is the least known of the masters of twentieth-century poetry.

MICHAEL WOOD : Unmistakably one of this century's major poets... Reading him for the first time is like discovering Svevo or Borges.

MARTIN SEYMOUR-SMITH : [Pessoa's poetry] makes for one of the most remarkable bodies of work of the century [...] Pessoa shows as great an awareness of the problems facing the twentieth-century poet as anyone of his time.

DAVID T. HABERLY : Fernando Pessoa is the greatest Portuguese poet since Camões, and one of the most complex and astonishing figures of twentieth-century literature.

DAVID H. ROSENTHAL : Carlos Drummond de Andrade (1902-87) and Fernando Pessoa (1888-1935) rank among the foremost poets of our century, yet neither has received much recognition in the United States.

OCTAVIO PAZ : Anglomanic, myopic, courteous, elusive, dressed in black, reticent and familiar, the cosmopolitan who preaches nationalism, the *solemn investigator of useless things*, the humorist who never smiles and makes our blood run cold, the inventor of other poets and self-destroyer, the author of paradoxes clear as water and, like water, dizzying: *to pretend is to know oneself*, the mysterious one who does not cultivate mystery, mysterious as the moon at noon, the taciturn ghost of the Portuguese midday – who is Pessoa?

ROY CAMPBELL : [Pessoa's] English prose was masterly, and equal in subtlety, delicacy, and accuracy to that of any living English master. His book of poems, *Mensagem*, is a paean to the maritime history of Portugal comparable in that respect to nothing since the *Lusiads*.

EDWARD HONIG : Pessoa shifts the course of poetic practice in Portugal by dramatising the lyric, stretching certain syntactic conventions, and often tilting the diction towards English. In giving it something foreign to digest, Pessoa slowly transforms traditional materials, dead styles, creating a Portuguese which at times sounds foreign even to the native reader.

ERNESTO GUERRA DA CAL : An Anglo-Saxon by education, (he spent twelve years in South Africa from the age of five), he was nevertheless fully Lusitanian in spirit. His prophetic bent and pre-occupation with the mystical, irrational, religious and occult relate him to Blok, Yeats, Unamuno, Rilke and George, and like some of them, he was obsessed by the nature and meaning of personal identity.

OCTAVIO PAZ : Pessoa's experience... takes its place in the tradition of the great poets of the modern age, from Nerval and the German romantics on... His work is a step toward the unknown... A passion.

NEW YORK TIMES : Eloquent, volatile and obsessed with life – and death – [Pessoa is one of the] modernist giants in whose shadow we live and who made our century one of extraordinary richness.

JONATHAN GRIFFIN : Fernando Pessoa is the extreme example of what may be the essentially modern kind of poet: the objective introvert. None has more consistently tried to find his real self with its multiplicity intact and to keep his poems impersonal... Pessoa was a pioneer of a new kind of long poem, which would in fact answer twentieth-century needs – an open-ended dramatic monologue. Besides being a singer on a par with Yeats, Pessoa created three of this century's viable long poems.

ERNESTO GUERRA DA CAL : For Pessoa, the only truth in poetry is that which the poet may arrive at after eliminating all sentimental accessories, all accretion of emotional and sentient experiences in everyday life. And this much the poet can accomplish during the gestation period, through voluntary self-control and through conscious exclusion of such 'objective truth', until he reaches the point at which he is able to simulate that other truth which is a genuine act of knowledge and a true vision of the world.

PETER RICKARD : ... Above all, Pessoa has the merit of questioning our assumptions, of delving deeper into the things we take for granted, of making us think along new lines, and of presenting things to us in a different and startlingly unconventional way. Many poets have written about suicide, but who ever treated the subject as he has treated it? Many poets have apostrophized Night, but who has done so as Pessoa did? Who ever compared himself with someone else's last look? Who yearned to kiss the harpist's gesture, not her hands? Who has ranged so widely, so originally, so multifariously and at the same time so agonizingly and so poignantly over so many aspects of the mystery of existence and man's quest for identity?

ALAIN BOSQUET : This man who reasons so brilliantly is the archetype of the modern poet, no longer able to ignore the urgent need to imagine the existence – between man and the universe – of a relationship that remains stubbornly unverifiable. That part of his work that is closest to us, and furthest from traditional poetic preoccupations, shows us a Fernando Pessoa haunted by *the shrinkage of man*, man dethroned by his own irony and by his feeling that the universe will no longer allow itself to be controlled, or reduced to a set of readily acceptable formulae.

JOSÉ AUGUSTO SEABRA : In modern Portuguese literature Fernando Pessoa stands at the crossroads of more than one revolutionary poetic movement. Did he not dream of becoming, all by himself, 'a whole literature?' Above all, he in his passing left so turbulent a wake that he has been in danger of becoming for us a kind of *monstre sacré*, already a victim of his own mythology. And yet this strange, protean poet might have remained almost unnoticed during his lifetime but for the outrageous circumstances surrounding his generation. His work itself, breaking so many frontiers, was slow to win the recognition it deserved. Now, at last, ever more widely translated, he is seen as one of the primary poets of our century.

JACQUES BOREL : Nowhere is it easier to understand the profound, almost organic unity of this singular voice – without which, after all, there cannot be a body of work – than in those very moments when the poet probes his own conscience, hesitates to come forward, or declines to commit himself: in those moments of corrosive humour and self-denunciation, in that vivid lucidity with which he lays bare his own and the world's bones and nerves, in the ironic, bitter or bewildered declaration of that Nothing in which he ultimately discerns his own truth, or in that way of questioning his own authenticity which is authenticity itself. Whenever this voice relentlessly announces the void, the nothingness, the intangibility, the atomization of the personality which are the fate and sick-bed of the poet – immediately the inspiration is unimpeachable, the dwelling-place itself of this being that creates itself by denying itself, or by 'going over to the other side'.

ARMAUD GUIBERT : No one has been more endowed with that long patience which is genius than this outstanding man. One begins to understand how much, behind the veil of his disguises, he was devoured by fire, fretted by intelligence, ironical and serious, superior to all the passions yet ignoring none...

C.K. WILLIAMS : At last, at last, at last, Pessoa again! More Pessoa! One of the very great poets of the twentieth-century, again and more! And one of the fascinating figures of all literature, with his manifold identities, his amazing audacities, his brilliance and his shyness.

R.W. HOWES : Fernando Pessoa is widely considered to be the greatest Portuguese poet of the twentieth century and a major writer of European stature. His enigmatic personality and the potent combination of poetic genius and metaphysics in his verse have fascinated a wide variety of readers both in Portugal and abroad.

PETER RICKARD : We are torn between the intuition which believes, and the reason which denies; that is the agonizing dilemma which Pessoa presents so vividly in his verse.

ARNALDO SARAIVA : Did Fernando Pessoa consider himself a genius? No doubt we have to say that he did – providing that we exclude the old sense of the word as denoting the guardian angel who presided over births and protected certain households. In all other senses the word suits him well: exceptional (literary) creator or inventor; seer and prophet; manufacturer of a community's myths; superior intelligence and sensibility; a model of wisdom; rare example of virtues. (…)

We no longer find it all that difficult, today, to believe in Pessoa's genius, even though the word – thanks to Romanticism – tends to raise doubts and suspicions in the modern mind.

Indeed, given the riches of his work, now that he is dead we perhaps will not find it difficult to admit that he has become also a genius in the old, first sense of the word. Perhaps now we might even say, without exaggeration or metaphor, that Fernando Pessoa seems more and more to resemble a higher spirit who through his voice incarnate keeps kindly watch over the condition of man, of nature, and of the Portuguese fatherland.

JEAN-PIERRE THIBAUDAT : Article in *Liberation* (about Pessoa's 'Tobacco Shop'.

JOSÉ RÉGIO : Truly, Fernando Pessoa seems able to bring the resources of his genius, his command of metre, his imagination, his emotion to bear upon any theme, pretext or motive for a poem, as well as those qualities which make him so admirable a translator (his version of 'The Raven' by Poe is sufficient testimony on its own) and so disconcerting a 'ventriloquist'; but the most profound roots of his poetry delve deep down into an apprehension of the underlying, metaphysical meaning of things, into the mystery that sustains all; and thence derives perhaps that magic we recognize in his poetry, despite some shortcomings and limitations.

MIGUEL TORGA : Fernando Pessoa is dead. As soon as I read the news in the paper, I closed my surgery and plunged into the mountains. There, with the pines and rocks, I wept for the death of the greatest poet of our times, whom Portugal watched pass by in his coffin, on his way to immortality, without even asking who he was.

Heteronymity and heteronyms

On Heteronymity

OCTAVIO PAZ : [The heteronyms] are a literary invention and a psychological necessity but also something more. In a certain way they are what Pessoa might have been or would have liked to be; in another, more profound sense, what he did *not* want to be: a personality.

F.E.G. QUINTANILHA : An introvert by disposition, Pessoa submitted himself to continuous analysis in a search for a common expression for the emotional chaos with which he felt himself affected. He kept oscillating between an idea and its opposite, and was clearly aware of the relativity of all truth. Hence his tendency to adopt an attitude of non-commitment, present throughout his poetry, and prose writings. Aware of his own limitations, together with his gift for empathy, Pessoa was led by his non-conforming, argumentative mind, and by his intellectual curiosity to attempt to synthesize the different facets of his character into a coherent scheme. Thus, what began as a state of chaos, aggravated after adolescence, became through a process of self-analysis and selection the aesthetic basis of his heteronymic theory.

JACINTO DO PRADO COELHO : I readily accept that Pessoa 'himself', Caeiro, Reis, Campos etc. were obeying different inspirations, that

Pessoa-author often felt himself possessed by Caeiro or Reis or Campos, or by the heroic rapture of *Mensagem*. But I also believe that in all that there was a subtle interplay of irrational impulses and deliberate intention. Whence come (and I am not talking about his undeniable readiness to pretend, to 'play tricks') the vacillations and contradictions we find when Pessoa refers to the nature and origin of his heteronyms; he claims either to have discovered them in a state of trance, so that he was simply acting as a medium when writing, for instance, the poems of Caeiro, or that he constructed them within himself; he considers them his 'split personalities' – but immediately corrects this by speaking of 'inventions'; sometimes he presents them as separate characters, as real as he is himself, and sometimes he acknowledges that they are only parts of himself, of what he is and of what he might or might not have been.

MARTIN SEYMOUR-SMITH : He dissected himself into three carefully constructed personalities, 'heteronyms', and another called Pessoa, and held private colloquies with himself [...] Nor was all this mere fun. But in the light of such wilful eccentricity Pessoa's self-knowledge was strangely profound, the intellectual plan behind his poetry is as remarkably lucid and uneccentric as that of any in the twentieth century.

ADOLFO CASAIS MONTERO : The poetry of Pessoa and of his heteronyms is that of a great poet. Upon this point at least there is complete unanimity between Pessoa himself, Álvaro de Campos, Alberto Caeiro and Ricardo Reis – yet another argument against the thesis of those who accept the total separation of the different heteronymous personalities: their works are, one and all, equally admirable.

SERGE FAUCHEREAU : The use of heteronyms puts an end to all notions of an individual body of work, of a personal stamp. By multiplying the ethical or aesthetic points of view, it enables the writer to escape the bounds of his personality. We move beyond the question of sincerity, and subjectivity is dissolved into a plurality of objectivities.

OCTAVIO PAZ : The relationship between Pessoa and his heteronyms is not the same as that between the dramatist or the novelist and his characters. He is not an inventor of poet characters but a creator of poet works.

CLAUDE MICHEL CLUNY : This intellectual, devotee of all games of wit, devoured by erudition, was the *inspired* maker of his inventions. To mention only some of these, he brought forth out of himself three new poets, Alberto Caeiro being, according to his laws of fictional creation, a sort of master for the other two. Each of them has his own biography, which is amusing; his own face, which is interesting... his own style, his lit-

erary territory: that is the miracle of Pessoa's creative *depersonalization.*
What we should also note is that, though Pessoa is elusive, and never takes
off one mask without putting on another, each of his heteronyms refrains
from all contrivance. The voice is pure behind the mask, each language
true – or it creates its truth as it speaks.

RONALD W. SOUSA : In connection with the exploration of the 'self',
it should be noted that 'Pessoa', a not-uncommon last name, means, as
common noun, 'person' or 'persona' and, by extension to its well-known
roots in Classical culture, 'mask', denotations upon which Pessoa constantly trades in his writing.

Alberto Caeiro

THOMAS MERTON : The interest of the poetic (or anti-poetic) experience of Alberto Caeiro lies in its Zen-like immediacy [...] Pessoa-Caeiro
may be numbered among those Western writers who have expressed
something akin to the Zen way of seeing – the 'knack of full awareness'.

OCTAVIO PAZ : Caeiro is everything that Pessoa is not, and more –
everything a modern poet could never be: a man reconciled to nature.
Before Christianity, yes, but also before work and history. Before consciousness. Caeiro denies, by the mere act of existing, not just the
Symbolist aesthetics of Pessoa but all aesthetics, all values, all ideas. Does
something remain? Everything remains, clean of the ghosts and the cobwebs of culture. The world exists because my senses tell me so; and by so
telling me they tell me I too exist. Yes. I shall die and the world will die, but
to die is to live.

PETER RICKARD : Some of Caeiro's ideas strikingly anticipate certain
aspects of modern existentialist thought: he would certainly have subscribed
to what Sartre was later to write in one of the first pages of *L'être et le néant.*

JONATHAN GRIFFIN : The style of Caeiro is an unostentatious anti-
poetry — this in 1914 [...] His teaching – according to some notes in the
name of Ricardo Reis – did for a moment seem to Pessoa 'the one source
of consolation' for those who feel like exiles in modern life.

F.E.G. QUINTANILHA : Pessoa wanted Caeiro to be the reinterpreta-
tion in twentieth-century terms of Man in a state of innocence. He is [...]
the man to whom the world of thought appears as an *illness of the senses.*

ARMANDO MARTINS JANEIRA : I have not found any references
to Zen in Fernando Pessoa's work and have no doubt that he never
encountered the thought of this Buddhist sect. Nonetheless, one can trace

profound similarities and numerous points of contact between Pessoa's thought and that of Zen [...] Freedom, the 'supreme joy', comes from experiencing communion with things, the placing of the ego within the Universe. Zen means thinking with one's body. This communion of the whole man with the Universe cannot be achieved by the intellect alone. Thus Caeiro declares that he has never committed 'the error of wanting to know too much' nor 'the error of wanting to know by means of the intellect alone'. [...] the coincidences of thought between Caeiro and Zen are to be found not only in the distrust of language and reason, but even in the suppression of dualism, in the annulment of the contradiction of opposites, which is fundamental to all Buddhist and Hindu thinking.

Ricardo Reis

F.E.G. QUINTANILHA : In opposition to Caeiro's constant discovery of things, Reis appears as the man within the tradition of the *sage*, for whom there is no more to learn, and to whom the world has nothing more to offer.

OCTAVIO PAZ : Reis's stoicism is a manner of not being in the world, without actually leaving it. His political ideas have a similar significance: they are not a programme but a negation of the present state of things. He neither hates Christ nor does he love Him; Christianity bores him although – aesthete to the end – when he thinks of Jesus he admit that 'his pitiful suffering form brought us something that was missing'. The true deity for Reis is Fate, and all of us, men and myths, are subject to its rule.

PETER RICKARD : The *Odes* of Ricardo Reis contain obvious reminiscences of Horace. Reis, like the Latin poet, treats the themes of the fleeting hour, the vanity of earthly goods, the snares of Fortune, the changing seasons, the brevity of human existence, life in the country, and even *aurea mediocritas* of a sort.

JONATHAN GRIFFIN : Reis is the nearest that Pessoa could come to being Caeiro. A disciple of Caeiro, Reis works paganism into an ethical doctrine, part epicurean, part stoic, yet conscious of, and kept clear of, a human environment conditioned by Christianity; a doctrine for people in the modern world to live by, so as to suffer as little as possible.

Álvaro de Campos

ROY CAMPBELL : It is strange that a person whose name, Pessoa, *means* 'person', should be at the same time so impersonal, and yet able to project such thundering personalities as Álvaro de Campos, whose character is so real that you have to pinch yourself while reading him to remind yourself that this amazing spouter of blood and thunder is fiction... The *Maritime Ode* is the loudest poem ever written.

PETER RICKARD : Campos, though far more strident and exclamatory in his early poems than Whitman himself, was on the other hand less enumerative, less sensual, less hearty, and far more thoughtful. Yet there was more than enough, in the poems of Pessoa's Whitmanesque phase, to shock and startle the Lisbon public... By 1917, Pessoa was already tired of futurism and its ethic of dynamism and even of violence, and had come to realize that he had much to say that would have occurred neither to Whitman nor to Marinetti... Now he becomes *par excellence* the poet appalled by the emptiness of his own existence, lethargic, lacking in will-power, seeking inspiration, or at all events finding it in semi-conscious states, in the twilight world between waking and sleeping, in dreams and in drunkenness.

R. CLIVE WILLIS : The Whitmanesque and futurist Álvaro de Campos was closer to Pessoa; in his noisy and tumultuous verse there was room for anything. His early verse thundered with the enthusiastic desire to identify the poet with the whole of creation but he ended pessimistically in isolationism.

JONATHAN GRIFFIN : But the repressed Dionysiac Pessoa did burst out: in modern dress, of course. The modern dress was Álvaro de Campos. Through Campos, Pessoa saved himself from settling down into Reis; it is as though Dionysus saved him from Apollo.

F.E.G. QUINTANILHA : Campos never attains a final harmony and it is in this oscillation between extremes that he becomes a more accurate reflection of the real personality of Pessoa. He reflects with lucidity the clash of tendencies, and the evolution of thought within both a scientific approach to life and a decadent and narcissistic attitude. This is at the root of Pessoa's work and is present in different degrees in all the heteronyms.

MARIA ALIETE GALHOZ : I have only truly loved Álvaro de Campos after I learned how to love Lisbon. Álvaro de Campos is Lisbon.

'Fernando Pessoa'

ROY CAMPBELL : Some of the best poetry of Pessoa, in his own name, often trembles on the very verge of silence, like Verlaine's.

R. CLIVE WILLIS : When writing under his own name Pessoa was essentially a metaphysical poet, a poet of subjective and introverted idealism who saw himself as an occultist medium seeking to penetrate the labyrinth of the individual consciousness and indulging frequently in childhood reminiscence. Like Jiménez in Spain he popularised in Portugal the short poem which sought to capture the fleeting moment, the passing sensation, the sudden emotion, especially when it struck a deeper, more intimate chord within him.

Bernardo Soares

WILLIAM BOYD : Soares is one of Pessoa's 'heteronyms' — false identities he created and inhabited in order to write. His three poetic heteronyms – Caeiro, Reis and de Campos – are the better known, but Soares comes closest to the writer himself, not simply because, like Pessoa, he was a lowly functionary whose life of tedium and routine was charged with fervid dreams of literature, but also because of his voice – plangent, heartfelt and ruthlessly bereft of self-pity – through which one gains a real sense of the complex personality of this astonishing chameleon of a poet... Pessoa's amazing personality is as beguiling and mysterious as his unique poetic output. We cannot learn too much about him.

P.J. KAVANAGH : In *The Book of Disquietude* the obsession of the man alone in the room is the question of identity: who am I and if I find the 'I' that I am what difference will that make, if any? Round and round he goes, up and down, until you want to shake him, implore him to go out into the street, get drunk, fall in love, anything; but impatience and boredom mysteriously give way to an almost hypnotised fascination. It is like watching a particularly slow-moving and convoluted oriental dance that makes a Westerner want to scream but which slowly draws him into his own timescale, and one he at last recognizes.

Pessoa is careful to keep himself distinct from his solipsistic character, who he calls 'Soares'... [However] there is no doubt that the book is an exploration of a part of Pessoa himself, and a part of most of us, which we try to keep in abeyance, that part which sometimes finds most of our public and external life unreal.

JOHN WAIN: *Alberto Caeiro*
                     Ricardo Reis
                     Álvaro de Campos
                     Fernando Pessoa
                     … what resounding Portuguese names!

Names full of cloud and seagulls, the surf-crash
of a South-Western coast, the tidal swing of the Tagus:
names full of the weather of Portugal,
the long empty roads, the eucalyptus trees,
the rice fields and the Atlantic promontories:
the sardines grilling over charcoal in side-street bars,
the street-markets, the churches full of God's calm shadow,
citizens with head-colds riding in the trams,
the yellow trams of Lisbon…

Fernando Pessoa, the Man

PIERRE HOURCADE : If it is sometimes true that a well-founded biography illuminates every aspect of a body of work – for instance in the case of certain Romantic poets – the opposite could almost be said to be true in the case of Fernando Pessoa. His life *ne nous regarde pas*, in both senses of the phrase: it is no concern of ours, and it is not turned towards us.

JORGE DE SENA : In private life, as I saw him and as all of his family, friends, and acquaintances can or did testify, he could be a delightful man, full of charm and good humour, a humour that was very British […] But this role was also that of a heteronym, which saved him from intimacy with anyone while allowing him to take a modest part in the normal feast of daily life. Certainly there was a kind of frightening cold – something of the terrifying cold that you feel sometimes when reading him – emanating from Pessoa for those not admitted to the inner sanctum.

RONALD W. SOUSA : Pessoa was well versed in various branches of esoterica: he had read in Theosophy, Astrology, Freemasonry, and Rosicrucianism and had progressed from them to other types of occultism, including spiritualism, automatic writing and, by the time of his death, alchemy and magic. He had read works dealing with the cabala and consequently knew of numerology. On at least one occasion he claimed the possession of certain psychic powers, including clairvoyance. He often stated that he felt he was controlled by dark forces.

MARIA ALIETE GALHOZ : Who is Fernando Pessoa exactly? The high flying poet? The perturbing virtuoso in the exercise of reasoning power? The intellectual humorist of *nonsense*? The dilettante occultist who made horoscopes? The impeccable aesthete of ironic insensitivity? The creator of prophetic and mathematic Fifth Empires of the Spirit? The uneasy and monotonous commentator on the absurdity and the miracle of life? We can question him in this way in the various lights of the kaleidoscopic combinations of his creative genius, and in this way, through his work, his intentions, his negations, he appears as if he is disclosing himself and at the same time preventing us from guessing, conjecturing or misinterpreting him.

AGOSTINHO DA SILVA : Fernando Pessoa deliberately confirmed the natural chance of his birth: he was and would be Portuguese because of his deeply-held conviction that God cannot abandon his other chosen people, and that once the domination of Europe is over and when technology has exhausted all its possibilities, when the Protestant economy has been found to be completely anti-human, when state centralization has shown itself to be sterile, Portugal will once again rise to build its world of peace, however great its sacrifice may have to be; a world of peace which will not proceed like a Roman peace or a British peace, i.e., from the exterior to the interior, from a Caesar to his subjects, from the law courts to human individuals. It will be a peace which will take place above all in souls. The law will be entirely non-written and at best, even unformulated. It will be the Kingdom of God which arises through the interior transformation of Man.

JOÃO GASPAR SIMÕES : It was written in the stars that he would be happy in that part of his life directly connected with the subconscious, his true home. Between birth and consciousness there is an intermediate zone in which a living human being does not yet belong to this world; years of life flow past, no longer life within the womb, but subconscious life, in the full sense of the word. It is during that uncertain period of our existence – early childhood – that is woven, out of cellular deposits of pre-human personality, the spiritual tissue that will cloak the adult consciousness. That is when Fernando Pessoa *unknowingly knew* the joys of earthly paradise, the gift of living, yet as if unaware that he was alive. And so it was that, when one day he became aware, he *felt* in a flash that consciousness was to be the great grief of his life.

ARMAND GUIBERT : Always dressed soberly, wearing clothes of an Anglo-Saxon style, he never lost the imprint of his adolescence in a British country, and in particular in his strict reserve of his privacy: nothing southern or Latin in this respect. He repressed, however, a great nervous febrility, noticeable in the way he would press his forehead against his hand. He smoked eighty cigarettes a day.

PIERRE HOURCADE : He was there, without warning, late or early – never to time – always unexpected, even when I had long arranged the meeting. And in the short moments of his presence, he seemed to live double, triple, as if to concentrate the time, and to recoup the non-existent time that had gone before.

PIERRE HOURCADE : He radiated a mixture of charm, malice and courtesy; a seductive, slightly feverish aura brightened by the nimbleness of his mind: it was as if the air we breathed around him was richer in oxygen than ordinary air. Fernando Pessoa quite firmly declined all shackles, and I believe that, no matter when or where, he would have erected that same watertight bulkhead between the part of himself he granted to others, and the essential part of his being, of which he was determined to be sole judge, and for which he was responsible to himself alone.

APOTHEOSIS

Page 313 (Opposite)
1 (Above & below) : Card cut-and-fold effigy.
2 : 100 Escudos banknote.
3 : Main staircase, University Fernando Pessoa, Oporto.
4 : Part of a map of Lisbon, for Pessoa pilgrims.
5 : Street sign.
6 : Symbol of Casa Fernando Pessoa (his last apartment, now his museum and arts foundation).

Page 314 (Overleaf)
The tomb at the Jerónimos monastery, Potugal's national pantheon, where Pessoa now lies, finally united with Alberto Caeiro, Richard Reis, Álvaro de Campos – a verse from each embellishes a face of the square memorial pillar.

Apotheosis

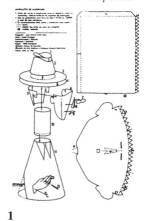

1

2

3

4

5

6

BIBLIOGRAPHY

**Selected bibliography in English
& some key works in Portuguese**

JOSÉ BLANCO

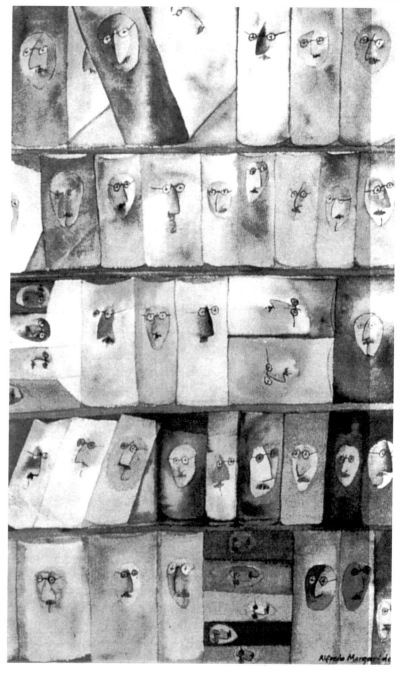

Detail of painting, *The Library* by Alfredo Margarido. See colour plate 12

TRANSLATIONS

I : POETRY

1. Book-length

GREEN, J.C.R.: **By Weight of Reason**. Translated by... Shirley, Solihull, Warks: The Aguila Publishing Co. Ltd., 1968. [6 poems by Alberto Caeiro, 3 poems by Fernando Pessoa, 1 poem from *Mensagem*].

GREEN, J.C.R.: **Álvaro de Campos. The Tobacconist**. Translated by... Breakish, Isle of Skye: The Phaeton Press, The Aguila Publishing Co. Ltd., 1975. [12 poems by Álvaro de Campos].

GREEN, J.C.R.: **Ricardo Reis. The Ancient Rhythm**. Translated by... Breakish, Isle of Skye: The Phaeton Press, The Aguila Publishing Co. Ltd., 1976. [23 poems by Ricardo Reis].

GREEN, J.C.R.: **The Stations of the Cross**. Translated by... Breakish, Isle of Skye: The Phaeton Press, The Aguila Publishing Co. Ltd., 1976. [22 poems by Fernando Pessoa, 2 poems from *Mensagem*, 1 fragment from *Fausto*].

GREEN, J.C.R.: **The Keeper of Flocks**. Translated by... Breakish, Isle of Skye: The Phaeton Press, The Aguila Publishing Co. Ltd., 1976. [19 poems by Alberto Caeiro].

GREENE, James; MAFRA, Clara de Azevedo: **Fernando Pessoa. The Surprise of Being**. Twenty-five poems translated by... Introduction by Jaime H. Silva. London: Angel Books, 1986. [23 poems by Fernando Pessoa and 2 poems from *Mensagem*. 2nd ed. 1987]. Bilingual.

GRIFFIN, Jonathan: **Fernando Pessoa I-IV**. Translated by... [4 vols: I – Alberto Caeiro, II – Ricardo Reis, III – Álvaro de Campos, IV – Fernando Pessoa]. Oxford: Carcanet Press, 1971. [21 poems by Fernando Pessoa, 22 poems by Alberto Caeiro, 11 poems by Álvaro de Campos, 17 poems by Ricardo Reis and 16 poems from *Mensagem* – total 87 poems].

GRIFFIN, Jonathan: **Fernando Pessoa. Selected Poems**. Translated by... London: Penguin Modern European Poets, Penguin Books, 1974. [65 poems by Fernando Pessoa, 14 poems by Alberto Caeiro, 10 poems by Álvaro de Campos, 14 poems by Ricardo Reis and 3 poems from *Mensagem* – total 106 poems. 2nd ed. with new Supplement, 1982; repr. 1988.].

GRIFFIN, Jonathan: **Fernando Pessoa. Message**. Translated by... Introduction by Helder Macedo. London: The Menard Press/King's College London, 1992. Bilingual. [44 poems (complete)].

HONIG, Edwin: **Selected Poems by Fernando Pessoa**. Including poems by his heteronyms Alberto Caeiro, Ricardo Reis, Álvaro de Campos, as well as some of his English sonnets and selections from his letters. Translated by... with an introduction by Octavio Paz. Chicago: The Swallow Press, 1971. [9 poems by Fernando Pessoa, 11 poems by Alberto Caeiro, 8 poems by Álvaro de Campos, 10 poems by Ricardo Reis – total 38 poems, plus 3 prose excerpts and 10 sonnets from *35 Sonnets*]. Bilingual.

HONIG, Edwin; BROWN, Susan M.: **The Keeper of Sheep by Fernando Pessoa**. Translated by... Riverdale-on-Hudson (New York): The Sheep Meadow Press, 1986. [Complete series – 44 poems].

HONIG, Edwin; Brown, Susan M.: **Poems of Fernando Pessoa**. Translated and edited by ... New York: The Ecco Press, 1986. [25 poems by Fernando Pessoa, 25 poems by Alberto Caeiro, 18 poems by Álvaro de Campos, 17 poems by Ricardo Reis and complete translation of *Mensagem* – total 129 poems, plus 22 English poems (3 poems by Alexander Search, 1 poem from *The Mad Fiddler*, 8 poems from *Inscriptions* and 10 sonnets from *35 Sonnets*)].

HONIG, Edwin; BROWN, Susan M.: **Fernando Pessoa. Message**. [Repr. from *Poems of Fernando Pessoa*, New York: The Ecco Press, 1986]. Translated by... Ed. by José Augusto Seabra. Lisbon: Edições Asa, 1991 [44 poems (complete). The volume includes French, German and Chinese translations].

MACEDO, Suzette: **The Tobacconist's. Tabacaria. A poem by Fernando Pessoa** (Álvaro de Campos). Translation by... Lisbon: Calouste Gulbenkian Foundation, 1987. Bilingual.

MONTEIRO, George: **Fernando Pessoa. Self-analysis and Thirty other poems**. Translation by... Lisbon: Calouste Gulbenkian Foundation, 1988 [9 poems by Fernando Pessoa, 5 poems by Alberto Caeiro, 12 poems by Álvaro de Campos and 5 poems by Ricardo Reis – total 31 poems]. Bilingual.

QUINTANILHA, F.E.G.: **Fernando Pessoa. Sixty Portuguese Poems**. Introduction, selection, English translation of the poems and notes by... Cardiff: University of Wales Press, 1971 [15 poems by Fernando Pessoa, 11 poems by Alberto Caeiro, 10 poems by Álvaro de Campos, 9 poems by Ricardo Reis and 12 poems from *Mensagem* – total 57 poems, plus 3 sonnets from *35 Sonnets*. Rep. 1973; 1st ed. in paperback, 1988]. Bilingual.

RICKARD, Peter: **Fernando Pessoa. Selected Poems**. Edited and translated by... Edinburgh and Austin: Edinburgh University Press and University of Texas Press, 1971. [15 poems by Fernando Pessoa, 17 poems by Alberto Caeiro, 14 poems by Álvaro de Campos, 21 poems by Ricardo Reis and 3 poems from *Mensagem* – total 70 poems]. Bilingual.

2. Special Editions

MONTEIRO, George: **Fernando Pessoa... A Tribute. 10 Poems Translated on the Occasion of the 100th Anniversary of His Birth**. Conceived, designed and illustrated by Walter Feldman. Providence (Rhode Island): Ziggurat Press, 1988. [*Fernando Pessoa*: 'Self-Analysis'; 'Reaper'; 'This'; 'Clearly Non-Campos'. *Alberto Caeiro*: 'Pity the flowers in the corner of formal gardens'; 'This morning, early, I went out'. *Ricardo Reis*: 'I fear Destiny, Lydia. Nothing is certain'; 'I fear for my fate, Lydia'. *Álvaro de Campos*: 'Psyche-Typing (Or Psycho-Typing)'. *Mensagem*: 'Ulysses'. Translated by ...].

3. In Books

AGNETA, Joseph Luke: [*Alberto Caeiro*. 'Virgil's shepherds played flutes and other things'; 'At twilight leaning over the window'. *Fausto*. 'Ah, all is symbol and analogy!' *Fernando Pessoa*. 'Unexpected hand of some hidden ghost'; 'Eros and Psyche'; 'Great mysteries live'; 'Death is the curve of the road'; 'Rest a moment'. *Mensagem*. 'Horizon'. Translated by...]. In

Américo da Costa Ramalho, **Portuguese Essays**. Lisbon: National Secretariat for Information, 1963, pp. 47-84. [2nd rev. 1968].

CAMPBELL, Roy: [*Fernando Pessoa*. 'The thing that hurts and wings'; 'Death comes before its time'; 'The poet fancying each belief'. *Álvaro de Campos*. 'Maritime Ode' (exc.) Translated by...]. In his **Portugal**. London: Max Reinhardt, 1957, pp. 157-160. [Chicago: Henry Regener, 1958; repr. in **The Collected Poems of Roy Campbell**, Vol. 3, Translations, with a foreword by Edith Sitwell, London: The Bodley Head, 1960, pp. 136-139; also in Roy Campbell: II, **Poetry Translations**, ed. Peter Alexander, Michael Chapman and Marcia Leveson, Craighall: Ad. Donker, 1985].

GRIFFIN, Jonathan: '*Fernando Pessoa. Notes for a Dramatic Poem on Faust'*. A selection translated with an Introduction by... In **Comparative Criticism. A Yearbook**, IV. Ed. by E.S. Shaffer. Cambridge: Cambridge University Press, 1982, pp. 281-320.

HONIG, Edwin: [Álvaro de Campos. 'Salutation to Walt Whitman'. Translated by...]. In **Walt Whitman. The Measure of His Song**. Ed. by Jim Perlman & Dan Campion. Introduction by Ed Folsom. Minneapolis: Holy Cow! Press, 1981, pp 32-39.

JENNINGS, Hubert D.: '*Fernando Pessoa. A Selection of the Poems'*. Translated by... in his **Fernando Pessoa in Durban**. Durban: Durban Corporation, [1986]. [18 poems by Fernando Pessoa, 17 poems by Alberto Caeiro, 6 poems by Álvaro de Campos, 11 poems by Ricardo Reis and 9 poems from *Mensagem* – total 61 poems].

LONGLAND, Jean R.: [*Fernando Pessoa*. 'The poet is a feigner'. *Alberto Caeiro*. 'I am not always consistent in what I write and say'. *Álvaro de Campos*. 'Lisbon Revisited (1923)'; 'On Lloyd George near Babylon's throne'. *Ricardo Reis*. 'When Lydia, our autumn comes'; 'As if each kiss should prove'. *Mensagem*. 'The Specter'; 'Night'. Translated by...] In Américo da Costa Ramalho, **Portuguese Essays**. Lisbon: National Secretariat for Information, 1963, pp. 55-70. [Repr. 1968].

MERTON, Thomas. [*Alberto Caeiro*. 'My gaze is clear as a sun flower'; 'Lightly, lightly, so lightly'; 'I do not bother with rhymes'; 'The Tagus is finer than the creek'; 'What we see of things is the things themselves'; 'If people insist on my having'; 'If I sometimes say that flowers smile'; 'Last evening a city man'; 'Rather the flying bird, leaving no trace; 'Poor flowers in geometric beds'; 'The mystery of things – where is it found?'; 'The bus has gone by'. Translated by...]. **The Keeper of the Flocks**. Kentucky: Abbey of Our Lady of Gethsemani, 1965. [Repr. in 'Fernando Pessoa. Twelve Poems from 'The Keeper of the Flocks', *New Directions in Prose and Poetry*, 19, ed. by J. Laughlin. New York, New Directions, 1966, pp. 299-307; also in **The Collected Poems of Thomas Merton**, New York: New Directions, 1977, pp. 987-996].

PARKER, John M. [*Fernando Pessoa*. 'This'; 'She sings, poor reaping girl'; 'O church-bell of my village'. *Albert Caeiro*. 'My Gaze is as clear as a sun-flower'; 'To-day I read almost two pages'. *Álvaro de Campos*. 'Tobacco Kiosk'; 'I have an awful cold'. *Álvaro de Campos*. 'Here, sit beside me Lydia'; 'Hold nothing in your hands'. Translated by...]. In his **Three Twentieth-century Portuguese Poets**. Johannesburg: Witwatersrand University Press, 1960, pp. 2-19.

4. In Periodicals

GRIFFIN, Jonathan: [*Fernando Pessoa*. 'To the Blind and the Deaf I Leave'; 'This Life Has Happened to Me'; 'The Counter-Symbol'; 'The Ancient Censer'; 'Between the Sleep and the Dream'. *Mensagem*. 'Dom Sebastião'; 'Affonso de Albequerque'; 'Night'. *Alberto Caeiro*. 'What we see of things are the things'; 'Rather the flight of a bird, which passes and leaves no trail'; 'One wildly clear day'; 'If, After I Die'. *Ricardo Reis*. 'The Bee'; 'I Want the Flower You Are'; 'A Better Destiny'; 'If I Remember'. *Álvaro de Campos*. 'Clouds'; 'Country Holiday'; 'There crossed My Path'; 'Huge are the Deserts'. Translated by...]. *Modern Poetry in Translation. 13/14. Portugal*, Compiled by Helder Macedo. London: Modern Poetry in Translation Limited, 1972, pp. 4-9. [20 poems].

GRIFFIN, Jonathan. *'Fernando Pessoa: a brief study of his dominant quest'* [*Fausto*. 'I stop at the edge of me and lean over...' *Fernando Pessoa*. 'Stations of the Cross I-V'; 'I've in me, like a cloud'; 'Still is not night and'; 'Lucky ones – someone waving'; 'They pass in the street, the processions'; 'If, by chance, estranged even from what I've dreamed'; 'At night I can't sleep'; 'Don't know how many souls I have'; 'The child I was is weeping in the street'; 'Day by day we change into the one'; 'My God! My God! who am I, I who don't'. Translated by...]. *Temenos*, 10, London, 1989, pp. 25-40. [30 poems].

HARVEY, Andrew. [*Álvaro de Campos*. 'The Ancients invoke the Muses'; 'Unfurling before an imaginary crowd of starred heavens'; 'I would love to love to love'; 'Wherever I am and go, where I am not, and don't go'; 'Tripe à la mode de Caen'. *Alberto Caeiro*. 'The Tagus is more beautiful than the river that runs through my village'; 'I've never understood how you could find a sunset sad'; 'When spring returns'; 'As, so you want a better light'; 'When the grass grows over my tomb'; 'It isn't enough just opening the window'; 'This is, perhaps, the last day of my life'; 'Sometimes, on days of perfect and exact light'; 'Lightly, lightly, very lightly'. *Ricardo Reis*. 'You are alone. You know that. Be quiet, and pretend'; 'I do not sing of night for in my song'; 'It is not you, Christ, whom I hate or do not love'; 'Innumerable beings live in us'; 'I await, with equanimity, the unknown'; 'I prefer roses, my love, to my country'. Translated by...]. *Normal, A Quarterly of Arts and Ideas*, 3, New York, Winter 1987, pp. 16-23. [20 poems].

HONIG, Edwin. [*Álvaro de Campos*. 'Maritime Ode'. Translated by...]. *New Directions in Prose and Poetry 23*, ed. by J. Laughlin, New York: New Directions, 1971, pp. 103-133.

JENNINGS, Hubert D.: *'The Many Faces of Fernando Pessoa'* [*Álvaro de Campos*. 'A Note'; 'Lisbon Revisited (1923)'; 'That Old Anguish'. *Ricardo Reis*. 'It is you, the living flower, I want'; 'I rest secure on the firm pillar'; 'Happy those whose ashes lie under the trees'. *Alberto Caeiro*. 'My glance is like that of the sunflower'; 'And there are poets who are artists'; 'Blessed the same sun of ours from other lands'; 'The astonishing reality of things'; 'I go inside and shut the window'. *Fernando Pessoa*. 'It is not yet night'. *Mensagem*. 'Horizon', 'Initiation'. Translated by...]. *Contrast*, 27, VII, November 1971, pp. 51-64. [14 poems].

LONGLAND, Jean R.: [*Fernando Pessoa*. 'The poet is a feigner'; 'Between the sleep and the dream'. *Ricardo Reis.* 'You believers in Christs and Marys'. *Álvaro de Campos.* 'I have a terrible cold'; 'Cross on the door of the tobacco shop'; 'At the wheel'; 'Tobacco Shop'. *Mensagem.* 'Dom Sebastiaõ, King of Portugal'. *Alberto Caeiro.* 'If my life were only an oxcart'; 'If I could be the dust of the road'. Translated by...]. *Poet Lore,* Autumn 1970, pp 280-292. [10 poems].

MONTEIRO, George: [*Álvaro de Campos.* 'A cross? on the door of the tobacco shop?'. *Ricardo Reis.* 'The God Pan did not die'. *Alberto Caeiro.* 'Today, I nearly read two pages'. *Álvaro de Campos.* 'Tripe, *Porto* Style'; 'An Instantly Venerable Sonnet'. *Fernando Pessoa.* 'Self-Analysis'. Translated by...]. *Translation,* XVII, New York, Fall 1986, pp. 225-230.

RITCHIE, George: '*Fernando Pessoa.* '*The Mariner'.* A '*static drama*' *in one act*'. Translated by... *Translation,* XXV, Portuguese Issue. Guest Editor Richard Zenith, New York, Spring 1991, pp. 38-56. [Repr. in *Performing Arts Journal,* May 1993, pp. 50-62].

ROBINSON, Peter; TWEDDLE, Christine. [*Álvaro de Campos.* 'At the Chevrolet's wheel on the road to Sintra'; 'A cross on the tobacconist's door!' 'Tripe in the Oporto Style'; 'Dactylography'; 'They didn't have any electricity there'. Translated by...]. *Numbers,* III, I, Cambridge, Spring, 1988, pp. 50-57.

WILMER, Clive; RICKARD, Peter. ['*Fernando Pessoa.* 'Abdication'; 'I leave to the blind and deaf'; 'I am a runaway'; 'There was a rhythm in my sleep'; 'It's love that is inescapable'. *Mensagem.* 'Prince Henry the Navigator'. *Alberto Caeiro.* 'I am a keeper of flocks'; 'Hey keeper of flocks,'; 'The amazing reality of things'. *Ricardo Reis.* 'You who, believing in your Christs and Marys'; 'Follow your fate'. Translated by...]. *Numbers,* III, I, Cambridge, Spring 1988, pp. 14-18, 44-49.

II : PROSE

1. Book-length

COSTA, Margaret Jull: **Fernando Pessoa. The Book of Disquiet.** Translated by... Ed. by Maria José de Lancastre. London: Serpent's Tail, 1991. [259 fragments from *Livro do Desassossego*].

HONIG, Edwin: **Always Astonished. Selected Prose by Fernando Pessoa.** Translated, edited and introduced by... San Francisco: City Lights Books, 1988. [*The Anarchist Banker* by Fernando Pessoa, 12 fragments of *Livro do Desassossego,* 4 texts by Álvaro de Campos and 8 texts by Fernando Pessoa, plus several English texts].

MAC ADAM, Alfred: **Fernando Pessoa. The Book of Disquiet.** Translated by... New York: Pantheon Books, 1991. [276 fragments from *Livro do Desassossego*].

WATSON, Iain: **Fernando Pessoa. The Book of Disquiet. A Selection.** Translated from the Portuguese and with an introduction by... London: Quartet Books, 1991. [141 fragments from *Livro do Desassossego*].

ZENITH, Richard: **Fernando Pessoa. The Book of Disquietude.** Translated and with an Introduction by... Manchester: Carcanet Press, 1991. [532 fragments from *Livro do Desassossego* (complete)].

2. In Books

GRIFFIN, Jonathan: *'Fernando Pessoa. Toward Explaining Heteronomy'.*
Translated by... In **The Poet's Work. 29 Masters of 20th Century Poetry on
the Origins and Practice of their Art**. Ed. by Reginald Gibbons. Boston:
Houghton Mifflin Company, 1979, pp. 5-15. [10 prose texts by Fernando
Pessoa].

3. In Periodicals

MACEDO, Suzette: *'"The Anarchist Banker". A translation of "O Banqueiro
Anarquista" by Fernando Pessoa'. Portuguese Studies*, 7, Department of
Portuguese, King's College, London, 1991, pp. 109-132.

CRITICISM

1. Book-length

Actas do 2º. Congresso Internacional de estudos Pessoanos: [Proceedings of
the 2nd International Congress on Fernando Pessoa, Vanderbilt
University, Nashville, Tennessee, 31 March-2 April 1983]. Centro de
Estudos Pessoanos: Oporto, 1985. [Includes 14 essays in English. Cf. Sol
BIDERMAN, Susan M. BROWN, Linda S. CHANG and Lorie
ISHIMATSU, Joanna CORTEAU, David T. HABERLY, Russel G.
HAMILTON, Hubert D. JENNINGS, George MONTEIRO, Enrique J.
NOGUERAS, William H. ROBERTS, Jaime H. da SILVA, Ronald W.
SOUSA and Erdmute Wenzel WHITE].

FERNANDO PESSOA: **A Galaxy of Poets**. Edited and with an Introduction
by José Blanco. Presented by the London Borough of Camden in association with the Portuguese Ministries of Foreign Affairs and Culture: Lisbon,
1985 [119pp.] [Chronology, Personal Documents, Critical Anthology,
Poetical Anthology, Selected Bibliography and Catalogue of the
Exhibition].

GUYER, Leland: **Spatial Imagery of Enclosure in the Poetry of Fernando
Pessoa**. Ph.D. Dissertation, University of California, Santa Barbara.
University Microfilms International: Michigan, 1979. [338 pp.].

JENNINGS, Hubert D.: **Fernando Pessoa in Durban**. Durban Corporation:
Durban[1986]. [188 pp.].

The Man Who Never Was. Essays on Fernando Pessoa. Edited with an intro-
duction by George Monteiro. Gávea-Brown: Providence, Rhode Island,
1982 [195 pp.]. [Papers presented at the International Symposium on
Fernando Pessoa, Brown University, Providence, Rhode Island, October
1977. Cf. Jorge de SENA, João Gaspar SIMÕES, Gilbert R. CAVACO,
Ronald W. SOUSA, Joanna CORTEAU, Francisco Cota FAGUNDES,
Catarina F. EDINGER, Carolina MATOS, Hellmut WOHL and José
Martins GARCIA].

TERLINDEN, Anne: **Fernando Pessoa: The Bilingual Portuguese Poet.
A Critical Study of 'The Mad Fiddler'**. Publications des Facultés
Universitaires Saint-Louis: Brussels, 1990. [236 pp.].

Three Persons in One. A Centenary Tribute to Fernando Pessoa. Edited and with an Introduction by Bernard McGuirk. Department of Hispanic Studies, University of Nottingham: Nottingham, 1988 [98 pp.]. [Includes 8 Essays and a Bibliography. Cf. Michael FREEMAN, Eugénio LISBOA, Bernard McGUIRK and John WAINWRIGHT].

2. In Books

BAKER, Badiaa Bourennane: 'Fernando Pessoa and Edgar Allan Poe. Fernando Pessoa and Walt Whitman'. In **Arquivos do Centro Cultural Português**, 15. Fundação Calouste Gulbenkian: Paris, 1980, pp. 247-321.

BLOOM, Harold: 'Borges, Neruda, and Pessoa: Hispanic-Portuguese Whitman'. In **The Western Canon. The Books and School of the Ages**. Harcourt Brace & Company: New York, San Diego, London, 1994, pp. 485-490.

BROWN, Susan M.: 'Whitmanian Fermentation and the 1914 Season'. In **Actas do 2º. Congresso**... Centro de Estudos Pessoanos: Oporto, 1985, pp. 99-109.

CAMPBELL, Roy: 'Portuguese Poetry'. In **Portugal**. Max Reinhardt: London, 1957, pp. 156-160.

CAVACO, Gilbert R.: 'Pessoa and Portuguese Politics'. In **The Man who Never Was**... Edited by George Monteiro. Gávea-Brown: Providence, Rhode Island, 1982, pp. 57-74.

CHANG, Linda S.; ISHIMATSU, Lorie: 'The Poet as Celebrant: Epic Ritual in "Mensagem"'. In **Actas do 2º. Congresso**... Centro de Estudos Pessoanos: Oporto, 1985, pp. 111-122.

CORTEAU, Joanna: 'The Quest for Identity in Pessoa's Orthonymous Poetry'. In **The Man Who Never Was**... Edited and with an Introduction by George Monteiro. Gávea-Brown: Providence (Rhode Island), 1982, pp. 93-107.

CORTEAU, Joanna: 'Contradiction in the poetry of Fernando Pessoa'. In **Actas do 2º. Congresso**... Centro de Estudos Pessoanos: Oporto, 1985, pp. 123-131.

DA CAL, Ernesto Guerra: 'Pessoa, Fernando (1888-1935, Portuguese poet)'. Entry in **Columbia Dictionary of Modern European Literature**. Horatio Smith, General Editor. Columbia University Press: New York, 1947, pp. 622.

DA CAL, Ernesto Guerra: [Note on the poems 'Autopsicografia' and 'Entre o sono e o sonho']. In **The Poem Itself**. Edited and with an Introduction by Stanley Burnshaw. Touchstone: New York, 1989, pp. 198-201. [1st ed. U.S.A., Holt, Rinehart and Winston, 1960; 2nd ed. Meridian Books: New York, 1963; U.K., Penguin Books, A Pelican Original: London, 1964.].

EDINGER, Catarina T.F.: 'The Sun vs. Ice Cream and Chocolate: The Works of Wallace Stevens and Fernando Pessoa'. In **The Man Who Never Was**... Edited and with an Introduction by George Monteiro. Gávea-Brown: Providence, Rhode Island, 1982, pp. 131-152.

FAGUNDES, Francisco Cota: 'The Search for the Self: Álvaro de Campos's "Ode Marítima"'. In **The Man Who Never Was**... Edited and with an

Introduction by George Monteiro. Gávea-Brown: Providence, Rhode Island, 1982, pp. 109-129.

FREEMAN, Michael: 'Messages from Pessoa: "Viriato"'. In **Three Persons in One**... Edited and with an Introduction by Bernard McGuirk. Department of Hispanic Studies, University of Nottingham: Nottingham, 1988, pp. 5-26.

FREEMAN, Michael: 'Portugal Past and Present: Aspects of Pessoa's Nationalism'. In **Three Persons in One**... Edited and with an Introduction by Bernard McGuirk. Department of Hispanic Studies, University of Nottingham: Nottingham, 1988, pp. 43-50. [1st. publ. in *Vida Hispanica*, (2) 36, Sutton-on-Derwent, 1987, pp. 23-37].

GARCIA, José Martins: 'A Biographical-Bibliographical Note on Pessoa'. In **The Man Who Never Was**... Edited and with an Introduction by George Monteiro. Gávea-Brown: Providence, Rhode Island, 1982, pp. 185-195.

GRIFFIN, Jonathan: 'Four in One'. In **Fernando Pessoa** (4 Vols.). Carcanet Press: Oxford, 1971, pp. 3-7 (Vol. I).

GRIFFIN, Jonathan: 'Four Poets in One Man'. In **Fernando Pessoa. Selected Poems**. Penguin Books (Penguin Modern European Poets): Harmondsworth, 1974, pp. 9-23. [2nd ed. with new Supplement, 1982; repr. 1988].

HABERLY, David T.: 'Pessoa'. Entry in **Great Foreign Writers**. Ed. by James Vinson and Daniel Kirkpatrick. St Martin's Press: New York, 1984, pp. 432-433.

HABERLY, David T.: 'Mythical History and Personal Revelation in Pessoa's "Mensagem"'. In **Actas do 2º. Congresso**... Centro de Estudos Pessoanos: Oporto, 1985, pp. 241-250.

HAMBURGER, Michael: 'Multiple Personalities'. In his **The Truth of Poetry. Tensions in Modern Poetry from Baudelaire to the 1960s**. Carcanet New Press Ltd.: Manchester, 1982, pp. 138-147. [1st ed. Weidenfeld & Nicholson, London, 1969; Harcourt Brace Hovanovich Inc., New York, 1969. Repr. by Methuen, 1982].

HAMILTON, Russell G.: 'Echoes of Pessoa in the Poetry of Lusophone Africa'. In **Actas do 2º. Congresso**... Centro do Estudos Pessoanos: Oporto, 1985, pp. 253-261.

HARLAND, Michael C.: '"Active Imagination" and Heteronymy in Fernando Pessoa'. In **Readings in Spanish and Portuguese Poetry for Geoffrey Connell**. Edited by G. Nicholas and D. Gareth Walters. Bibliography by David G. Frier. University of Glasgow, Department of Hispanic Studies: Glasgow, 1985, pp. 67-79.

HONIG, Edwin: 'Introduction. Some Words in the Entryway'. In **Always Astonished. Selected Prose by Fernando Pessoa**. City Lights Books: San Francisco, 1988, pp. i-ix.

HONIG, Edwin; BROWN, Susan M.: 'Introduction'. In **The Keeper of Sheep by Fernando Pessoa**. The Sheep Meadow Press: Riverdale-on-Hudson (New York), 1986, pp. [9 unnumbered pages].

HONIG, Edwin; BROWN, Susan M.: 'Preface'. In **Poems of Fernando Pessoa**. The Ecco Press: New York, 1986, pp. xi-xviii.

JENNINGS, Hubert D.: 'That Long Patience Which is Genius...'; 'Judica Me

Deus...'. In **The D.H.S. story** 1866-1966. The Durban High School and Old Boys' Memorial Trust, Brown, Davis & Platt Ltd.: Durban, 1966, pp. 99-110, 111-116.

JENNINGS, Hubert D.: 'The South African Episode'. In **Actas do 2º. Congresso**... Centro de Estudos Pessoanos: Oporto, 1985, pp. 310-331.

JOSIPOVICI, Gabriel: 'Fernando Pessoa, 1888-1935'. In his **The Lessons of Modernism and Other Essays**. M: New York, 1977, pp. 26-50.

LISBOA, Eugénio: 'A Violent Tranquility'. In **Three Persons in One**... Edited and with an Introduction by Bernard McGuirk. Department of Hispanic Studies, University of Nottingham: Nottingham, 1988, pp. 27-35. [Translated by Manucha Lisboa].

LISBOA, Eugénio: 'Revisiting the Modernisms'. In **Three Persons in One**... Edited and with an Introduction by Bernard McGuirk. Department of Hispanic Studies, University of Nottingham: Nottingham, 1988, pp. 65-79.

LOPES, Teresa Rita: 'Preface'. In **Fernando Pessoa. Lisbon: what the Tourist should see/O que o turista deve ver**. Livros Horizonte: Lisbon, 1992, pp. 17-19. [Translated by Richard Zenith].

MAC ADAM, Alfred: 'Introduction'. In **Fernando Pessoa. The Book of Disquiet**. Pantheon Books: New York, 1991, pp. vii-xxii.

MACEDO, Helder: 'Introduction'. In **Fernando Pessoa. Message**. Translated by Jonathan Griffin. The Menard Press/King's College London: London, 1992, pp. 4-7.

MATOS, Carolina: 'Edwin Honig and Jean Longland: Two Interviews'. Conducted by... In **The Man Who Never Was**... Edited and with an Introduction by George Monteiro. Gávea-Brown: Providence, Rhode Island, 1982, pp. 153-165.

McGUIRK, Bernard: 'Pessoa's Wordsworth: Two "figures of capable imagination"'. In **Three Persons in One**... Edited and with an Introduction by... Department of Hispanic Studies, University of Nottingham: Nottingham, 1988, pp. 51-64.

McGUIRK, Bernard: 'Pessoa and the "affective fallacy"'. In **Three Persons in One**... Edited and with an introduction by... Department of Hispanic Studies, University of Nottingham: Nottingham, 1988, pp. 36-42.

MILBURN, A.R.: 'Pessoa, Fernando (Lisbon 1888-Lisbon 1935)'. Entry in **The Penguin Companion to Literature. 2– European**. Edited by Anthony Thorlby. Penguin Books: Middlesex, 1969, pp. 608.

MONTEIRO, George: 'Fernando, Old Artificer'. In **Actas do 2º. Congresso**... Centro des Estudos Pessoanos: Oporto, 1985, pp. 407-427.

MONTEIRO, George: 'Ophélia's Lovers'. In **Selected Proceedings. The Thirty-fifth Annual Mountain Interstate Foreign Language Conference**. Edited by Ramón Fernandéz-Rubio. Furman University: Greenville, South Carolina, 1987, pp. 245-253.

MONTEIRO, George: 'Introduction'. In **Fernando Pessoa. Self-analysis and Thirty Other poems**. Calouste Gulbenkian Foundation: Lisbon, 1988, pp. 11-14.

NOGUERAS, Enrique J. :'Notes on the Concept of Heteronym'. In **Actas do 2º. Congresso**... Centro de Estudos Pessoanos: Oporto, 1985, pp. 446-455.

PARKER, John M.: 'Fernando Pessoa'. In his **Three Twentieth-century Portuguese Poets**. Witwatersrand University Press: Johannesburg, 1960, pp. 2-19.

PAZ, Octavio: 'Introduction. Fernando Pessoa or the Imminence of the Unknown' [abridged]. In **Selected Poems by Fernando Pessoa**. Translated by Edwin Honig. The Swallow Press: Chicago, 1971, pp. 1-21. [Translated by Edwin Honig. Original essay in Octavio Paz, **Cuadrivio**, Barcelona: Biblioteca de Bolsillo, 1991].

PILLING, John: 'Fernando Pessoa (1888-1935)'. In his **An Introduction to Fifty Modern European Poets**. Pan Books: London and Sydney, 1982, pp. 173-180.

QUINTANILHA, F.E.G.: 'Fernando Pessoa. The Man and His Work'. In **Fernando Pessoa. Sixty Portuguese Poems**. University of Wales Press: Cardiff, 1971, pp. xi-xlix. [Rep. 1973; 1st ed. in paperback, 1988].

RAMALHO, Américo da Costa: 'Fernando Pessoa, Portugal's Greatest Modern poet'. In his **Portuguese Essays**. National Secretariat for Information: Lisbon, 1963, pp. 47-84. [Repr. 1968].

RICKARD, Peter: 'Fernando Pessoa. An Introduction'. In **Fernando Pessoa. Selected Poems**. Edinburgh University Press: Edinburgh, 1971, pp. 1-61. [Repr. by University of Texas Press, 1972].

RICKARD, Peter: '**Pessoa**, Fernando António Nogueira. 1888-1935. Portuguese Poet'. Entry in **Makers of Modern Culture**. Edited by... Routledge & Kegan Paul Ltd.: London, 1981. [Concise edition in paperback: **Dictionary of Modern Culture**, Ark Paperbacks, London and Boston, 1984].

ROBERTS, William H.: 'Messianic Forebears of Sebastian and Pessoa'. In **Actas do 2°. Congresso**... Centro de Estudos Pessoanos: Oporto, 1985, pp. 479-486.

SENA, Jorge de.: 'Fernando Pessoa: The Man Who Never Was'. In **The Man Who Never Was**... Edited and with an Introduction by George Monteiro. Gávea-Brown: Providence, Rhode Island, 1982, pp. 19-31.

SEVERINO, Alexandrino Eusébio: 'Fernando Pessoa in Durban'; 'The Importance of Fernando Pessoa's South African Education' 'The Poet Fernando Pessoa'; 'Fernando Pessoa – a Modern Lusiad'. In **Fernando Pessoa e O Mar Português**. Ed. by... Fundação Eng°. António de Almeida: Oporto, 1988, pp. 23-26, 119-126, 151-163.

SEYMOUR-SMITH, Martin: 'Pessoa, Fernando (1888-1935)'. Entry in his **Who's Who in Twentieth Century Literature**. Weidenfeld & Nicholson: London, 1976, pp. 279-280.

SILVA, Jaime H. da.: 'Between English and Portuguese: Fernando Pessoa, the Estrangeirado'. In **Actas do 2°. Congresso**... Centro de Estudos Pessoanos: Oporto, 1985, pp. 548-568.

SILVA, Jaime H. da.: 'Introduction'. In **Fernando Pessoa. The Surprise of Being**. Twenty-five poems translated by James Greene and Clara de Azevedo Mafra. Angel Books: London, ;1986, pp. 9-14. [2nd ed. 1987

SIMÕES, João Gaspar: '*Presença*'s Pessoa'. In **The Man Who Never Was**... Edited and with an Introduction by George Monteiro. Gávea-Brown: Providence, Rhode Island, 1982, pp. 33-56.

SOUSA, Ronald W.: 'Pessoa: The Messenger'; 'The Rediscoverers: A Retrospect Passion'. In his **The Rediscoverers. Major Writers in the Portuguese Literature of National Regeneration**. Pennsylvania State University Press: University Park and London, 1981, pp. 130-160 and 161-168.

SOUSA, Ronald W.: 'Ascendant Romanticism in Pessoa'. In **The Man Who Never Was**... Edited and with an Introduction by George Monteiro. Gávea-Brown: Providence, Rhode Island, 1982, pp. 74-91.

SOUSA, Ronald W.: 'Fernando Pessoa "Ele-Mesmo" as Cultural Being'. In **Actas do 2º. Congresso**... Centro de Estudos Pessoanos: Oporto, 1985, pp. 588-601.

STODDARD, Roger E.: 'The Books of Poems that Fernando Pessoa Published in his Lifetime: A First-Hand Account of the Harvard Copies by OLISIPO'. In **A Grass of Green Tea – with Honig**. Ed. by Susan Brown, Thomas Epstein and Henry Gould. AlephoeBooks: Providence, Rhode Island, 1994, pp. 193-197.

TERLINDEN, Anne: 'The Concept of the "Além" in Fernando Pessoa's Heteronyms and in "The Mad Fiddler": A Comparative Study'. In **Arquivos do Centro Cultural Português, XXII**. Fundação Calouste Gulbenkian: Paris, 1986, pp. 347-405.

Twentieth-century Literary Criticism. Excerpts from Criticism of the Works of Novelists, Poets, Playwrights, Short Story Writers, and Other Creative Writers Who Died between 1900 and 1960, from the First Publish. 'Fernando (António Nogueira) Pessoa. 1888-1935'. Gale Research Company, Book Tower: Detroit, Michigan, 1988, pp. 291-325. [Repr. criticism by several authors and an additional bibliography. Cf. Edouard RODITI, Michael HAMBURGER, F.E.G. QUINTANILHA, Octavio PAZ, Peter RICKARD, Michael WOOD, Marcia SMILACK, Jonathan GRIFFIN, Marilyn Scarantino JONES, Ronald W. SOUSA, and Joanna CORTEAU.].

WAINWRIGHT, John: 'Fernando Pessoa: An Introductory Bibliography'. In **Three Persons in One**... Edited and with an Introduction by Bernard McGuirk. Department of Hispanic Studies, University of Nottingham: Nottingham, 1988, pp. 80-98.

WATSON, Iain: 'Introduction. The I as a Ventriloquist'. In **Fernando Pessoa. The Book of Disquiet. A Selection**. Quartet Books: London, 1991, pp. vii-xi.

WHITE, Erdmute Wenzel: 'Beyond Objectivity: Fernando Pessoa, Heteronymic Poet'. In **Actas do 2º. Congresso**... Centro de Estudos Pessoanos: Oporto, 1985, pp. 644-656.

WOHL, Hellmut: 'The Short Happy Life of Amadeo de Souza Cardoso'. **The Man Who Never Was**... Edited and with an Introduction by George Monteiro. Gávea-Brown: Providence, Rhode Island, 1982, pp. 167-184.

ZENITH, Richard: 'Introduction'. In **Fernando Pessoa. The Book of Disquietude**. Carcanet Press: Manchester, 1991, pp. vii-xvii.

3. In periodicals

BACARISSE, Pamela: 'Fernando Pessoa: Towards an Understanding of a

Key Attitude'. *Luso-Brazilian Review*, (17) 1, University of Winsconsin Press, Winsconsin, Summer 1980, pp. 51-61.

BIDERMAN, Sol: 'Mount Abiegnos and the Masks: Occult Imagery in William Butler Yeats and Fernando Pessoa'. *Alfa*, 10, Faculdade de Filosofia, Ciêncis e. Letras, Marília (Brazil), 9/1966, pp. 37-56. [Rep. in *Luso-Brazilian Review*, (5) 1, University of Winsconsin Press: Winsconsin, 1968, pp. 58-74. An abridged version was published in **Actas do 2º. Congresso**... Centro de Estudos Pessoanos, Oporto, 1985, pp. 79-90].

BRODSKY, Joseph: 'How to Read a Book'. *The New York Times. Book Review*, New York, 6/12/1988.

BURGESS, Anthony: 'The nothingness is all'. *The Observer*, London, 10/6/1991. [Review of *The Books of Disquiet* by Ferdinand [sic] Pessoa. Edited by Maria José de Lancastre. Translated by Margaret Jull Costa].

CARREÑO, António: 'Suggested Bases for a Comparative Study of Pessoa and António Machado'. *Romance Notes*, (20) 1, Fall 1979, pp. 24-28.

COELHO, Joaquim-Francisco: 'On Moonlight in Álvaro de Campos'. *Portuguese Studies*, 1, Department of Portuguese, King's College, London, 1985, pp. 116-120.

COURTEAU, Joanna: 'The Desacralization of the World in the Poetry of Fernando Pessoa'. *Revista de História das Ideias*, 8, Faculdade de Letras. Instituto de História e Teoria das Ideias. Universidade de Coimbra, 1986, pp. 557-564.

FRIER, David: 'Camilo and Álvaro de Campos: The Grass is Always Greener'. *Portuguese Studies*, 7, Department of Portuguese, King's College, London, 1991, pp. 86-95.

GARCIA, Rubén: 'The Unexpected Affinities: W.B. Yeats and Fernando Pessoa'. *Journal of the American-Portuguese Society*, (10) 1, New York, 1976, pp. 29-37.

GRIFFIN, Jonathan: 'Fernando Pessoa: A Brief Study of His Dominant Quest'. *Temenos*, 10, London, 1989, pp. 25-40.

GUYER, Leland: 'The Gardens of Fernando Pessoa and Andrew Marvell'. *Selecta. Journal of the Pacific Northwest Council on Foreign Languages*, 5, Oregon State University, Corvallis, 1984, pp. 85-91.

HOLLAND, Jonathan: 'Not so much a city, more a state of mind'. *The European*, London, 11/4-10/1994, [Review of Fernando Pessoa, **Lisbon: What the Tourist should see**].

HOWES, R.W.: 'Fernando Pessoa, Poet, Publisher and Translator'. *The British Library Journal*, (9) 2, London, 1983, pp. 161-170.

JONES, Marilyn Scarantino: 'Pessoa's Poetic Coterie: Three Heteronyms and an Orthonym'. *Luso-Brazilian Review*, (14) 2, University of Winsconsin Press, Winsconsin, Winter 1977, pp. 254-262.

JOSIPOVICI, Gabriel: 'Losing Balance'. *The Times Literary Supplement*, 4471, London, 12/9-15/1988., [Review of *Fernando Pessoa. Selected Poems*. Translated by Jonathan Griffin].

KINSELLA, John: 'Resisting Eliot: A Reading of Álvaro de Campos' "Tabacaria"'. *Portuguese Studies*, 7, Department of Portuguese, King's College, London, 1991., pp. 96-105.

LOURENÇO, Eduardo. 'Fernando Pessoa or The Absolute Foreigner'. *Translation. The Journal of Literary Translation*, Vol. XXV, New York, Spring 1991, pp. 58-62. [Translated by David Alan Prescott].

MERTON, Thomas: 'Translator's Note', in 'Twelve Poems. Fernando Pessoa'. *New Directions In Prose and Poetry*, 19, Edited by J. Laughlin. New York, 1966, pp. 299.

MONTEIRO, Adolfo Casais: 'Theory of Impersonality: Fernando Pessoa and T.S. Eliot'. *The Journal of the American Portuguese Cultural Society*, 6-7, New York, 1971-1973, pp. 40-45.

MONTEIRO, George: 'Fernando Pessoa's Ontological Poem'. *Concerning Poetry*, (9) 1, Western Washington State College, 1976, pp. 15-18.

MONTEIRO, George: 'Poe/Pessoa'. *Comparative Literature*, (40) 2, pp. 134-149.

MONTEIRO, George: 'The Song of the Reaper: Pessoa and Wordsworth'. *Portuguese Studies*, 5, Department of Portuguese, King's College London, 1989, pp. 71-80.

PAZ, Octavio: 'Unknown to Himself: Fernando Pessoa'. *Numbers*, (III) 1, Cambridge, Spring 1988, pp. 66-93. [Translated by Michael Schmidt. Original essay in Octavio Paz, **Cuadrivio**, Barcelona: Biblioteca de Bolsillo, 1991].

PRING-MILL, Robert D.F.: 'The Themes of Fernando Pessoa's English Sonnets'. *Studies in Modern Portuguese Literature*, 4, Tulane University, New Orleans, 1971, pp. 9-37.

RABASSA, Gregory: 'Fourth Person Plural'. *Parnassus. Poetry In Review*, 1-2, New York, Spring-Summer 1973, pp. 133-139.

RICKARD, Peter: 'Fernando Pessoa. 1888-1935'. *Numbers*, (III) 1, Cambridge, Spring 1988, pp. 8-13.

RICKARD, Peter: 'Four Poets in One'. *The Times Literary Supplement*, 4471, London, 9-15 December 1988., [Review of several books on Fernando Pessoa].

RODITI, Édouard: 'The Several Names of Fernando Pessoa'. *Poetry*, (87) 1, Chicago, October 1955, pp. 40-45.

RODITI Édouard: 'Fernando Pessoa, Outsider Among English Poets'. *The Literary Review*, (6) 3, Farley Dickinson University, Spring 1963, pp. 372-391.

ROSENTHAL, David H.: 'Unpredictable Passions'. *The New York Times. Book Review*, New York, 12/13/1987, pp. 32-33. [Review of *The Keeper of Sheep* by Fernando Pessoa and *Poems of Fernando Pessoa*, translated and edited by Edwin Honig and Susan M. Brown].

VIEIRA, Yara F.: 'From Pessoa's Laboratory: The Creation of the "Mostrengo"'. *Portuguese Studies*, 9, Department of Portuguese, King's College, London, 1993, pp. 214-223.

WILMER, Clive: 'Poetic Puzzles from the Portuguese'. *The Times*, London, 1/11/1992., [Review of *The Book of Disquietude* by Fernando Pessoa, translated by Richard Zenith (Carcanet), *The Book of Disquiet*, translated by Margaret Jull Costa (Serpent's Tail) and *The Book of Disquiet. A Selection*, translated by Iain Watson (Quartet)].

WOOD, Michael: 'Mod and Great'. *The New York Review of Books*, (19) 4, New York, 8/21/1972, pp. 19-22. [Review of *Fernando Pessoa: Selected Poems*, translated by Peter Rickard and *Selected Poems by Fernando Pessoa*, translated by Edwin Honig].

WOOD, Michael: 'The Sorcerer's Apprentice'. *The New York Review of Books*, (37) 17, New York, 10/24/1991, pp. 20-21. [Review of *The Book of Disquiet* by Fernando Pessoa, translated by Alfred MacAdam and *The Year of the Death of Ricardo Reis* by José Saramago, translated by Giovanni Pontiero].

SELECTED CRITICISM IN PORTUGUESE :
50 basic books

ALMEIDA, Luis Pedro Moitinho de.: **Fernando Pessoa. No cinquentenário da sua morte.** Coimbra Editora: Coimbra, 1985.

ALMEIDA, Onésimo Teotónio de.: **Mensagem. Uma tentativa de interpretação.** Direcção Regional dos Assuntos Culturais: Angra do Heroismo (Azores), 1987.

ANTUNES, Alfredo: **Saudade e profetismo em Fernando Pessoa.** Faculdade de Filosofia: Braga, 1983.

BLANCO, José: **Fernando Pessoa. Esboço de uma bibliografia.** Imprensa Nacional/Casa da Moeda: Lisbon, 1983.

CENTENO, Yvette K.: **Fernando Pessoa e a filosofia hermética.** Presença: Lisbon, 1985.

CIRURGIÃO, António: **O 'Olhar Esfíngico' da 'Mensagem' de Pessoa.** Instituto de Língua e Cultura Portuguesa/Ministério da Educação: Lisbon, 1990.

COELHO, António de Pina: **Os fundamentos filosóficos da obra de Fernando Pessoa** (2 vols.). Verbo: Oporto, 1971. [1st ed. 1968].

COELHO, Jacinto do Prado: **Diversidade e unidade em Fernando Pessoa.** Editorial Verbo: Lisbon, 1982 (7th ed.) [1st ed. 1949].

COELHO, Jacinto do Prado: **Camões e Pessoa, Poetas da Utopia.** Europa-América: Lisbon, 1984.

COELHO, Joaquim-Francisco: **Microleituras de Álvaro de Campos.** Publicações Dom Quixote: Lisbon, 1987.

COSTA, Dalila Pereira da.: **O esoterismo de Fernando Pessoa.** Lello & Irmão: Oporto, 1971.

COSTA, Eduardo Freitas da.: **Fernando Pessoa. Notas a uma biografia romanceada.** Guimarães Ed.: Lisbon, 1951.

FRANÇA, Isabel Murteira: **Fernando Pessoa na intimidade.** Publicações Dom Quixote/Livraria Paisagem: Lisbon and Rio de Janeiro, 1987.

GALHOZ, Maria Aliete: 'Fernando Pessoa, Encontro de Poesia'. In **Fernando Pessoa. Obra poética.** Ed. José Aguilar: Rio de Janeiro (Brazil), 1960, pp. XI-XLV. [Several repr.].

GARCEZ, Maria Helena Nery: **Alberto Caeiro descobridor na natureza?** Centro de Estudos Pessoanos: Oporto, 1985.

GARCIA, José Martins: **Fernando Pessoa: Coração despedaçado** (Subsídos para um estudo da afectividade na obra de Fernando Pessoa). Universidade dos Açores: Ponta Delgada (Azores), 1985.

GIL, José: **Fernando Pessoa ou a metafísica das sensações.** Relógio de Água Editores, Col. Filosofia: Lisbon, no date.

GUERRA, Maria Luísa: **Ensaios sobre Álvaro de Campos. Vol. I.** No publisher: Lisbon, [1969].

GUNTERT, Georges: **Fernando Pessoa. O eu estranho.** Publicações Dom Quixote: Lisbon, 1982. [Translated by Maria Fernanda Cidrais. 1st publ. in German, **Das fremde ich. Fernando Pessoa.** Walter de Gruyter & Co.: Berlin, 1971].

KUJAWSKI, Gilberto de Melo: **Fernando Pessoa, o outro**. Ed. Vozes: Petrópolis (Brazil), 1979. [1st ed. 1967].

LANCASTRE, Maria José de.: **Fernando Pessoa. Uma fotobiografia.** Imprensa Nacional/Casa da Moeda: Lisbon, 1984. [1st ed. 1981].

LIND, Georg Rudolf: **Estudos sobre Fernando Pessoa**. Imprensa Nacional/Casa da Moeda: Lisbon, 1981.

LOPES, Teresa Rita: **Pessoa por conhecer. I – Roteiro para uma expedição. II – Textos para um novo mapa** (2 vols). Editorial Estampa: Lisbon, 1990.

LOPES, Óscar: 'Fernando Pessoa'. In his **Cifras do tempo**. Caminho: Lisbon, 1990, pp. 123-166.

LOURENÇO, Eduardo: **Fernando Pessoa revisitado. Leitura estruturante do drama em gente**. Moraes: Lisbon, 1981. [1st ed. 1973].

LOURENÇO, Eduardo: **Poesia e metafísica: Camões, Antero, Pessoa**. Sá da Costa: Lisbon, 1983.

LOURENÇO, Eduardo: **Fernando, Rei da nossa Baviera**. Imprensa Nacional/Casa da Moeda: Lisbon, 1986.

MARTINHO, Fernando J.B.: **Pessoa e a moderna poesia portuguesa. Do 'Orpheu' a 1960.** I.C.A.L.P., Biblioteca Breve, Vol. 82: Lisbon, 1991. [1st ed. 1983]/

MONTEIRO, Adolfo Casais: **A poesia de Fernando Pessoa**. Imprensa Nacional/Casa da Moeda: Lisbon, 1985. [1st ed. 1943].

MOURÃO-FERREIRA, David: **Nos passos de Pessoa**. Ed. Presença: Lisbon, 1988.

PADRÃO, Maria da Glória: **A metáfora em Fernando Pessoa**. Limiar: Oporto, 1981. [1st ed. 1973].

PERRONE-MOISÉS, Leyla: **Fernando Pessoa: aquém do eu, além do outro**. Livraria Martins Fontes: São Paulo (Brazil), 1982.

QUADROS, António: **Fernando Pessoa. Vida, personalidade e génio. O homem e a obra**. Publicações Dom Quixote: Lisbon, 1984. [1st ed. 1981].

SACRAMENTO, Mário: **Fernando Pessoa, poeta da hora absurda**. Ed. Vega: Lisbon, 1985. [1st ed. 1958].

SEABRA, José Augusto: **Fernando Pessoa ou o poetodrama**. Ed. Perspectiva: São Paulo (Brazil), 1974.

SEABRA, José Augusto: **O heterotexto pessoano**. Dinalivro: Lisbon, 1985.

SENA, Jorge de: **Fernando Pessoa & Cª. heterónima** (2 vols.). Edições 70: Lisbon, 1982.

SERRÃO, Joel: **Fernando Pessoa, cidadão do imaginário**. Livros Horizonte: Lisbon, 1981.

SILVA, Agostinho da: **Um Fernando Pessoa**. Guimarães Ed.: Lisbon, 1988. [1st ed. 1959].

SILVA, Luis de Oliveira e.: **O materialismo idealista de Fernando Pessoa**. Clássica Editora: Lisbon, 1985.

SIMÕES, João Gaspar: **Heteropsicografia de Fernando Pessoa**. Inova: Oporto, 1973.

SIMÕES, João Gaspar: **Vida e obra de Fernando Pessoa** (7th ed.). Publicações Dom Quixote: Lisbon, 1991. [1st ed. 1950].

SOUSA, João Rui de: **Fotobibliografia de Fernando Pessoa**. Organização, Introdução e Notas de... Prefácio de Eduardo Louranço. Imprensa Nacional-Casa da Moeda/Biblioteca Nacional: Lisbon, 1988.

TABUCCHI, Antonio: **Pessoana mínima**. Imprensa Nacional-Casa da Moeda: Lisbon, 1984.

Actas do I Congresso Internacional de Estudos Pessoanos (Proceedings of the 1st International Congress on Fernando Pessoa. Oporto, 3-5 April 1978). Brasília Editora: Oporto, 1979 [Includes essays in Portuguese by: Arnaldo SARAIVA, José Augusto SEABRA, Adélia SILVESTRE, Alexandrino E. SEVERINO, Ana HATHERLY, Ana Paula Quintela Ferreira SOTTOMAYOR, Carlos Felipe MOISÉS, Cleonice BERARDINELLI, Dalila Pereira da COSTA, E.M. de Melo e CASTRO, Eduardo LOURENÇO, Fernando GUIMARÃES, Fernando J.B. MARTINHO, Georg Rudolf LIND, Helder MACEDO, Jacinto do Prado COELHO, João CAMILO, Joel SERRÃO, Jorge de SENA, José-Augusto FRANÇA, José Clécio Basílo QUESADO, Julia CUERVO-HEWITT, Leodegário A. de AZEVEDO FILHO, Leyla PERRONE-MOISÉS, Maria Aliete GALHOZ, Maria de Fátima MARINHO, Maria de Fátima de Sá e Melo FERREIRA, Maria da Glória PADRÃO, Maria Leonor Machado de SOUSA, Maria Luísa GUERRA, Maria Teresa Schiappa de AZEVEDO, Norma Backes TASCA, Óscar LOPES, Pedro Araújo FIGUEIREDO, Stephen RECKERT, Vasco Graça MOURA and Y.K. CENTENO].

Actas do 2º. Congresso Internacional de Estudos Pessoanos (Proceedings of the 2nd International Congress on Fernando Pessoa. Vanderbilt University, Nashville Tennessee, 31st March-2nd April 1983). Centro de Estudos Pessoanos: Oporto, 1985. [Includes essays in Portuguese by: Anoar AIEX, Carlos D'ALGE, Vilmae AREAS, Maria Tereza Camargo BIDERMAN, Roxana EMINESCU, Luisa TRIAS FOLCH, Maria Aliete GALHOZ, Maria Helena Nery GARCEZ, Frederick C. Hesse GARCIA, José Martins GARCIA, Maria Luisa GUERRA, Ana HATHERLY, Julia CUERVO-HEWITT, Dorel-Neagu JACOBESCU, Teresa Rita LOPES, Eduardo LOURENÇO, Maria de Fátima MARINHO, Fernando J.B. MARTINHO, Luise Filipe Barata MONTEIRO, António QUADROS, William P. ROUGLE, Maria Irene Ramalho de Sousa SANTOS, Arnaldo SARAIVA, Joel SERRÃO, Jorge Fernandes da SILVEIRA, João Gaspar SIMÕES, Ricardo da Silveira Lobo STERNBERG, Nicolás EXTREMERA TAPIA and Norma Backes TASCA].

Actas [Do] IV Congresso Internacional de Estudos Pessoanos. Secção Brasileira (Proceedings of the 4th International Congress on Fernando Pessoa. Universidade de São Paulo (Brazil), 27-30 April 1988). Fundação Eng. António de Almeida: Oporto, 1990. [2 vols. Includes essays in Portuguese by: Carlos D'ALGE, Maria Aliete GALHOZ, Maria Helena Nery GARCEZ, Maria Luísa GUERRA, Julia CUERVO-HEWITT, Eduardo LOURENÇO, Fernando J.B. MARTINHO, Alexandrino E. SEVERINO, Almir de Campos BRUNETTI, António CIRURGIÃO, Beatriz BERRINI, Berta WALDMAN, Carlos PORTO, Cleonice BERARDINELLI, Duílio COLOMBINI, E.M. de Melo e CASTRO, Edgar PEREIRA, Elisabeth ARRIBAT-PAYCHERE, Eneida Maria de SOUZA, Ettore FINAZZI-AGRO, Fábio LUCAS, Fernando ALVARENGA, Fernando SEGOLIM, Flavio AGUIAR, Francisco

Casado GOMES, George MONTEIRO, Gersey Georgette Bergo YAHN, Haquira OSAKABE, Helder MACEDO, Hiudéa Rodrigues BOBERG, Horácio COSTA, Ivo CASTRO, J.L. FONTENLA, Jaime FERNANDES, Joanna COURTEAU, João Alves das NEVES, João DÉCIO, José Augusto SEABRA, José BLANCO, José G. Herculano de CARVALHO, José Luís GARCIA MARTIN, José Roberto Whitaker PENTEADO FILHO, Lênia Márcia de Medeiros MONGELLI, Leodegário A. de AZEVEDO FILHO, Leonor S. CABRAL, Leopoldo SCHERNER, Leyla PERRONE-MOISÉS, LINHARES FILHO, Luís de Sousa REBELO, Luísa FREIRE, Maria Aparecida RIBEIRO, Maria Fernanda de ABREU, Maria de Loudes Abreu de OLIVEIRA, Maria Luísa Scher PEREIRA, Maria de Lourdes BELCHIOR, Marleine Paula Marcondes TOLEDO, Monsenhor Primo VIEIRA, Nádia Batella GOTLIB, Odette Penha COELHO, Onésimo Teotónio de ALMEDIA, Pedro LYRA, Philadelpho MENEZES, Pires LARANJEIRA, Regina ZILBERMAN, Roberto de Oliveira BRANDÃO, Robson Pereira GONÇALVES, Salvato TRIGO, Sérgio CORREA, Silvano PELOSO, Sílvio ELIA, Tânia Franco CARVALHAL, Teresa Cristina Cerdeira da SILVA, Teresa Sobral CUNHA, Vera VOUGA, Victor JABOUILLE, Wanda Melo MIRANDA, Yara Frateschi VIEIRA and Yvonne de Oliveira SILVEIRA].

Um Século de Pessoa. Encontro Internacional do Centenário de Fernando Pessoa. (Proceedings of the Fernando Pessoa Centennial International Conference. Lisbon 5-7 December 1988). Secretaria de Estado da Cultura: Lisbon, 1990 [Includes essays in Portuguese by: Cleonice BERARDINELLI, Ivo CASTRO, Joaquim-Francisco COELHO, João DIONISIO, Guilia LANCIANI, Óscar LOPES, Luciana STEGAGNO-PICCHIO, Guiseppe TAVANI, Álvaro Cardos GOMES, Pavla LIMIDLOVA, Teresa Rita LOPES, Carlos Felipe MOISÉS, Leyla PERRONE-MOISÉS, Massaud MOISÉS, José Rodrigues de PAIVA, Maria Alzira SEIXO, Gersey Georgette Gergo YAHN, Carlos D'ALGE, Fernando ALVARENGA, Nelly Novaes COELHO, Lélia Parreira DUARTE, Vergílio FERREIRA, Michael FREEMAN, José GIL, Maria Luísa GUERRA, Julia CUERVO-HEWITT, Santiago KOVADLOFF, Fábio LUCAS, Augustina BESSA-LUIS, Suzette MACEDO, Alfredo MARGARIDO, Bernard McGUIRK, José Augusto SEABRA, Alexandrino E. SEVERINO, Luís de Oliveira e SILVA, João Rui de SOUSA, Satoru YABUNAKA, Onésimo Teotónio de ALMEÍDA, Leodegário de AZEVEDO FILHO, Maria Helena Néry GARCEZ, João Medina, Pedro Teixeira da MOTA, José Carlos Seabra PEREIRA, António QUADROS, Ettore FINAZZI-AGRO, Beatriz BERRINI, Fernando GUIMÃRES, Yara Frateschi VIEIRA, Brian F. HEAD, Gilberto de Mello KUJAWSKI, Georg Rudolf LIND, Álvaro Manuel MACHADO, Fernando Manuel Cabral MARTINS, Amina di MUNNO, Américo Costa RAMALHO, Maria Irene Ramalho de Sousa SANTOS, José SASPORTES, Regina ZILBERMANN, Dalila Pereira da COSTA, Silvina Rodrigues LOPES, Fernando J.B. MARTINHO, Helena RIAUSOVA, E.M. de Melo e CASTRO, Almeida FARIA, Eugénio LISBOA, George MONTEIRO, João Alves das NEVES and Eduardo LOURENÇO; in French by Robert BRÉCHON, Patrick QUILLIER,

Pierre LÉGLISE-COSTA, André COYNÉ, Armand GUIBERT, Michael CHANDEIGNE and Dominique TOUATI; in Spanish by Pilar GOMEZ BEDATE, Ángel CRESPO, Pablo del BARCO and José-Ángel CILLERUELO].

Fernando Pessoa: **'Mensagem'. Pemas Esotéricos.** Edição crítica. José Augusto Seabra, Coordenator. Archivos/Fundação Eng. A. Almeida: Madrid, 1993 [Includes essays in Portuguese by: Onésimo Teotónio de ALMEIDA, José Edil de Lima ALVES, José BLANCO, Yvette K. CENTENO, Dalila Pereira da COSTA, Maria Aliete GALHOZ, Teresa Rita LOPES, Eduardo LOURENÇO, Maria Helena da Rocha PEREIRA, José Caro PROENÇA, António QUADROS, Américo da Costa RAMALHO, Clara ROCHA, Adrien ROIG, José Augusto SEABRA and Luis Filipe B. TEIXEIRA].

Pessoa Personae. Watercolour, 1995. By Alfredo Margarido